Also by the Authors

Failing at Fairness
Teachers, Schools and Society
Gender in the Classroom
Sex Equity Handbook for Schools
Now Upon a Time:
A Contemporary Approach to Children's Literature

STILL FAILING AT FAIRNESS

How Gender Bias Cheats Girls and Boys
in School and What We Can Do About It

**DAVID SADKER, MYRA SADKER,
AND KAREN ZITTLEMAN**

SCRIBNER

New York   London   Toronto   Sydney

Scribner
A Division of Simon & Schuster, Inc.
1230 Avenue of the Americas
New York, NY 10020

This Scribner edition April 2009

SCRIBNER and design are registered trademarks of The Gale Group, Inc.,
used under license by Simon & Schuster, Inc., the publisher of this work.

For information about special discounts for bulk purchases,
please contact Simon & Schuster Special Sales:
1-866-506-1949 or business@simonandschuster.com

The Simon & Schuster Speakers Bureau can bring authors to your live event.
For more information or to book an event, contact the Simon & Schuster
Speakers Bureau at 1-866-248-3049 or visit our website at www.simonspeakers.com.

Manufactured in the United States of America

1   3   5   7   9   10   8   6   4   2

ISBN-13: 978-1-4165-5247-5
ISBN-10: 1-4165-5247-2

An earlier edition of this title was originally published in 1994 as *Failing at Fairness*.

To our first teachers, our parents

Jacob Miller, Jerome and Evelyn Sadker
Shirley and Lou Pollack
Kenneth and Norma Zittleman

Contents

STILL FAILING
AT FAIRNESS

Authors' Note

"Didn't we solve this sexism thing years ago?"
"I heard that girls are doing fine now, really better than the boys!"
"It's all about biology. Girls' and boys' brains are hardwired differently."
"I read that single-sex schools are best because students focus on their work instead of each other."
"Isn't there a boys' crisis? Aren't women the majority of college students?"

A "charmingly naïve belief" that women have achieved equality is how *Newsweek* columnist Anna Quindlen describes the current state of affairs. Today, men comprise over 90 percent of the top executives at Fortune 500 companies—not exactly equity in the business world. In the military culture, female leadership is viewed as an oxymoron. Great strides in politics and journalism? Hardly. Women comprise an underwhelming 20 percent of our leading journalists. Female representation in the U.S. House of Representatives ranks a disheartening sixty-ninth in the world, behind Iraq and North Korea. Even in prestigious careers such as medicine and law, it does not take long for women to realize that their earnings lag well behind male colleagues. At big law firms, women make up less than 20 percent of the partners. Female doctors confront a gender wage gap that is actually greater than other women in the workforce.

Have you visited a Toys 'R' Us (or any toy store) lately? They are like time machines with blue aisles for boys and pink aisles for girls, a sort of *Back to the Future*, 1950s style. True, a few toys target both genders, but most toys project blue and pink worlds that engulf the very young in "gender-appropriate" activities and futures.

1

College majors are not found in blue and pink aisles, but some might as well be. Forty years ago, 75 percent of students studying to be elementary teachers were female. Today, 90 percent are female. Teaching is getting pinker. Only one in five engineers is female, two-thirds of physics majors are male, and a lower percentage of females are studying computer science today than a decade ago. These are the blue majors. Even when women break free of gender stereotypes, as they have in many math and science courses, too few actually find careers in science or math.

So if females continue to be dogged by sexism, is it safe to assume that boys and men are the beneficiaries? Not at all. Gender equality is neither a competition nor is it only about females. Breaking news: boys and men have a gender. Few males even consider the heavy price they pay because of gender stereotyping. Truth is, boys are gender stereotyped earlier and more harshly than girls, and their stereotype has tighter boundaries. Careers from teaching to social work, from dance to nursing are routinely denied to countless boys. Surveys reveal that first-year college men view themselves as talented students who will earn higher grades than females, despite the fact that they read less and study less than their female peers. Why is it a revelation that they earn lower grades? Male hubris comes with a high cost.

Yet there are those who do not believe that gender bias is a problem. They believe males and females are "wired" differently, have different brains, and that is all part of nature's plan. Across America today, hundreds of public schools have bought into this argument and created separate classrooms and different instructional strategies for males and females, setting coeducation back a century.

We have written *Still Failing at Fairness* to shine a light on these and other gender issues that have become so prevalent in today's schools. This new edition differs from the original in several ways:

- In many recent books on gender, the focus has been on "boys in crisis." Before that, the focus was on "schools cheating girls." Such approaches set the reader up for such questions as: "Who is worse off, girls or boys?" "Are boys further behind now?" "Do girls no longer need to worry about gender bias?" It is time we understood that gender bias and stereotypes are persistent problems for both males and females. It is not one or the other gender that is the problem; gender bias is the problem.
- The original edition of *Failing at Fairness* focused primarily on girls because most people assumed that girls' good grades and grad-

uation rates meant that they were doing well in school. Some still make this assumption. But the 1994 edition documented how those good grades often masked persistent problems that short-circuited girls in school. The earlier edition of *Failing at Fairness* also included a chapter on the male stereotype and the gender barriers boys and men confront. This time, David and Karen have worked to integrate male and female issues throughout the book.

- This new edition is also more inclusive than the first in that we have tried to integrate gender research from different racial, ethnic, and socioeconomic backgrounds. Whenever possible, we view gender through cultural and racial lenses, recognizing that each group interprets gender roles differently.
- Naturally, we have updated the research throughout the book, but readers will note that we continue to include classic studies that date from the 1980s and 1990s. It is important for the reader to understand that the federal government has been an unreliable partner in exploring and dismantling gender barriers in schools. Unsympathetic administrations have eliminated much research funding. We hope that in the years ahead, the federal government will once again become a more positive force for eliminating gender bias in schools.
- We are often asked, "Is this still a problem? I heard about gender bias years ago. Isn't this old news?" We respond with a question: "Why wouldn't gender bias still be a problem? We are training teachers today in much the same way we did thirty years ago. While the curriculum is less gender biased than decades ago, it is still very biased. So yes, somewhere in most people's brains there is knowledge of gender bias in schools, but without specifics and without training, we have a new generation of teachers and students who are repeating many of the gender-stereotyped lessons of those who preceded them." In this revision, we cite many sad yet current statistics that make it all too clear that gender bias is very much an issue. And the fact that some people think it is no longer a problem is reason enough to write *Still Failing at Fairness*.
- Each chapter now concludes with a brief section we call "Succeeding at Fairness." After *Failing at Fairness* was originally published in 1994 a number of readers asked for practical advice, ideas, and online resources to help them create equitable home and school environments for both girls and boys. We have taken their recommendations to heart and now conclude each chapter with such suggestions.

In 1994, Myra and David coauthored *Failing at Fairness*. Both were professors and Myra was Dean of the School of Education at American University. That same year, Myra was diagnosed with breast cancer, and in nine months, our world changed. Myra died while undergoing a bone marrow transplant at Georgetown Hospital. She was fighting breast cancer, but it was the "cure" that took her life. Her words, her thoughts, and her spirit are on every page of this revision.

In 1999, a new doctoral student came into David's office at American University, and it was clear to David that she would be an important voice for equality. Karen Zittleman brings incredible commitment and insight to this project, and she is now a coauthor of this book. To keep things as clear as possible for the reader, when we use the term *we* in this book, we are referring to the two current authors, David and Karen. When the reference refers to work done by David and Myra, we will say so.

We want to acknowledge several people who have helped immeasurably with this revision. New parent Audra Prewitt interviewed other parents and uncovered some insightful anecdotes that appear in the book. Teachers Amy Wolfson, Eleni Vagelatos, and Andrea Bilotto replicated several gender studies in their classrooms, documenting just how painfully slow positive gender changes can be. Lynn Rosen has been a supportive literary agent for both editions of this book. Our editor, Samantha Martin, read every page and provided thoughtful recommendations. While we are responsible for what is written here, this book is undoubtedly stronger for all their contributions. Finally, we extend our thanks to friends, family, colleagues, and of course our students, for their insights and support.

CHAPTER 1

Didn't We Solve This Problem Years Ago?

By 1994, Myra and David Sadker had already been researching classrooms for over a decade, documenting what so many missed: despite girls' terrific report cards and cheery smiles, subtle sexist practices at home and at school were sapping their future potential. Many of the lessons girls were learning in school would actually thwart their success as adults. Gender bias was not about girls only: boys were also being shortchanged and confined to an even tighter gender role of what was, and was not, acceptable behavior. The Sadkers saw the challenge in simple terms: publicize unfair treatment (in this case sexism in schools), create awareness of the problem, and surely teachers and parents would demand change. The Sadkers shared their decades of research in the original 1994 edition of *Failing at Fairness*.

While there has been significant progress in the past few years, sexism not only persists, but has become both more puzzling and more virulent than ever. Political pundits and far-right foundations have fueled a concerted effort to turn back the clock, to degrade feminist efforts, and to reestablish more restrictive gender roles. They argue that men and women are so different that they should be educated in different ways and for different life roles. Today, the need for a revised *Failing at Fairness* could not be clearer.

More Public Schools Dividing Boys and Girls
Houston Chronicle (2007)

Harvard President Shocks with Comments on Gender Differences
University Wire (2005)

Civil Rights Commission Turns into Heated Debate on Title IX
CBS Sportsline.com (2007)

The Math Myth: The Real Truth about Women's Brains and the Science Gender Gap
Time, February 27, 2005

Study Casts Doubt on the "Boy Crisis"
Washington Post, June 26, 2006

Study Notes Lack of Female Professors
University Wire, February 23, 2004

Many teachers, parents, and students are confused. College students in our classes often view sexism as a vestige of a bygone era, more about political correctness than actual inequities. They arrived on the scene after the most egregious examples of sex bias were eliminated, and have yet to recognize how gender bias can (and likely will) inhibit their options. For them, the word *feminist* is a label to be avoided at all cost. They are not alone.

Just before revising this book, David received a call from a young reporter who wanted to speak to him about his work "in making women superior to men." This reporter had already constructed his own definition of gender equity, one built on fear, and his writing will likely fuel fear in others. He viewed gender bias in school as boys versus girls. Some authors and media pundits find that combative metaphor useful. We do not. Gender bias short-circuits both boys and girls, and both move forward when gender restrictions are removed. We need to remove the fear of change, of moving forward. Marianne Williamson wrote about such fear.

Our deepest fear is not that we are inadequate. Our deepest fear is that we are powerful beyond measure. It is our light, not our darkness that most frightens us. We ask ourselves, who am I to be brilliant, gorgeous, talented, fabulous? Actually, who are you *not* to be? You are a child of God. Your playing small does not serve the world. There is nothing enlightened about shrinking so that other people won't feel insecure around you. We are all meant to shine, as children do. We were born to make manifest the glory of God that is within us. It's not just in some of us; it's in everyone. And as we let our own light shine, we unconsciously give other people permission to do the same. As we are liberated from our own fear, our presence automatically liberates others.[1]

There is no doubt that political and social opposition to gender equity has grown in recent years. The critics, often referred to as the *backlash,* touch a "darkness that most frightens us" by drawing gloomy scenarios of how society will be harmed, boys hurt, and our future imperiled if traditional gender roles are changed. Our purpose is quite the opposite: to encourage parents and educators to help each child grow in a world free of stereotypes, to welcome the light. We hope that *Still Failing at Fairness* will reinforce Williamson's idea that each of us is "powerful beyond measure."

BIAS IN THE CLASSROOM

The media floods us with restricted gender images of female beauty and male macho. Blatant sexist images inundate movies, television, and advertising, but it is the even more subtle sexist messages that can shape how we view our world. When *Failing at Fairness* was first published, Myra and David focused on these subtle, all but invisible, examples of sexism in school. But it was their appearances on *Dateline* in 1992 and in 1994 (before the "To Catch a Predator" epidemic had set in) that underscored the challenge of "seeing" subtle sexism in school.

Jane Pauley, the show's coanchor at the time, wanted to visit classrooms, capture these covert sexist lessons on videotape, and expose them before a television audience. The task was to extricate sound bites and video clips of sexism from a fifth-grade classroom where the teacher, chosen to be the subject of the exposé, was aware she was being scrutinized for sex bias. The teacher agreed to be the focus so that she could learn and improve her already strong teaching skills. What a great idea!

Dateline had been taping her class for two days when David received a concerned phone call from the show's producer: "This is a fair teacher. How can we show sexism on our show when there's no gender bias in this teacher's class?" David and Myra drove to the NBC studio in Washington, D.C., and found two *Dateline* staffers, intelligent women concerned about fair treatment in school, sitting on the floor in a darkened room staring at the videotape of a fifth-grade class. "We've been playing this over and over. The teacher is terrific. There's no bias in her teaching. Come watch."

The teacher was terrific. She was also a classic example of the many skillful, well-intentioned professionals who inadvertently teach boys better than girls. The NBC staffers, like most people, simply could not detect the bias. One literally has to learn to see again, to remove the cultural blinders. The Sadkers froze the tape, pointed out the sexist behaviors, and then replayed it. The producers were amazed that they looked so hard and saw so little. The examples of sexism were like micro inequities: fleeting but persistent, brief but powerful, flying under our conscious radar. Once the hidden lessons of unconscious bias are made visible, classrooms never look the same again.

Much of the unintentional gender bias in that fifth-grade class could not be shown in the short time allowed by television, but the video clips of sexism selected for broadcast were powerful. *Dateline* showed a math group with boys sitting on the teacher's right side and girls on her left. Informal segregation by race would likely be addressed, but when done by gender is routinely ignored—with compelling consequences. After giving the math book to a girl to hold open at the page of examples, the teacher turned her back to the girls and focused on the boys, teaching them actively and directly. Occasionally she turned to the girls' side, but only to read the examples in the book. This teacher, although aware that she was being observed for sexism, had unwittingly transformed the girls into passive spectators, an audience for the boys. All but one, that is: the girl holding the math book had become a prop.

Dateline also showed a lively discussion in the school library. With both girls' hands and boys' hands waving for attention, the librarian chose boy after boy to speak. In one interaction she peered through the forest of girls' hands waving directly in front of her to acknowledge the raised hand of a boy in the back of the room. Startled by the teacher's attention, the boy muttered, "I was just stretching." In the fast pace of classroom give-and-take, such behaviors are difficult to detect, much less change. Sexist interactions are part of our everyday culture, imbedded in how we talk and behave. It is much easier to discuss sexism in the abstract than it is to eliminate specific sexist behaviors—especially when you are the teacher.

Sitting in the same classroom, reading the same textbook, listening to the same teacher, boys and girls receive very different educations. From grade school through graduate school, female students are more likely to be invisible members of classrooms. Teachers interact with males more frequently, ask them better questions, give them more precise and helpful feedback, and discipline them more harshly and more publicly. Over the course of years the uneven distribution of teacher time, energy, attention, and talent shapes both genders. Girls learn to wait patiently, to accept that they are behind boys on the line for teacher attention. Boys learn that they are the prime actors shaping classroom life. If frustrated, boys quickly discover that they can call out or act out. Teachers learn that the way to "manage" a class is to control the boys. In today's sexist school culture, boys assume that they are number one, and begin to understand the inherited power of entitlement. This sense of entitlement is a two-edged sword: soaring boyhood hopes often crash into adult realities. Boys are led to expect much from the world, often too much in the way of power and material wealth. Few boys will become president or an astronaut or a millionaire or a sports star. Many boys will become men who sell life insurance, fix furnaces, or work long hours on two jobs. School teaches girls what society expects from them: patience, waiting, a second-class citizenship, and quiet frustration (and too often depression). Sexism sends both girls and boys into the world with these powerful lessons—lessons they would be better off unlearning.

After several decades of research and thousands of hours of classroom observation, the stubborn persistence and subtlety of sexist lessons are startling. When Myra and David began their first research project in the early 1980s, they visited one of Washington, D.C.'s most elite (and expensive) private schools. Uncertain of exactly what to look for, David and Myra decided to write nothing down, but simply sit quietly and observe. They felt like meditating monks in the midst of a whirlwind of activity. So much happening at once! Classroom life is so fast paced that one could easily miss a vital phrase or gesture, a tiny inequity that might hold a world of meaning. Sometimes, subtlety was not the problem. On the second day, they witnessed their first clear example of sexism, a quick, jarring flash within the hectic pace of the school day:

Two second graders are kneeling beside a large box. They whisper excitedly to each other as they pull out wooden blocks, colored balls, counting sticks. So absorbed are these two small children in examining and sorting the materials, they are visibly startled by the teacher's impatient voice as she hovers over them. "Ann! Julia! Get your cotton-pickin' hands out of the math box. Move over so the boys can get in there and do their work."

Isolated here on the page of a book, this incident is not difficult to interpret. Some might not even find the comment particularly offensive.

But if race rather than gender was the distinction, the injustice is brought into sharper focus. Picture Ann and Julia as African-American children asked to take their "cotton-pickin' hands" away so white children "can get in there and do their work." Whether the child was black or female, if Ann and Julia's parents had observed this exchange, they might justifiably wonder whether their tuition dollars were well spent. But few parents actually watch teachers in action, and fewer still have learned to interpret the meaning behind fast-paced classroom events.

While the teacher talked to the two girls, she was also keeping a wary eye on fourteen other active children. Unless you actually shadowed the teacher, stood right next to her as we did, you might miss the event entirely. After all, it lasted only a few seconds. The incident unsettles, but it must be considered within the context of numerous interactions this harried teacher had that day. Perhaps the teacher feared that without some constructive activity, the boys might have gotten into mischief. Keep them on task and the girls will mind themselves. But the hidden lesson to those students was obvious.

Most sexist behaviors are far less obvious. It took Myra and David almost a year to develop an observation system that would register the hundreds of daily classroom interactions, teasing out the imbedded gender bias. Trained raters went into classrooms in four states and the District of Columbia, recording the dialogue of teachers and students. They observed students from different racial and ethnic backgrounds as they attended math, reading, English, and social studies classes. They saw lessons taught by women and by men, by teachers of different races. In short, they analyzed America's classrooms. By the end of the year, there were thousands of observation sheets, and after another year of statistical analysis, a syntax of sexism emerged, one so elusive that most teachers and students were completely unaware of its influence.[2] Boys had become the center of teacher attention; girls had become quiet spectators.

BREAKING THE SOUND BARRIER

Women who have spent years learning the lessons of silence in elementary, secondary, and college classrooms have trouble regaining their voices. David often sets up a role play to demonstrate classroom sex bias. Four volunteers, two women and two men, are asked to pretend to be students in a middle school social studies lesson. They have no script;

their only direction is to take a piece of paper with them as David, playing the part of the social studies teacher, ushers them to four chairs in front of the room. He tells the audience that he will condense much of the research on classroom sexism into a ten-minute lesson so that the bias will be more obvious, even overwhelming. The job of parents and teachers in the audience is to detect the different forms of egregious sexism. He begins the lesson:

"Today we're going to discuss the chapter in your book, *The Gathering Clouds of War,* about the American Revolution. But first I'd like you to take out your homework so I can check it." David walks over to Sarah, the first student in the line of four. (In real life she is an English teacher at the local high school.)

"Let's see your paper, Sarah." He pauses to look it over. "Questions three and seven are not correct." Sarah looks concerned.

David moves to Peggy (who is a communications professor at a state college). "Oh, Peggy, Peggy, Peggy!" She looks up as everyone stares. David holds up Peggy's paper. "Would you all look at this? It is sooo neat. You print just like a typewriter. This is the kind of paper I like to put on the bulletin board for open school night." Peggy looks down, smiles, blushes, looks up wide-eyed, and bats her eyelashes. Before our eyes she is reliving the lessons of her childhood, the stereotypical good girl with pretty penmanship. The lessons have been well learned.

Next David stops by Tony (who is a career and vocational education teacher) and looks at the blank paper he is holding. "Tony, you've missed questions three, seven, and eleven. I think you would do better on your assignments if you used the bold headings to guide your reading. I know you can get this if you try harder." Tony nods earnestly as David moves to Roy. Sarah, who missed questions three and seven, looks perplexed.

David scans Roy's paper and hands it back. "Roy, where's your homework?"

Roy (a college physics teacher) stammers, "Here it is," and again offers the blank paper that served as homework for the others in the role play.

"Roy, that's not your history homework. That's science." Roy still looks puzzled. "Trust me, Roy," David says. "No matter what you come up with, it won't be history homework. Now, where is it?"

"The dog ate it," Roy mutters, getting the picture and falling into the bad boy role. He smirks a bit and laughs along with the others.

Next David discusses revolutionary battles, military tactics, and male leaders—George Washington, John and Samuel Adams, Paul Revere,

Benjamin Franklin, Thomas Jefferson, and more. He calls on Roy and Tony more than twenty times each. When they don't know the answer, he probes, jokes, challenges, offers hints. He calls on Sarah only twice. She misses both her questions because David gives her less than half a second to speak. After effusively praising Peggy's pretty paper, David never calls on her again. As the lesson progresses, Sarah's face takes on a sad, almost vacant expression. Peggy keeps on smiling.

When the scene of blatant sexism is over, many in the audience want to know how the two women felt.

"That was me all through school," Peggy blurts out. "I did very well. My work was neat. I was always prepared. I would have had the right answer if someone had called on me. But they never did."

"Why did you watch the two males get all the attention?" we ask. "If you weren't called on, why didn't you call out?"

"I tried. I just couldn't do it."

"Why? You weren't wearing a muzzle. The men were calling out."

"I know. I felt terrible. It reminded me of all those years in school when I wanted to say something but couldn't."

"What about you, Sarah?" we ask. "Why didn't you just shout out an answer?"

"It never occurred to me to do it," Sarah says, then pauses. "No, that's not true. I thought about it, but I didn't want to be out there where I might get laughed at or ridiculed."

David has taught this role-play class hundreds and hundreds of times in workshops in big cities and small towns all across the United States. Each time he demonstrates sex bias by blatantly and offensively ignoring female students, and almost always the adult women, put back into the role of twelve-year-olds, sit and say nothing; once again they become the nice girls watching the boys in action. Inside they may feel sad or furious or relieved, but like Sarah and Peggy, they remain silent.

The men who volunteered for the role-play did not bargain for their role, either: in the spotlight. Most were not history experts, but with David's clues and cues, they managed to answer the seemingly endless stream of questions he directed at them. They were also singled out for discipline, although they had done nothing wrong. When that happened, familiar bells rang and they nodded and smiled at the other participants. They knew the class clown routine. When David needed students to come to the front of the class to demonstrate "guerrilla warfare," he recruited the two boys. Most teachers do the same, asking boys to take part in demonstrations to keep them active and engaged. The men, like the women, have cell memories of their student behaviors. They remembered the misplaced discipline or the stream of academic questions cascading on them when they were young. They chuckle now, for they have learned how to "take it like a man." But as boys, those were difficult times.

Women must work to be heard in such classes, but the rewards are often not worth the effort. Instead, some sit patiently and take notes, some doodle or write letters or pass notes, or simply wait for the teacher to notice them. It can be a long wait. In a California workshop, one parent who was playing the part of a student developed an elaborate pantomime. She reached into her large purse, pulled out a file, and began to do her nails. When that failed to attract David's attention, she brought out a brush, makeup, and a mirror. But David continued to ignore her, talking only with the two males.

"I was so mad I wanted to hit you," the woman fumed at the end of the role play when she was invited to express her feelings.

"What did you do to show your anger?" David asked.

"I didn't do anything." Then she paused, realizing the passive-aggressive but ultimately powerless strategy she had pursued. "No, I did do something—my nails," she said sadly.

After hundreds of these role plays, we are still astonished at how quickly the veneer of adulthood melts away. Doing the role play in 2008 creates the same reactions as it did twenty years ago. Despite a general awareness of gender equity, the *gender culture* of schooling persists; many girls find solace in classroom silence, and many boys still feel the need to clown around in class, or dominate the discussion. Women and men continue to replay behaviors they learned as children at school, and teachers continue to teach the way they were taught. These role plays are revealing, funny, sad, and sometimes, they take a troubling twist.

At a workshop for college students at a large university in the Midwest, one of the young women ignored in the role play did not exhibit the usual behavior of silence or passive hostility. Instead, in the middle of the workshop in front of her classmates, she began to sob. She explained later in private that as one of only a few girls in the university's agricultural program, she had been either ignored or harassed. That week in an overenrolled course an instructor had announced, "There are too many students in this class. Everyone with ovaries—out!"

"What did you do?"

"What could I do? I left. Later I told my adviser about it. He was sympathetic but said if there was no room, I should consider another major."

BIAS IN BOOKS

Among Schoolchildren written by Tracy Kidder, chronicles real-life educator Chris Zajac. A thirty-four-year-old teacher in Holyoke, Massachusetts, Mrs. Zajac is a no-nonsense veteran of the classroom. She does not allow her fifth-grade students to misbehave, forget to do their homework, or give up without trying their hardest. Underlying her strict exterior is a woman who cares about schoolchildren. Our students admired her dedication and respected her as a good human being, and it took several readings and discussions before they discovered her inadvertent gender bias. Then came the questions: Does Mrs. Zajac work harder teaching boys than girls? Does she know there is sex bias in her classroom?

These questions probably do not occur to most readers of *Among Schoolchildren* and might jolt both Chris Zajac and the author who so meticulously described the classroom. Here's how Tracy Kidder begins the story of a year in the life of this New England teacher:

> Mrs. Zajac wasn't born yesterday. She knows you didn't do your best work on this paper, Clarence. Don't you remember Mrs. Zajac saying that if you didn't do your best, she'd make you do it over? As for you, Claude, God forbid that you should ever need brain surgery. But Mrs. Zajac hopes that if you do, the doctor won't open up your head and walk off saying he's almost done, as you said when Mrs. Zajac asked you for your penmanship, which, by the way, looks like who did it and ran. Felipe, the reason you have hiccups is, your mouth is always open and the wind rushes in. You're in fifth grade now. So, Felipe, put a lock on it. Zip it up. Then go get a drink of water. Mrs. Zajac means business, Robert. The sooner you realize she never said everybody in the room has to do the work except for Robert, the sooner you'll get along with her. And . . . Clarence. Mrs. Zajac knows you didn't try. You don't just hand in junk to Mrs. Zajac. She's been teaching an awful lot of years. She didn't fall off the turnip cart yesterday. She told you she was an old-lady teacher.[3]

Swiftly, adroitly, Kidder introduces the main characters in the classroom—Clarence, Claude, Felipe, Robert, and back to Clarence, the boy in whom Mrs. Zajac invests most. But where are the girls?

As the students analyzed the book and actually examined whom Mrs.

Zajac was speaking to, they saw that page after page she spent time with the boys—disciplining them, struggling to help them understand, teaching them with all the energy and talent she could muster. In contrast, the pages that showed Mrs. Zajac working with girls were few and far between.

When we ask teachers at our workshops why they spend more time helping boys, they say, "Because boys need it more" or "Boys have trouble reading, writing, doing math. They can't even sit still. They need me more." In *Among Schoolchildren,* Chris Zajac feels that way, too. Kidder describes how she allows boys to take her over because she thinks they need her.

Teachers of good intention, such as Chris Zajac, respond to boys and teach them more actively, but their time and attention are not limitless. While the teachers are spending time with boys, the girls are being ignored and shortchanged. The only girl clearly realized in *Among Schoolchildren* is Judith, a child who is so alert that she has a vast English vocabulary even though her parents speak only Spanish. But while Judith is a girl of brilliant potential, she rarely reaps the benefit of Mrs. Zajac's active teaching attention. In fact, rather than trouble her teacher and claim time and attention for herself, Judith helps Mrs. Zajac, freeing her to work with the more demanding boys. Mrs. Zajac knows she isn't giving this talented girl what she needs and deserves: "If only I had more time," she thinks as she looks at Judith.

On a field trip to Old Sturbridge Village, the children have segregated themselves by sex on the bus, with the boys claiming the back. In a moment of quiet reflection, Mrs. Zajac realizes that in her classroom "the boys rarely give her a chance to spend much time with her girls." She changes her seat, joins the girls, and sings jump rope songs with them for the remainder of the trip.[4]

But her time spent with the girls is short-lived—the length of the daylong field trip—and her recognition of the gender gap in time and attention is brief: a paragraph-long flash of understanding in a book of more than three hundred pages. On the whole, Chris Zajac does not invest her talent in girls. But nurturing children is not unlike tending a garden: neglect, even when benign, is withering; time and attention bear fruit. Mrs. Zajac and other caring teachers across the country are unaware of the full impact of uneven treatment. They do not realize the high academic and emotional price many girls pay for being too good.

In our own classroom observations, we have seen many scenes like those described in *Among Schoolchildren.* In today's classrooms, bias in school textbooks is often a springboard for sexist classroom discussions.[5] Imagine yourself as the teacher in the sixth-grade science class described below. The scenario is based on our observations in a Maryland classroom, but this time we will highlight the gender inequities in the scene to help you spot them.

The teacher begins by writing a list of inventors and their discoveries on the board:

Elias Howe	sewing machine
Robert Fulton	steamboat
Thomas A. Edison	lightbulb
James Otis	elevator
Alexander Graham Bell	telephone
Cyrus McCormick	reaper
Eli Whitney	cotton gin
Orville and Wilbur Wright	airplane

A girl raises her hand and asks, "It looks like all the inventors were men. Didn't women invent anything?"

Possible Responses:

- The teacher smiles, and says, "Great point!" Then the teacher adds several female inventors to the list.
- The teacher explains how new scholarship recognizes the role of scores of women inventors who have been overlooked. (If the name Eli Whitney sparks cotton gin in your mind, you need to learn more about Catherine Littlefield Greene.)
- The teacher explains the social and economic constraints on women in past eras. He describes how social conventions had inhibited women from obtaining patents in their own names.
- The teacher jumps on this "teachable moment" and explains how textbook authors use the word *inventor* when they should use *patent holder*. The truth is we may never know how many female (or black or other) inventors are excluded from the pages of our history books because they did not hold the patents.

Actual Response:

The teacher grins, winks, and says, "Sweetheart, don't worry about it. It's the same with famous writers and painters. Men create and women inspire." Several boys laugh. A few clown around by flexing their muscles as they exclaim, "Yes!" One girl rolls her eyes toward the ceiling and shakes her head in disgust. The incident lasts less than a minute, and the discussion of male inventors, many of whom will become questions on the all-important test, continues.

We sometimes ask our college students to list twenty famous women from American history. There are only a few restrictions. They cannot include figures from sports or entertainment. Presidents' wives are not allowed unless they are clearly famous in their own right. Most students cannot do it. Many struggle to name ten. (How many can you name?) The seeds of this ignorance are sown in our earliest years of schooling.

In the 1970s, researchers analyzed the most common school history textbooks. They discovered a biological oddity: male pregnancy and birth, and no women involved.[6] Founding fathers were everywhere; founding mothers were nowhere in sight. In one text, more space was given to the six-shooter than to the women's suffrage movement. In fact, the typical history text gave only two sentences to the political movement that enfranchised half the population. Change is slow. In a popular history text published in 2005, there were eight full-page biographies of men, and only one female biography. (If you are wondering, it was Anne Hutchinson's fight for religious freedom in Colonial America that was included.) Not that the stories of women who made a difference are lost. Their stories are accessible. For example, a year earlier, in 2004, television commentator Cokie Roberts had written a bestseller, appropriately titled *Founding Mothers*. Her stories of Colonial women who fought for and created this nation can be found in most bookstores, but these stories are still missing from school texts.[7]

Science and math texts continue the narrative of a one-gender world. For example, a study of elementary mathematics software in the 1990s found that things were not much better than the 1970s, when Madame Curie was pictured standing behind her husband, peering over his shoulder as he looked into a microscope.[8] In mathematics software, only 12 percent of the characters were female, and careers were marked by gender stereotyping.[9]

At our workshops we ask teachers and parents to tell or write about any sexism they have seen in their schools. We have been collecting their stories for years.[10] A Utah teacher told us: "Last year I had my U.S. history classes write biographies about famous Americans. When I collected all one hundred and fifty, I was dismayed to find only five on women. When I asked my kids why, they said they didn't know any famous women. When I examined their textbook more closely, I saw there were few females in it. And there were even fewer books on famous American women in our school library."

Teachers add to textbook bias when they produce sexist materials of their own. One parent described her continuing efforts to stop a teacher-made worksheet that perpetuated stereotypes:

> A few years ago my daughter came home upset over her grade. When I looked at her paper, I got more angry than she was. At the top of the worksheet were the faces of a man and a woman. At the bottom were different objects—nails, a saw, a sewing needle, thread, a hammer, a screwdriver, a broom. The directions said to draw a line from the man to the objects that belong to him and a line from the woman to the objects that go with her. In our house my husband does the cooking and I do the repair work, so you can imagine what the lines on my daughter's paper looked like. There was a huge red F in the middle of her worksheet. I called the teacher right away. She was very under-standing and assured me the F wouldn't count. A small victory, I thought, and forgot about it.
>
> This year my son is in her class. Guess what he brought home last week. Same worksheet—same F. Nothing had changed at all.

When children do not see girls and women in the pages of textbooks and teachers do not point out or confront the omissions, our daughters and our sons learn that to be female is to be an absent partner in the development of our nation. Teachers can do a great deal to neutralize omissions or even stereotypes, but too often they were never taught about women's experiences themselves.

In a 1992 survey in *Glamour,* 74 percent of those responding said that they had "a teacher who was biased against females or paid more atten-tion to the boys." Math class was selected as the place where inequities were most likely to occur. Fifty-eight percent picked math as the most sexist subject. Physical education was second, and science came in third, selected by 47 percent of the respondents.[11] By 2000, researchers found little had changed: almost three out of four male teachers believed that boys were more interested and more talented than girls in computer tech-nology.[12] Most primary and secondary teachers believed males to be more competent in mathematics.[13]

A study of high school STEM classes (science, technology, engineering, and math) demonstrated how teacher assumptions can play out in the classroom. In one computer science class, boys made comments about girls and their bodies, appearance, and competence. The male teacher did nothing to stop the harassment. In the same class, a girl asked why the teacher always used football examples for assignments. Instead of varying his examples, the teacher told the girl that she could choose another topic if she wanted. The boys in the class laughed and suggested that the girl "do it on sewing." Again, the teacher did nothing. Not surprisingly, female enrollment in these advanced computer science classes continued to fall.[14] The *Chronicle of Higher Education* described another high school class where the boys repeatedly told one of two girls in the class that she was not good at programming. "One of the guys I grew up with and was in all of the classes with told me that, scientifically, girls were not programmed to do math like guys could," she said. "And I believed him."[15] Girls and women are more likely than males to internalize such criticism and biased comments.[16]

Sometimes a school staff allows humiliating comments and sexist behaviors in the school:

> The New England high school was having an assembly during the last period on Friday, and the auditorium was packed with more than a thousand students, who were restless as they listened to announcements. A heavy, awkward tenth grader made her way across the stage to reach the microphone located in the center. As she walked, several male students made loud barking noises to signify she was a dog. Others oinked like pigs. Later a slender, long-haired senior walked to the mike; she was greeted by catcalls and whistles. Nobody attempted to stop the demeaning and hurtful public evaluation of the appearance of these teenage girls.

Too many teachers look the other way, shrug their shoulders, and mumble "boys will be boys" during such events. Sexually denigrating comments, even pinching, touching, and propositioning, have become part of the fabric of classroom life. Sensitive and insecure about their appearance, some girls are intimidated into silence. Many girls don't even realize they have a right to protest. And when they muster the courage to bring sexual harassment in school into the open, their bravery is rarely rewarded. Such charges are routinely swept under the rug or even turned against the girl who had the courage to complain. A teacher at a workshop in Indiana told us: "In our school a girl was pinched on the derriere by two boys and verbally harassed. When she reported the incident to the principal, she was told that her dress was inappropriate and that she had asked for it."

A 2001 study by the American Association of University Women found that girls are not the only targets of such attacks; boys are almost as likely to be sexually harassed. Much of that harassment is in the form of a masculinity test. Boys must act tough, strong, and stoic to survive; avoiding the taint of anything female is essential to male identity (and safety). A feminine boy is a walking target. As one seventh-grade female summed it up: "Some of them are called gay, fags. They get picked on and fight for survival."[17] To survive, many boys choose a path of extreme masculinity. Their macho toughness sparks teachers' attention. In her 2005 study, Karen found that most students, both girls and boys, believe that teachers overreact to boys. Students accuse teachers of "picking on boys" and witness innocent boys caught and disciplined unfairly. As a seventh-grade middle schooler explains, "Boys joke around too much so teachers pay more attention by disciplining rather than helping them to learn."[18] We have created an amazingly dysfunctional classroom climate: sexual harassment thrives while discipline is seen as unfair.

Intimidating comments and offensive sexual jokes are even more common in college, sometimes becoming part of a classroom discussion. A female faculty member, teaching at a university that was historically all male, described one of the most popular teachers on campus, an economics professor:

> He would show slides illustrating an economic theory and insert women in bikinis in the middle "to keep the students interested." He illustrated different phases of the economic cycle by showing a slide of a woman's breast and pointed out how far away from the nipple each phase was. When a number of female students complained, the local newspaper supported the professor and criticized the "ultrasensitive coeds." That semester the university gave the professor the Teacher of the Year award.

Although sexually harassing remarks, stories, and jokes occur in classrooms, female silence is a typical response. During the Sadkers' two-year study of colleges, raters found that girls grew quieter as they grew older. In coeducational classes, college women are even less likely to participate in discussions than elementary and secondary school girls. In the typical college classroom, 45 percent of students do not speak; the majority of these voiceless students are women.[19]

THE COSTS OF ENTITLEMENT

When adolescent boys and girls were asked what it would be like to be born a member of the other sex, how do you think they responded? As you might suspect, girls saw some enticing possibilities if they were born male: wealth, strength, political power, and athleticism. Boys were repulsed at even the idea of being born a female, or living in a female body, or facing female life choices. A significant percentage of the boys said they would kill themselves, that they would rather be dead than female. Male entitlements are obvious even to children.[20]

While most teachers would disapprove of gender inequities and male entitlement, they are unaware of how their own teaching patterns contribute to the problem. Because teachers mean no harm, they believe they cause none, but their interactions can accentuate gender differences. Teachers talk less to girls, question them less, praise, probe, clarify, and correct them less. Female students accept the leftovers of teacher time and attention, and morsels of amorphous feedback. As a result, most girls learn to mind themselves, stay out of mischief, and settle for a quiet role in the classroom. Girls quickly learn to smile, work quietly, be neat, defer to boys, and talk only when spoken to. The school curriculum reinforces lessons of female docility with womanless histories, male-oriented science and math classes, and school sports programs that create heroes of male athletes. Girls even feel at risk in their schools, avoiding certain hallways or stairwells if at all possible. Little wonder that so many girls lose their voice, confidence, and ambition, a problem likely to haunt them in adulthood.

Boys, even those who struggle in school, recognize that while they may not be tomorrow's power players, they are still better off than the girls. Whether it is on the athletic field, in a classroom discussion, or in the principal's office, boys are expected to compete and win, or be tough and "take it" if they do not. Teachers understand that to manage their classes, they must manage the boys. So teachers direct more questions at boys to keep them on task. Teachers roam the classroom, positioning themselves nearer boys to keep an eye on their behavior, and at the same time, check the quality of their work. If necessary, the teacher can reseat students to separate boys, or move them up front where they can be closely monitored. Teachers get it; controlling boys keeps the classroom orderly. But in the process, boys are given more public attention and active instruction.

Not all boys thrive in the public spotlight of control and competition. For the artistic boy, the unathletic boy, the quiet boy, the rambunctious boy, life can be difficult. For the feminine or gay boy, school life can be near impossible. For good reasons or bad ones, boys live in the spotlight of attention, expectation, and restraint. Most boys survive, a few even thrive, but others find the glare too bright and drop out of school.

Even those boys who seem to do well in this environment may only be delaying the day of reckoning. The high school or college star athlete with dreams of glory in professional sports will eventually discover that only a tiny fraction of such athletes make it to the pros. Boys with visions of future wealth will likely see their dreams dissolve into middle-class lives. Boys voted "most likely to succeed" may one day settle for a brass ring rather than a gold one. The dreams we encourage boys to dream are self-centered and materialistic. Few boys are encouraged to focus on the joy of parenting, to fully appreciate loving relationships, to find meaningful work that satisfies their hearts rather than just their wallets, or simply to delight in life's everyday joys and gifts. In the end, the traditional male gender role is often shallow and unfulfilling, even for the winners.

In 2008, two new books were flying off bookstore shelves: *The Dangerous Book for Boys* and *The Daring Book for Girls*. Offering nostalgic trips to an earlier, simpler life, the books taught parents and children old-fashioned pastimes, such as Dutch jump rope and building racing go-carts, attractive alternatives to sedentary video games. But the books were more than nostalgia; they also told a gender tale. The turquoise-covered *Daring Book for Girls* encouraged girls to explore their world, all of their world, from changing tires to weaving a daisy chain. Girls were encouraged to read about the male hero in *Robinson Crusoe* as well as the female hero in *Island of the Blue Dolphins*. They were learning about all kinds of possibilities. Not so the boys. The bright red cover of *The Dangerous Book for Boys* included many exciting and even dangerous activities, but one activity was evidently too dangerous: learning about girls. The boys' book did not feature the breadth and variety of the girls' book. There were war stories to read, hunting to try, and bows and arrows to make. Boys were learning that being male (circa 1950s—or is it 1850s?) was all they needed to know. *The Dangerous Book for Boys* reminds us not only of the persistence and pervasiveness of sexism, but that male entitlements come with a cost.[21]

Author and attorney Riane Eisler argues that male entitlements put all of society in danger. She notes that our culture revolves around historical male priorities such as violence, which occupies local news stories, international events, and too many daily interactions. Traditional female values such as nonviolence, caring for one another, nurturing children, and helping those in need become devalued. The struggle for our future, she believes, is between those trying to maintain a system of male domination, and those working toward a new system, one she calls "partnership," which recognizes the values and contributions of women.[22] She offers as examples countries like Sweden, Finland, and Norway, where caring is more valued, the status of women higher, and the quality of life better. Perhaps if we want males and females to value fairness and justice for others, we must create schools in which they experience justice—in their classes, relationships, school experiences, and outcomes.[23]

THE COST OF SEXISM

In the past decades, we have seen great progress in battling sexism. Women now have access to virtually all colleges and are taking full advantage of that opportunity. The majority of college students, the presidents of several prestigious Ivy League universities, and about half the enrollment of medical and law schools are female. Today, boys are making impressive progress as well. More boys are scoring higher on standardized tests, taking advanced placement exams, graduating from high school, and going on to college than ever before. (However, for poorer and minority boys and girls, the situation is less encouraging.) Given these gains, it is not surprising that some believe that gender bias in school is no longer a problem, simply a relic of a bygone era. That is a false sense of confidence. Here are just a few of the gender challenges that we face today:

- *Boys and Schools:* Poor school achievement, overdiagnosis and referral to special educational services, athletic overinjury, bullying, peer harassment, disciplinary problems, and violence remain common school problems plaguing boys. Some now use the term "boys' crisis" to refer to this issue, but it is not a new crisis. Poor boys and boys of color especially continue to struggle in school. Many believe that the socialization of boys sets the stage for this conflict.[24]

- *Girls and Schools:* Gender socialization may explain in part why girls appear to do so well in school. Girls receive higher report card grades, have fewer disciplinary problems, and are more likely than boys to become valedictorians and go on to college. But the purpose of school is less clear. In 2006, over a third of students in grades three through twelve reported "people think that the most important thing for girls is to get married and have children."[25]
- *Test Scores:* In the early years, girls are ahead of or equal to boys on most standardized measures of achievement. By the time they graduate from high school or college, they have fallen behind boys on high-stakes tests such as the SAT, ACT, MCAT, LSAT, and GRE, all the key exams needed to gain entrance (and scholarships) to the most prestigious colleges and graduate schools.[26]
- *Instruction:* Perhaps one reason why female test scores tumble is that from elementary school through higher education, female students receive less active classroom instruction, both in the quantity and in the quality of teacher time and attention. Female grades may be less a sign of academic gifts than a reward for following the rules, being quiet, and conforming to school norms.[27]
- *Anti-Achievement Attitudes:* Boys often view reading and writing as "feminine" subjects that threaten their masculinity. Many boys, especially minority and poor boys, view school as irrelevant to their futures.[28]
- *Sexual Harassment:* Incidents of school-based sexual harassment are now reported with alarming frequency, with nearly nine in ten students (85 percent) reporting that students harass other students at their school, and almost 40 percent of students reporting that school employees sexually harass as well. Some are surprised to learn that boys are the targets of such harassment almost as frequently as girls.[29]
- *Self-Esteem:* As girls go through school, their self-esteem plummets, and the danger of depression increases. Eating disorders among females in schools and colleges are rampant and increasing, and some boys are beginning to display body image issues, including dieting and steroid abuse.[30]
- *College:* Men had been the majority of college students from the Colonial period to the early 1980s. Today women are the majority, but put into perspective, there is a higher percentage of both women and men attending college today than ever before. It is revealing to note that women who graduate from highly selective colleges earn

less than men from those colleges, but about the same as men from minimally selective colleges.[31]

- *Earnings:* Women also earn less at every level of education. In 2005, the median annual earnings of a female high school graduate were at least 34 percent less than that of her male counterpart. The median annual earnings of a woman with a bachelor's degree were almost 31 percent (or $15,911) less than that of a similarly qualified man; and a woman with a master's degree earned 32 percent (or $21,374) less than a man with a master's degree. The median annual earnings for a woman with a professional degree were $65,941 while men earned over $100,000. A woman with a doctoral degree earned at least 29 percent (or $22,824) less than a similarly qualified man. Women who work full-time and year-round earn on the average 77 cents for every dollar men earn. For African-American women, the figure is 72 cents, for Latinas, 58 cents, and for Asian Americans, 87 cents. When we consider all women, including those who work part-time or have taken time off to have children, the figure is 34 cents.[32]

- *Careers:* Many careers are hypersegregated by gender. In 2006, 91 percent of registered nurses, 82 percent of all elementary and middle school teachers, and 98 percent of all preschool and kindergarten teachers were women. In comparison, only 12 percent of all civil engineers, 8 percent of electrical and electronics engineers, and 2 percent of all aircraft pilots and flight engineers were female.[33]

- *Child Care and Women:* The availability or lack of affordable child care has a large impact on a family's income, and on a woman's ability to work. Child-care responsibilities continue to fall disproportionately on women. Estimates of child-care costs for two children in the United States could be as much as 37 percent of a single parent's income. Even for two-parent families of all income brackets, child care tends to be the second-largest household expenditure.[34]

- *Changing Family Earning Patterns:* The familiar family structure of a husband wage earner and a wife as a stay-at-home nonworker characterized 66 percent of families in the 1940s and '50s. By 2005, it described only 19 percent of families.[35]

- *Politics:* Women's representation in legislative bodies around the world puts America's democratic principles to the test. While almost half of Sweden's and Rwanda's legislators are women, in the United States the figure is under 17 percent, putting us ahead of Turkmenistan but trailing Zimbabwe.[36]

SUCCEEDING AT FAIRNESS:
SUGGESTIONS FOR STUDENTS, PARENTS, AND TEACHERS

We conclude each chapter with a section titled: "Succeeding at Fairness." Here we offer suggestions and activities for children, parents, and teachers to create a more equitable and humane childhood. We also recommend some books and online resources. Here are a few ideas for beginning to explore gender issues in and beyond school.

1. Observe people interacting in business or social settings. What gender differences do you note in their words, their topics, and their behaviors? Who is talking more? Who asks more questions? What adjectives are being used to describe males and females? How would you compare body language? How do such gender differences reinforce cultural stereotypes?

2. Now do the same thing in a school setting. Observe how adults talk to and treat students. What gender differences do you detect?

3. Now for the biggest challenge: Observe your own family and friends. What gender differences can you see in how males and females are treated? Perhaps an example might help. The Sadkers once watched two moms in the park as their children, a son and a daughter, learned to ride two-wheelers. Inevitably, each took turns falling. When the girl tumbled, the mom ran to her and in a sweet voice explained, "It's all right dear." She carefully brushed off the girl's knees and clothes, and gave her a hug. When the boy went down, the mother yelled, "That's okay, try again." There was no running, no brushing off, and no hug. One child was learning dependence and perhaps compassion, and the other independence and suppressing feeling, although neither mother seemed to note the gender training taking place.

4. Walk down the hallway of a school building. Look at the displays, the exhibits, the athletic trophies and other awards, the lists of students doing well or poorly. What gender lessons are being taught to the students who every day travel those halls? Are there any indications that the school is making an effort to break down traditional gender roles?

5. Parents and teachers can visit the library and check out nonsexist books to read to their children, or older students can check them out themselves. Librarians are a great source of information for such books for both boys and girls. When children are a bit older, there are some

fine nonsexist Newbery Award winners that the librarian can help recommend. As a related suggestion, there are magazine subscriptions that adults can purchase in a child's name. *New Moon* is a fine magazine for preteen girls. Science and math periodicals for young girls or short story collections and literary magazines for young boys can also widen gender options. Here, too, the librarian can be a big help.

6. Check out Title IX. This is the federal law that protects girls and boys, teachers and staff from sex bias in school. Unfortunately, few teachers or parents are aware of these protections, or how to get help if there are violations. Visit www.titleix.info/ or the National Women's Law Center (www.nwlc.org) online for information, activities, and suggestions. You might want to meet your school district's Title IX liaison. If they don't have one, they are already in violation and need to appoint someone.

7. Sexist practices can begin at nursery school (and often do) and continue through graduate school. Parents, teachers, and friends should discuss school life to make certain that discrimination is not occurring.

8. Clothing and toys purchased for young children send messages about what society says is "okay" for them to do. So when girls have rough-and-tumble clothes and are encouraged to engage in all kinds of physical activities, and when boys are encouraged to paint or read or care for younger siblings, parents and teachers are encouraging them to go beyond traditional notions of gender. Our society often emphasizes differences—among cultures, races, and genders. It is helpful for adults to find similarities among groups, those characteristics that define us all as part of humanity, and to share those similarities with children. As John F. Kennedy put it when talking about the dispute between communism and the West, "For in the final analysis, our most basic common link is that we all inhabit this small planet. We all breathe the same air. We all cherish our children's futures. And we are all mortal." Sharing our commonalities while not denying what makes us individuals may prove more helpful and truthful than dividing us by skin color, language, or gender.

9. Visit the website listed at the end of the chapter to track gender issues in school, in society, and in other nations. Adults can explore with youngsters why such problems and bias persist in our culture.

Resources

The Real Wealth of Nations: Creating a Caring Economics, by Riane Tennenhaus Eisler

Discusses the impact of female values versus traditional male values on public policy and the quality of citizens' lives.

Backlash: The Undeclared War Against American Women, by Susan Faludi
While this book is no longer new, it still offers a highly engaging account of the backlash against the women's movement. It may be the perfect time for a new generation to learn about this chapter of history.

Boys Will Be Boys: Breaking the Link Between Masculinity and Violence, by Myriam Miedzian
This book will help boys to see how the culture sends them messages of what is acceptable and unacceptable behavior.

For additional resources, see *Still Failing at Fairness*'s page on www.simon andschuster.com.

CHAPTER 2

Opening the Schoolhouse Door

Although a woman donated the plot of ground for a free school in New England, girls were forbidden to attend. In 1647, the town council of Farmington, Connecticut, voted money for a school "where all children shall learn to read and write English." However, the council quickly qualified this statement by explaining that "all children" meant "all males." Wealthy, white boys were the focus of America's schools for hundreds of years. Poor, female, and darker-skinned children were for the most part blocked at the schoolhouse door. Colonial Americans were, as a society, suspicious of educating these groups. Community leaders felt that educated women in particular "posed a danger to the social order and even to their own sanity."[1]

Education in this country took root slowly, and was informal, practical, and limited. Homeschooling was often the only option, and young boys and girls were taught lessons in reading, values, manners, social graces, and vocational skills. Sometimes, one home became a center of school activities. Led by a well-respected woman (or dame), this was called a "dame school." While both boys and girls were educated in dame schools, their educations were quite different. Girls were taught basic homemaking skills, while boys received a stronger emphasis on academics, including writing and arithmetic. Beyond the dame school, education was essentially a white male monopoly. Viewed as mentally and morally inferior, girls and women were relegated to learning only domestic skills, though they hungered for more.

While formal histories say little, letters and diaries hint of women's desire for learning and the lack of opportunity to fulfill that desire. In the early 1700s a Virginia girl wrote to her brother, who had been sent to England to study: "I find you have got the start of me learning very much, for you write better already than I expect to do as long as I live."[2] The parents of another Virginia girl, Mary Ball, searched to find a tutor for their able daughter. After four years they finally found a minister who agreed to live in their home and teach young Mary, the woman who would later give birth to George Washington.

But these were the lucky girls. Most received little or no formal education. Documents reveal that only 30 percent of women in Colonial America could even sign their names.[3] While the school door was closed, the house door was wide open. The home, serving as the girl's classroom, was where she learned the practical domestic skills for her inevitable role as wife and mother—inevitable, that is, as long as Providence took a hand and a mate was found. And, in Colonial America, there were ways to assist Providence. To attract suitors a girl needed a graceful carriage and erect posture. Special chairs complete with harnesses, stocks, and rigid backs were designed to align properly the female backbone. Committed to attaining that desirable graceful and erect carriage, girls were strapped into these chairs for hours. Unable to move—and usually unable to read—they just sat. A popular gift item, the restraining chair served as a harbinger of the restricted adult life to come.[4]

But by the late 1700s, new ideas were brewing. Some public schools actually opened their doors to girls, but with severe restrictions. In 1767 a school in Providence, Rhode Island, advertised that it would teach both reading and writing to female children. The small print noted the hours of instruction: from six to seven-thirty in the morning and from four to six-thirty in the afternoon. Each female student was charged a hefty sum for this inconveniently timed education. By fitting girls' education around the boys' regular hours, the teachers acquired needed additional income. Other elementary schools provided winter instruction for boys and allowed the girls to attend in the summer, an off-season education at a discount rate. Thus, slowly, as the concept of democracy was taking root, so was the notion that girls as well as boys should receive an education.[5]

REVOLUTIONARY IDEAS

The new democracy enlarged the European view of women, for while a woman's place was still in the home, in America her role took on new dimensions. In those revolutionary times she was to nurture her children's intellectual development. America's mothers were the nation's first teachers, and it didn't take long for people to realize that before a woman could enlighten children, she had to be enlightened herself.

The current debate over "school choice" would pale in comparison to the entrepreneurial array of schools that flourished in America's early years. Some schools began to open their doors to girls, at least those whose parents were able and willing to pay. Noted educator Benjamin Rush created the Young Ladies' Academy in Philadelphia to transform girls into strong and intellectually able mothers. Religious orders spread their educational philosophies in girls' schools built by Quakers, Moravians, and Catholics.

It was not until the first half of the nineteenth century that the ideas of a formal education for all girls and boys took root. Horace Mann, secretary of education for Massachusetts, became the nation's leading advocate for the "common school"—today's public elementary school—where Americans of all backgrounds could attend a public school supported not by charging fees but by tax dollars. Poor, middle-class, and wealthy children of all races would all receive a "common education," an experience necessary to build a united nation.[6]

By the first half of the nineteenth century, some communities in Massachusetts began to experiment with the radical concept of high school education for girls. A high school for boys had already been established in Boston, and in the late 1820s the public demanded one for girls, too. But city leaders underestimated the interest, and there were far more applicants than spaces available. Three out of four girls were turned away. Facing growing public unrest, Boston's mayor had to explain why 75 percent of the girls applying could not attend high school, and he came up with a brilliant but painful solution: disappointing everyone equally, he played no favorites and closed the high school. Girls who thirsted for more education would have to wait until after the election; with the mayor's defeat, their high school was finally reopened.[7]

While large cities struggled to establish separate high schools, smaller communities could not afford to build one high school for boys and another for girls. With true American ingenuity, towns and rural communities built one high school and then pretended that they had built two. Entering by separate doors, boys and girls went directly to their assigned single-sex area. Sometimes they went to different floors, or boys went to one side of the building and girls to the other. Frequently the girls were taught by women and the boys by men, so they continued to learn in their own sex-segregated worlds. But they were in the same school building at the same time—a revolutionary development!

These "mixed" schools, as they were called, stirred emotional debate. Critics worried that boys and girls learning together in one place would have dire consequences. Such a combustible mix, they warned, required close supervision. These worries only increased as, over several decades, "mixed" schools became "mixed" classrooms. Opponents to this burgeoning coeducation charged that boys and girls were headed for different destinies, and they should be educated separately for their distinct life paths. Offering girls and boys identical lessons would do little to encourage womanly interest and skill in domestic activities. Critics also predicted that the tough academic exchanges and standards of all-male classroom discussion would soften in deference to females and that schools would be feminized.

Advocates of coeducation argued that the presence of girls would refine boys' rough behavior and that these mixed schools and classrooms would develop better-educated females who, when they became mothers, could teach their own children more effectively. But the winning argument was economic: separate schools and programs for boys and girls were simply too costly, and taxpayers proved unwilling to pay the bill. By 1900, 98 percent of high schools were coeducational, and coeducation was all but universal in American elementary and secondary public schools.[8]

Some families rejected coeducation, however. For them the seminary became the school of choice.

MORALS, MIND, MANNERS, AND MOTHERHOOD

If the word *seminary* conjures up images of an austere, cloistered, and religious world, you are not far off at all. Historians have summarized seminary curriculum as "the three M's: morals, mind, and manners." These institutions provided protected educational environments, safe havens for high-school-age girls to learn to become fit companions for their husbands, the first teachers of their children, and the moral and spiritual cornerstone of the family. These seminaries were dedicated to the tricky proposition of expanding women's educational options while keeping their role in life limited.

To the three M's of seminary education we could add a fourth: motherhood. In 1821, when Emma Willard was struggling to establish the Troy Female Seminary, she wooed adherents and financial backers with her claim to "professionalize motherhood": "O how immensely important is this work of preparing the daughters of the land to be good mothers."[9] Her tactics were effective, and she built her seminary. After all, who would not support motherhood?

In her seminary, Willard raised domesticity to a science. Willard explained to New York's governor, DeWitt Clinton, "It is believed that housewifing might be greatly improved by being taught not only in practice but in theory."[10] Girls in seminaries learned the secrets of managing homes to make them healthier and more efficient.

For many of these schools, the spiritual and moral development of their students was paramount. This relationship helped formal schooling for girls gain legitimacy, for if females' knowledge was tied (and mostly constrained) to the Bible, then the knowledge would not be so dangerous; few educators wanted children to question the curriculum, and even fewer wanted women to investigate the lots in which their sex was cast.[11] In this tradition, Mary Lyon established Mount Holyoke Female Seminary in 1837, organizing it around her evangelical beliefs. Students lived and studied in one building along with their instructors, who carefully monitored students around the clock. Bells signaled every step the girls took—prayers in the morning, classes during the day, and prayers again in the evening. Self-denial and strict discipline were considered important tools in molding devout wives and moral mothers.

Mount Holyoke provided students with an intellectually challenging program as well, including Latin, mathematics, ancient history, chemistry, and philosophy. Academic offerings of the stronger seminaries compared favorably with those of the first two or even four years of college. Some seminaries were far less impressive, however; they avoided rigorous courses and provided instruction in traditional women's crafts instead. Some of the strongest and some of the weakest schools in America shared the name "seminary."

With help from the Quakers and Harriet Beecher Stowe, Myrtilla Miner, a white woman from New York, mounted the first organized effort to provide higher education for black women. As a result, in the 1850s the Miner Normal School for Colored Girls was established in Washington, D.C., with a curriculum that was typical of respected seminaries at the time. Eventually the school's mission focused on education, and it became Miner Teachers College. In 1881, Sophia Packard and Harriet Giles, two New England missionaries and teachers, brought Bibles and schoolbooks to Atlanta, Georgia, and started the Spelman Female Seminary, whose curriculum emphasized the liberal arts, practical skills, and teacher preparation. Today the former seminary is Spelman College, a highly regarded school for African-American women.[12]

Although seminaries were intended to prepare a woman for "her own sphere" as wife and mother, they opened up different paths for women to take. At Troy and Mount Holyoke, over 80 percent of the graduates entered teaching. Viewed as an extension of the home, the classroom was another setting in which to raise and guide children, and women were welcome—at least until they decided to marry.

The seminaries undertook teacher education with missionary zeal, creating both innovative and effective teacher training programs. While male graduates of academies and colleges taught by recitation and memorization, seminaries developed more dynamic strategies and stressed reasoning and creativity. Seminary leaders such as Emma Willard and Catharine Beecher wrote textbooks on teaching methods. Seminary graduates promoted student cooperation, avoided corporal punishment, and created more humane classrooms. Female teachers did more than fill a role, they restructured a profession.

Horace Mann was a great supporter of this new breed of teacher. "That woman should be the educator of children I believe to be as much a requirement of nature as that she should be the mother of children."[13] Mann had good reason to validate these recent recruits to the classroom: he desperately needed them. During the first half of the nineteenth century, Mann had initiated the common school movement. The supply of male teachers was insufficient to staff these new public schools, so women were welcomed, especially given the cost factor. Women could be paid significantly less than men. With more of them in the classrooms, school costs and thus taxes could be kept low.

From these humble beginnings there slowly emerged a more professional program for teacher education. In 1823, the Reverend Samuel Hall established a normal school (derived from the French *école normale,* a school that establishes model standards or norms) in Concord, Vermont. This private school provided elementary school graduates with formal training in teaching skills. Reverend Hall's modest normal school marked the beginning of teacher education in America. Sixteen years later, in 1839, Horace Mann was instrumental in establishing the first state-supported normal school, in Lexington, Massachusetts. Normal schools typically provided a two-year teacher training program consisting of academic subjects as well as teaching and methodology. Normal schools are not relics of the past. Many of today's noted universities began as normal schools a century ago.

SPINSTERS, BACHELORS,
AND GENDER BARRIERS IN TEACHING

One poignant thread of stories in our nation's history concerns how gender and sexuality have been used to short-circuit the contributions of both women and men in education. While some teachers have courageously fought such confining social conventions, many others have been victimized. Their stories are worth remembering.

Although today teaching is predominantly a female career, in fact men dominated teaching well into the mid-nineteenth century. Although a few women taught at home in dame schools, the first women to become teachers in regular school settings, earning a public salary, were viewed as gender trespassers, "unsexed" by their ambition, and considered masculine. Concerned by this negative characterization, early feminists such as Catharine Beecher implored female teachers to accentuate their feminine traits, highlight their domestic skills, and continue their preparation for marriage.[14] Despite the national reluctance to allow women into the workforce, and despite the perception that teachers should be male, the demand for more and inexpensive teachers made the hiring of women teachers inevitable.

By the early part of the twentieth century, women constituted upwards of 90 percent of teachers. But not all women were equally welcome. School districts preferred "spinsters," women unmarried and unlikely to marry. Such women would not suffer the dual loyalties inherent in "serving" both husband and employer. Unmarried women were hired so frequently in the late nineteenth and early twentieth centuries that teaching and spinsterhood became synonymous. Cartoonists, authors, and reporters made the spinster schoolteacher a cultural icon. Rooming and boardinghouses, and eventually small apartments, sometimes called teacherages, were built to provide accommodations for this new class of workers. Teaching was gendered "female."

As women came to dominate teaching, a new concern arose: the fear that female teachers were feminizing boys. There were demands to bring men back to teaching, and to halt the feminization of young schoolboys. President Theodore Roosevelt added a touch of racism to the debate, arguing that since so many white women were choosing teaching over motherhood, they were committing "race suicide," and the continuance of the white race was in jeopardy.[15] School districts responded by actively recruiting male teachers, and male educators carved out their own niches in school systems. Administration, coaching, vocational and certain high school departments, specifically science and math, became male bastions.

For women, teaching meant economic and financial liberation—but at a cost. The dedicated teaching spinsters of the nineteenth century became the object of ridicule in the twentieth century. Women choosing teaching over motherhood were considered unnatural by a mostly male cadre of psychologists, physicians, and authors. Articles and books began to appear early in the twentieth century arguing that being unmarried caused women to be spiteful, hateful, and disgusting. The eminent psychologist G. Stanley Hall wrote an article titled "Certain Degenerative Tendencies among Teachers," explaining why unmarried women were frustrated, bitter, and otherwise unpleasant. Political opinions parading as research soon appeared claiming that as many as half of all single teachers were lesbians. Stage shows and movies picked up the theme, portraying lesbian relationships in and beyond school settings. But when the Great Depression hit in the 1930s, the idea of hiring wives and creating two-income families was anathema: the scarce jobs were to be funneled to women living alone or to men, the family "breadwinners." It was not until the end of World War II that most school districts even employed married women.

Men who remained in teaching also paid a price. Conventional wisdom early in the twentieth century held that effeminate men were gay men, and that gay men were naturally drawn to teaching. Worse yet, gay men were considered to be a teaching time bomb, since they would be poor role models for children. All male teachers became suspect, and few were drawn to teaching. School districts avoided hiring men who did not possess a clearly masculine demeanor. (Married men with children were preferred.) The Cold War and the accompanying McCarthy anticommunist scare of the 1950s declared war on liberal ideas and unconventional choices: homosexuality was seen as a threat to America. "There was a list of about twenty-one things that you could be fired for. The first was to be a card-carrying Communist, and the second was to be a homosexual."[16] Single teachers declared their "healthy" heterosexuality, and gay teachers stayed hidden. During this time, the number of married teachers doubled.

Recent years have witnessed a loosening of gender straitjackets, but sex stereotypes, myths, and bigotry against gays continue to restrict and confine both women and men. Men drawn to teaching young children and women seeking leadership roles confront both barriers and social sanctions. Gay and lesbian teachers (and students) frequently endure hurtful comments and discriminatory treatment. As long as these gender and sexual barriers persist, we are all the poorer.

KNOCKING AT THE COLLEGE DOOR

Efforts to break gender barriers in education cast long shadows. Women studying at normal schools and seminaries opened the door to teaching for women. But some women wanted and worked for full educational citizenship. Their efforts were rewarded in Oberlin, Ohio, where the cult of domesticity was brought to the college campus.

Considered a radical, even dangerous place, Oberlin was the first American college to admit both women and men. Then in 1833 this higher education institution became not only a "mixed" college but one that admitted racial minorities as well. In fact, Mary Jane Patterson, the first African-American woman to graduate from college, received her degree from Oberlin in 1862. But along with opportunities there were problems.

Daily practice mocked Oberlin's lofty ideals; religious and social restrictions were everywhere. Oberlin women experienced a distinctly second-class education; they attended the "Ladies Course," a sub-college-level program focused on gender-limited options. The ladies were closely supervised and always segregated from the men.

Older than most students who attended Oberlin, Lucy Stone saw more clearly the injustice of the college's gender restrictions. "Oberlin's attitude," she wrote, "was that women's high calling was to be mothers of the race." As a result, female students at Oberlin were "washing the men's clothes, caring for their rooms, serving them at table, listening to their orations, but [were] themselves remaining respectfully silent in public assemblages."[17] Stone was not one to accept this role. Although she found her public voice later and became a noted public speaker for antislavery and women's rights, she was not allowed to speak at Oberlin. For the graduation ceremony she was awarded the honor of preparing the commencement address. She was elated until she discovered that she was expected to author the speech, not deliver it. A male student would give the oration. She declined the "honor."

The tension between the liberating effect of education and the restricting nature of sexism soon spread beyond Oberlin's campus to other battlegrounds. When Kentucky moved to upgrade a female secondary school to a college in 1835, a Massachusetts newspaper thought that the proposed degrees, Mistress of Music, Mistress of Instruction, and the like, were inappropriate. While the "Mistress" title was often used to distinguish female degrees from the bachelor's degrees awarded men, the newspaper recommended a new genre of titles: the M.P.M. for Mistress of Pudding Making, M.D.N. for Mistress of Darning Needles, and the M.C.S. for Mistress of Common Sense. Honorary degrees included the R.W.H.H., Respectable Wife of a Happy Husband, and M.W.R.F., Mother of a Well-Regulated Family. Underlying this satire was a serious question: Should a woman's education be expanded beyond that for her role as wife and mother?[18]

As at the seminaries, women in these small, church-related colleges were closely supervised and were housed and educated separately from the men. Female students did well academically at Oberlin and Antioch, and this added to the pressure to admit them to other colleges, especially the larger, state-supported universities. After all, state universities were funded by state taxes and had a moral obligation to admit all state residents. If moral arguments did not persuade opponents, practical ones did. Few states were financially able to fund a separate state university for women. In addition, female tuition dollars would help pay the bills at the state university. As more than one cost-conscious advocate pointed out, "You can lecture to one hundred students as cheaply as fifty."

In 1858 three women formally applied to the University of Michigan, one of the largest and most prestigious state universities. Their applications were given national attention. Would the elite University of Michigan become coeducational? A committee formed to decide their fate and wrote to college administrators across the nation for advice. University presidents in the East were united in their opposition. Even Oberlin and Antioch, both already coeducational, warned of the difficulty in monitoring women and maintaining sex-segregated activities. Michigan's president also voiced his opposition: "Men will lose as women advance, we shall have a community of defeminated women and demasculated men. When we attempt to disturb God's order, we produce monstrosities." Finally, the committee reached its decision: the University of Michigan would not enroll women.[19]

One of the major forces that ultimately opened college doors for women was the Civil War. The loss of male students, casualties of war, created economic pressures for female tuition dollars, so it was not surprising that, in 1870, Michigan finally relented. But even then women were not very welcome. Male students often jeered when females entered class, avoided them on campus, and made their lives difficult. And professors openly ridiculed women. One disgruntled professor stopped his students from removing a dog that had wandered into his class. "The dog is a resident of Michigan," he said. "Don't you know that we now recognize the right of every resident of the state to enjoy the privileges afforded the university?"[20]

Opposition to coeducation continued and intensified across the nation. The University of Rochester's story is the stuff of reality TV, perhaps called "Education for Ransom." Women had fought for more than thirty years to open the university's doors. The trustees finally agreed to admit them, but only if they raised $100,000 within two years to pay for additional classrooms and instructors. It was a combination of *Beat the Clock* and *Dialing for Dollars;* by the spring of 1900 they had raised $40,000. With the deadline just a few months away, the trustees reduced the target goal to $50,000. The women struggled and reached $42,000. With only weeks to go, Susan B. Anthony entered the fray. Prior to this she had kept her name out of the crusade to admit women because "feminists" were perceived as radical by many Americans, and she feared her reputation might hurt the cause. But now time was running out. She mounted a brave effort and feverishly drove around Rochester asking friends for contributions. She cashed in her own life insurance policy, a gift for her work in women's suffrage, and donated it to the cause. In the nick of time, the $50,000 goal was met and women were admitted.

This happy result was changed, however, when the new president voiced his opposition. Encouraged by the official cold shoulder, male students responded by stamping their feet when a woman entered a classroom, physically blocking classroom doors, and by mocking and jeering women whenever they appeared on campus. By 1913 the university's administration said enough was enough: a separate women's college was organized, and female students were once again isolated and had fewer educational resources. The men had their university back.

Male educators voiced many different reasons why women should not go to school with men. Some predicted that the brisk give-and-take of classroom debate would be softened in deference to the ladies. Other critics feared the loss of romance, arguing that if men and women learned together, the "mysterious" attraction between the sexes would evaporate. As a result, women would marry late or not at all. (In fact, there is evidence that women who graduated from college did marry later, were more particular in choosing their husbands, and may have avoided uncongenial marriages altogether.)[21] But the real reason behind such strong opposition was that education was devalued as women were included. If a woman could do college-level work, then the whole system of higher learning became less prestigious and less exclusive.

IVY LEAGUE SPIN-OFFS

The most elite eastern colleges were slow to jump on the coeducation bandwagon. At prestigious Harvard, an invisible college for women took shape. Professors taught men in Harvard Yard, then walked a few blocks to rented homes where they repeated their lectures to women—for an extra fee, of course. There were no permanent buildings for the women, an arrangement that pleased President Charles W. Eliot, an adamant opponent to their admission. The Harvard professors and their female students became known as the "Annex," and women who graduated were awarded certificates that indicated they had accomplished academic work equivalent to that of Harvard men.

In 1893 the invisible college finally achieved visibility and was named Radcliffe after a woman who had contributed funds to Harvard in 1641. Two hundred and fifty-two years after the gift, the college was offering a halfhearted thank-you, for women still had only limited access to the university's impressive resources. After the Harvard library closed each evening, messengers slipped in to obtain books for the Radcliffe women to study. The books had to be returned before the library opened the next morning. Burning the midnight oil was not an expression to be taken lightly at Radcliffe.

Although not equal partners, Radcliffe at Harvard and the newly opened Barnard at Columbia represented progress. In these "coordinate colleges" women moved closer to acceptance in America's most prestigious institutions. But at other colleges, such as Tufts, the coordinate college was actually a step back. Women had been admitted to Tufts in 1892; at the same time, enrollment dropped. The college president identified the admission of women as the cause. "The future of the academic department of Tufts College as a man's college depends upon the immediate segregation of the women into a separate department or college," he proclaimed. "I regard this as the most pressing education problem we have before us. . . . I have no doubt that a failure to solve it would involve imminent disaster to the College of Liberal Arts."[22] To avoid "disaster," Jackson College was founded in 1910, and women were removed from the Tufts campus. Resegregation occurred at other colleges, such as Brown and Pembroke. Wesleyan took more drastic measures: in 1912 the college reversed its open-door policy but did not segregate women; it barred them from attending at all.

A COLLEGE OF HER OWN

Frustrated with the struggle to receive equal education at the existing universities, some women and men envisioned a bold alternative. These visionaries did not want a breakaway branch of a male university, a less-than-equal education in a coeducational institution, or even a "near" college experience at some of the more rigorous female seminaries. They wanted "to build and endow a college for young women which shall be to them what Yale and Harvard are to young men." While still a radical idea in the 1850s, it was not new. Two centuries earlier, in the year that Harvard was founded, Lucy Downing had shared her vision of education for women with Massachusetts governor John Winthrop: "I would build far off from men a college like a man's," she wrote. "And I would teach them all that men are taught."[23]

In 1855, Matthew Vassar's search for a way to immortalize himself resulted in the advancement of Lucy Downing's visionary idea. Impressed with the beautiful hospitals he had seen in Europe, Vassar decided to build one here in America that would be a lasting monument to his achievements. All this changed when his friend Milo Jewett convinced him that a great hospital in the small town of Poughkeepsie, New York, would be mostly unused, a waste of Vassar's hard-earned brewery fortune. Jewett suggested that Vassar build the first "real" college for women, one with ample resources, qualified faculty, and an endowment. Vassar became convinced that a women's college would be an appropriate legacy—unique, necessary, and "more lasting than the Pyramids."[24] And so Vassar College was established.

As the college grew, so did its founder's commitment to education for women. When Vassar College opened in 1865, critics might have accused it of having a patronizing form of government, similar to that of the female seminaries, complete with bells, prayers, and monitors. But there was nothing condescending about the curriculum, which was undoubtedly at college level. Most of the early students were not prepared for this degree of rigor. Two-thirds arrived without the necessary academic background, and they were redirected to the preparatory department where they enrolled in high-school-level prerequisites.

Wellesley was founded by Henry Fowle Durant, a successful Boston lawyer whose life changed when his young son died. Durant turned to religion, became an evangelical Christian, and sought a vehicle to spread his beliefs. As a great supporter of the Mount Holyoke seminary, Durant decided to invest his fortune in building a similar religious women's college on his magnificent country estate near Boston. He believed in the power and competence of women and appointed them not only as trustees of the new school but as the entire faculty, a courageous move at that time and, many believed, unworkable. He launched a recruiting expedition and hired women graduates from Mount Holyoke, Oberlin, Vassar, and the recently coeducational University of Michigan. Still, Durant could not fill the thirty faculty positions. Devising his own affirmative action plan, one that was more effective than many of today's attempts, Durant identified intellectually talented women who had not received an official college education and paid their way for additional schooling. When they completed their studies, they joined the Wellesley faculty.

Smith College was established in another part of Massachusetts in September 1875; it was the first women's college endowed by a woman. Sophia Smith had inherited a large fortune and turned to her pastor for advice. John Greene suggested that she establish a college for women, but one that differed dramatically from the seminary model.

At the time Smith College was planned, large institutional buildings were being criticized as sources of physical and mental stress, so Smith was developed as a college of small, intimate cottages. Also, John Greene, Sophia Smith's adviser, feared the dangerous ideas that might result from so many women confined in a large building. He worried that these isolated structures would encourage rejection of social norms and roles, or even worse. Such fears were described in 1884 by J. G. Holland, an editor at Scribners: "No consideration would induce us to place a young woman—daughter or ward—in a college which would shut her away from all family life for a period of four years. The system is unnatural, and not one young woman in ten can be subjected to it without injury."[25]

Holland feared that the seminary model, while it might protect young women from men, left them vulnerable to the advances of other women. Sophia Smith chose to avoid these potential "hot beds" by building smaller cottages, supervised by adults, to better reflect a natural family environment. Contact with the townspeople would also dissuade the students from developing radical notions and visionary ideas. But visionary ideas are difficult to contain, as M. Carey Thomas would show.

Among the first women to graduate from Cornell University, in 1877, Thomas was ahead of her time. She was accepted, reluctantly, by the graduate school of Johns Hopkins, but she was barred from attending seminars. After Hopkins, she set sail for Germany, where she spent three years earning her doctorate. When she heard about plans to create Bryn Mawr, she wrote letters promoting herself as the president of the new college. She might have seemed the perfect candidate for the Quaker College for Women: she was a Quaker woman returning from Europe with her new doctorate and was the daughter, niece, and cousin of various members of the board of trustees. But being an inexperienced administrator, a woman, and something less than a devout Quaker all worked against her. Instead, she was selected as dean and a faculty member. Several years later, when the male president died, the board saw the wisdom of her arguments, and she became more than president: she was the force that shaped Bryn Mawr.

The quality of the faculty at Wellesley, Smith, and Vassar fell far short of Thomas's expectations. At Bryn Mawr she envisioned a women's college with the standards, curriculum, and scholarship of Johns Hopkins. She recruited a largely male faculty that had been newly trained in German universities and were dedicated to academic excellence. By 1885, Bryn Mawr's faculty was comprised of highly promising scholars, including Woodrow Wilson. Promising students were also valued. Applicants who did not pass the strict entrance requirements and examinations were not accepted. Bryn Mawr's standards would not be diluted by enrolling students in a high-school-level preparation program as Vassar had done.

Carey Thomas rejected not only inferior academic standards but inferior life standards for women. She broke with the Victorian notion of a woman's sphere; Bryn Mawr women did not perform domestic chores. They wore caps and gowns to class, as did male scholars at that time. Protective buildings, guardians, and monitoring were abandoned. Bryn Mawr students enjoyed privacy and lived in buildings similar to the quadrangle design of many men's campuses.

The Seven Sisters—Smith, Mount Holyoke, Wellesley, Vassar, Barnard, Radcliffe, and Bryn Mawr—were founded to transform young women, but over time they themselves were transformed. Students created their own clubs, organizations, and traditions. Evangelical fervor and religious conformity were replaced by diversity of opinion and culture. Faculty members discovered their own voice as well. They refused to serve as the eyes and spies of the administration, constantly supervising student behavior. Increasingly they recognized and confronted their own exploitation. Vassar's distinguished astronomer, Maria Mitchell, felt the pain of sexism when the college president asked for a list of faculty publications but sent the request to male instructors only. Female faculty at women's colleges were systematically paid less than males, were housed in more modest living quarters, and sometimes were even barred from participating in faculty meetings. At Smith, women faculty members of all ranks were called teachers; men were called professors. This treatment in colleges dedicated to women's advancement became a painful public reminder of the continuing inequality between women and men.

Despite this sexism, the influence of these colleges was enormous. A critical mass of educated women had been brought together to learn about their world, but many of them did not like what they saw. Women's colleges, so focused at their inception, were spinning off in new directions, unleashing forces unimagined by their original founders.

CHOICE: OVARIES OR ALGEBRA?

By the second half of the nineteenth century, education for girls and women had undergone a revolution. Beyond the campus, a national women's movement gained momentum; its agenda included political rights, social reforms, and economic equity. More and more women entered the labor market. Much like the 1970s, the 1870s marked tremendous progress for women and a period of conservative backlash followed.

Nineteenth-century women had proven themselves in the formerly forbidden realm of higher education. Several colleges reported that they earned higher grades than men. Since women were succeeding academically, concern about their intellectual inadequacies almost disappeared.

Some women knocked on the doors of the professional schools. Julia Ward Howe, the well-known social reformer, looked beyond college education to professional and graduate studies as "the keystone to the arch of women's liberty."[26] But opposition to women in the professions was fierce. The medical profession offered especially stiff resistance.

Although Elizabeth Blackwell worked as a teacher for years to support herself, she had always dreamed of becoming a doctor. The fact that no woman had ever attended a medical school did not deter her from applying. As she anticipated, the rejection letters piled up. Except for one—the Geneva Medical School in upstate New York. She graduated two years later, in 1849, with the first medical degree awarded in this country to a woman. Harriet Hunt was less fortunate. She had practiced medicine without a diploma for years when she applied to medical schools. At this time Hunt was forty-five and viewed by the Harvard faculty "as a dignified matron who would not enflame the sexual passions of the male students."[27] Her skills and efforts were recognized in her admission to Harvard Medical School, along with three male African-American students. Actually, her admission limited her to attendance at lectures while the African-Americans were admitted to the full degree program. When word of her impending lecture attendance spread, students protested, and she was forced to withdraw. The African-American students remained.

In 1870, Mary Hovey attempted to open medical schools to women such as Harriet Hunt. She offered Harvard a $10,000 gift (in the grand old tradition of a bribe) if it would admit women. She believed that if prestigious Harvard opened its doors, others would follow. Similar to the strategy that would be used at the University of Rochester, Hovey's "creative philanthropy" or "education for ransom" approach caused a yearlong debate. Finally, Harvard refused the money and rejected female applicants. In 1891, Mary Ganett tried the same scheme with a promise of a $60,000 gift to Johns Hopkins Medical School. That was worth a two-year debate, and eventually the gift was increased to $306,000. That price was right; Hopkins saw the value of women students.

Faced with such extraordinary educational advances, opponents of education for women needed new ammunition. They found it in one of the oldest positions: Biology is destiny. Their arguments suggested that below the skin and under the skull lurked the real reasons women did not belong in higher education. Their problems were in their brains and in their ovaries.

Americans today are intrigued by reports on the mysteries of the brain. Our curiosity is not new. In the nineteenth century, craniology was considered a science. Liberating in its simplicity, craniology taught that brain size revealed intelligence. Since large brains required large skulls, measuring cranial size revealed a person's intellect. Craniology confirmed popular biases of the day. The brightest race was Caucasian, with a definite skull-size advantage over smaller-headed Africans and Asians. Measurements also showed northern Europeans with bigger skulls than southern Europeans, confirming another widely held prejudice. Unfortunately, childbirth stunted women's evolutionary development. Their brains would never be as big or as complex as those of men.

Because craniology reflected the prejudice of the times, it withstood problems that should have rapidly toppled it. Errors were commonplace, measurements were taken incorrectly, male-female brains were mislabeled, women were discovered with larger skulls than very bright men; and finally, investigations showed that brain size was not related to intelligence. By the early twentieth century, craniology was on the way out, but during the late 1800s it provided opponents of women's educational progress with a biological explanation for the intellectual supremacy of males. But the anatomy lesson was not over.

Other adversaries moved to the reproductive organs to explain why women should avoid higher education. In a slim volume titled *Sex in Education* (1873), Dr. Edward Clarke asserted that prolonged coeducation was physically dangerous to the reproductive health of females. During the teenage years girls developed their reproductive organs, and "periodicity" (menstruation) was of central importance. If young women attended school during formative adolescence, blood would be diverted from these reproductive organs to the brain. The result would be "monstrous brains and puny bodies . . . flowing thought and constipated bowels."[28] If Clarke's beliefs were reduced to a warning label, it would be: WOMEN BEWARE: HIGH SCHOOL AND COLLEGE MAY BE HAZARDOUS TO YOUR HEALTH. As historian David Tyack suggested, Clarke was forcing girls to choose between algebra and ovaries.

But Clarke had a solution to this dilemma: Replace coeducation with less demanding, sex-segregated schools. Girls should attend schools that were sensitive to the needs of their reproductive organs: less study, less stress, easier curriculum, no competition, and "rest" periods during menstruation. Separate girls' education would ensure the future of the Anglo-Saxon race. To continue coeducation was to flirt with "race suicide." The vast majority of girls attending high schools and colleges in the 1870s and 1880s were white, affluent, and Anglo-Saxon. Like the craniologists, Clarke accepted Darwin's belief of Anglo-Saxon superiority, and his recommendations focused on protecting the "fittest" of womanhood. The reproductive damage done to black women by long hours spent working in the fields or to immigrant women by extraordinary hours of labor in crowded factories and sweatshops did not concern him. In fact, lowering their reproductive abilities while increasing the fertility of the superior Anglo-Saxon women was the genetically correct position, according to Darwin and Clarke.

Clarke's book enjoyed brisk sales as people debated the reproductive cost of educating females. Even advocates of coeducation worried about the health of girls. In 1889 the superintendent of Detroit's public schools pleaded for elevators because climbing stairs was "a menace to normal functional development" of women. An editorial in a college newspaper warned: "A woman . . . cannot afford to risk her health in acquiring knowledge of the advance sciences, mathematics, or philosophy for which she has no use. . . . Too many women have already made themselves permanent invalids by overstrain of study at schools and colleges."[29]

The seeds of doubt were planted. Even intellectually gifted, fiercely independent women such as M. Carey Thomas, president of Bryn Mawr, confided the fears she experienced from Clarke's thesis: "I remember often praying about it, and begging God that if it were true that because I was a girl, I could not successfully master Greek and go to college, and understand things, to kill me for it."[30] As late as 1895, more than twenty years after Clarke's work first appeared, the University of Virginia faculty concluded that "women were often physically unsexed by the strains of study."

While education put ovaries in danger, evidently it did not threaten male reproductive health. Imagine how concerned men would be if a renowned medical authority discovered an inverse relationship between college credits and sperm count. Research findings that tie law degrees to male impotence might also have a chilling effect. But according to Clarke, there were no such dangers. Men appeared to be biologically fit for every intellectual endeavor.

Like the theories of the craniologists, Clarke's arguments appealed strongly to prejudice but fell short on evidence. In 1885 the Association of Collegiate Alumnae, which later became the American Association of University Women, feared for the worse and sponsored a nationwide survey of women's health. While 78 percent of college women reported good health, only 50 percent of noncollege women made such a claim. As the decades wore on, evidence to support either Clarke or the craniologists became increasingly more difficult to find. Women of all skull sizes were doing well academically, and their ovaries remained intact.

VOCATIONAL DESTINY

In the decades that followed the Clarke controversy, coeducation flourished and school attendance soared. But coeducation did not mean equal education. Part of the problem can be traced to an influential reform effort to modernize the secondary school.

In 1918 the Commission on the Reorganization of Secondary Education was about to steer America on a new course of schooling. Members of the commission viewed the high school college preparation curriculum—Latin, Greek, German, philosophy, algebra—as out of date with the more practical needs of the country. Although schools prepared students for college, most of them never went. It was suspected that this classical curriculum contributed to the high dropout rate as students lost interest, performed poorly, or both. The commission called for a new American high school, one more responsive to non-college-bound students and to the real demands of the world of work. To education's historical mission of providing students with a classical education, a new responsibility was added—preparing youth for the world of work. Eventually, vocational education became a new high school track.

The aim of vocational education was progressive and forward-looking, but for coeducation it meant a step backward. The adult world of work was highly sex segregated, so vocational education courses separated students, sending girls into one sphere of study and boys into another. Girls took home economics and business courses. Boys went into the more profitable trades and industrial arts. Even college-bound girls who were not enrolled in the vocational curriculum were required to take domestic science or home economics while boys took manual training or industrial arts. For black and minority women, home economics became vocational training, a form of preparation for domestic work.

As the century moved on, new electives proliferated that allowed girls and other students to skip courses like math and science. Simultaneously, classes such as physics were made "girl friendly," as was shown by San Jose, California's course offering: "The Physics of Home Plumbing and Lighting." Physical education expanded, with sports and athletics becoming more central for boys and less important for girls. Even extracurricular activities were marked by sex segregation. In clubs, boys were the "Future Farmers of America" and girls were the "Future Homemakers." Dr. Clarke's concern for the well-being of a woman's ovaries never restructured schools, but he probably would have taken some solace in this resegregation of the sexes.

When Myra and David asked women to recall what it was like to be educated during the 1950s and 1960s, they shared stories like these:

Here's how my 1960s high school chemistry class was taught: Boys were seated by the male teacher on the side of the room with the teacher's desk. Girls were seated on the far side of the room. Girls were told to be quiet and not cause trouble and they would not fail the class. When "dangerous" experiments were conducted, the boys went into the lab while the girls watched through the windows.

In 1965 I was sixteen years old, and I wanted to study architecture at Iowa State University. My father took me to talk with an architecture faculty member about their program. All I can remember is that he said he would have to admit me but that I would never graduate. He said that girls didn't graduate in architecture at Iowa State. I didn't enter that program. Instead I received a degree in art education. Even today I still dream about being an architect. I never used my art education degree.

Women shared countless stories, often with an intensity that revealed a wound still not healed.

THE ERA OF NEW HOPE

In 1972, Shirley McCune of the National Education Association organized a unique gathering. She invited every American educator who had voiced a public concern or written an article or book about sexism in schools to a meeting in Warrenton, Virginia. There were about 150 of us. Everyone in the nation working for gender equity in schools could easily fit into a single large room. Myra and David felt "a sense of energy and commitment" from these people, individuals who had been working in isolation and now discovered they were not alone. We came as individuals and left as part of a critical mass. By the end of the decade, our numbers grew. From Hawaii to Maine, sex equity in education had become a popular cause.

Congress had passed Title IX in 1972, and certainly this law provided the momentum, the official approval that what we were doing was all right. Our cause was welcomed by the American government. Those committed to gender equity in education were elated. There was now a legal weapon to fight schools that treated girls and boys unfairly. Many forget that these changes, which some see as radical today, occurred during the Republican administrations of Presidents Nixon and Ford. Within a decade, during the Reagan and later in the first and second Bush years, the federal government would switch sides, question the cause of gender equity, and eventually work to weaken Title IX. But in the 1970s, we had a miracle in our hands, a federal law making sex discrimination in schools illegal. Title IX outlawed sex bias in school athletics, career counseling, medical services, financial aid, admissions practices, and the treatment of students and employees. From elementary school through the university, Title IX violators were threatened with the loss of federal funds.

Then federal dollars began to flow for sex equity research and training. In 1974, Congress passed the Women's Educational Equity Act (WEEA) to fund research, materials, and training to help schools eliminate sex bias. The few million dollars given to WEEA, one of the tiniest of federal programs, resulted in a wealth of resources to help schools comply with Title IX, to recruit girls into math and science, to analyze gender bias in books, and to train nonsexist teachers. In 1978, Congress broadened the Civil Rights Act to include sex equity work in ten desegregation assistance centers (now called equity assistance centers). These centers assist teachers, parents, and students in developing nonsexist as well as nonracist educational and community programs. By 1980 even the National Institute of Education, the federal research agency, was providing limited funding to investigate the nature of sex bias in schools. Compared to most government programs, the budget for sex equity was modest, a blip on the federal radar screen, but for those who had been working with nothing, such support was incredibly meaningful.

More and more schools made changes. Better (but not equal) athletic programs for girls developed. Teachers took creative steps to shatter the gender lines separating home economics and industrial arts. Girls were urged to take more courses in math and science, and some schools even checked to make sure that encouraging words translated into enrollment. Teachers learned how to analyze books for sex bias and lobbied publishers for better, fairer instructional materials.

But as the 1970s drew to a close, it became evident that educators overestimated the power of a law to change people's lives. Many schools chose to ignore the law, especially schools in conservative communities. In one school, only boys were allowed into advanced math courses. In another, vocational programs remained segregated with cosmetology and secretarial courses only for women and electrical and automotive courses only for men. In another community, pregnancy became grounds for expelling teenage mothers, but not teenage fathers. School districts were spending fifteen and even twenty times more funds on male than female sports. One college awarded ten times as many scholarships to men, although the women denied the scholarships were equally qualified. Complaints were lodged, paperwork piled up, delays were common, and penalties became a new mythology, for they were rarely applied. Decades after Title IX was passed, despite the fact that most districts were to one degree or another violating the law, it was difficult to find even a single school district that was actually fined for such violations.

REVOLUTION INTERRUPTUS

Today, we live during a time of a virulent backlash movement. Some argue that girls have not only achieved equality, but superiority. *Backlash* is actually a mechanical term to describe a sharp recoil; but the *backlash* in this case describes a human recoil from social change in general, and gender equity efforts in particular. Backlash critics fight against the liberalization of male and female roles, and challenge studies that report how sexism harms girls, arguing that female bias in schools is a fabrication of liberals and feminists. They claim that feminists are waging a "war on boys," and squandering precious resources on helping girls in science and math. Backlash critics argue that feminism has gone too far. Boys, they insist, are the new "victims" of doctrinaire feminists.[31] The endless parade of talk shows and conservative publications promote backlash pundits as experts. Many in the public who listen to such "experts" are led to believe that traditional sex stereotypes and inequities that once impacted girls are a thing of the past.[32] Still others are threatened by the implications of abandoning traditional gender roles. Gender equity is at a crossroads.

While many of the blatant sexist practices of the past are gone, sexism is not. Subtle and pervasive bias continues to plague schools, shortchanging both females and males. Title IX itself is often under attack and its enforcement has been sporadic at best. Federal programs designed to assist girls and women have been reduced or eliminated. Indeed, sex-segregated classes are now reappearing, a potentially dangerous step back in time. In high school and college, gender-segregated futures are still commonplace. Women are rarely found in engineering, physics, and computer science. In nursing, teaching, library science, and social work, it is the men who are a distinct minority. Even in high-status careers such as medicine and law, where tremendous progress has been made for women, bias persists. Women are often channeled into the least prestigious, least profitable medical and legal specialties, and the wage gap for women in law and medicine is actually greater than it is in many other careers. The slow rate of change may be due to gender fatigue.

Signs of gender fatigue began to appear in the 1980s with the Reagan administration. Feminists were cast as cartoon figures, bitter, humorless women who believed that "all men are pigs, all women are saints, and women who stay home with kids are wasting their lives."[33] Tradition-minded leaders in the federal Department of Education fought to elim-inate programs and to restrict Title IX enforcement. Charges were made that feminism was a threat to the traditional family—the patriarchal model with a husband and father at its head. A well-educated woman of independent thought and means was a challenge to that patriarchal sys-tem. Education's leaders set out to regress more than a century of femi-nist ideas, back to the notion of the home as the only right and proper sphere for women.

Susan Faludi wrote, "Just when women's quest for equal rights seemed closest to achieving its objective, the backlash struck it down."[34] Just when schools became the wedge for unleashing female potential, support was cut off. Research was terminated, funds were curtailed, and Title IX, a paper tiger, was declawed. High on the backlash agenda for termination was the Women's Educational Equity Act and its director, Leslie Wolfe. WEEA was a federal program that began in 1976 to help local schools enforce Title IX and encouraged the achievement of girls and women in education, especially science, math, and nontraditional careers. For most of its existence, WEEA was woefully underfunded, typically one to three million dollars a year to fund all its gender programs nationally, as well as pay its staff. Nevertheless, the Heritage Foundation's 1981 "Mandate for Leadership" targeted WEEA as "an important resource for the prac-tice of feminist policies and politics." As such it had to be crushed.

A civil service employee for more than a decade, Wolfe was attacked in magazines and on talk shows as a "radical feminist," and WEEA was denounced as a "money machine for a network of openly radical femi-nist groups." "We were not a very large program," Wolfe said. "In a fed-eral budget of billions, we had $10 million to try to achieve equity for girls across the nation. But I was a feminist, and our program was getting results. We drove them crazy."

Within a year the Women's Educational Equity Act program was downgraded, its budget cut, and its staff reassigned, and Leslie Wolfe was no longer working for the government. By 1992, under President George H. W. Bush, the agency's budget dwindled to half a million dol-lars, and the administration was still requesting its elimination. Under the second Bush administration, WEEA funds were redirected to study such issues as single-sex education. When this study funded with WEEA dollars found for the most part that single-sex education lacked solid research support, the results were ignored. Despite the findings, an administration comfortable with single-sex education changed Title IX to permit separating students on the basis of sex.

Thinking back to the Reagan era, Wolfe recalls: "I was so naïve. I kept my feminist posters up in my office when people advised me to take them down. But I didn't want the thought police to intimidate me. If they had silenced me, they would have won." The results of two decades of research findings, curricular materials, and training were available to educators nationally and around the world through the WEEA Equity Resource Center in Massachusetts. By 2003, center funds were cut, and years of work was no longer available to the public.

In 1982, Myra and David had just completed the second year of a three-year federal contract to explore the impact of gender in classrooms. Preliminary findings were in, and the Sadkers gave an interview to the *Washington Post*. The next day they opened the newspaper to see an article about their gender equity research. Then the phone calls began. "What are you doing giving interviews?" The caller was someone from the National Institute of Education, a friend who had supported gender research. "You have to keep a low profile. Here they are searching for gender equity projects so they can kill them, and there you are in the *Washington Post*."

Like Leslie Wolfe, Myra and David had been naïve and believed that they could discuss the idea of gender equity in a free press in a free society. They were new to this kind of politics. They tried to continue their research, and received some friendly NIE phone calls: " 'Equity' is on a list of unacceptable words. They're doing computer searches of all grants. When they find 'equity' in your grant title, they'll eliminate your project. I'm changing 'equity in classrooms' to 'effectiveness in classrooms.' Effectiveness is not on the list."

Later the Sadkers found out that *ecology* was another unacceptable word. A nationally renowned early childhood educator used the phrase "ecology of the child" in his grant description, and when the computer targeted his "liberal"-sounding research for termination, he had to fight to keep his project.

Myra and David changed their title and then the abstract describing the project, but it was too late: characterized as antifamily radical feminists, they were blacklisted. The next calls were not friendly; their grant was to be terminated. "There must be some mistake," they protested. "We've spent two years of time, effort, and money collecting data. In the third year we're supposed to analyze all the information and come up with our findings. It will be a terrible waste to cut the contract now." "There is no mistake," they were told.

People who supported the Sadkers' research called their congressional representatives. This time, fighting back worked. Their contract was reinstated, and they were able to complete the research described in countless articles, in the first version of *Failing at Fairness,* and now in this updated edition. Yet, opposition to gender equity continues.

Funding and Implementation Woes

Gender equity funding was under attack throughout both Bush administrations, and was not a priority during the Clinton administration. As we go to press, the Obama administration is taking office and we await their policies. Clearly, much work needs to be done. Title IX regulations, for example, call for schools to "designate at least one employee to coordinate its efforts to comply with and carry out Title IX responsibilities." However, as Dr. Sue Klein, education equity director of the Feminist Majority Foundation, and her colleagues have discovered, there are nowhere near the estimated 150,000 active Title IX coordinators called for. In fact, their 2008 update of a Web list of state gender equity coordinators revealed that not a single state had a full-time Title IX coordinator, and two states, Texas and Indiana, were not able to identify even a part-time coordinator.[35] Amazingly, WEEA is still alive with minimum funding, and a continued favorite target of those who see gender equity as the problem rather than a good idea. But with virtually no budget, its wings have been clipped.

Gender Research

Fewer gender bias studies are being reported today but that does not mean that gender bias is no longer a major problem. Past administrations have stifled this research. What are today's gender issues? In this book, we use recent research from doctoral studies and professional organizations including the National Women's Law Center and the American Association of University Women, but we are all the poorer for the lack of federal funding in this area. Sound research has in part been supplanted by the rise of publications and pundits arguing that females no longer face gender bias. Unfortunately, as we document here, reports of the death of gender bias are premature.

Single-Sex Schooling

"We conclude that in the field of public education the doctrine of 'separate but equal' has no place. Separate educational facilities are inherently unequal."[36] Since 1954, this principle has been part of the fabric of United States constitutional law, and indeed, our society. Notwithstanding this cornerstone, in the mid-2000s, the Department of Education's Office for Civil Rights reintroduced segregation into public education—this time in the form of segregation by sex.[37]

Title IX law previously allowed school districts to create single-sex schools or classes only under very specific circumstances. Schools were always allowed to separate boys and girls for choirs, sex education, and contact sports such as football in physical education. Schools could also offer single-sex programs to compensate for a learning problem. For example, a school might offer an all-girls science class or all-boys writing class if that helped student performance. But the recent changes to Title IX are far more dramatic. Schools can now sex-segregate students without any specific reason (and certainly without any research supporting its effectiveness).[38] The single-sex school trend has many supporters of gender fairness worried. According to representatives from the National Women's Law Center:

> This opens the door to sex stereotypes that should not be perpetuated into the next generation—for example, that boys can only learn when away from girls, who slow them down, or are too inactive. Or that girls are fragile creatures who can only achieve in environments that don't challenge them in fast-paced math or science classes, or that do not place too much emphasis on competition.[39]

Trying to educate girls and boys in the same classroom is seen by some as a disservice, and single-sex schools and classrooms are springing up across the nation. In fact, between 1991 and 2005, there was a 23 percent increase in all-girls private schools, but it did not stop there. While only five public single-sex high schools were still operating in 1996, a decade later, that number had jumped to over 30.[40] In addition to new single-sex schools, school districts are also creating something very new: single-sex classrooms within coed schools. Coeducation, once seen as a beacon of democracy and equality, is now attacked as a barrier to effective teaching and learning. We shall devote a chapter in this book to this pressing issue.

Title IX Attacks

Another symptom of "gender fatigue" is the movement to roll back Title IX protections. While Title IX bars sex discrimination in most educational areas, it is best known for creating dramatic increases in the number of girls and women participating in high school and college athletics. Opposition to gender equity in sports often comes from football coaches and athletes who fear that putting more resources into women's programs will mean taking away money from football. In fact, when Title IX was first passed, the National Collegiate Athletic Association (NCAA) led a campaign to have football exempted from gender equity requirements, arguing that football teams produce profits that fund other sports. However, few football teams make a profit and most run at a large deficit: at about two-thirds of all NCAA Division I and Division II institutions, football does not pay for itself. Among the competitive big-time football programs in Division I, 36 percent of football programs average $1 million in losses annually. Men's basketball is not much better: 30 percent of all Division I men's basketball programs run annual deficits averaging $290,000 a year, and 66 percent of all other Division I men's basketball programs accrue annual deficits over $200,000.[41]

Opposition to women's sports also arises from men's teams that generate low revenues and media attention, such as wrestling, golf, and gymnastics. These critics argue that as more women become athletes, there are fewer opportunities for men to play. This argument is also misleading. While female athletes at the high school level have increased substantially since Title IX—from 295,000 to more than three million—male athletes have also grown and now exceed four million. At the college level approximately 29,500 women participated in athletics prior to Title IX, compared with nearly 167,000 today, a 456 percent increase. At the same time, collegiate male participation has climbed to more than 222,800 athletes. Still, females are only little more than 40 percent of high school and college athletes and their participation rates are below male pre–Title IX levels.[42] Evidently, for some male coaches, athletes, and administrators, 40 percent is too much.

In 2002, the National Wrestling Coaches Association filed a federal lawsuit alleging that Title IX is a quota system, requiring equal participation by males and females. Furthermore, the wrestlers charged that increased participation of females in sports causes men's teams to be unfairly eliminated or underfunded. In an important victory to support Title IX's civil rights protections, a federal court affirmed that Title IX is far from a quota system, and instead requires equitable opportunities and funding based on male and female enrollments.[43] Schools are not required to offer identical sports or fund males and females equally. Few do. Schools have *three* methods described in Title IX to demonstrate fair athletic opportunities. A school can show that organized sports participation roughly reflects the proportion of male and female students in the school, that the athletic interests and needs of female students are fulfilled, *or* that they are expanding to meet those needs. Despite popular opinion, Title IX does not require equal participation or quotas. Schools *are* expected to provide an equal opportunity for females to play in sports of interest.

The George W. Bush administration, however, took aim at Title IX and made it easier for schools to legally ignore the interests of its female athletes. If you called this change "civil rights by email," you would not be far off. In March 2005, the Department of Education decided that colleges can claim compliance with Title IX based solely on the results of an online survey of female students' interest in sports. Schools need not send such emails to males to determine their interest. Moreover, schools are allowed to declare that lack of survey response means lack of interest.[44] So now a school can send out an email about athletic interests, and if females do not respond, then it is assumed they are not interested in athletics. Given the low response rates to email surveys (it's rather easy to hit the delete button) and the glitches with electronic communications, it is safe to say that this policy will allow schools to significantly underestimate females' interests in athletic participation, and then reduce athletic opportunities for females. Did you ever imagine that protection of your civil rights might be determined by a mass email? Evidently, the U.S. Department of Education considered it a good idea.

But even if no changes were made to the law, the reality is that Title IX has never been well enforced and even current requirements are often ignored.[45] Too often, sexist school practices persist because teachers, parents, and students are unaware of their rights under the law, school administrators are unresponsive or uninformed, or the Office for Civil Rights is less than vigorous in enforcement. When we asked nearly one hundred middle and high school teachers and more than five hundred middle and high school students about their knowledge of Title IX, almost half of the teachers and over 95 percent of the students volunteered that they had no knowledge of the law. If these teachers and students had heard of Title IX at all, it was most often for creating more athletic opportunities for women and girls. Less than 10 percent of teachers and not a single student knew that the Department of Education was responsible for enforcing the law, and less than 5 percent of teachers and not one student could name the Title IX coordinator for their school or district.[46] The sad reality is that schools regularly break the law by not appointing the requisite Title IX coordinators or putting in place grievance procedures or even informing students and teachers of their rights. But no government official seems to mind. It is like driving on a highway without traffic laws and no police force: a formula for disaster.

One assignment we give to our students at American University is to visit local schools and evaluate their compliance with Title IX. A free lunch is the prize for any students who can find a school not violating the law. Our lunch fund is undiminished. We invite you to do the same, to visit your local school and look for remnants of a law called Title IX.

AT THE CROSSROADS

Many believe we are at a crossroads: to accept the progress to date, or to risk the progress by continuing to press for gender equity. David and Karen decided to seek the experts' advice, to ask children themselves how they see gender issues in their schools. Here are some typical responses of the more than four hundred middle school students we questioned.[47]

"Girls do everything for men in marriage." —eighth grade, Hispanic male

"Boys have more sports available and can play them better. It's fair to say that we are better athletes than girls." —seventh grade, white male

"Boys are listened to much more than girls are. Boys' ideas matter." —seventh grade, black female

"Girls don't have to pay for dates." —seventh grade, white female

Sexism is still a way of life in our schools, although many boys do not see it. "Gender" has become synonymous with females and feminism; the male role also inhibits options. Sexist notions of masculinity limit male careers, activities, interests, emotions, and longevity. Gender equity progress in the last few years has slowed down for women; for men, it has barely started.

Failing to connect with so many men may well be the feminist movement's greatest political and social failure. Some of the responsibility lies with a few vocal radical feminists who have angrily accused males of being oppressors, and targeted all men as the enemy. But the opponents of feminism bear responsibility as well, for they have promoted the idea that gender equity is antimale. Fanning the flames of fear has sent up a smoke screen preventing many from seeing that gender stereotyping limits the lives of men and boys, although male economic, social, and political entitlements can make this reality more difficult to see. Particular careers (teaching, nursing, social work, and others) are not viewed as "gender appropriate" for men. Boys and men who pursue these careers, or who are unathletic, enjoy the arts, or are not heterosexual, all risk scorn and worse. Parenting and family responsibilities traditionally assigned to women may leave men alienated from the very family they work so hard to support. And that wage earner role can be costly, leading to health problems and an earlier death. The truth is, the quality of men's lives could be greatly enhanced by unlocking conventional gender roles.

Many of us have grown disheartened working on gender equity during the backlash. At its worst, it felt as if our years of effort and personal struggle had been wasted. But while the backlash may have cut off the flowers, the plant has taken root. In huge cities and small towns in every part of America, parents and teachers continued to become aware of sexism in school and in countless small ways fought back. Through them the historic struggle for the full education of America's girls and boys goes on.

SUCCEEDING AT FAIRNESS:
SUGGESTIONS FOR STUDENTS, PARENTS, AND TEACHERS

1. *Timeline:* Using the people and events mentioned in this chapter, teachers (and parents and children!) can share the salient events and individuals who worked to bring full educational opportunities for women. From Horace Mann and Emma Willard to Edith Green (whom we discuss later in the book) and Title IX, this often missed civil rights struggle can be portrayed as a timeline and posted on the classroom (or child's room) wall. Older students can use both print and nonprint sources as well as the Internet to add new insights and entries to the timeline. It may be helpful that each entry includes a year as well as a brief description to inform others who view the timeline. The timeline can also include the struggle of other groups—poor, minority, special needs students—to receive an education.

2. *Boys Are a Gender, Too!* In what ways are boys restricted and stereo-typed? Some adults puzzle over this question, but students see prob-lems pretty quickly. Ask both boys and girls to share school norms and behaviors that they consider unfair to boys. The same can be done for out-of-school activities. Personal stories and incidents can be collected and then categorized into common areas of male stereotyping. Teachers or parents could find such lists insightful, and perhaps work to elimi-nate these sexist behaviors from their classrooms and homes. And of course, the same exercise can be done with girls. Seeing sexism through personal experiences provides students with meaningful insights. For adults, such insights provided by children can help them become aware of their own unfair behaviors, and work on eliminating them.

3. *"I have learned . . ." Statements:* This can be a short follow-up to any of the activities described here or in the other chapters. After any of these exercises, ask the students to write down and complete an *I have learned* statement. What have they learned from this activity and what do they take away with them?

4. *Role Play:* The struggle to gain access to school, vocational training, math and science courses, sports, colleges, and eventually professional schools represents a real-life drama that can be emphasized through a role play. Two students can be selected to reenact one of these dramas in the front of the class. The students can be on-the-spot volunteers or can be given some time to prepare for their role play at home. Students can be instructed to put themselves in the roles of the characters described, and be prepared to continue the role play for a few minutes. Here are a few examples:

   • *A girl excited about her first day in elementary school meeting a boy who resents the intruder and prefers the way it was before girls entered his class.*
   • *A girl who wants to study auto mechanics and enters an all-boys voca-tional class, and they are not happy.*
   • *A man who arrives in a class to train preschool teachers, becoming the only man in the class.*
   • *Elizabeth Blackwell arriving at medical school, to the astonishment of the male professors and male students.*

These are only a few suggestions, but these role-play settings offer students the opportunity to put themselves in another's shoes, to better *feel* what these challenges were like. Teachers or students can suggest others.

Teachers can add yet another dimension to these role plays by creating what some call an *alter ego* role play. For any of the situations described above, select two more students. One stands next to the male, and the other next to the female. Each follows the situation and speaks out to the whole class what thoughts and feelings might be going on inside their character. The alter ego role players are voicing to the public what is typically kept personal. These alter ego voices speak while the role play is on going, speaking over the actions and words of the characters, the way thoughts actually occur during conversations. Alter ego role play can help students of all ages to consider other people's perspectives. (And it often makes for a pretty interesting role play!)

5. *Backlash:* The backlash against feminists and feminism has tainted those words. Many people today, especially the young, are confused about what those words mean. Do feminists want superior treatment? A few radical feminists might argue for this, but most feminists advocate for fundamental equity. Explore how today's students and children describe feminists and feminism. You might begin by asking them to complete a sentence such as:

"A feminist is . . ."
"Feminism means . . ."

Some students might suggest that all feminists want is more rights than males. Others may suggest they advocate for quotas. After they have completed their sentences, it might be helpful to share with them how others have defined such terms and viewed the issue of gender equity:

"A feminist is anyone who recognizes the equality and full humanity of women."

—GLORIA STEINEM

"In the end anti-black, and all forms of discrimination are equivalent to the same thing—anti-humanism."

—SHIRLEY CHISHOLM

You might also want to ask them why Susan B. Anthony described the challenge this way:

"Men and their rights and nothing more; women and their rights and nothing less."

(This might be a good time to ask students to look up these people and identify Gloria Steinem, Shirley Chisholm, and Susan B. Anthony.)

Resources

Campus Life: Undergraduate Cultures from the End of the Eighteenth Century to the Present, by Helen Lefkowitz Horowitz
> This comprehensive social history redefines the terrain of campus life, past and present. Through insightful stories, learn how "the College Men, the Rebels, and the Outsiders" of the past have shaped today's college experience

Herstory: Women Who Changed the World, by Deborah Ohrn
> Did you know that Wolfgang Amadeus Mozart had an older sister who was also a musical genius? Some believe she composed several of her brother's greatest works. Nannerl Mozart is just one example of how women and their accomplishments have been ignored or erased entirely from world history. This book seeks to amend that gaping absence in history books and popular culture with 120 biographies of women whose contributions made a difference to modern society.

In the Company of Educated Women, by Barbara Miller Solomon
> This monumental book chronicles the social, cultural, and economic circumstances that have shaped the development of women's higher education. After considering Colonial America, when women were outsiders to liberal arts institutions, Solomon traces the creation of women's and coeducational colleges and describes the process by which women of different ethnic, racial, religious, and social groups became collegians.

Learning Together: A History of Coeducation in American Public Schools, by David Tyack and Elisabeth Hansot
> Written with intelligence, wit, and reason, this book is a remarkable exploration of how race, class, religion, ethnicity, and gender have shaped—and been shaped by—public education at all levels.

For additional resources, see *Still Failing at Fairness*'s page on www.simonandschuster.com.

CHAPTER 3

The Beginning of the Classroom Compromise: The Elementary School Years

Reality TV would have a field day in elementary school. No need to create embarrassing situations or survival challenges, just set up a time-lapse video camera to record every few minutes or so and watch the strange world of classroom life unfold. What you would see is a world of persistent gender lessons and compromises, perhaps something like this:

Snapshot #1 Emma and Alicia sit with hands raised while Kenton answers a question. Alicia moves her arm over her head to help hold up her raised hand, which appears to be getting heavier.

Snapshot #2 Madison answers a question as the teacher frowns at two boys who are talking.

Snapshot #3 Olivia looks disappointed as the teacher chooses Roberto to demonstrate how to use a microscope.

Snapshot #4 The teacher praises Marcus for his skill in constructing a classroom display.

Snapshot #5 The teacher explains that the homework assignment will be kept brief if everyone pays careful attention for the next fifteen minutes.

Snapshot #6 The teacher helps Ethan with a spelling mistake.

Snapshot #7 The teacher compliments Alicia on her neat paper.

Snapshot #8 Students are in lines for a spelling bee. Boys are on one side of the room and girls are on the other.

As Ted Sizer wrote in *Horace's Compromise*, classroom life often means compromise, an academic *Let's Make a Deal*. Here's the deal: if the students do not challenge the teacher or cause disruption, if the teacher can get through the day's lesson plan, then the students will be rewarded with less work, less pressure, and a more relaxed classroom climate. If teachers and students can meet each other's needs, a comfortable life for all is the reward. Sizer believed that when one or the other breaks this unspoken contract, trouble is likely to follow.

So if some students want to talk, letting them talk can head off potential discipline problems. And if some students do not want to talk, putting them in the spotlight can lead to a whole new set of woes. You probably remember this unspoken compromise from your own school days. If you wanted to speak, you knew just what to do to get called on. Raising a hand might be your first move, but waving your hand would signal that you *really* wanted to talk. Eye contact with the teacher was always a good idea, but a few strategically placed grunts could work miracles in getting attention. Once called on—assuming you had the right answer (not always a sure thing)—you got to speak, your needs were met, and the teacher's needs were met as well. By calling on the eager and willing students, the teacher moves the lesson along at a good pace, the main points are all "covered," and there are smiles all around.

Remember when you did not want to talk? Perhaps you did not have a clue to the right answer. Or perhaps you were incredibly shy, frightened at speaking in front of peers who could make or break your social world. Maybe you were new to the country and to the language, embarrassed to show that you did not always understand what was being said, or how best to formulate your sentences. Then you wanted to be silent, hidden, and if at all possible, invisible. So you honed your invisible techniques: you would disappear in your book and avoid eye contact with the teacher. Most often your prayers would be answered and you would be left alone. But some teachers would push the comfort zone, break the classroom compromise, and ask you a question. Perhaps you endured just a few seconds of silent discomfort, social embarrassment, hopefully mumbling enough words so the teacher would move on. Although the memories of these embarrassing moments linger, they are probably rare. Truth is, most teachers call on students who want to talk, and leave the others alone, and everybody is comfortable. So what's the problem?

Although it *sounds* awfully good, the purpose of school is not to make everyone comfortable. Schools are for education, for stretching, for learning new and sometimes uncomfortable skills. Talented teachers know that if they select only students who quickly volunteer, reticent students will be relegated to the sidelines, unable or unwilling to participate while talkative students will be reinforced for talking even more. The students who may be most in need of the teacher's attention will be least likely to get it. The students who most need to learn the lesson of how to talk in public are least likely to have that opportunity. Students who need a little more time to think—because they are by nature thoughtful, or because English is a new language, or because their cultural background encourages a slower response, or because they are shy—become spectators to rapid classroom exchanges. Females lose out, children of color lose out, English language learners are left behind, and shy boys are silenced. The classroom compromise creates an attractive comfort zone that moves the lesson forward at a good clip, but too often leaves many students behind.

The gendered nature of the classroom compromise can be subtle and is often ignored. Male students frequently control classroom conversation. They ask and answer more questions. They receive more praise for the intellectual quality of their ideas. They get criticized more publicly and harshly when they break a rule. They get help when they are confused. They are the heart and center of interaction. Watch how boys dominate the discussion about presidents in this upper elementary class.

The fifth-grade class is almost out of control. "Just a minute," the teacher admonishes. "There are too many of us here to all shout out at once. I want you to raise your hands, and then I'll call on you. If you shout out, I'll pick somebody else."

Order is restored. Then Stephen, enthusiastic to make his point, calls out.

STEPHEN: I think Lincoln was the best president. He held the country together during the war.

TEACHER: A lot of historians would agree with you.

KELVIN (seeing that nothing happened to Stephen, calls out): I don't. Lincoln was okay, but my Dad liked Reagan. He always said Reagan was a great president.

DAVID (calling out): Reagan? Are you kidding?

TEACHER: Who do you think our best president was, Dave?

DAVID: FDR. He saved us from the Depression.

MAX (calling out): I don't think it's right to pick one best president. There were a lot of good ones.

TEACHER: That's interesting.

REBECCA (calling out): I don't think the presidents today are as good as the ones we used to have.

TEACHER: Okay, Rebecca. But you forgot the rule. You're supposed to raise your hand.

The classroom is the only place in society where so many different, young, and restless individuals are crowded into close quarters for an extended period of time day after day. Teachers sense the undertow of raw energy and restlessness that threatens to engulf the classroom. Few successfully redirect all this energy for learning. Most try to contain it with conventions such as "Raise your hand if you want to talk." Yet even a fraction of a second is too long for some students to wait to be heard. Very active and animated students challenge the rule and simply shout out the answer.

Intellectually, teachers know they should apply rules consistently, but when the discussion becomes fast-paced and furious, rules are often swept aside. When this happens, it is an open invitation for male dominance. The Sadkers and others have found that boys call out significantly more often than girls. Sometimes what they say has little or nothing to do with the teacher's questions. Whether male comments are insightful or irrelevant, teachers respond to them. However, when girls call out, there is a fascinating phenomenon. Perhaps the teacher sees this as a warning sign and suddenly remembers the rule about raising your hand before you talk. And those not as assertive as the animated male students are deftly and swiftly put back in their place.[1]

Not being allowed to call out like her male classmates during the brief conversation about presidents will not psychologically scar Rebecca; however, the system of silencing operates covertly and repeatedly. It occurs several times a day during each school week for twelve years, and even longer if Rebecca goes to college, and, most insidious of all, it happens subliminally. This micro inequity eventually has a powerful cumulative impact.

In many ways, girls appear to be doing well in school. They get better grades and receive fewer punishments than boys. Quieter and more likely to conform, they are a school's ideal students. "If it ain't broke, don't fix it" is often the school's operating principle as girls' good behavior frees the teacher to work with the more difficult-to-manage boys. In fact, some see quiet, conforming girls as a sign that they are doing well, as proof that schools work well for girls but not for boys. Hardly. Take a more thoughtful look. Girls receive less instructional time, less help, and fewer challenges. Reinforced for passivity, their independence and self-esteem suffer. Girls are penalized for "following the rules." Perhaps because they mature sooner than boys, or because of socialization, most girls tolerate a sedentary learning style better than boys do. In contrast, boys get reinforced for breaking the rules; they are rewarded for grabbing more than their fair share of the teacher's time and attention. Even when teachers remember to apply the rules consistently, boys are more likely to get noticed.

The Sadkers observed hundreds of classes and watched as girls typically raised their hands, arms bent at the elbow in a cautious, tentative, almost passive gesture. At other times they pause or stop to think before raising their arms straight and high. Educator Diana Meehan calls this phenomenon the "girl pause": If a teacher asks a question, a girl pauses to think, *Do I know this?* Meanwhile, a boy blurts out an answer, and the class moves on.[2] In contrast, when boys raise their hands, they fling them wildly in the air, up and down, up and down, again and again. Sometimes these hand signals are accompanied by strange noises, "Ooh! Ooh! Me! Me! Ooooh!" Occasionally they even stand beside or on top of their seats and wave one or both arms to get attention. "Ooh! Me! Mrs. Smith, call on me." In the social studies class about presidents, we saw boys as a group grabbing attention while girls as a group were left out of the action.

Another way to observe the gender dimension of the classroom compromise is to focus on individual children and record and describe their behavior for an extended period of time. Here is what we found when we watched two children for a forty-five-minute class. Perhaps you will see yourself in their behavior. Maybe you will see your son or daughter.

The fifth-grade boy sits in the fourth seat, second row. Since there are more than thirty other children in the class, getting the teacher's attention is a very competitive game.

First the boy waves his hand straight in the air so that the teacher will select him from the surrounding forest of mainly male arms. He waves and pumps for almost three minutes without success. Evidently tiring, he puts his right arm down only to replace it with the left. Wave and pump. Wave and pump. Another two minutes go by. Still no recognition. Down with the left hand, up with the right. He moves to strategy two—sounds: "Ooh, me. C'mon. C'mon. Pleeze. Oooooh!" Another minute without being noticed. Strategy three: He gets out of his seat, stands in front of his desk, and waves with sound effects for another thirty seconds. He slumps back into his seat, momentarily discouraged. Five seconds later there's the strategy four effort: He holds his right arm up in the air by resting it on his left as he leans on his elbow. Three more minutes go by.

"Tom." His name. Recognition. For a brief moment he has the floor. The eyes of the teacher and his classmates are on him, the center of attention. He has spent more than nine minutes in his effort to get a half-minute in the sun. Post-response: He sits for four quiet minutes. Then up shoots the arm again.

There is another student in the same class on the other side of the room, a little more toward the front. She begins the class with her arm held high, her face animated, her body leaning forward. Clearly she has something she wants to say. She keeps her right hand raised for more than a minute, switches to the left for forty-five seconds. She is not called on. She doesn't make noises or jump out of her seat, but it looks as though her arm is getting tired. She reverts to propping the right arm up with the left, a signal she maintains for two more minutes. Still no recognition. The hand comes down.

She sits quietly, stares out the window, plays with the hair of the girl in front of her. Her face is no longer animated. She crosses her arms on the desk and rests her head on them, which is how she spends the final twelve minutes of class time. Her eyes are open, but it is impossible to tell if she is listening. The period ends. The girl has not said a word.

When we videotape classrooms and play back the recordings, most teachers are stunned to see themselves teaching subtle gender lessons along with math and spelling. The teacher in the social studies class about presidents was completely unaware that she gave male students more attention. Only after several viewings of the videotape did she notice how she let boys call out answers but reprimanded girls for similar behavior. The teacher who taught Tom and the silent girl did not realize what effort it took to get attention. Surprised and saddened, he watched how his initially eager female student wilted and then faded from the activities of the classroom.

In our workshops for educators we call boys like Tom "star students" or "green-arms." Teachers smile with weary recognition as we describe students whose hands are up in the air so high and so long that the blood could have drained out. They want to be called on and are comfortable in the spotlight. The Sadkers' research shows that in a typical class of twenty-five students, two or three green-arm students may capture 25 percent of the teacher's attention.[3] The lesson moves forward, but with the momentum of only one-fourth of the class.

Most students are not so salient. Rather, nominally involved, they are asked one or two questions by the teacher each class period. Even though nominal students don't wave arms and make birdlike noises, they do exhibit their own distinct patterns. If you were a nominal student, you can probably remember the following from your own school days: As the teacher approaches, you tense. The question is asked. Your shoulders rise, your adrenaline pumps, and your heart pounds so loudly that the teacher's voice is barely audible. You answer. Correct! You exhale with relief. The teacher's shadow moves on. You've paid your dues. If the teacher asks you another question, you're likely to think, *He's picking on me.*

When teachers ask students to read aloud one after the other down the row, one paragraph after another, nominal students count ahead and practice their upcoming paragraph silently. Can you remember industriously working on an impending passage only to have the student in front of you flub his, leaving you to stumble over unknown literary ground? If you can picture yourself in this scene for at least part of your school career, you were probably a nominal student.

In the typical classroom the Sadkers found that approximately 10 percent of students are green-arms and 70 percent are nominal. Who's left? The remaining 20 percent, about four or five students in most classrooms, do not say anything at all. Of course some boys are shy and some girls are assertive, but in their observations of more than one hundred classrooms, the Sadkers found that male students are more often heard and female students are more often stifled.[4] Others have also found that no matter the subject or grade level, boys command classroom attention.[5]

Boys cast in starring classroom roles are often high achievers. Bright boys answer the questions, and their opinions are respected by the teacher. Low-achieving boys also get plenty of attention, but more often it's negative. In general, girls receive less attention, but there's another revelation: unlike the smart boy who flourishes in the classroom, the smart girl is the student who is least likely to be recognized.[6] (Yet being "too smart" can create difficulties for males and females, especially in middle and high schools. Gifted students often face ridicule from peers, and consequently work hard to hide their intelligence by underachieving and withdrawing from classroom interactions.)

Analyzing their interaction data, the Sadkers discovered another intriguing trend: The students most likely to receive teacher attention were white males; the second most likely were males of color; the third, white females; and the least likely, females of color. In school, receiving attention from the teacher is enormously important for a student's achievement and self-esteem. Later in life, in the working world, the salary received is important, and salary levels parallel the classroom: white males at the top and minority females at the bottom. In her classroom interaction studies, Jacqueline Jordan Irvine found that black girls were active, assertive, and prominent in the primary grades, but as they moved up through elementary school, they became the most invisible members of classrooms.[7] Researcher Linda Grant witnessed that even the energy of black girls in the early grades is channeled into stereotypical roles that stress service and nurture. In the first- and second-grade classrooms she observed, black girls were cast in the roles of teacher helpers and monitors of disruptive peers.[8]

THE "OKAY" CLASSROOM IS NOT

As part of our work at American University, David, Myra, and Karen supervised student teachers. During one of these visits by the Sadkers, a young woman, one of the most talented in our teacher preparation program, confronted a sexist incident:

The teacher flicks on the overhead projector, and a poem in the shape of a seesaw draws the third graders' attention. Another transparency and a new image, this time in the shape of a candy bar. The children giggle and whisper. More images—a kite poem, and even one looking like a giraffe. The youngsters are captivated.

"What do these poems have in common?" the teacher says to open the discussion. Through skillful questions and explanations she teaches concrete poetry and motivates the children to write their own poems. "What are some topics you might want to write about?" The third graders are eager to share their ideas: Trucks. A cat. Dogs. TV. My doll.

"That's so dumb." A boy's comment breaks the collegial brainstorming. "I bet all the girls will draw girly Barbie dolls."

"Not me," a girl shoots back. "I'm doing a horse poem."

Not about to let sexism mar her lesson, this teacher confronts the comment. "There's nothing wrong with dolls. A lot of girls and boys like to play with them, which is nice because they learn how to take care of people that way. Not all girls like dolls, just like not all boys like football. Now me—I like teddy bears. [The children laugh.] I'm going to write my concrete poem about a teddy bear."

As the class settles down to write, the teacher walks from desk to desk giving reactions and offering suggestions.

First stop, a boy's desk (twenty seconds): "That's good. I like the way you use describing words."

Second stop, a boy's desk (two minutes; the teacher kneels so she can be eye to eye with the student): "You can't think of anything to write about? What are some of your hobbies?" (There are several more questions about hobbies, and then the boy's interest is sparked and he begins to write.)

Third stop, a boy's desk (fifteen seconds): "That's great! A deck of cards. I never would have thought of that."

Fourth stop, a boy's desk (two minutes): "Tony, this isn't right. It's not supposed to be in straight lines. A concrete poem is in the shape of something. (More discussion that is inaudible. Tony seems to have gotten the idea and starts to write.)

Fifth stop, a girl's desk (four seconds): "Okay."

"I was so nervous. I can't believe that boy's comment about the doll," the student teacher said, shaking her head as she talked with us after the lesson. "How do these kids come up with this stuff? Did I handle it well? What do you think?"

David and Myra assured the student teacher that she had handled the doll incident skillfully. Many instructors would not even have picked up on the comment, and even fewer would have challenged it. Ironically, even as this talented beginning teacher confronted the sexist comment of one of her young male students, she inadvertently doled out insidious gender lessons herself.

In studies of sexism in classroom interaction, we have been particularly fascinated by the ways teachers react to student work and comments because this feedback is crucially important to achievement and self-esteem. The Sadkers found that teachers typically give students four types of responses.

Teacher *praises:* "Good job." "That was an excellent paper." "I like how you developed the characters in your short story."

Teacher *remediates,* encouraging a student to correct a wrong answer or expand and enhance thinking: "Check your addition and remember the carry method." "Review the causes of the Civil War and try again."

Teacher *criticizes,* giving an explicit statement that something is not correct: "No, you've missed number four." This category also includes statements that are much harsher: "This is a terrible report."

Teacher *accepts,* offering a brief acknowledgment that an answer is accurate: "Uh-huh." "Okay."

Teachers praise students only 10 percent of the time. Criticism is even rarer—only 5 percent of comments. In many classrooms teachers do not use any praise or criticism at all. About one-third of teacher interactions are comprised of remediation, a dynamic and beneficial form of feedback.

More than half the time, however, teachers slip into the routine of giving the quickest, easiest, and least helpful feedback—a brief nonverbal nod, a quick "okay." They rely more on acceptance than on praise, remediation, and criticism combined. The bland and neutral "okay" is pervasive, another sign of the classroom compromise where students are not challenged with more difficult questions, or "pushed" to think more carefully. The prevalence of the "Okay Classroom" is another sign that comfort rather than academic rigor is a classroom norm.

In the scene above, it is clear that the compromise is not shared equally by both genders. Boys received not only more instruction but also better instruction. Two boys were praised, a response that promotes their confidence and self-esteem, and alerts them to what they do well. Through constructive criticism, another boy learned that he was not completing the assignment accurately, and he corrected his mistake. The teacher gave another boy remediation, helping him develop ideas for his poem. The only feedback given to a girl was bland and imprecise, without direction or information. "Okay" can leave her to wonder, "How am I doing? Is my poem good? Can I make it better? Were you really listening? Do you care? Tell me more, please."

The Sadkers' research in more than one hundred classrooms found that while boys received more of all four reactions, the gender gap was greatest in the most precise and valuable feedback. Boys, especially the high achievers, were more likely to be praised, corrected, helped, and criticized—all reactions that foster student achievement. Additional studies show that lower-achieving boys and those with discipline problems are not praised as much as their "starring" peers; yet they still receive more teacher interactions, remediation, and criticism.[9] No matter whether they were high or low achievers, girls received the more superficial "okay" reaction, one that packs far less educational punch. In her research, Jacqueline Jordan Irvine also found that black females were least likely to receive clear academic feedback.[10]

At first teachers are surprised to learn that girls are "okayed" and boys gain clear feedback. Then it begins to make sense. "I don't like to tell a girl anything is wrong because I don't want to upset her," many say. "What if she cries? I wouldn't know how to handle it."

The "okay" response is well-meaning, but it kills with kindness. If girls, and boys, don't know when they are wrong, if they don't learn strategies to get it right, then they will never correct their mistakes. And if they rarely receive negative feedback in school, they will be shocked when they are confronted by it in the workplace and in life.

THE BOMBING RATE

"How long do you wait for students to answer a question?" When we ask teachers to describe what they do hundreds of times daily in the classroom, their answers are all over the map: One minute. Ten seconds. Five seconds. Twenty-five seconds. Three seconds. How long do you think teachers wait for a student to answer?

Three decades ago, Mary Budd Rowe was the first researcher to frame this question and then try to answer it. Today, many continue her work and uncover an astonishingly hurried classroom. On average, teachers wait only nine-tenths of a second for a student to answer a question. If a student can't answer within that time, teachers call on another student or answer the question themselves.[11]

When questions are hurled at this bombing rate, some students get lost, confused, or rattled, or just drop out of the discussion. "Would you repeat that?" "Say it again." "Give me a minute. I can get it." Requests such as these are really pleas for more time to think. Nobody has enough time in the bombing rate classroom, but boys have more time than girls. It is not unusual for boys to get double the wait time.[12]

Waiting longer for a student to answer is one of the most powerful and positive things a teacher can do. It is a vote of confidence, a way of saying, "I have high expectations for you, so I will wait a little longer. I know you can get it if I give you a chance." Since boys receive more wait time, they try harder to achieve. As girls struggle to answer under the pressure of time, they may flounder and fail. Less assertive in class and more likely to think about their answers and how to respond, girls may need *more* time to think. In the real world of the classroom, they receive less. For female achievement and self-esteem, it is a case of very bad timing.

PRETTY IS—HANDSOME DOES

Ashley Reiter, a national winner of the Westinghouse Talent Search for her sophisticated project on math modeling, remembers winning her first math contest. It happened at the same time that she first wore her contact lenses. Triumphant, Ashley showed up at school the next day without glasses and with a new medal. "Everyone talked about how pretty I looked," Ashley remembers. "Nobody said a word about the math competition."

One area where girls are recognized more than boys is appearance. Teachers compliment their outfits and hairstyles. We hear it over and over again—not during large academic discussions but in more private moments, in small groups, when a student comes up to the teacher's desk, at recess, in hallways, at lunchtime, when children enter and exit the classroom: "Is that a new dress?" "You look so pretty today." "I love your new haircut. It's so cute." While these comments are most prevalent in the early grades, they continue throughout school, into the workplace, and throughout life: "That's a great outfit." "You look terrific today."

Many teachers do not want to emphasize appearance. "They pull you in," a preschool teacher says. "The little girls come up to you with their frilly dresses and hair ribbons and jewelry. 'Look what I have,' they say and wait for you to respond. What are you supposed to do? Ignore them? Insult them? They look so happy when you tell them they're pretty. It's a way of connecting. I think it's what they're used to hearing, the way they are rewarded at home."

Like girls, boys in the early grades also ask teachers how they look, but teachers respond to boys and girls differently. And in these differences there is a world of meaning:

A first-grade classroom: A girl approaches the teacher and holds up the locket that is hanging around her neck. "See my new necklace?" The teacher smiles. "That's beautiful. Did your mother give it to you?" The little girls nods. "You look so pretty today."

The same first-grade classroom: A boy comes up to the teacher and points to his sneakers. "These are new," he says. "That's neat," the teacher responds. "I'll bet you can jump really high in those."

A kindergarten classroom: The teacher walks over to a boy who is playing with small, round plastic hoops. He has slipped his hand through them and holds out his arm, circled in red, blue, green, and yellow "bracelets," for the teacher to admire. The teacher finds a plastic peg that stands on the floor. "Look. Here's what you should do with these." The teacher and the boy spend the next several minutes removing the hoops from the boy's arm and putting them around the peg. "First we'll put blue," says the teacher. "What color shall we put on next? What color is that? Right, yellow. Are all the rings the same size? Let's see if any are bigger than the others."

When teachers talk with boys about appearance, the exchanges are brief—quick recognition and then on to something else. Or teachers use appearance incidents to move on to a physical skill or academic topic. In the scene just described, the teacher used the bracelet incident to teach about size, shape, and color. In another exchange, a little boy showed the teacher his shiny new belt buckle. Her response: "Cowboys wore buckles like that. They were rough and tough and they rode horses. Did you know that?"

When teachers talk to girls about their appearance, the conversations are usually longer, and the focus stays on how pretty the girl looks. Sometimes the emphasis moves from personal appearance to papers and work. When boys are praised, it is most often for the intellectual quality of their ideas. Girls are twice as likely to be praised for following the rules of form. "I love your margins" or "What perfect handwriting" are the messages.[13]

Girls learn these appearance lessons early and well, and with lasting impact. When we asked more than four hundred middle school students from diverse cultural and economic backgrounds to describe the best thing about being female, appearance topped the list. One seventh grader declared, "Being pretty is important because it helps me get people's approval." Another seventh grader described how "THE perfect outfit can make you feel pretty and worth something." Yet another girl noted that her favorite after-school activity is "receiving beauty treatments to feel better about myself." Sadly, such comments underscored how girls learn to seek approval and validation of their worth based on appearance.[14]

DIFFERENT WORLDS

This chapter began with a series of brief video clips that revealed the classroom compromises and gender lessons imbedded in everyday teaching. If the camera were to go beyond the classroom and take pictures throughout the school, we might see something like this:

Snapshot #1 Leaving the library, a single caterpillar line crawls along—its first half all female, its second half all male.

Snapshot #2 At a long rectangular lunchroom table a group of fifth and sixth graders eat lunch together, black and white, Hispanic and Asian. Every child is male.

Snapshot #3 On the playground, a large all-male soccer game is in play. It stretches out to take over most of the schoolyard.

Snapshot #4 A few girls jump rope at the edge of the schoolyard.

If you look again at these scenes but substitute white and black for male and female, the segregation screams out. A racial inequity would be unacceptable, but a gender inequity is not even noticed. We must freeze the action to even see the divisions. A separate boy world and a separate girl world is just education as usual. Many of us were schooled in these gender-divided worlds, and it didn't seem to hurt us. Or did it?

BOY BASTIONS—GIRL GHETTOS

Raphaela Best spent four years as an observer in an elementary school in one of Maryland's most affluent counties. She helped the children with schoolwork, ate lunch with them, and played games in class and at recess. As an anthropologist, she also took copious notes. After more than one thousand hours of living with the children, she concluded that elementary school consists of separate and unequal worlds.[15] She watched gender segregation in action firsthand, and with each year saw the walls grow higher and more entrenched.

In the first grade, when so much about school seems gigantic and fearful, children look to adults for safety. Best found that both boys and girls ran to their first-grade teacher for hugs, praise, and general warmth and affection. But by the second grade, boys had begun to place more importance on their peer group. To ensure privacy from the female world, the meeting place became the boys' bathroom, where the boys talked about kids at school and decided what to play at recess.

By grades three and four the playground also became increasingly sex-segregated, as blacktop and grassy areas were reserved for active boys' ball games. The girls were often found on the sidelines, where they stood talking, played hopscotch, and jumped rope. Occasionally an athletic girl breached the cultural divide and played with the boys, yet her status as tomboy was always a limiting and noninclusive role. A powerful male culture had evolved, one of privileged entitlement. Excluded from this all-male society were not only girls but also some boys who were considered "sissies."

Girls spent the first few years of school helping the teacher, not switching their allegiance to the peer group until the fourth grade. Then, instead of joining a club, they formed best-friend relationships. Sometimes fights broke out, when two girls argued over having a third as best friend. Being a good student and having a pleasing personality were seen as important, but, by the upper elementary grades, appearance had become the key to social status.

Best found the lunchroom to be a key area of increasingly formal segregation. In the first grade boys and girls sat together, talking and playing. By second grade they sat at the same table, but it was as if an invisible line had cut it in half, with girls on one end and boys on the other. By the third grade the boys burst into the cafeteria at a dead run to claim their male-only table.

These cafeteria gender hierarchies can haunt students for years. A student at American University remembers his school lunchroom in Brooklyn:

> At lunch our class all sat together at one long table. All the girls sat on one side, and the boys sat on the other. This was our system. Unfortunately, there were two more boys in my class than seats on the boys' side. There was no greater social embarrassment for a boy in the very hierarchical system we had set up in our class than to have to sit on the girls' side at lunch. It happened to me once, before I moved up the class social ladder. Boys climbed the rungs of that ladder by beating on each other during recess. To this day, twenty years later, I remember that lunch. It was horrible.

Other men speak, also with horror, of school situations when they became "one of the girls." The father of a nine-year-old daughter remembered girls in elementary school as "worse than just different. We considered them a subspecies." Many teachers who were victims of sexist schooling themselves understand this system and collaborate with it; they warn noisy boys of a humiliating punishment: "If you don't behave, I'm going to make you sit with the girls."

Girls are hurt by these gender divides, too. A third grader described it this way: "Usually we separate ourselves, but my teacher begins recess by handing a jump rope to the girls and a ball to the boys." Like the wave of a magic wand, this gesture creates strict gender lines. "The boys always pick the biggest areas for their games," she says. "We have what's left over, what they don't want."

"When it's recess time," an elementary school girl observed, "the boys run to the closet and get out the balls and bats and mitts and other stuff."

"Does the teacher ever say anything about the boys taking all the balls?" we asked her.

"Never."

"Would you like to play ball in the big area of the playground?"

"Sometimes I would like to. And sometimes girls do play kickball, but mostly not. This is just the way it is in our school."

Every morning at recess in schoolyards across the country, boys fan out over the prime territory to play kickball, football, or basketball. Sometimes girls join them, but more often it's an all-male ball game. In the typical schoolyard, the boys' area is bigger than the girls'. Boys never ask if it is their right to take over the territory, and it is rarely questioned. Girls huddle along the sidelines, on the fringe, as if in a separate female annex. Recess becomes a spectator sport.

Teachers seldom intervene to divide space and equipment more evenly, and seldom attempt to connect the segregated worlds—not even when they are asked directly by the girls.

> "The boys won't let us play," a third grader said, tugging at the arm of the teacher on recess duty. "They have an all-boys club and they won't let any girls play."
>
> "Don't you worry, honey," the teacher said, patting the little girl's hair. "When you get bigger, those boys will pay you all the attention you want. Don't you bother about them now."

As we observed that exchange, we couldn't help but wonder how the teacher would have reacted if the recess group had announced "No

Catholics" or if white children had blatantly refused to play with Asians. The world of children and the world of adults is comprised of *different* races, but each gender is socially constructed as so different, so alien that we use the phrase "the *opposite* sex."

Most girls—five, six, seven, or eight years old—are much too young to truly understand and challenge their assignment as the lower-caste gender. But without challenge over the course of years, this hidden curriculum in second-class citizenship sinks in. By upper elementary and middle school, nearly one in five students see second-class status as the biggest disadvantage of being a girl. Boys and girls describe a society that expects females to serve males by cleaning and cooking, and see girls as the weaker sex. Students further report that teachers and coaches listen less and expect less from girls than boys. One girl remarked, "People think you aren't as good at 'a whole lot of things' if you are a girl." Another told us:

> Our basketball coach told our parents that the girls' practice was shorter than the boys' team practice because girls did not have the "attention span" or the "interest" to focus on basketball for two hours at a time and were more interested in socializing than in the game. Our coach is wrong.[16]

Schools and children need help—intervention by adults who can equalize the playing field. The first step is for parents and teachers to question education-as-usual. A Milwaukee teacher recalls when she finally understood she was questioning too little and accepting too much:

> As I walked my assigned area of the playground on a recent Monday, I looked at the boys playing basketball on the far end and the girls huddled or walking in small groups along the side. No one was fighting or swearing, so I figured it was a good day. And then I caught myself. No, all was not well because I knew that some of the girls huddled in the groups liked to play basketball. So why weren't they playing? And what was I doing about it? Why did I allow a "might-makes-right" playground where the boys decided where they would play and with whom, which in practice meant no girls on the basketball or soccer teams. What was the hidden message I was giving to the girls on the playground? That the boys decide, and that's that?[17]

MALE MAGNETS

We are often asked to talk to classes about sexism in school. In one visit to a sixth grade, a thoughtful African-American girl talked about how baffled she was by boys. "What thoughts go on inside their heads?" she asked. Her classmates began to giggle until they realized her question was completely honest. "No, I mean it. I know they don't think like I do. Something different goes on inside their heads, but I can't figure out what it is." Her sincerity drew in others:

"Yeah, guys are totally different. They're like aliens."

"When I go to the movies and something sad happens, I cry. But a guy doesn't cry. It's not that they have *different* feelings. They don't have *any* feelings."

"I don't think that's true. They have feelings, they just don't let anyone know it."

"Girls are strange, too. We don't get them at all," one boy said, getting the boys into the discussion.

A popular African-American male student addressed his reaction directly to the girls in the classroom: "You don't talk about normal things like we do. All you talk about is hair and makeup, and what to do if you get your period."

Several students glanced up quickly to catch our reaction to this taboo topic. But the boy was not after shock effect; he was being honest, too. We were struck by the confusion of these eleven-year-olds. They did not understand one another because they had so little opportunity to really interact. We asked the sixth graders to look around their classroom and see if they noticed anything that might lead to miscommunication and misunderstanding. The classroom was arranged in eight groups of six. In each group, African-American, Asian, Hispanic, and white children sat together. The students were amazed to see that not a single group was integrated by gender.

We have found that sex segregation in the lunchroom and schoolyard spills over into the classroom. In the Sadkers' three-year, multistate study of one hundred classrooms, researchers drew "gender geography" maps of each class they visited. They found that more than half of the classes were segregated by gender. There is more communication across race than across gender in elementary schools.[18]

We have seen how sex segregation occurs when children form self-selected groups. Sometimes the division is even clearer, and so is the impact on instruction.

> The students are seated formally in rows. There are even spaces between the rows, except down the middle of the room where the students have created an aisle large enough for two people standing side by side to walk down. On one side of the aisle, the students are all female; on the other side, all male. Black, white, Hispanic, and Asian students sit all around the room, but no student has broken the gender barrier.
>
> The teacher in this room is conducting a math game, with the right team (boys) against the left team (girls). The problems have been put on the board, and members of each team race to the front of the room to see who can write the answer first. Competition is intense, but eventually the girls fall behind. The teacher keeps score on the board, with two columns headed "Good Girls" and "Brilliant Boys."

The gender segregation was so formal in this class that we asked if the teacher had set it up. "Of course not." She looked offended. "I wouldn't think of doing such a thing. The students do it themselves." It never occurred to the well-meaning teacher to raise the issue or change the seats.

Here is another segregation episode, this one involving affluent independent school students during a swimming lesson.

> The pool is divided by a rope into two lap lanes. No one has tested the children or divided them by ability to make faster and slower lap lanes, but all the girls are in one lane and all the boys in another. Although many of the girls swim as fast or faster than the boys, gender alone created the division.
>
> A male teacher and a female teacher supervise the swimming. The male teacher stands at the end of the pool directly in front of the boy lane. He gives boys suggestions and advice as they come across the pool: "Good stroke, Tom." "Sean, watch your breathing." "Michael, don't forget to kick." "Tim, bend your arm forty-five degrees, like this." The boys find these comments helpful, so they call out questions and clamor for more attention. "Is this it?" "Look at my stroke and tell me if it's good." The female teacher comes over to the male side of the pool to help answer the avalanche of male requests.
>
> Meanwhile, the girls talk to each other, splash, jump up and down

to keep from getting cold. Finally, too bored to wait for more directions, several start swimming to the other end of the pool. Others follow. Not a single girl has received instruction on how to improve her performance.

In our research we have found that gender segregation is a major contributor to female invisibility. In sex-segregated classes, teachers are pulled to the more talkative, more disruptive male sections of the classroom or pool. There they stay, teaching boys more actively and directly while the girls fade into the background.

THE SPOTLIGHT ON BOYS

When teachers are asked to remember their most outstanding students, boys' names dominate the list. Teachers say males are brighter, better at science and math, and more likely to become the nation's future leaders. When students are asked to choose outstanding classmates, they also name boys. But boys are also on another roster. When teachers remember their worst students—the discipline problems, the ones most likely to create a classroom disturbance or to flunk out of school—they still list boys.[19] As one teacher at a workshop put it, "Boys at school are either in the process of becoming the Establishment or fighting it. Either way, they are the center of attention."

In the classroom, attention is the prize. But not every boy can be at the head of the class. Only a few rise to the very top. We watched two boys fight for star status in a suburban elementary school:

Twenty-eight students file into the room, hang up their coats, and take their seats. The teacher, a nine-year veteran of the classroom, reviews the day's agenda. Math is first on the schedule.

It is then we meet Jim and Matt, without being formally introduced. With the teacher's first question their hands shoot up. First Matt answers, then Jim, as each competes to be the center of attention. Hands waving, they edge out of their seats. Jim sits on his knees, gaining a full six inches and a visible advantage over Matt. The next question goes to the now-elevated Jim, stirring Matt to even greater heights—literally. He stands beside his chair and waves his arm. "Settle down, guys, and give someone else a chance," the teacher says. Several other students are called on, but within a few minutes the "Matt and Jim Show" returns. When the teacher writes difficult problems on the board, the questions no one else can answer, she turns to her two male stars for answers. "Matt and Jim will be great mathematicians when they grow up," the teacher comments as math class ends and she erases the problems from the board.

Evidently, Matt will grow up to be a great historian as well, for he dominates social studies, too. With Jim less involved, Matt has the floor all to himself. During language arts, the class works in small groups on stories for a school newspaper, and the achievements of Jim and Matt are featured in several articles. The last class before lunch is science, and Matt is called up for a demonstration. As he stands in front of the room and reads the results of the science experiment, the other students dutifully copy his calculations into their notebooks.

During lunch we review our observation forms. Although almost evenly divided between boys and girls, males in this class have benefited from a more active learning environment; but Matt and Jim were in a class of their own. Matt received more of the teacher's time and talent than anyone else, with Jim coming in second. Calling these two boys future mathematicians, the teacher further distanced them from the rest of the class. At the end of three hours, Matt and Jim have answered almost half of the teachers' questions, leaving the other twenty-six students to divide up the remainder of the teachers' attention. Nine students, six girls and three boys, have not said a single word.

Warmed by the academic spotlight, students like Matt and Jim reap school rewards. In the elementary grades their future careers are the talk of the teachers' room. By high school, prestigious colleges and scholarships loom on the horizon. But school life can be marred by clouds even for stars. Since their performance is head and shoulders above the other students, boys like Matt and Jim no longer compete with their classmates; they are vying with each other. These superstar students, who are more likely to be male, face ever-increasing pressure and cutthroat competition in their fight to get to the top—to win state honors, the most lucrative scholarship, a place at an Ivy League college. From Jim's vantage point, although ahead of his classmates, he just can't seem to catch up with Matt. Frustration and despair often haunt and depress smart boys who find themselves "runners-up" in the competition for top prizes.

Star students are not the only ones who capture the teacher's attention. When schools are not able to meet their needs, some boys cross the line and go from calling out to acting out. On the classroom stage these males take the bad-boy role, sometimes using it as a passport to popularity. Interviewing elementary school students, researchers have found that many of the most admired males are those ready to take on the teacher. Here's how two fourth graders described these popular boys:

MARK: They're always getting into trouble by talking back to the teacher.

TOM: Yeah, they always have to show off to each other that they aren't afraid to say anything they want to the teacher, that they aren't teacher's pets. Whatever they're doing, they make it look like it's better than what the teacher is doing, 'cause they think what she's doing is stupid.

MARK: And one day Josh and Allen got in trouble in music 'cause they told the teacher the Disney movie she wanted to show sucked. They got pink [disciplinary] slips.

TOM: Yeah, and that's the third pink slip Josh's got already this year, and it's only Thanksgiving.[20]

If teachers were asked to "round up the usual suspects"—the class clowns, troublemakers, and delinquents—they would fill the room with boys. Teachers remember these boys for all the wrong reasons. In fact, so pervasive is the concern over male misbehavior that even when a boy and a girl are involved in an identical infraction of the rules, the male is more likely to get the penalty. Scenes like this one are played out daily in schools across America:

Two seniors, Kyle and Michelle, arrive at their high school English class fifteen minutes late. The teacher stares at them as they enter the room. "Kyle, do you need a special invitation? Is it too much to ask that you get here on time? Never mind. Sit down and see me after class. [Pause; voice softens.] And Michelle, I'm disappointed in you."

Boys' disorderly conduct sets into motion a chain reaction with steep costs and lasting impressions. When men at our workshops looked back on their school days, some of their most unpleasant memories were of the tough disciplinary incidents they experienced. A man who is now a high school teacher in New England said: "I was in fifth grade, and it was the first time I had a male teacher. This teacher would treat the girls almost like princesses, but when the boys were disciplined, it was very physical and very rough. He would grab us by the hair and slam our heads down on the desk."

Marissa, a student teacher in a Maryland middle school, is already learning the disaster potential of problem students, mainly male. Observing her class, we keep track of which students she calls on, what she says, and where she moves in the room. When we show her our notes, she sees that most of her questions went to six boys sitting at two tables near her desk.

"I know I usually call on those boys up front. I put them there so I can keep an eye on them."

"Did you realize that more than half of the questions you asked went to those six boys?"

"I didn't think I was talking with them that much, but I do use questions to keep them on task."

"Were they on task?"

"At the beginning, but toward the end they weren't paying attention."

"What about the other twenty-four students, the rest of the class? How were they doing?"

Marissa looks confused. "I don't even know," she says. "I was so concerned about that group of boys, so worried they would act out, I didn't pay much attention to the rest of the class."

Marissa was devoting her energy to boys at the bottom, the ones with potential to undermine her authority and throw the class into turmoil. So powerful was their influence, they determined where she walked, whom she questioned, and even how the room was arranged and where students sat.

While boys grab teacher attention by acting out, the consequences of such misbehavior can reveal a racial mismatch. African-American males are punished more often and more harshly than their white peers, setting a pattern of black male footsteps out of the classroom and into disciplinary spaces.[21] In her book, *Bad Boys,* sociologist Ann Ferguson provides a window into this troubling inequity. She spent three years observing African-American fifth and sixth graders in a racially and economically diverse California public elementary school. She concluded that in the eyes of many teachers, black males set the standard for inappropriate behavior, too often seen as "one step away from becoming a troublemaker."[22]

Ferguson argues that male misbehavior is often characterized as "boys will be boys: they are mischievous and naughty by nature. As a result, rule breaking on the part of boys is looked at as something-they-can't-help."[23] We have seen how male misbehavior gets attention, yet Ferguson witnessed that teachers give their attention for very different reasons. When African-American boys acted out in class, the "boys will be boys" idea was quickly cast aside as black boys earned the distinction of "troublemakers," children with character flaws needing to be controlled. Within the school, academic expectations of the "troublemakers" quickly plummeted. Yet teachers admitted that their attitudes shifted when a white boy misbehaved. They believed in his academic promise and their discipline was designed to keep him on task.

Racial inequities were further revealed when teachers were asked to describe their typical students. On one end of the spectrum was the ideal student, a studious yet mischievous white male. A sixth-grade teacher offered this description:

> The ideal student is one that can sit and listen and learn from me—work with their peers, and take responsibility on themselves and understand what is next, what is expected of them. He's not really Goody Two-shoes, you know. He's not quiet and perfect. He'll take risks. He'll say the wrong answer. He'll fool around and have to be reprimanded in class. There's a nice balance to him.[24]

In contrast to the ideal students are those devoid of this nice balance, the at-risk, unsalvageable ones. Who are these unsalvageable students? Most often African-American boys. Here is one teacher's explanation:

> He's a boy with a lot of energy and usually uncontrolled energy. He's very loud in the classroom, very inappropriate in the class. He has a great sense of humor, but again it's inappropriate. I would say most of the time that his mouth is open, it's inappropriate, it's too loud, it's disrupting. But other than that [dry laugh] he's a great kid. You know if I didn't have to teach him, if it was a recreational setting, it would be fine.[25]

In both teacher accounts, boys are acting out in class. But a troubling contrast emerges when we examine the meaning attached to the misbehavior. The teachers Ferguson interviewed believed that by acting out the ideal student—the white male—achieves a healthy balance between academic prowess and being a "real boy." Not so for African-American boys. Their classroom disruption was seen as deviant. Boys at the bottom and boys at the top are magnets that attract a teacher's attention either as a reward or as a mechanism for control. Teachers hope their male stars will become tomorrow's corporate presidents, senators, and civic leaders, but they do not hold high hopes for the boys at the bottom. Instead they fear those males could become involved in very serious trouble. Both groups are taught very different lessons and socialized into distinct aspects of the male role in America. Often these roles are created by the complex intersection of gender, race, and socioeconomic class. Whether they are first or last, boys pay a price.

CHARACTERS OF THE CURRICULUM

Few things stir up more controversy than the content of school curriculum. Teachers, parents, students—all seem to be intuitively aware that schoolbooks shape what the next generation knows and how it behaves. In this case research supports intuition. When children read about people in nontraditional gender roles, they are less likely to limit themselves to stereotypes. When children read about women and minorities in history, they are more likely to feel these groups have made important contributions to the country. As one sixth grader told us, "I love to read biographies about women. When I learn about what they've done, I feel like a door is opening. If they can do great things, maybe I can, too."

But what if your identity is misrepresented, misremembered, or just plain missing from the school curriculum? For more than four decades, parents and educators have conducted studies to document objectively how men and women are portrayed in the curriculum.

In their landmark 1975 study *Dick and Jane as Victims*, Lenore Weitzman and her colleagues studied 2,760 stories in 134 elementary texts and readers, looking at the pictures, stories, and language used to describe male and female characters and found the following ratios:[26]

Boy-centered stories to girl-centered stories	5:2
Adult male characters to adult female characters	3:1
Male biographies to female biographies	6:1
Male fairy-tale stories to female fairy-tale stories	4:1

Females of color, portrayed half as frequently as their male counterparts, were truly invisible.

Weitzman and her colleagues also reviewed award-winning children's literature, Caldecott winners from 1953 through 1971. These picture books, chosen as the best of the year by the American Library Association, had eleven times as many boys and men pictured as girls and women.[27] When girls and women were included, they were typecast. They looked in mirrors, watched boys, cried, needed help, served others, gave up, betrayed secrets, acted selfishly, and waited to be rescued. While men were involved in 150 different jobs, women were housewives. When they took off their aprons and discarded their dishtowels (the actual costume of the textbook housewife), they worked outside the home only as teachers and nurses.

Children's literature and school texts routinely included derogatory comments about being female.[28] For example:

From Harper & Row's *Around the Corner:* "Look at her, Mother, just look at her. She is just like a girl. She gives up."

From Scott Foresman's *Ventures:* "We are willing to share our great thoughts with mankind. However, you happen to be a girl."

It was not a pretty picture. The negative publicity over sexist books jolted publishers. In the 1970s and 1980s, textbook companies and professional associations, such as the American Psychological Association and the National Council of Teachers of English, issued guidelines for nonracist and nonsexist books, suggesting how to include and fairly portray different groups in the curriculum.[29] Such efforts are important: students spend as much as 80 to 95 percent of classroom time using textbooks, and teachers make a majority of their instructional decisions based on these texts.[30] And given the nearly $1 billion worth of children's books purchased every year by family and friends, how gender is represented on the pages of what children read deserves careful attention.[31]

So how are books doing today? We can celebrate some changes. Females appear more often in textbooks and children's literature, are more likely to demonstrate traditional male traits such as assertiveness and athleticism, and are depicted with wider career options. Yet problems persist.

No matter the subject, the names and experiences of males continue to dominate the pages of school books. Men are seen as the movers and shakers of history, scientists of achievement, and the political leaders. Boys are routinely shown as active, creative, brave, athletic, achieving, and curious. In striking contrast, girls are often portrayed as dependent, passive, fearful, docile, and even as victims, with a limited role in or impact on the world. For example, in a study of elementary mathematics software only 12 percent of the characters were female. In their limited appearances, they were presented as mothers and princesses. Male characters, on the other hand, experienced occupational action and variety as heavy equipment operators, factory workers, shopkeepers, mountain climbers, hang gliders, garage mechanics, and even a genie providing directions.[32] Such gender imbalances are not limited to math, but are found across the curriculum.

Studying history is a journey through time, but mostly a male journey. In telling the story of our national history, current elementary and high school social studies texts include five times more males than females.[33] When women are included, it is not always a positive development. For instance, the nineteenth-century diplomat Klemens von Metternich is described in the popular high school history book *World History: Patterns of Interaction* as a man whose "charm" worked well with "elegant ladies"—words and facts of dubious historical import, but not without prurient interest.[34] Such gender and linguistic insights are frequently left unexplained in texts.

Recently, a colleague remarked to us that "while half the country is female, the fact is that most 'notable' history-making acts have involved men. History books *should* feature more men because there *were* more men in important roles. That's not gender bias; that's the truth." Such a comment sounds down-to-earth and reasonable, but it reflects our own lack of learning. Most adults were taught a conventional historical narrative with few women. Many adults believe that there is not much of a story to tell about women. But our ignorance should not become the standard for the next generation. To paraphrase Winston Churchill, history is written by those in power, and women are not in power.

Here is a simple example. Paul Revere's courageous ride through the night to alert a sleeping countryside of the coming of the British troops is known by virtually every American. But how many know the tale of Sybil Ludington? She undertook an equally heroic ride when she was but a sixteen-year-old farm girl. On the night of April 26, 1777, Sybil Ludington rode into the damp hours of darkness and through enemy-infested woods to summon soldiers to halt a British raid on Connecticut and New York. When she returned home more than four hundred soldiers were ready to march. Sybil rode forty miles, more than twice the distance of Paul Revere. How do textbooks recount her exploits? Usually, not at all. But in the rare school history text that does mention her, she is referred to as the "female Paul Revere."[35]

History texts rarely mention the women soldiers who also fought in the American Revolution, or those women who made their contributions on the home front. During war, women were left to care for their families and manage businesses and farms on their own. In fact, women from Abigail Adams in the Revolutionary War to Rosie the Riveter in World War II can be viewed as a "disposable labor force." Women were hired when the nation needed them, and fired when the war was over, and little is said about the matter in textbooks. Nor is much said about female courage. We honor the courage of soldiers in the Revolutionary army who bravely fought the British, as well we should. But women facing childbirth at that time also showed courage. Imagine what it must have been like to feel the joy of bringing a child into the world, while realizing that childbirth might very well end your life. We ask our students if they think more men died in the Revolution fighting for our nation's independence, or if more Colonial women died during childbirth bringing forth the next generation of Americans? We do not pretend to know the answer, but we do ask students to recognize that male courage in war is how we tell our history, and female courage in childbirth does not even merit a sentence in that history. Shouldn't both forms of courage be honored?

Social, cultural, and legal barriers are often omitted or glossed over in texts. For example, in our classes and workshops we ask, "Has anyone ever heard of Catherine Littlefield Greene?" Silence follows. Most have heard of her husband, Revolutionary War general Nathanael Greene. After her husband's death, she met Eli Whitney, a Yale-educated tutor. Whitney, as we learn from our history texts, refined the cotton gin (although some texts give him full credit for inventing it!). He worked on this project while living on Catherine Greene's Mulberry Grove plantation in Savannah. But his design was flawed: although seeds were pulled from the cotton, they became clogged in the rollers. It was the unmentioned Catherine Greene who came up with the breakthrough idea of using hairbrushes to remove the seeds. Her insight made the difference, and copycat gins sprang up on other plantations. Lawsuits followed. Who really held the patent to the cotton gin? Once again, Catherine Greene sprung to the rescue and paid Whitney's legal bills to defend his right to the cotton gin. It took seven years for Eli Whitney to win full title to the cotton gin, and the legal fight cost Catherine her estate.[36] You will likely look in vain for her name in school history books.

"Why wasn't the patent taken out in both names?" students ask us when we tell the story. It is an excellent question that reflects another untaught history lesson. At a time when it was unseemly for women to write books (many female authors took male names), it was especially unlikely for a "lady" to patent an invention. So men took out the patents. Remember the time you learned about the industrial revolution and had to memorize the seemingly endless list of inventors—Fulton, Edison, Whitney, Singer, the Wright brothers, Samuel Morse, Charles Goodyear, George Pullman, and George Washington Carver? The official lesson you were being taught was to connect each inventor with his invention; the hidden lesson you were learning was that inventive genius resides in male brains, usually white male brains. We can do better today. Newer books need to tell of the women inventors (and there were many) who were left out of the history books that so many of us read. We owe our children a more complete history.

Let's look at language arts: Is literature more gender fair than it was thirty years ago? To find out, Lorraine Evans and Kimberly Davies examined thirteen current elementary basal readers. They found that male characters continue to dominate, outnumbering females 2 to 1. They also were stunned to learn how males are still strikingly bound by traditional standards. For example, in a story from a fifth-grade book, the display of male aggressiveness is noteworthy: A boy wants to be in charge of the fair project; he is the biggest and looks at his raised fist while glancing at the other children to signify no one was to argue. No one did. In other stories, the adult males are shaking their fists at other males, shouting and often chasing them.[37]

These lessons in gender bias extend beyond the pages of academic texts, reinforced by award-winning, popular children's books read daily in classrooms and nightly at home. Mykol Hamilton and David Anderson explored sexism in two hundred distinguished children's books published between 1995 and 2001. The books are American Library Association award winners, Caldecott selections, and top-selling children's picture books. Hamilton and Anderson wondered if decades of research documenting gender bias in schools and society might have led to a more balanced female-to-male character ratio and less stereotyped portrayals of the sexes. They were disappointed. Contemporary children's books tell twice as many male-centered tales than female, and illustrations depict 50 percent more males. Although female characters appear in newer roles such as doctors, lawyers, and scientists, they are more often passive observers, watching their active brothers at work and at play. A passage in *Johnny and Susie's Mountain Quest* highlights the rigid roles of a brave boy and a helpless girl: " 'Oh, please help me, Johnny!' cried Susie. 'We're up so high! I'm afraid I'm going to fall.' "[38]

Females are not the only ones often missing from the pages of children's literature. Fathers are, too, appearing in less than half of the two hundred books. When present, fathers are depicted as stoic, hands-off parents, rarely seen hugging or feeding their children. Mothers are shown more often as affectionate caregivers capable of expressing a range of emotions from happiness to sadness. And surprisingly, mothers in these stories discipline children and express anger more often than do fathers.[39]

Hamilton and Anderson also discovered that occupational stereotyping has not gone underground. In the two hundred books they reviewed, women are given traditional jobs ten times as often as nontraditional ones. For example, the lead adult female character in *Alligator Tales* is a stewardess, a maid in *Mr. Willowby's Christmas Tree,* and a librarian in *Hopping Hens Here!* Males in children's books remain in traditional roles as well. Boys tend to have roles as fighters, adventurers, and rescuers. They are also overwhelmingly shown to be aggressive, argumentative, and competitive.[40]

These are just books. Does it really matter if girls are cast in passive roles, boys in active ones, fathers are absent, or if male characters outnumber female characters? It matters. Gender stereotypes and the lack of female characters contribute negatively to children's development, limit their career aspirations, frame their attitudes about their future roles as parents, and even influence personality characteristics. Following her study in the 1970s, Lenore Weitzman argued that the dearth of female characters teaches both sexes that girls are less worthy than boys.[41]

Today, forty years later, some still do not get that message. Several contemporary writers, such as Peg Tyre, Leonard Sax, and Michael Gurian, recommend that schools acquire many more books with male characters than female characters in order to help boys improve their reading skills.[42] They call for adventurous characters and stories that will appeal to boys. Forgetting the lessons of the past when male characters and stories dominated school libraries, these authors see fewer female stories and characters as a solution rather than a problem. Perhaps they do not recall when males outnumbered females 6 to 1 or 10 to 1 or even 95 to 1 in these books. Nor do they seem to recall that such one-sided libraries worked for neither gender. School libraries filled with boy books did not improve boys' reading scores and they did little to help girls feel good about themselves or their futures. Neither boy books nor girl books need to be expunged from libraries, but good books do need to be acquired. Children enjoy exciting, well-written books, and such books can include characters from different races and ethnicities and from both genders. In fact, books should offer children both a mirror and a window. Students should see themselves in their books, and they should see the real world around them through those books.

DOUBLE JEOPARDY

When the Sadkers wrote the first edition of *Failing at Fairness,* they wanted to see firsthand how women's invisibility impacted student learning. They visited sixteen fourth-, fifth-, and sixth-grade classes in Maryland, Virginia, and Washington, D.C., and gave students this assignment:

> In the next five minutes write down the names of as many famous women and men as you can. They can come from anywhere in the world and they can be alive or dead, but they must be real people. They can't be made up. Also—and this is very important—they can't be entertainers or athletes. See if you can name at least ten men and ten women.

At first the students wrote furiously, but after about three minutes, most ran out of names. On average, students generated eleven male names but only three women's. While the male names were drawn directly from the pages of history books, the female names represented far greater student creativity: Mrs. Fields, Aunt Jemima, Sarah Lee, Princess Di, Fergie, Mrs. Bush, Sally Ride, and children's book authors such as Beverly Cleary and Judy Blume. Few names came from the pages of history. Betsy Ross, Harriet Tubman, Eleanor Roosevelt, Amelia Earhart, Sojourner Truth, Sacajawea, Rosa Parks, Molly Pitcher, and Annie Oakley were sometimes mentioned.

Several students could not think of a single woman's name. Others had to struggle to come up with a few. In one sixth-grade class, a boy identified as the star history student was stumped by the assignment and obviously frustrated:

"Have you got any girls?" he asked, turning to a classmate.

"Sure. I got lots."

"I have only one."

"Think about the presidents."

"There are no lady presidents."

"Of course not. There's a law against it. But all you gotta do is take the presidents' names and put Mrs. in front of them."

In a fourth-grade class, a girl was drawing a blank. She had no names under her Women column. A female classmate leaned over to help. "What about Francis Scott Key? She's famous." The girl immediately wrote the name down. "Thanks," she said. "I forgot about her."

As the Sadkers were leaving this class, one girl stopped them. "I don't think we did very well on that list," she said. "It was too bad you didn't let us put in entertainers. We could've put in a lot of women then. I wrote down Madonna anyway."

Given a timeline extending from the earliest days of human history to current events, and given no geographic limits whatsoever, these upper-elementary schoolchildren came up with only a handful of women. The most any single child wrote was nine. In one class the total number of women's names given didn't equal ten.

That all happened in 1992. Fifteen years later, in the spring of 2007, David and Karen decided to repeat the experiment. We thought that even the limited improvements in textbooks along with our nation's increased diversity would make a difference. We were stunned by the results.

We asked 164 students in elementary and secondary schools to participate in the "famous men and women" challenge. These students were racially and ethnically diverse, in urban and suburban schools, and from lower to upper middle class backgrounds. We gave the same instructions as the Sadkers did in 1992, with one difference: We had caught on to the clever trick of adding Mrs. to male presidents' names. So along with athletes and entertainers, no "Mrs." were allowed. (Try it yourself and compare your list with student selections.)

Students listed an average of 12 men and 5 women, compared to 11 men and 3 women that were identified in 1992. Thirty-four was the highest number of men recorded by a single student. The most women listed by one student was nine, the same as the Sadkers originally found fifteen years ago.

Political figures dominated the male list with George W. Bush, George Washington, Martin Luther King, Jr., Abraham Lincoln, and Bill Clinton grabbing the most votes. But students went well beyond politics in naming famous men. Making the list were artists, inventors, writers, and religious figures such as Picasso, Thomas Edison, Albert Einstein, Bill Gates, Langston Hughes, Stephen King, Nelson Mandela, Gandhi, and Jesus.

Who was the most famous woman? Rosa Parks landed on top of these students' lists, followed by Harriet Tubman, Hillary Clinton, Condoleezza Rice, Maya Angelou, and Princess Diana. Some students included *Harry Potter* author J. K. Rowling, offering a bit of irony. Before Rowling's first book was released, publishers feared that boys would not read a book written by a woman and urged her to disguise her gender by using initials rather than her first name, Joanne.

Coretta Scott King, Mother Teresa, Queen Elizabeth, and Madame C. J. Walker (an entrepreneur who built her empire developing hair products for black women and became the first African-American female millionaire) also frequently appeared. We found the famous women lists particularly intriguing because they included many women of color. Why? Perhaps because each February many schools celebrate Black History Month, followed by National Women's History Month in March. African-American women get two opportunities to be included in the school curriculum. Yet even with such attention, we are saddened that simply naming any famous women is still so difficult.

Some students struggled to think of a single woman. They voiced frustration at their empty pages, and decided to write in "grandma, mom, and me." Creativity also helped fill in the lists: Betty Crocker, Sara Lee, and Little Debbie were popular write-ins, highlighting the timeless stereotype of women's role in the kitchen.

When we asked students why it was easier to name more famous men than women, their answers revealed the pervasive nature of sexism in and beyond schools. A fifth grader asked, "How can we expect women to be famous when men go out and work while women stay home, do housework, and have children?" A sixth grader offered this insight: "Women help others more, but men make discoveries and rules so they are seen more on television and the books we read." Another student hopefully suggested, "There are probably more famous women but we haven't discovered them or we haven't read information on them."

Many students also complained about not being allowed to use the names of entertainers or athletes. Some became so frustrated that they wrote the names down anyway, desperate to avoid a blank sheet of paper, names like Will Smith, Judge Joe Brown, Jerry Springer, Shaquille O'Neal, Peyton Manning, Beyoncé, Alicia Keys, and Judge Judy. Although we did not count these names, we were concerned that students seemed so wrapped up in popular culture. One sixth grader wrote, "I thought this assignment was hard and ridiculous because there's not really anyone who's famous that is not an athlete or in entertainment."

But this assignment also created a "teachable moment" when a classmate shared this insight: "I discovered that there are a lot of people who are famous in different ways, not just as athletes and entertainers. Amazing!"

When girls and women are systematically excluded from curricular material, students are deprived of information about half the nation's people. The result is that both boys and girls lower their opinions about the value of females. When a sexist curriculum is compounded by sexist teaching, the damage increases exponentially. We see it over and over in our school observations, including this elementary classroom: In a third-grade language arts classroom, the children were sitting on a carpet, clustered around the teacher who was putting cartoon characters on a felt board. At first glance it was a charming scene, but after looking more closely we could see how biases in curriculum and instruction merged to put girls and boys in double jeopardy.

> TEACHER: What is a noun? (More than half the class waves their hands excitedly.)
> TEACHER: John?
> JOHN: A person, place, or thing.
> TEACHER: Correct. (She places a large cartoon dragon on the felt board.) What part of the definition is this? Antonio?
> ANTONIO: A thing.
> TEACHER: Good. (She places a castle on the felt board above the dragon.) What part of the definition is this? Elise?
> ELISE: A place.
> TEACHER: Okay. (She puts a tiny princess in front of the dragon. The face of the princess is frozen in a silent scream.) Here is a person. Now, what is a verb? Seth?
> SETH: An action word.
> TEACHER: I'm glad to see you remember your parts of speech. (She posts a cartoon of an enormous knight riding a horse.) What are some action words that tell what the knight is doing? Mike?
> MIKE: Fight?
> TEACHER: Right. What else?
> PETER (calling out): Slay.
> TEACHER: Good vocabulary word. Any others? Al?
> AL: Capture.
> TEACHER: Excellent verbs. What is an adjective? Maria?
> MARIA: A word that describes something.

TIM (calling out): Adjectives describe nouns.

TEACHER: Good, Tim. (The teacher posts a minstrel strumming a lute. A large bubble is drawn, cartoon style, showing that the minstrel is singing the words "Oh, she is beautiful.") What is the adjective in this sentence? Donna?

DONNA: Beautiful.

TEACHER: Now we are going to see how parts of speech can be used in stories. Each one of you will write your own fairy tale about how the brave knight slays the dragon and rescues the beautiful princess.

For the next twenty minutes the children write their stories as the teacher and a student teacher, placed in the classroom as part of her training program, circle the room and assist. Then:

TEACHER: You have written wonderful stories. I want each and every one of you to get a chance to read them out loud. All the girls should go to Miss McNeil [the student teacher]. If you talk very softly and don't bother anyone, you can read your stories in the hall. The boys will stay in the classroom with me.

This lesson lasted only an hour, but it taught far more than parts of speech. The children learned that men in the Middle Ages were creative and bold. They wrote songs and fought dragons. They worked as minstrels and knights. Women in the Middle Ages were tiny, beautiful princesses who could not take care of themselves; no other role was shown.

As the lesson progressed, the students were funneled into a narrower vision of the world. First they heard and watched as the teacher validated stereotypes, and then—and this was where the psychological backlash turned truly troubling—they were taught to make those stereotypes their own. The children created their *own* stories about the pretty, passive princess and the big, brave knight. They read their stories, their versions of the stereotypes, to one another. If the teacher had schemed to indoctrinate the children in the stereotypes, she could not have done it more brilliantly.

But of course there was much more going on. Donna, Maria, Elise, and the other third-grade girls were not called on as often as John, Antonio, Seth, Mike, Al, Tim, and the other male students. Like the active knight on the felt board, many of the boys in the class were active, too. When the teacher did not call on them, they called out and were praised for their assertive effort. During the entire lesson, no girl called out. Like the passive little princess, their voices were also frozen and unheard. When boys answered, the teacher took the time to offer evaluations in the form of praise. Indifferent and imprecise reactions—"Uh-huh," "okay," or no comment—were reserved for the girls.

The sexist messages continued. When the teacher divided the class, she did it by gender. The girls were allotted second-class space and an inexperienced assistant. There was also a parting shot: The female children were told to read their stories quietly so that no one would even know they were there. The boys were instructed by the real teacher and read their stories outloud.

The teacher, a female who could have served as a role model for the girls, both accepted and facilitated the male dominance of the classroom. She herself had been a victim of years of sexist schooling and had no idea that she collaborated with a system that stunts the potential of female students. The girls, knowing no better, did not realize that little by little, lesson by lesson, day by day they were being robbed. The student teacher was also indoctrinated into the sexist curriculum and instruction. She would be licensed to teach the following year, and it is quite likely that she will teach gender-biased lessons in a classroom of her own.

Every day in America girls lose independence, achievement, and self-esteem in classes like this. Boys gain an unfair sense of entitlement and face a pressure cooker of high expectations. Subtle yet persistent, the gender-biased lessons result in quiet catastrophes and silent losses. But the casualties—tomorrow's women and men—are very real.

SUCCEEDING AT FAIRNESS:
SUGGESTIONS FOR STUDENTS, PARENTS, AND TEACHERS

1. Famous Men and Women Activity

Ask your child or students to list famous men and women. Do they have an equal number of women and men? More women? More men? Does the list include individuals of diverse racial and ethnic backgrounds? Discuss with them what their list means and what might be done to learn more about famous men and women from diverse racial and cultural backgrounds.

2. Classroom Interactions: Who's Talking?

Call on different students. Many teachers are so focused on getting an answer, and getting it quickly, that they call on the "quickest hand," which is usually attached to a male. This typically keeps the same students involved and slower hand-raisers and thoughtful thinkers remain outside the conversation.

Instead of calling on the first hand in the air, choose instead to pick the third or fifth or seventh hand raised. Teachers may also ask students to choose among their peers to answer questions so that one student calls on another. Whatever strategies are used, the key is to keep all students actively involved.

Use wait time deliberately. Wait time can be a big help in promoting equitable participation. Giving themselves three to five seconds before calling on a student allows teachers more time to deliberately and thoughtfully choose whom to call on. The extra wait time also allows students more time to develop an answer. Teachers should also give themselves more wait time after a student speaks. Waiting provides the opportunity to think about the strengths and weaknesses of a student's answer and to provide specific feedback.

3. Classroom Organization

Put walls to work. Do you remember the phrase "If these walls could speak"? In a sense they do. What messages are the classroom walls sending to your students? Walls decorated mostly with pictures of white men in math, science, and technology (or in history, literature, and athletics) send one message; displays that include females and males from diverse racial and ethnic groups engaging in a variety of activities send quite another. Survey school displays for equity. Should you find resources to supplement materials and create a more equitable learning climate? Ask students to work with you—let them know that you make gender equity a priority.

Segregation. Avoid segregated seating patterns or activities. Sometimes teachers segregate: "Let's have a spelling bee: boys against the girls!" Other times, students segregate themselves. Gender, race, or ethnic groups that are isolated alter the dynamics of the classroom and create barriers to effective communication among students, as well as obstacles to equitable teaching. It's okay to move students around to create a more integrated class. There are also times when children need to be in same-gender clusters. If there are only two or three girls (or boys) in a class, separating them can actually increase the sense of isolation. Diversity and good judgment are both important as teachers group and organize students.

Mobility. Students sitting in the front row and middle seats of the classroom—often dubbed the Terrific T—receive the majority of the teacher's attention. This is because the closer you are to students, the more likely you are to call on them. If you move around the room, you will get different students involved. By the way, students are mobile, too. You may want to change their seats on a regular basis to disperse classroom participation more equally.

4. Balancing the Books

While yesterday's stark sexist texts are thankfully gone, subtle bias persists. How can parents and teachers detect gender bias in books? Here are descriptions of seven forms of bias that emerge in today's texts. These forms of bias can be based not only on gender, but also on race, ethnicity, the elderly, people with disabilities, gays and lesbians, and limited-English speakers. By teaching your students and children about the forms of bias, you can help them to become critical readers, an important skill they can take into adulthood.

Invisibility: *What You Don't See Makes a Lasting Impression*
When groups or events are not taught in schools, they become part of *the null curriculum.* Textbooks published prior to the 1960s largely omitted African Americans, Latinos, and Asian Americans, and many of today's textbooks continue to give minimal treatment to women, those with disabilities, gays and lesbians, and others. A similar case can be made for the invisibility of males in parenting and other roles nontraditional to their gender.

Stereotyping: *Glib Shortcuts*
When rigid roles or traits are assigned to all members of a group, a stereotype is born, which denies individual attributes and differences. Examples include portraying all African Americans as athletes, Mexican Americans as laborers, and women only in terms of their family roles.

Imbalance and Selectivity: *A Tale Half Told*
Curriculum sometimes presents only one interpretation of an issue, situation, or group of people, simplifying and distorting complex issues by omitting different perspectives. A description of women being *given*

the vote omits the work, sacrifices, and physical abuse suffered by women who *won* the vote.

Unreality: *Rose-Colored Glasses*
Curricular materials often paint a Pollyanna picture of the nation (and this goes for any nation!). Our history texts often ignore class differences, the lack of basic health care for tens of millions, as well as ongoing racism and sexism. For example, when the nuclear family is described only as a father, mother, and children, students are being treated to romanticized and sanitized narratives, an *unreality* that omits the information they will need to confront and resolve real social challenges.

Fragmentation: *An Interesting Sideshow*
Did you ever read a textbook that separates the discussion of women in a separate section or insert? For example, many of today's texts include special inserts highlighting certain gender topics, such as "What If He Has Two Mommies?" or "Ten Women Achievers in Science." Such isolation presents women and gender issues as interesting diversions and implies that their contributions do not constitute the mainstream of history, literature, or the sciences.

Linguistic Bias: *Words Count*
Language can be a powerful conveyor of bias, in both blatant and subtle forms. The exclusive use of masculine terms and pronouns, ranging from our *forefathers, mankind,* and *businessman* to the generic *he,* denies the full participation and recognition of women. More subtle examples include word orders and choices that place males in a primary role, such as "men and their wives."

Superficial Equity: *Pretty Wrapping*
Superficial equity offers an "illusion of equity." Beyond the attractive covers, photos, or posters that prominently feature all members of diverse groups, bias persists. Examples include a science textbook that features a glossy pullout of female scientists, but precious little narrative of the scientific contributions of women.

Until publishers and authors discuss relevant gender issues and the strategies needed to eliminate gender bias, it will be up to the creativity and commitment of teachers and parents to fill in the missing pages. Here are just a few suggestions to start:

1. Review books and identify each of these seven forms. In what ways can you remove the bias and create more equitable textbooks? Ask your students and children to do the same.
2. Extend this activity by identifying these forms of bias in magazines, television programming, and on the Internet.
3. Such bias can impact many different groups. Find examples that negatively impact males, or people of color, or the poor. Suggest ways to overcome the bias.

5. Media Matters

Children are heavy media consumers. In one year, children spend more than a thousand hours watching television and will see twenty thousand commercials. Movies on DVD are also popular in American homes. Children as young as six years old own at least twenty DVDs.[43] These media bombard our children with characters and commercials filled with gender lessons. Children, in the process of discovering their identity, are particularly vulnerable to such messages.

Fortunately, children can be taught to analyze and deflect the media's sexist messages, enabling them to distinguish myth from reality, and healthy messages from exploitive ones. Families and schools can take active roles in changing the narrow portrayals of females and males seen in children's television and movies. Award-winning actor Geena Davis is one parent showing us how. She started the Geena Davis Institute on Gender in Media, an organization that advocates for better gender equity in movies for children.

One of the many questions researchers at the Geena Davis Institute ask is how movies answer children's perennial question "What can I be when I grow up?" They studied the 101 top-grossing G-rated films released from 1990 through 2004 and found stereotypes abounding. Female characters in these popular children's movies are most often secretaries, princesses, or entertainers. On the flip side, male characters are only half as likely as females to have children or be married.

When you watch movies with your son or daughter, track the occupations of female and male characters. You can get children thinking about what they see in their favorite movies by asking if the jobs in the movies reflect the jobs people have in real life. See if your children would like to have those jobs. Ask how your daughter or son would do things differently if they were making the movie.

Resources

Boys Will Be Boys: Breaking the Link Between Masculinity and Violence, by
Myriam Miedzian

> A powerful examination of the way boys are taught and raised in
> today's society. This book describes how a "masculine mystique" of
> toughness, dominance, and extreme competitiveness harms boys,
> and offers specific, practical suggestions for parents and educators to
> promote healthy development.

*Dads and Daughters: How to Inspire, Understand, and Support Your Daugh-
ter When She's Growing Up So Fast,* by Joe Kelly

> *Dads and Daughters* does what a good advice book should do: respect
> its readers while offering them real guidance and help. This is a book
> that will make fathers want to learn how to stay close to their daugh-
> ters, and it is a book that will show them how.

Founding Mothers: The Women Who Raised Our Nation, by Cookie Roberts

> Cookie Roberts brings to life the extraordinary accomplishments of
> women who laid the groundwork for our nation and for a better soci-
> ety. While their men were away serving as soldiers, statesmen, or
> ambassadors, the women managed property, raised their children,
> and made their own contributions to the cause of liberty.

Gender Play: Girls and Boys in School, by Barrie Thorne

> The author describes her daily observations of children in the class-
> room and on the playground to show how children construct and
> experience gender. She also shares what children think about their
> gendered lives, offering fresh insights into the social lives of elemen-
> tary schoolers.

*Mothers of Invention: From the Bra to the Bomb: Forgotten Women and
Their Unforgettable Ideas,* by Ethlie Ann Vare and Greg Ptacek

> Over one hundred brief biographies of unheralded women reveal
> their discoveries, ranging from the theory of nuclear fission to Wite-
> Out.

For additional resources, see *Still Failing at Fairness*'s page on www.simon
andschuster.com.

CHAPTER 4

Self-Esteem Slides:
The Middle Years

When viewing an exhibit of photographs, we were drawn to one particular image, that of a six-year-old girl. She had climbed arduously to the top of a tall playground slide, and there she stood on her sturdy legs, with her head thrown back and her arms flung wide. As ruler of the playground, she was at the very zenith of her world. The image aroused us because the camera had captured a proud and perfect time, and for too many girls such times are short-lived.

Poised between preschool and adolescence, the girl in the photo is full of energy, self-reliance, and purpose. She feels confident about what she can do and who she can become. Barbara Kerr, who studies the underachievement of gifted women, highlights the "I can do it" assurance of girls in the early elementary grades. She says they are "like birds in spring . . . in their most colorful phase."[1] Ready to try anything, their daily routine is the unexpected. They think they can be archeologists, detectives, clowns, authors, bungee jumpers—consecutively or maybe all at once. Side by side with their brothers, these spunky girls rush forward eagerly to seek new challenges to test their mettle. Their world is wide and packed with possibilities. They love their lives, but they do not want to hold back time. They choose to keep going and to keep growing. They cannot see ahead to the mind- and body-altering changes yet to come.

Like the tightening of a corset, adolescence closes around these precocious, authoritative girls. They begin to restrict their interests, confine their talents, pull back on their dreams. As they work on blending in with other girls, they move toward the end of their colorful phase.

We can also easily imagine a boy standing strong at the crest of the slide: head held high, twinkling eyes and wide smile exuding confidence. Indeed, to much of the world boys appear to be the favored gender, heirs apparent to society's rewards. Schools mirror this gendered value system as boys receive the lion's share of teacher time and attention in class, and read textbooks that describe male accomplishments. Sitting atop high-stakes test scores such as the SATs, boys haul in the majority of scholarship dollars and are destined for high salaries and leadership roles in honored professions. Just looking at those boys as they stand at the crest of the slide, one gets the feeling that at some level, they, too, already sense their entitlements. But when they become adults, these now men will discover that entitlements carry a hefty price tag in health, relationships, and happiness. Many will look back on these boyhood years of unlimited possibilities as the happiest time of their lives.

Not all boys will feel this hopeful optimism or enjoy a sense of entitlement. While some boys rise to the top, often the white and wealthy, many others fall to the bottom, in school and in life. Raised to be active, aggressive, and independent, these not-so-entitled boys enter schools with energy, enthusiasm, and hope, unprepared for the controlling and passive school life they will encounter. In this new, complicated school culture, boys walk a tightrope between compliance and rebellion. Some successfully walk that tightrope to graduation; others fail and fall.

When Myra and David first wrote *Failing at Fairness* in 1994, girls' self-esteem was in the national spotlight. Groundbreaking research showed that as girls made the passage into adolescence, their self-esteem plummeted. To help parents and teachers better understand this phenomenon, Myra and David devoted a chapter to girls' self-esteem slide. In this revision, we now confront self-esteem struggles of both girls and boys. We also take a more critical look at the different dimensions of self-esteem: academic, physical, and social. For example, researchers have found that academic success plays a much smaller role in forming the self-esteem of boys; boys often build their self-esteem on "being able to do things."[2]

Race, class, and culture are also factors. While boys of all races and socioeconomic backgrounds enjoy higher self-esteem than girls, black males and females consistently report higher self-esteem than their white, Asian, and Hispanic peers. Here again, academics is less central than physical prowess, family support, and community connections. In fact, it is a strong racial identity that helps black youth sustain positive feelings about themselves in the face of academic struggles and discrimination.[3]

We are also learning how self-esteem can change with age and life experiences. The gender gap in self-esteem is relatively small in the early grades but widens as students progress through school. Throughout life, females *and* males struggle with discovering self-confidence, with celebrating their unique authenticity. In this chapter, we explore the myriad of challenges children face as they work to cultivate a healthy self-esteem. We will also suggest ways teachers and parents can nourish a healthy self-image.

GIRLS' COSTLY FREE FALL

If the camera had photographed the girl on the slide half a dozen years later, at twelve instead of six, it would have likely captured a very different pose: She would be looking at the ground instead of the sky; her sense of self-worth would be accelerating downward. She would have moved from self-confidence to self-consciousness. She would also have moved from elementary school to middle school.

Do you recall your own transition from elementary to middle school? Was it filled with the excitement of new friends and the joy of freely moving from one class to another? Did you experience some angst as you navigated a new building, a myriad of teachers, and more demanding friendships? Middle school is part of growing up, a sign of emerging independence. Relatively new, middle schools were created to help the transition from childhood into adulthood, to respond to children's emotional, psychological, and social needs as they go through puberty and prepare for high school. But many critics charge that these "connecting schools" are simply not working, that they overemphasize emotional development at the expense of academic rigor. Others argue the opposite: that they are not meeting their own goals of responding to the social and emotional issues adolescents face.[4] In fact, some educators have given up on these schools and advocate a return to just two schools, the K–8 elementary school and the high school. While the future of middle schools is in doubt, the period of life that middle schools encompass, that critical time of sexual development, ego formation, and self-concept, remains an ever-present challenge.

For both girls and boys, adolescence is a time of confusion as their bodies and lives go through jarring transformations. Most males view this physical change as a change for the better. When boys describe what happens to their bodies during adolescence, images of size, growth, strength, and physical talent dominate. Boys learn they can do more, and they are in charge: "You get to be in control. . . . If you're a boy, you don't have to worry about girls beating up on you. You're bigger than the girls." As girls' bodies mature, they see themselves as more vulnerable and grow less confident. Some work hard to avoid becoming a "target."[5]

The transition from elementary to middle school may be the most damaging period of a girl's young life because it coincides with physical changes and increased social and cultural pressures. Girls are caught in bodies that swell and expand in puzzling ways just as they are dealing with the shift from elementary to middle school. In this more chaotic and alienating school, with new rules and unchartered social norms, it is easy to become both physically and emotionally lost.

The American Association of University Women conducted one of the largest studies on self-esteem to learn how boys and girls from ages nine to fifteen viewed themselves and their present and future lives. The study sample included three thousand children in grades four through ten in twelve locations nationwide. When the results were tallied for the many different questions asked by the researchers, several striking findings emerged, including how adolescence is difficult for both girls *and* boys. But the survey also revealed how as boys and girls mature, troubling differences emerge in how they feel about themselves.[6]

In response to the statement "I'm happy the way I am," 67 percent of the boys responded affirmatively in elementary school, but by the time they reached high school, only 46 percent agreed with the statement, a self-esteem slide of 21 points. For girls the slide was more of a free fall, especially between elementary and middle school, with a total drop of 31 points. While 60 percent of girls said they were happy about themselves in elementary school, 37 percent answered affirmatively in middle school, and only 29 percent in high school. Little surprise then that in the AAUW study, girls were less likely than boys to agree with the statement "I like most things about myself." They were more likely to say, "I wish I were somebody else," and to admit, "Sometimes I don't like myself."

In elementary school, young girls are proud of their schoolwork, but adolescence brings a whole new "look" to their lives. Being attractive becomes more important than being intelligent. Girls become immersed in media portrayals of women consumed with thinness, makeup, style, and fashion. Young girls seek popularity from their peers and learn not only what to wear and how to look, but also how to "work" their peer group to increase their status. The current flows differently in middle school, and many girls change course; some even "dumb down." Even gifted girls can redirect their intelligence and creativity to diet schemes, shopping, and grooming rituals.[7]

Typically, boys also struggle with the changes during puberty, but for them they come later in life, after they have made the shift to middle school, so they can cope with one change at a time. Not so for girls, who must deal simultaneously with the metamorphosis of puberty and the adjustment to a new, more difficult school. Little wonder that their self-esteem suffers dramatically.[8]

Hispanic girls may suffer the greatest self-esteem loss. The AAUW study reported that in elementary school, 68 percent of Hispanic girls said they always felt happy about themselves, but this sense of contentment faded, and by high school only 30 percent said they were always happy with themselves, a 38-point drop. Also troubling was the steep decline in their confidence. Fifty-one percent of elementary Hispanic girls agreed that they "are pretty good at most things"; by high school only 18 percent voiced such self-assurance. The number of Hispanic girls who agreed with the statement "I feel good about myself when I'm with my family" tumbled an eye-opening 41 points—from 79 percent in elementary school to 38 percent in high school.[9] Hispanic girls, like those in other traditional families and cultures, are expected to do an "adolescent about-face" in the middle school years: on the road to puberty, a girl's intelligence is often considered a positive characteristic; after puberty, the expectation is that she will conform to traditional family roles.[10] Adolescent Hispanic girls look away from school and to home to see their futures, and what they see is far from comforting. Hispanic girls care for younger siblings, help with housework, and perhaps prepare for marriage while Hispanic boys earn money, enhancing the family income. Boys' value in the family increases; girls' decreases.

While Hispanic girls suffer this dramatic esteem decline, African-American females do not. In fact, their self-esteem rises. In elementary school, 46 percent said, "I like most things about myself." But rather than tumble in middle and high school, the percentage improved to 50 percent. In elementary school 59 percent of African-American girls considered themselves "important," a percentage that climbed to a healthy 74 percent by high school. African-American males also exhibited a solid sense of self-esteem, one that put them ahead of black girls in general happiness and confidence in their ability to do things. So what is going on here?

To find out, Sharlene Hesse-Biber and colleagues interviewed seventy-eight black girls ages nine to eighteen.[11] For these girls, a solid connection with their families and racial identity helped to strengthen their self-esteem. Academic work did not. As their racial self-esteem increased, overall self-esteem increased. The girls described a clear distinction between being black and being female.

INTERVIEWER: What do you consider yourself, Black first or female first?
EVERYONE: Black first.
INTERVIEWER: Why?
CRYSTAL: 'Cause anybody can be a female, if you think about it . . .
KEYETT: Not everybody can be Black.
SASHA: I consider myself Black before female. Because if God wanted us to be just female, he wouldn't have created all these wonderful colors we have in this world.

When asked to describe what it means to be a "black female," the girls used words such as "strong, independent, smart, and caring." The voices of Naomi and Joy captured the authentic confidence and inner beauty these girls feel.

NAOMI: I have a lot of self-esteem. I got it from my parents, my family, my brother and my sister. . . . They listen to me, they listen to the things that I have to say and that makes me feel good—that someone is paying attention to me. And they say that I am okay the way I am and they are proud of me and my friends love me.
INTERVIEWER: What does having high self-esteem mean to you?
JOY: It means not caring about whatever anyone else says, just worrying about yourself, loving yourself.

We wish all girls—and boys—could learn to love themselves as they are, not as the dominant culture or media would construct them.

SHORT-CIRCUITING GIRLS

Education is rarely the mirror boys peer into to gauge their self-esteem; they peer into a mirror of "How well can I do things?" In elementary school, 55 percent of boys said they were always "good at a lot of things." This declined to 48 percent in middle school and to 42 percent in high school. For girls the drop was far more precipitous: 45 percent of girls in elementary school said they were always "good at a lot of things," 10 points behind the boys. Girls' belief in their ability to do things tumbled an extraordinary 16 points between elementary and middle school and then declined another 6 points to 23 percent in high school.[12] One reason for this self-esteem gap is that males have more confidence in their athletic abilities. Adolescent boys have twice the confidence in their athleticism than do girls.[13]

But even beyond the football field, basketball court, or baseball diamond, there is a subtle and persistent self-esteem vampire stalking girls. Whether at home or school, girls are interrupted—short-circuited—as they try to do things on their own. The short-circuiting begins early. It was first documented thirty years ago by Lisa Serbin and Daniel O'Leary when they were analyzing early childhood and kindergarten classes. Teachers, Serbin and O'Leary found, gave boys extended directions on how to accomplish tasks for themselves. When it came to girls, teachers were less likely to offer explanations and directions as to how to do things but instead would do *for* them. For example, children went up to the teacher's desk to staple handles onto party baskets. When a boy couldn't work the stapler on his own, the teacher showed him. When a girl couldn't staple on her own, the teacher took the handle and the basket and stapled it for her.[14]

The short-circuit syndrome continues today. Marta Cruz-Janzen studied gender lessons in a kindergarten classroom. She visited a class of Hispanic children, seven boys and eight girls, several times over the course of a year. At the beginning of the year both boys and girls went to the teacher aide for assistance. Whenever girls wanted to view tapes on the VCR in this classroom, a male aide agreeably set it up for them. When boys wanted to watch a video, he explained to them how to insert the tape, turn on the machine, rewind the tape when the video was finished, and put the tape away. At the end of the year, girls still went to the aide to play their tapes, but the boys operated the VCR by themselves.[15]

Short-circuiting is found on all levels of education. A recent study of more than a dozen elementary classrooms found that by the third grade, 51 percent of boys used a microscope in class, in contrast to 37 percent of girls. The microscope lesson of male doers and female observers becomes all too familiar as students advance through school.[16] With exasperation, a seventh-grade girl told us, "Teachers don't expect us to be good in science. That's why I think we have less time on instruments like the microscope than do boys. Instead we are in charge of cleaning and putting away the equipment. If we are lucky, we get to write the results on the whiteboard. Not much fun."[17]

We see short-circuiting again and again in classrooms. Here's how it looked in the upper-elementary and middle school grades:

A fourth-grade girl doesn't know how to put a CD into the computer. She raises her hand for help. The teacher stops at her desk for a few seconds and puts the CD in for her.

A sixth-grade girl is having trouble working out a math problem. The teacher takes the pencil out of her hand and quickly does the problem for her.

In a ninth-grade science lab, a girl gets squeamish when dissecting a frog. The teacher asks a boy to do it for her.[18]

In none of these cases were the girls ignored, but they were dismissed. After years of being short-circuited, girls lose faith in their skills and hang back while boys take over.

When a teacher or a parent does *for* a girl instead of teaching her *how* to do for herself, education is turned off. Independence and self-esteem are short-circuited as well. The key word here is *do*. It doesn't work to just tell a girl that she is good at something. When a girl becomes competent in something, she internalizes that knowledge, which boosts her confidence and self-esteem. Girls need to understand that it is okay to struggle when facing a new challenge. And adults need to put the brakes on their impulse for the "quick fix" and allow girls to "just do it." Her growing confidence will keep her from feeling inferior and help to discover true talents.

Girls learn the short-circuit lesson well, often too well. Rather than celebrating their intelligence, girls often work hard to hide it. They describe short-circuiting their own academic achievements, fearful that success will make them unpopular with friends or threaten potential boyfriends. A white, sixth-grade girl wrote of the pressure she felt from her parents and teachers to excel in school. But when she did well, she had trouble finding a date to the school dance and her peers called her a "nerd." She started to participate less often in class discussions and no longer studied as much. One young Asian middle schooler admitted to us, "Girls more and more are getting teased for being too successful and superstars. Sometimes I don't turn in assignments so I won't get ridiculed for being too smart." A Hispanic peer poignantly shared how she wished "girls could be popular by being smart rather than looking pretty. I like math, but did not take advanced math because none of my friends did."[19]

"HELP ME, GOD. I'M A GIRL."

"Suppose you woke up tomorrow and found you were a member of the other sex. How would your life be different?" Almost eleven hundred children in Michigan wrote essays about what life would be like if they experienced a gender change. Forty-two percent of the girls found many good things to say about being male: they would feel more secure and less worried about what other people thought, they would be treated with more respect, they looked forward to earning more money at better jobs. Ninety-five percent of the 565 boys saw no advantage at all to being female. Only twenty-eight boys saw any benefits. Some of the reasons offered by this 5 percent were sincere. They talked about not being punished as much, getting better grades, not needing to pay for dates, and not getting hurt in fights. But the advantages were often phrased as stereotypic put-downs: "crying to get out of paying traffic tickets" and getting out of trouble by "turning on the charm and flirting my way out of it."

Sixteen percent of the Michigan boys wrote about fantasy escapes from their female bodies, with suicide the most frequent getaway selection:

"I would *kill* myself *right away* by setting myself on fire so no one knew."

"I'd wet the bed, then I'd throw up. I'd probably go crazy and kill myself."

"And I would never wake up again and would be heading over to the cemetery right now and start digging."

"If I woke up tomorrow as a girl, I would stab myself in the heart fifty times with a dull butter knife. If I were still alive, I would run in front of a huge semi in eighteenth gear and have my brains mashed to Jell-O. *That would do it.*"[20]

During the past decades we have posed that same question to hundreds of students across the country and found themes similar to those revealed in the Michigan study. The question fascinates students; their answers reveal the value they place on each gender as well as on themselves.[21]

Girls' reactions run the gamut when it comes to changing their gender. Many would rather stay girls. As an eleven-year-old said, "Being female is what I'm all about. It would be confusing to be a boy." Still, girls are intrigued at the thought of becoming boys, at least for a little while. "I don't think being a boy would be that bad," said twelve-year-old Hannah. "I would not want to be a boy permanently, but I would like to try it for a week to see how it feels. If I liked it, I would stay longer."

Other girls embrace their new roles enthusiastically; they see many advantages. "When I grow up, I will be able to be almost anything I want, including governor and President of the United States," wrote twelve-year-old Dana. "People will listen to what I have to say and will take me seriously. I will have a secretary to do things for me. I will make more money now that I am a boy." Anita said, "I would feel sort of more on top. I guess that's what a lot of boys feel."

For boys the thought of being female is appalling, disgusting, and humiliating; it was completely unacceptable. "If I were a girl, my friends would treat me like dirt," said a sixth-grade boy from a rural school. "My teachers would treat me like a little hairy pig-headed girl," said Michael from an urban classroom. The essays of desperate horror continue:

"If I was a girl, I would scream. I would duck behind corners so no one would see me."

"I would hide and never go out until after dark."

Again, many choose the final exit: "If I were turned into a girl today, I would kill myself."

Boys took imaginative, desperate measures to get out of being girls. Stephen would "walk around the world on hot coals," and Jesse offered to "jump out of a plane into a glass of milk to get my boy body back."

As girls move into adolescence, being popular with boys becomes overwhelmingly important, the key to social success. They look to males for esteem, hoping to see approval and affirmation in their eyes. But if the attitudes expressed in the male stories of gender changing are any measure, girls are seeking comfort in a carnival mirror, one sending back an image so grotesque and misshapen that its distortion is startling. Although we have read hundreds of boys' stories about waking up as a girl, we remain shocked at the degree of contempt expressed by so many. If the students were asked to consider waking up as a member of a different religious, racial, or ethnic group, would rejection be phrased with such horror and loathing?

When we talked with students about these essays, we tried to understand why the boys made such disparaging comments about girls, why their stories were marked by such jolting themes of revulsion. Part of the reason appears to lie in boys' perception of the female body as fragile, limited, and incompetent, especially in athletics and sports. More than one in four middle school boys regards athletics as the best thing about being male.[22] An eighth-grade Hispanic male declared to us, "Sports is what it is all about." One regret that repeatedly emerged in boys' essays of gender change was loss of the ability to play sports. Boys said: "Being a girl sucks. Now instead of basketball I have to play boring jump rope." "Now that I'm a girl, they won't let me play football. But I'll play it anyway. I'll play in a dress if I have to." Eleven-year-old Keith told how becoming female meant losing the most important fantasy of his life: "So many times I wish I was still a boy because of all my dreams to become a baseball player. But now they've perished into the night, and I'm just a little old bag lady sitting in a cardboard box. And whenever I go to a baseball game I cry my eyes out because my dreams have been lost forever."

Students lamented about another girl peril—loss of freedom. By adolescence, students easily describe girls as the "second-class gender." Girls feel restricted in where they are allowed to go, and one in five middle schoolers see personal freedom as boys' prized advantage. Hispanic girls are especially aware of restraint and confinement: one in three describe their lack of freedom as "a bad thing about being a girl." One Hispanic young woman asked us, "Do I have to cook for boys and men all my life?"[23]

Our society often seems obsessed with physical appearance, and the pressure to look "right" profoundly harms girls' self-esteem. In one landmark nationwide study, 31 percent (a troubling low number itself) of white girls in elementary school said they liked the way they looked. This feeling of appearance satisfaction took a 20-point dive to 11 percent in middle school; in high school it remained level as only 12 percent said they were satisfied with their appearance. Between elementary and middle school, pride in appearance took a 26-point plunge for Hispanic girls, from 47 percent to 21 percent. Another 10-point drop occurred between middle school and high school when only 11 percent of Hispanic girls always liked the way they looked. While African-American girls took more pride in their appearance, they also expressed more concern about pregnancy.[24]

Adolescence means pregnability. For some, menstruation is a moment of triumph, a signal of maturity; for others, it is humiliating, even scary. The normal weight gains of puberty tend to have positive meaning for boys—"he's maturing"—and less than positive implications for girls—"she's getting fat." These very different gender expectations help explain why boys may gain self-confidence and social status as their bodies change while girls often lose confidence and status.

Even for young women considered attractive in their own cultural communities, few can measure up to the standards of the media. Whiteness, blondness, and thinness mark the worth of women and girls. Yet, compared to white, Asian, and Hispanic girls, African-American girls resist these messages.[25] In their interviews with black girls, Sharlene Hesse-Biber and colleagues discovered that although many girls had been teased about their appearance as children (for being fat, for having big lips, for being too dark, about their hair or their height), almost all the girls expressed pride and/or satisfaction in their appearance when asked.[26] Naomi, one of the girls interviewed, captured this resilience:

> When I was little I used to get into some arguments and the kids used to call me ugly, like the little boys so I used to go home and ask my mother, "Mommy am I ugly?" and she used to be like "no you're not ugly you're pretty." And I used to ask my father, "Daddy am I ugly, this little boy said I was ugly." And he was like "you're not ugly, he's just jealous, maybe he likes you." That's what they would say. . . . My looks don't bother me, it's just my personality. I wanna have a good personality and have people like me, if they don't like me for my personality or just because of my looks then they must be missin' out on something.

Maturing adolescent bodies became the topic of discussion when we talked with a racially diverse and unusually forthright eighth-grade class about essays they had written on gender.

"What are some advantages of being a girl?" we ask. We start a list on the board. Several girls shout from different parts of the room:

> "Going shopping."
> "Going to the mall."
> "Talking on the phone."
> "Looking gorgeous."
> "You get to wear better clothes—boy clothes and girl clothes."

The initial burst of enthusiasm is over, and the room grows quiet. Then a Hispanic girl raises her hand and says softly, "You get to bring new life into the world. I would never want to give that up."

No boy has yet offered an advantage, so we call on a group sitting together toward the back of the room to name one good thing about being female. "Nothin'," they say. "There's nothin' good at all."

"Not a single thing?" we probe.

"Well, you don't get into as much trouble," one boy finally volunteers. "The girls just bat their eyelashes, and we get blamed for everything."

We ask for the disadvantages. This list grows more quickly, and it is much longer. Both males and females contribute:

> "Going through labor."
> "Getting periods."
> "Cooking and cleaning."
> "Sexual harassment."
> "Getting raped."
> "Not getting respect."
> "Weaker."
> "Not as good in sports."
> "Can't be president of the United States."
> "Don't have as much freedom."
> "Don't have as much fun."
> "Diet all the time."
> "Don't get as many jobs or make as much money."
> "Have to spend all your money to look pretty."

"Did any of you write your essays about these?" we ask. An Asian boy raises his hand and reads his paragraph about the work it takes to maintain the female body: "I'd have to douche, wear tampons, shave my legs, and wear heels. I'd buy a ThighMaster, but every day I would grow more cellulite."

Other boys laugh, but Nelson is now serious. "I think the worst thing is that you're vulnerable," he volunteers. "In this school boys are always touching girls. They bump into them in the halls and touch their behinds. If you're a girl, you've got to worry about being sexually harassed or raped. I couldn't stand it if people messed with me like they do with girls."

"Do you feel that way?" we asked the girls. Almost all of them nodded. "What do boys do that frightens or embarrasses you?"

"They say things like 'Look at that juicy behind.' "

"They snap our bras in gym."

"Sometimes they squeeze breasts."

"They say mean things, like if you're not developed, they say, 'You're about as curvy as that blackboard up there.' "

"They say, 'You're so fat and ugly. Get outta my face.' "

"They say, 'Your bra is showing.' " The girl who volunteers this comment turns beet red. "I never wore that bra again."

"Like Nelson said, they bump into us in the hallway, and they pinch us and touch us."

"Did any of you write your essays about these things?" The girls nod. "Would you read them?"

Thirteen-year-old Latoya volunteers: "If I were a boy, I think my life and relationships would be totally different. People would respect me more. As it is now, I think people look at me and see a target. I also bet my mother would let me do more on my own—walk to my friends' houses, ride my bike where I want. She is very worried that when older men see a young girl like me, they see me as an easy target."

"Let me read mine," says Charlene. She saunters to the front of the room, smiles, and reads: "I wouldn't mind being a boy. I'd order *Playboy*. Knock the shower down. Buy beer. Get a car. Have parties. Have a body-building workout. Talk dirty. Pig out. Walk like an ape. Nobody would dare fool with me. I wouldn't have to deal with date rape. I wouldn't mind it for a change."

Several girls laugh and cheer. Others raise their hands to read, but the bell rings. As we leave, a slight girl, an immigrant from Vietnam, runs to catch up with us. "I'm the only child in my family, and my father wishes I was a boy. I worry, but I never have anybody to talk to. It helps to speak about these things in class. I'm glad we did it."

SUPERGIRL: FEELING THE PRESSURE

The image of these eighth graders stays with us because the students so honestly spoke of the daily challenges and stereotypes girls confront. They are not alone in their opinions and ideas; in fact, their words seem timeless.

When junior high teachers were asked to describe their good female and male students, they easily crafted long lists of admirable adjectives. *Appreciative, calm, conscientious, considerate, cooperative, mannerly, poised, sensitive, dependable, efficient, mature, obliging,* and *thorough* characterized the girls. Boys were seen as *active, adventurous, aggressive, assertive, curious, energetic, enterprising, frank, independent,* and *inventive*.[27] Look closely at these lists. Like us, you might be astonished that they do not share one common adjective. Through teachers' eyes, these students learn and live in two very different worlds: a passive, well-behaved life for girls and an active, exciting world for boys. This study was completed in the early 1960s, before the civil rights and women's movements. It seems fair to expect that such stereotypes are now history.

Girls Inc. decided to find out. In 2006, they asked 2,065 female and male students in grades three through twelve how gender stereotypes and expectations shape their lives. Their words are strikingly familiar to the gender adjectives of the 1960s. In the Girls Inc. survey, students described how boys are expected to be aggressive and protective: 88 percent of girls and 94 percent of boys believe that males are "supposed to protect themselves and others." Girls, on the other hand, are seen as nurturers and caretakers: 84 percent of girls and 87 percent of boys believe females are "supposed to be kind and caring."[28]

Yet this Girls Inc. study also revealed that girls see themselves as much more than kind caretakers. They want to seize the opportunities available to them, with 71 percent aspiring to go to college full-time. "Girls want their future open to any dreams they might have for themselves," one third grader proudly proclaimed.

But girls are also well aware of the gender barriers they face. As early as elementary school, they feel they need to be "supergirls"— everything to everyone all the time. Three-quarters of the girls in the study described feeling "a lot of pressure" to please everyone. A ninth grader shared her frustration: "There is way too much pressure, especially from the media, to be skinny, popular, athletic, and have a boyfriend. Girls should be respected more as people than so-and-so's girlfriend." An eighth grader poignantly concluded, "Even today, society values beauty in girls over intelligence and talent."

The girls also spoke about the mounting expectations they face from family, peers, and educators as they struggle to understand confusing messages from the media and reject traditional gender stereotypes. One twelfth-grade girl wrote, "There's an insane amount of media and peer pressure on girls to be thin, to be beautiful, to be airheaded and only care about going shopping, to always be wearing the latest trends . . . most girls won't have the courage to go against the media and do what they love, be it considered 'feminine' or not." While friends and family can bolster self-esteem, one in five middle and high school girls report that they do not know three adults to whom to turn when they have a problem.

We are struck by the words of these girls because they are so candid and outspoken. Yet if girls cannot confide in a trusting adult, who will they talk to? Or will they even talk at all?

SELF-CENSORED

In their studies of classroom interaction, Myra and David documented the public silence of girls from grade school through graduate school. A wealth of other studies confirms that girls are quieter, more hidden.[29] In one study, almost half of the boys, 48 percent, but only 39 percent of the girls said they speak up in class. The gender gap was wider on the question of arguing with teachers. Almost twice as many boys as girls, 28 percent versus 15 percent, said they always argued with teachers when they thought they were right.[30] We recently asked students why boys' voices dominate the classroom. An Asian seventh-grade girl told us, "Boys are listened to much more than girls are. Boys' ideas matter." A white seventh-grade girl summed up the interaction imbalance: "It's a man's world."[31]

Lyn Mikel Brown and Carol Gilligan interviewed nearly one hundred girls between the ages of seven and eighteen at the single-sex Laurel School in Cleveland, Ohio.[32] Over four years they watched as girls learned to censor themselves. Younger children spoke in clear, strong, authentic voices. As they moved up in grade, their voices became modulated, softened, sometimes obliterated. Lively, outspoken, and able to express a range of feelings at seven and eight, they became more reticent as they grew older; they monitored themselves and one another with adult prescriptions for "good girl" behavior: "Be nice," "Talk quietly," "Be calm," "Cooperate."[33] As Jesse explained, "You should be nice to your friends and communicate with them and not . . . do what you want." While Jesse harbored strong feelings and felt the need "to get my anger out of me," she was "terrified" that speaking her feelings would "cause a ruckus,"[34] disrupt the peace and quiet, anger others, or make them turn away and withdraw their love and attention. So she concealed her feelings.

As the Laurel School girls grew older, they began to mask and deny their feelings with the phrase "I don't know." When Judy was interviewed at nine, she used "I don't know" four times. Her interview at ten years of age was riddled with the phrase. When the interviewer asked Judy if there was a way to talk over problems before they exploded, Judy stumbled and was disconnected from the feelings she had concealed within her: "I don't know. It's just like if—I don't know, it's like—I don't know. I can't even begin to explain it because I don't even know if I know what it is. So I can't really explain it. Because I don't know. I don't even know, like in my brain or in my heart, what I am really feeling. I mean, I don't know if it's pain or upsetness or sad—I don't know."[35]

Girls who have spent years submerging their honest feelings, afraid to speak them aloud, eventually become confused; they begin to wonder whether their feelings are real. Neeti, a quiet, pretty girl of Indian descent who was popular and had good grades, was shocked to discover that by fifteen she couldn't write an answer to the essay question "Who am I?" This was her explanation for not being able to respond: "The voice that stands up for what I believe in has been buried deep inside me."[36]

When we speak with girls about what they do to avoid talking in class, they share their creative strategies: They take inconspicuous seats in the back of the room or in the corners. They check where the teacher never looks and then sit there. They raise their hands tentatively, halfway. If it looks as though the teacher might actually call on them, they change their raised arm to a yawn, a stretch, or some other movement. They use the once-in-a-while approach to classroom interaction: consciously self-regulating their speech, they answer every now and then so that the teacher will think they are making an effort.

Astute adults understand the connection between speaking up and self-esteem. Parents at our workshops have said that they worry when their children are quiet, shy, silent, or withdrawn: "I wish she'd come out of her shell." "Why doesn't she talk more?" "She's like a little mouse. Nobody even knows she's there." After a workshop in the Midwest, one woman told us how she consciously worked on regaining her own voice as part of her journey toward self-esteem: "I wanted to talk in class so badly, but I just couldn't get up the courage to hear my own voice. How I envied those who seemed to shout out whatever was on their minds. I rehearsed my comments, filtered them so carefully that by the time I was ready to raise my hand, the discussion had moved on—and I was left behind."

This woman told us how she had sat silently through year after year of elementary, middle, and then high school. By the time she got to college, she knew she had to find her voice to save her sense of self. With the help of a supportive boyfriend, she developed a plan to make at least one comment in each of her classes. Whether it was an answer, a question, a piece of new information, or a personal anecdote didn't matter. She just had to say something: "At first I was terrified. I thought I would say something stupid, and the professor would get angry—or just be amazed at my dumbness. The other students would laugh at me or resent me. But none of that happened. Nothing at all happened really, except that each time I talked, it got a little easier. And the more I talked, the more I realized I had good ideas and the more I liked myself."

LOSING THEIR MINDS

Winners of the Westinghouse Talent Search from across the country go to Washington where, as part of their program, they have the chance to interview professionals in different fields. Most of these academic super-stars request meeting with mathematics and science experts. But Ashley Reiter, a national first-place winner for her mathematics research, wanted to discuss sexism in school, so she talked with Myra and David. A soft-spoken young woman of extraordinary perceptiveness, she remembered middle school as a smart girl's torture chamber. "No one would speak to me," she said. "I wouldn't even go into the cafeteria for lunch. Long tables stretched the length of the whole room, but wherever I sat, people acted as if I wasn't in the right place. It wasn't so much cliques as a long social scale, and I couldn't figure out where I was supposed to fit. So I just decided it was easier not to go."

"What did you do about lunch?" we asked.

"I skipped it. I would go to the library. Or I scheduled meetings—I was in a lot of activities—and ate a sandwich then. It was definitely not cool to be smart in seventh and eighth grade, especially for a girl. Some kids thought they would lose their reputation just by speaking to some-one smart."

With the help of supportive parents and special programs that recog-nized her gifts, Ashley struggled through adolescence. Today she is a young woman of poise, apparent assurance, and outstanding achieve-ment. But just below the surface, the scars are still there. Ashley defied the social consequences and refused to hide her intellectual talent, but too many other girls cope with middle school by appearing dumb, learn-ing less, and giving up academic achievement.

In interviews girls told us what it takes to get into the popular crowd: being pretty or cute, wearing the right clothes, having a bubbly person-ality. Not mentioned were the following qualities: independence, courage, creativity, honesty, intelligence. In fact, brains were a barrier. Here is one African-American ninth grader's experience: "I am a pressure cooker ready to explode. I hide my good grades so my boyfriend doesn't get insulted."

In her observations and interviews with gifted girls, Linda Kramer documented how the girls denied being bright.

LYNN: Some people say, "Look at the brain! She knows all the answers." Some of these people could be just as smart as us if they'd study. They just don't want to take the time.

OBSERVER: Are you sure studying is the only reason?

LYNN: (Pause.) I don't know. I try to be nice to everyone. I don't want to be a brain. I try to have fun.[37]

Over and over during interviews these very bright sixth-, seventh-, and eighth-grade girls denied their intelligence. "We are not 'brains,' " they would say, "We're 'normal.' " As Lynn's comment shows, they attributed their spot in the gifted program to studying hard. The gifted boys were different; they were "real brains." Gifted girls were like everybody else; they just worked a little harder. As Debbie, another of the girls, explained, "Tom and Bob [gifted boys] don't have to try as hard. Their whole life is brains. . . . Their talk is scientific notation."[38]

The gifted girls in this study were successful at hiding their intelligence. Kramer found that teachers were readily able to identify gifted boys but were often amazed to learn a girl was considered particularly smart. "I have trouble looking at these girls as gifted," one teacher admitted. Another commented, "Gifted girls aren't superstudents in math. They tend to do well in language." After a pause she added, "I guess it's okay to do well in language." The general consensus among the teachers was that gifted girls were "just like all little girls growing up."[39]

In this lack of perception, the teachers in Kramer's research were similar to teachers everywhere. Study after study has shown that adults, both teachers and parents, underestimate the intelligence of girls.[40] Teachers' beliefs that boys are smarter in mathematics and science begin in the earliest school years, at the very time when girls are getting better grades and equal scores on the standardized tests. Many adults think that boys possess innate mathematical and scientific ability. Girls can also achieve, they believe, but they have to try harder. These perceptions persist throughout every level of education and are transmitted to the children. Girls, especially smart girls, learn to underestimate their ability.

Beliefs shape behavior and create a chilly climate in the classroom. Teachers at our workshops described how it happens: A young woman who did her student teaching in Wisconsin said, "A lot of my female students complained about a science teacher who persisted in referring to them as 'dizzy' or 'ditzy' or 'airhead.' He often told the class, 'You can't expect *these girls* to know anything.' " A Louisiana educator told us about a science teacher who called the boys "Mr." or "Professor" but called the girls by their first names, or worse, "Blondie."

Educators who are aware of subtle sexism often tell of their frustration with parents who are not. A middle school principal described a father, a college math professor, who came in for a conference. "He was worried that the math program wasn't rigorous enough for his son, but he never called or came in to talk about his daughter even though she was a much better math student." A Vermont teacher said, "At my last parent-teacher conference, a mother praised her daughter for being a real 'go-getter.' She said that her daughter wanted to be a doctor. I was shocked when she went on to say that she told her daughter to try being a nurse first, and then if she liked it, she could become a doctor."

One mother who was consciously trying to raise a daughter with non-traditional attitudes found herself backing off when her socialization program actually began to work:

> In a toy store my daughter won't walk down the pink-purple aisle with the Barbie dolls. She says, "Yuck." She won't have anything to do with ballet or anything frilly, and won't choose anything feminine as a Halloween costume. Her current ambition is to be a paleontologist when she grows up.
>
> My reaction to this is interesting to me. I have written graduate papers on several aspects of sexism and spent years as a teacher trying not to perpetuate sex stereotypes. I provided my daughter with a variety of toys—dolls, building blocks, and cars—when she was younger. But now just writing this gives me a knot of fear in my stomach because I see her as a social misfit. She would rather play with boys than girls. I don't know whether to push her to make more girl friends or to stay out of it and leave her be. I love her the way she is. I just worry that she'll be hurt.

Few adults maliciously stunt girls; most are simply unaware of how attitudes and expectations slip, inadvertently and subconsciously, into behavior that creates a self-fulfilling prophecy. For example, one study found that seven out of ten male teachers are more likely to attribute boys' success in technology to talent, while dismissing girls' success as due solely to luck or diligence.[41] Such signals are unobtrusive but powerful.

When boys do well, adults generally say, "Great job on that exam. Straight A! You're really good in science." Again, the intimation is subtle but potent. Boys learn that they achieve because they are smart. When girls do well, they are also praised: "Great job on that exam. Straight A!" But an important piece of the message is often missing—the attribution to ability. The girl does not learn she did well because she is intelligent.

Children pick up on these subtle cues and internalize the attitudes of adults. When boys achieve, they usually attribute their success to ability. "I'm pretty good in math," they will admit. When they fail, they attribute it to lack of effort. If they receive a low test grade, they don't think it's because they're stupid: "I can't believe it," they say. "I guess I studied the wrong stuff. I should have done better than this." When girls bring home the A, they are more likely to attribute their success to effort. "I really worked hard on this," they say to themselves. When girls get bad grades, they attribute failure to lack of ability: "I'm just not smart in math," they conclude.

Recent research clarifies the connection between self-esteem and academic achievement, especially in math and science. Most girls and boys who enjoy science and math consider themselves more important, like themselves more, and feel better about their schoolwork and family relationships. In elementary school, both males and females report that they like math and science, and their test scores are comparable. Girls continue to score as well as boys on standardized math tests in middle and high school. Yet, by the twelfth grade, girls report less positive attitudes and consider math and science harder subjects than do boys.[42] This self-confidence slide is especially steep for low-income or disadvantaged girls, girls with learning disabilities, and girls who are learning English as a new language. And girls make up only a third of Advanced Placement (AP) physics students and only 15 percent of AP computer science classes. Boys score higher on math and science sections of competitive tests, such as the AP tests, the SAT, and the ACT.[43]

But there are positive signs as well. Female enrollment in most high school and college mathematics and science courses has increased dramatically. Girls are the majority in biology, chemistry, algebra, and pre-calculus courses, but still lag behind boys in calculus and physics participation.[44] Unfortunately, the connection between girls and science and math remains tenuous. Girls are more anxious and less confident about their abilities than boys. They perceive math and science as cold, impersonal, and with little clear application to their lives or to society.[45] After graduation, fewer women gravitate to the math and science workplaces. For example, only 10 percent of engineers and 28 percent of computer scientists are women. Sadly, we are not likely to realize the scientific talents of girls any time soon: a 2006 survey by the Society of Women Engineers found that 75 percent of American girls have no interest in pursuing a career in science, math, or technology. Why? The girls repeatedly expressed little confidence in their abilities to succeed.[46]

Schools cannot remedy this alone. Researchers at the University of Michigan followed more than eight hundred children and their parents for thirteen years, and found that traditional gender stereotypes greatly influence parental attitudes and behaviors related to children's success in math. Parents provided more math-supportive environments for their sons than for their daughters, including buying more math and science toys. They also spent more time on math and science activities with their sons. Parents, and dads especially, held more positive perceptions of boys' math abilities than those of their daughters. So it is not surprising that boys' interest in math increases as their dads' expectations increase, while girls' interest in math decreases as their fathers' expectations lower.[47]

It is within the family that a girl first develops a sense of who she is and who she wants to become. Committed parents can create a climate of possibilities—or of limitations. Girls poised on the edge of adolescence struggle to retain their authenticity and vitality, for pitfalls are everywhere: physical vulnerability, the emphasis on thin, pretty, and popular; the ascendancy of social success over academic achievement; the silencing of their honest feelings; the message that math and science are male domains; the short-circuiting of ability that renders them helpless; the subtle insinuations that boys are naturally smart while girls' good grades are simply a sign of their hard work. Girls who succumb to these messages are at emotional and academic risk, in danger of losing their confidence, their achievement, and the very essence of themselves.

BOY BRAVADO

What's the best thing about being a boy? When we asked middle school boys that question, "not being a girl" was the second most popular response (just after sports).[48] It is an open secret that boys, even boys not doing well in school, believe that they are better, more valued, than girls. When all else is gloom, there is a light—they are not female. From their earliest days at school, boys learn to separate themselves from girls, and those who do not can quickly lose respect. Once the school world is divided, boys can strive to climb to the top of the male domain, thinking that even if they fall short, they are still in the top half, ahead of the girls.

But the boy world has its own struggles. In the elementary grades, boys are four times more likely to be sent to child psychologists and two and a half times more likely to be labeled hyperactive. Throughout school, boys are underdiagnosed for depression and are more likely to commit suicide. Boys make up two-thirds of students in special education, including 80 percent of those diagnosed with emotional disturbances or autism. The National Assessment of Educational Progress, the "Nation's Report Card," indicates that males of all races and ethnicities perform below females in writing and reading achievement, and boys often regard reading and writing as "feminine" subjects that threaten their masculinity. Boys receive lower report card grades than girls throughout the school years.[49]

Boys of color confront more frightening statistics. Compared with their white peers, black and Hispanic boys are two to three times more likely to land in special education programs. Boys of color are also disciplined more harshly than their white and Asian peers, achieve less academically, and drop out at higher rates.[50]

Given these serious challenges, it is no shocker then that boys' self-esteem drops. The perplexing question is why it falls less than girls'. Are boys more resilient? Are they tougher?

Carol Gilligan and others have described girls who "lose their voices" in adolescence; girls who retreat to a quieter, and hopefully safer, refuge. Boys take a different voice lesson, and find a voice of bravado. They grow up learning lines and practicing moves from a timeworn script that is supposed to guarantee male self-confidence: be cool, don't show emotion, repress feelings, be aggressive, compete and win. As the script is internalized, boys project an outward appearance of strength and security, of strong self-esteem. William Pollack calls this bravado the "boy code" or the "mask of masculinity"—a kind of swaggering posture that boys embrace to hide their fears, suppress dependency and vulnerability, and present a stoic, impervious front.[51] The rules for this bravado were described more than three decades ago by psychologist Robert Brannon, but have a much longer history:[52]

1. *No sissy stuff.* Masculinity avoids anything remotely feminine.
2. *Be a big wheel.* Masculinity is measured by wealth, power, and status.
3. *Be a sturdy oak.* Masculinity requires emotional imperviousness.
4. *Give 'em hell.* Masculinity requires daring, aggression, and risk-taking in our society.

Boys are keenly aware of the strict behavioral boundaries set by the masculine ideal and the high price that is exacted from them for playing "out of bounds." Listen to the disheartening experiences of one male middle schooler:

> I am not an athlete. In fact, I would rather make jewelry in the metals lab. But I am teased for being a girly-girl. I have had cigarettes thrown at me and people call me vulgar names almost daily. The words "fag," "dyke," "queer," "lesbo," and others ring through our hallways, locker rooms, and classrooms. Neither teachers nor students have been able to stop the control of a culture that continues to label, demean, and sort through who "belongs" and who is "outside" the gender box.

Staying a member of the boys' club is critical, and of all the cruel epithets boys hurl at one another, none is more devastating than being tossed out of the entitlements of boyhood by being called a "girl," "sissy," "fag," or "queer." In fact, it is the most common boy-to-boy harassment.[53] Boys work hard to purge themselves of any taint of femininity. Parents, teachers, and other adults also draw gender lines, training boys to avoid toys, games, or behavior associated with girls. Again and again participants in our workshops describe how that distancing takes place, and we hear how boys' sense of worth and security is shaken when they take even small steps beyond the rigid male borders:

> As a young boy I was slow to learn how to throw a baseball. One day in his haste to have me learn, my father yelled at me, "You throw like a girl!" There was such a negative twist to that statement. I still hear it in my mind whenever I go to throw a ball. Needless to say, I never did learn how to throw very well.

> I was student teaching in Washington, D.C., when Jim, one of my third graders, came in crying. He said that Brian called him names because he was wearing a pink shirt. When Jim began to cry, my supervising teacher scolded him: "Stop crying, Jim. Be a man!"

Studies show that adults worry about cross-sex behavior for both boys and girls, but parents and teachers believe girls will grow out of male behavior while boys will carry female traits into adulthood.[54] For girls to be called a "tomboy" is a backhanded compliment. Our language has no word with a nonpejorative connotation for a boy acting like a girl. "Janegirl" is not in our lexicon. Fearing boys who play with dolls or who try on makeup or jewelry will become homosexuals or transsexuals, adults watch them with intense concern and preoccupation:

> It was my first year teaching, and there was one four-year-old boy who was the talk of the school. We had a dramatic-play area, and whenever this boy went there, he would put on women's clothes. Every teacher who saw this (some came especially to see it) said it was queer. On the playground this boy would be a "hairdresser" and do my hair. Over the course of the year he changed; he played more with the boys and stopped assuming female roles. What I thought was so peculiar was that although the boy changed, the teachers never stopped talking about the time he acted female.

While most males will follow this rigid boy code, they will experience these rules differently based on their race, class, ethnicity, sexuality, and age. As sociologist Michael Kimmel explains, "What it means to be a 71-year-old, black, gay man in Cleveland is probably radically different from what it means to be a 19-year-old white, heterosexual farm boy in Iowa."[55] But not all manhood is equal, as sociologist Erving Goffman explained nearly half a century ago:

> In an important sense there is only one complete unblushing male in America: a young, married, white, urban, northern, heterosexual, Protestant, father, of college education, fully employed, of good complexion, weight, and height, and a recent record in sports. . . . Any male who fails to qualify in any one of these ways is likely to view himself—during moments at least—as unworthy, incomplete, and inferior.[56]

The unrealistic requirements of this male code become a prescription for failure: virtually all boys and men come up short. Not all boys are strong, or athletic, or successful, or fearless candidates for foolish risks. So while boy bravado speaks of strength, success, and toughness, a boy's inner voice quietly lives with the knowledge that he is falling short. A boy who wants to share emotions must break the code; boys' close friendships may signal vulnerability, again breaking the code. A boy who likes art or music or who is not athletic also breaks the code. And for those few who manage to keep the code intact through childhood, adulthood will bring greater challenges. Adulthood is when most young men realize that despite their loyalty to the code, very few of them will become millionaires, or astronauts, or sports stars. Some boys will grow to be men selling appliances at Sears, or teaching, or working on an assembly line. Many will become husbands, partners, and fathers, and emotional connection will be needed to help create these healthy relationships. What are men to do when reality rejects their boyhood bravado?

Michael Kimmel believes many boys deal with this frustrating conflict by working harder at the boy code, by repressing their emotions while doubling their efforts to prove that they are "real men." Kimmel believes it is a strategy that can quickly become violent.[57] From an early age, boys learn that aggression is sometimes acceptable, and often admired. Movies and television offer an endless stream of action heroes violently enforcing their will. And boys watch. The nation's power is projected abroad through military strength and widespread destruction. And boys watch. Let's not forget about violent computer games, misogynous MTV rappers, and the popularity of wrestling on television. These are the violent images that boys absorb, and take to school.

Picture a disruptive classroom, and you are likely to envision a boy at the center. Boys are also more likely to be fighting in the hall, and bullying on the school yard. One-half to two-thirds of America's children report being bullied at least once a month and ten percent feel continually targeted. In a classroom of twenty students, two or three come to school every day in fear of bullies. The most likely targets are gay students, or students perceived as gay. While girls can be bullies as well, boys are more likely to use physical violence or threats. One in twenty students reports being a victim of crime at school, with males more likely to be involved with such violence. Three times as many boys as girls carry weapons, and twice as many have been threatened, injured with weapons, or hurt in physical fights. Half of all teen boys get into a physical fight each year, four times more teenage boys than girls think fighting is appropriate when someone cuts in line, and more than 70 percent of school suspensions are boys. Even more troubling, men and boys are responsible for more than 90 percent of all violent crimes.[58]

While some boys and men explode from repressed emotion, others collapse inward with stony silence. Mothers ask their sons, "What's bothering you?" Children plead, "What's wrong, Daddy?" But the questions go unanswered. Since expressing emotion is considered "feminine," males hide their emotions from others—and often from themselves. Detachment, silence, and aggression are signs that the code is terribly broken.

BEYOND THE BRAVADO

Boys yearn for something more than these traditional gender restrictions. When a group of researchers interviewed kindergarten through fourth-grade boys in Ohio and Pennsylvania, they heard voices that were sensitive and caring in the younger grades. Boys were willing to admit feelings of fear and vulnerability. Trying to adjust to a new room, one confessed, "I can't see the whole room in the dark . . . and when the garage door goes up, it sounds like a dragon. So I just shut my eyes and hold my pillow." Another described the anxiety he feels just before falling asleep: "At night I get all scared and I think I see smoke, and I get under my covers and I get all scared." When the interviewer asked what he did to keep from being frightened, he answered, "I hug my stuffed animals."

The boys also talked about how much they valued friendship. One said, "A friend is someone who's willing to do something if you ask him to . . . like if it was a tie in a vote, then he would give in and say, 'Well, you can have it this time.' " Some boys described caring for make-believe companions instead of real-life friends. A first grader described a whole classroom of imaginary friends passed on to him by his sister. They lived behind a secret door in his house, and he was their teacher. "They like to learn," he said, "and I like to help them."[59] But this sensitive side is forced underground as the boys grow older. They learn to be careful about showing how deeply they care, even to themselves.

When researchers asked middle school girls and boys to recall whether they had felt afraid, sad, disgusted, or guilty in the last month, most males denied experiencing these emotions. But when the boys were asked to keep a daily diary of their feelings, then guilt, sadness, disgust, and fear all appeared in their personal accounts.[60] Clearly, boys could profit from developing what Daniel Goleman calls "emotional intelligence." He believes that people benefit when they are aware of their emotions, know how to manage them, and are able to recognize the emotions of others.[61] It seems that boys are routinely encouraged to bury such knowledge. Psychologist Howard Gardner sees emotional intelligence as consisting of two separate intelligences. He believes children and adults do well if they are able to analyze their own strengths and abilities, mental and emotional, and learn how to manage their skills. He calls this "intrapersonal intelligence," knowing oneself. Gardner also calls for "interpersonal intelligence," the ability to understand the perceptions and motivations of others, to think beyond oneself and to relate well with others. While we measure IQs, we do not measure EQs (emotional intelligence), the SATs do not measure inter- or intrapersonal intelligences, and we rarely teach them in schools. Perhaps we should. Studies show that individuals with strong social skills, such as empathy, conscientiousness, and cooperation, are more likely to advance in their careers than their peers who had similar test scores in school but fewer emotional skills.[62]

While parents encourage empathy in daughters, they fear that caring boys may be seen as too gentle. Psychologist Phyllis Berman videotaped forty-eight male and female two- and three-year-olds as they pretended to take care of their dolls. The parents, a sophisticated group of professionals, praised the girls with comments such as "You're such a good mommy," but they failed to encourage similar nurturing behavior in boys. This was a missed opportunity for teaching boys that being a father is more than a biological act. Research indicates that boys who care for younger brothers and sisters become less aggressive and more nurturing in their relationships.[63]

Schools and teachers can take an active role in developing such empathy and nurturing skills in boys. On the eve of those middle school years, in a fourth-grade class, we watched a teacher encouraging boys to push the borders of the male stereotype. As we observed her lesson, we were struck by how much effort it took to stretch outmoded attitudes. She began by writing a letter on the board.

> Dear Adviser:
>   My seven-year-old son wants me to buy him a doll. I don't know what to do. Should I go ahead and get it for him? Is this normal, or is my son sick? Please help!
>
>   Waiting for your answer,
>   Concerned

"Suppose you were an advice columnist, like Ann Landers," the teacher said to the class, "and you received a letter like this. What would you tell this parent? Write a letter answering 'Concerned,' and then we'll talk about your recommendations."

For the next twenty minutes she walked around the room and gave suggestions about format and spelling. When she invited the students to read their letters, Andy volunteered.

Dear Concerned:

You are in big trouble. Your son is sick, sick, sick! Get him to a psychiatrist fast. And if he keeps asking for a doll, get him bats and balls and guns and other toys boys should play with.

Hope this helps,
Andy

Several other students also read their letters, and most, like Andy, recommended that the son be denied a doll. Then the teacher read Charlotte Zolotow's *William's Doll,* the story of a boy who is ridiculed by other children when he says he wants a doll. Not until his grandmother visits does he get his wish so that, as the wise woman says, he can learn to be a father one day.

As the teacher was reading, several students began to fidget, laugh, and whisper to one another. When she asked the fourth graders how they liked the book, one group of boys, the most popular clique in the class, acted as if the story was a personal insult. Their reaction was so hostile, the teacher had trouble keeping order. We heard their comments:

"He's a fag."
"He'd better learn how boys are supposed to behave, or he'll never get to be a man."
"If I saw him playing with that baby doll, I'd take it away. Maybe a good kick in the pants would teach him."
"Dolls are dumb. It's a girly thing to do."

Next the teacher played the song "William Wants a Doll" from the *Free to Be You and Me* album. Several boys began to sing along in a mocking tone, dragging out the word *doll* until it became two syllables: "William wants a do-oll, William wants a do-oll." As they chanted, they pointed to Bill, the star athlete of the class. Both boys and girls whispered and laughed as Bill, slumped in his chair, looked ready to explode.

Belatedly the teacher realized the problem of the name coincidence; she assured the class that there was nothing wrong with playing with dolls, that it teaches both girls and boys how to become parents when they grow up. When the students began to settle down, she gave them her next instructions: "I'd like you to reread your letters and make any last-minute corrections. If you want to change your advice, you may, but you don't have to."

Later we read the students' letters. Most of them said a seven-year-old boy should not get a doll. But after listening to William's story, six modified their advice, having reached a similar conclusion: "Oh, all right. Give him a doll if you have to. But no baby dolls or girl dolls. Make sure it's a [Ninja] Turtle or a G.I. Joe."

Such innovative practices are rare. Most schools are locked in a more traditional model, one that promotes competition over cooperation, aggression over nurturing, and sports victories rather than athletic participation. Some boys thrive on this traditional male menu, but many do not.

In *American Manhood,* Anthony Rotundo writes that men need to regain "access to stigmatized parts of themselves—tenderness, nurturance, the desire for connection, the skills of cooperation—that are helpful in personal situations and needed for the social good."[64] Studies support Rotundo's contention: males who can call on a range of qualities, tenderness as well as toughness, are viewed by others as more intelligent, likable, and mentally healthy than rigidly stereotyped men.[65] As author Joseph Campbell noted, "The privilege of a lifetime is being who you are." It is time we let boys move beyond the false bravado of boyhood and enjoy that privilege.

SUCCEEDING AT FAIRNESS: SUGGESTIONS FOR STUDENTS, PARENTS, AND TEACHERS

Too often, parents and teachers feel like throwing up their arms in the face of powerful media and influential peers that reinforce traditional gender stereotypes. Adults can help both girls and boys build healthy self-esteems that trump such gender-restrictive stereotypes and messages. Here are a few suggestions:

1. Adults have some homework to do. They have been shaped by society's traditional view of gender roles. Teachers and parents reading this and similar books are taking the first step to freeing themselves from gender stereotypes. It will take a constant effort.
2. Teachers and parents should monitor and eliminate sexist terms and comments. Instead of focusing on girls' and boys' physical attributes, adults could emphasize more important issues such as character, caring, and compassion.
3. Books can broaden horizons, and there are several terrific nonsexist

books available for girls and boys of all ages. Librarians can help you find them. The Anti-Defamation League website also has a wonderful collection of multicultural and nonsexist books: www.adl.org/bibliography/default.asp.

4. Model nonsexist behaviors at home and at school. Fathers who cook, mothers who know how to work technology, and parents who share home chores are sending important messages. A teacher who asks a girl to work the audiovisual equipment or set up a lab experiment while asking a boy to take attendance or help in the school's day-care center is also sending a message that sharing tasks is part of life.

5. Catch children doing things well and compliment them. Whether it is schoolwork, or helping a friend, or being responsible, recognize positive efforts and build self-esteem.

6. Encourage girls and boys to explore nonsexist interests and toys. A chemistry kit for a girl or an art kit for a boy broadens options. Avoid walking those oh-so-subtle pink and blue toy store aisles.

7. Let girls do things on their own and avoid those short circuits. When a girl is old enough to drive, for example, she is also old enough to change a tire. Letting her change the tire (rather than watching her father or even her mother do it for her) can build self-esteem, confidence, and independence.

8. Encourage students to enroll in a full range of courses. Girls who avoid advanced math or science or boys who do not enroll in advanced literature, art, and music courses are limiting their futures.

9. Monitor the friends of both daughters and sons: peer groups are influential. Aggressive friends of either gender can be a source of problematic behavior.

10. Girls' involvement with sports and physical activity has positive health effects. Female athletes do better academically, have lower school dropout rates, lower levels of stress and depression, and develop a sense of competence that builds self-esteem.

11. Boys involved in athletics can benefit from friendships and a sense of teamwork. But male athletics can spiral out of control and have a negative impact on boys. Adults should monitor male athletics to emphasize sportsmanship, fairness, and the importance of effort rather than winning at any price. All boys should leave the field feeling good about their efforts, if not always good about the outcome.

12. Give children the freedom to experiment, and eliminate the fear of failure. A sense of security at school and at home can go a long way in building self-esteem.

And . . . here are some of our favorite books and resources to help parents and educators improve boys' and girls' self-esteem.

Resources

Best Friends, Worst Enemies, by Michael Thompson, Catherine O'Neill Grace, and Lawrence Cohen

> From thought-provoking observations to practical suggestions, this book offers an engaging, readable developmental perspective on how children's social lives and friendships are created from toddlerhood to adolescence. The book concludes with advice to teachers and parents on how to improve social life in schools and support children's friendships.

Growing a Girl, by Barbara Mackoff

> This insightful book offers parents hundreds of strategies to shatter stereotypes that limit girls' growth while nurturing girls' growing sense of self with tools to nourish her strength and spirit.

The Pressured Child: Helping Your Child Find Success in School and Life, by Michael Thompson

> The pressure to excel is transforming childhood as never before. This book explores how the culture we live in has redefined our definition of successful kids and created an obsession with superachieving.

Real Boys, by William Pollack

> This book takes us into the daily worlds of boys, not only to show how society's outdated expectations force them to mask many of their true emotions, but also to let us hear how boys themselves describe their isolation, fears, depression, love, and hope. Challenging traditional notions of manhood and masculinity, *Real Boys* guides parents and teachers to help boys develop emotional skills to effectively deal with issues such as relationships, peer pressure, violence, and sexuality.

For additional resources, see *Still Failing at Fairness*'s page on www.simon andschuster.com.

CHAPTER 5

Life in High School

Remember your high school days? (Are you smiling or grimacing?) Were you an *innie,* a popular kid with lots of friends, wondering if these may be the best years of your life? Or were you an *outie,* a social reject, living on the perimeter, hardly ever noticed, and wondering in your heart of hearts if you would ever get a real life? That's the world Ralph Keyes paints in his book *Is There Life After High School?*[1] Keyes's question may be rhetorical, but many of us are still influenced by the joys and scars of our high school years. High school can be a pressure cooker where teenagers are shoved into close quarters with twenty-five or thirty others of their age whom they may love, hate, care little about, or hardly know. Rushing from class to class, adolescents create a world of unique norms, rituals, and vocabulary, a place where even time is transformed from hours and minutes to periods. Adults are rarely allowed into the high school culture, but if we listen closely, we can learn a lot about how students see their world.

When high schoolers were asked to identify the best thing about their school, they usually said, "My friends." Sports activities ranked second. "Nothing" ranked higher than "classes I'm taking" and "teachers." When asked to describe her school, a junior provided this insight:

> The classes are okay, I guess. Most of the time I find them pretty boring, but then I suppose that's the way school classes are supposed to be. What I like most about the place is the chance to be with my friends. It's nice to be a part of a group. I don't mean one of the clubs or groups the school runs. But an informal group of your own friends is great.[2]

In *Posing, Pretending, Waiting for the Bell,* K. M. Pierce also found that peer relationships, not academics, are central to school life. Todd, a high school junior, poignantly admitted that class material is the least of what students learn:

> It's interesting how different atmospheres and the presence of certain individuals in the class can really determine how someone acts and feels in the room. I see a lot of hurt in these halls . . . kids struggling, being harassed, ridiculed, teased. . . . It appears that the courses in school aren't really the hardest part about it. And the material taught in classes is probably the least of what is learned within these walls. But what kids learn, is it helping them or pulling them apart? School is more of a war zone—a place to survive.[3]

In *A Tribe Apart: A Journey Into the Heart of American Adolescence,* Patricia Hersch shares the story of three years she spent with seventh through twelfth graders in suburban Reston, Virginia.[4] What Hersch discovered was troubling: an increasingly isolated, intense, and perilous adolescent culture, where drugs, alienation, and violence represent ongoing threats. It is a teenage society unknown to many parents (and teachers). Contemporary high school friendships appear to be more fluid: teenagers may have one group of friends in a drama club, another from math class, and a third set from sports activities. Today cross-gender friendships are also more common as boys and girls do a better job of developing relationships without the need for a romantic attachment.

But even as the number of friendships grows, the quality of adolescent relationships remains a problem. Today's teenagers, both girls and boys, report that although they have many friends, they lack intimate, close friends. Teenagers say that there is no one that they can really confide in, no one with whom to share their deepest thoughts. In the midst of a crowd, they feel alone. It is a disturbing admission.

THE LOOKING-GLASS SELF

In the central drama of adolescence, high school is when girls and boys begin their quests to develop an adult identity. They experiment with different roles in ways that bewilder their parents. As one mother told us:

> My daughter comes home from school exhausted. She doesn't say much usually, but yesterday she couldn't stop talking. First she was so happy because the cast names were up for the play and she got a part.

Then she learned that this girl was spreading rumors about her, and she was upset and angry. Next she got her chemistry test back and bombed it. She was depressed and wouldn't talk to anybody. After school she and a group of her friends went to McDonald's; they were so happy and having the best time. I can still see her face as she asked me, "How is it possible to have so many different feelings and be so many different people in such a short time? Sometimes I don't even know who I am!"

As youth struggle to reconcile different parts of their personalities, they look to parents, teachers, classmates, and friends for reactions. Reactions offer a yardstick to measure themselves, pooling and reflecting them in a process Charles Horton Cooley called "the looking-glass self."[5] By high school the mirror held up by peers is the one youth look into most to learn who they are and what they can become.[6] The looking-glass self is far from a new phenomenon; indeed it seems timeless. Take a moment to look back upon your own high school experience. What did you see reflected in the looking-glass?

In his classic 1961 study *The Adolescent Society,* James Coleman found that in the 1950s high school boys wanted overwhelmingly to be remembered by peers as "top athletic stars," second choice was "brilliant student," and third was "most popular." Girls wanted to be remembered as a "leader in activities," closely followed by "most popular." "Brilliant student" ranked a distant third.[7] For boys, athletics was mentioned again and again as the gateway to high school status. When girls were asked how they reached the leading crowd in school, they referred to appearance and personality: "Wear just the right things," they said. "Money, clothes, a flashy appearance. Date older boys, get fairly good grades, but don't be too smart. Flirt with boys. Be cooperative on dates."[8]

When Ralph Keyes interviewed adults who had attended high school during the 1970s, he found that status—on the athletic field and in the classroom—still reigned paramount for boys. He described Luke, a star athlete in high school, and the winner of eight varsity sport letters. Years after graduation, Luke still vividly dreamed of horsing around in class, throwing spitballs, winning a fight in his senior year, and running up and down the football field. Even though he'd get out of bed and try to walk them off, the dreams kept right on coming—every week or so. Luke admitted that he had done little of consequence as an adult. "My life's been pretty mediocre since high school." Even for those rich and famous, whose lives are far from mediocre, high school has made an indelible imprint: *Peanuts* cartoonist, Charles Schulz, never forgot the day the yearbook staff rejected his cartoon; actor Gregory Peck was regarded as least likely to succeed; former president Gerald Ford lost his bid to become senior class president; and former secretary of state Henry Kissinger was called "fatso" by his peers and ate lunch alone.[9]

The women Keyes interviewed also described the power of peers in their high school life. Being popular was still a top priority, and even famous personalities were haunted by memories of high school rejection. Actress Ali MacGraw remembered never having a date in high school. Author of *The Feminine Mystique* Betty Friedan recalled going out infrequently, mostly with "misfits like myself."[10] When writer Nora Ephron was asked what she wished she had been like in high school, her answer was immediate:

> Beautiful, feminine, popular with the boys, popular with the girls. . . . The one thing I would like to get across about my whole feeling regarding high school is how I was when I was fifteen: gawky, always a hem hanging down, or a strap loose, or a pimple on my chin. I never knew what to do with my hair. I was a mess. And I still carry that fifteen-year-old girl around now. A piece of me still believes I'm the girl nobody dances with.[11]

Ephron not only described what it felt like to be fifteen and awkward, she also told how she improved her popularity by dating boys who weren't too bright. She took her most important step toward status when she stopped raising her hand so that classmates wouldn't realize she knew the answers. She told Keyes:

"It made a tremendous difference."

"You were asked out more?"

"Oh, yeah. Instantly." She grimaced. "I realize the kind of patheticism of it—(a) that I stopped raising my hand, (b) that I felt I had to, and (c) that it worked."[12]

In today's adolescent society many girls still think that being bright conflicts with being popular. To go to the prom with the right date, to be a cheerleader, to be chosen as most popular, to be elected class officer—such is the stuff of high school dreams. The assertive style that leads to intellectual achievement does not mesh with the passive, noncompetitive role many boys desire and expect from girls. Since competing with boys—and winning—can result in being home alone on Saturday night, some girls put the brakes on academic success and cloak or camouflage their talent; not trying hard in school is just one step away from "playing dumb." One female high school senior we spoke to admitted, "When a girl asks me what grades I got last semester, I answer, 'Fair, only one A.' When a boy asks the same question, I act surprised. 'I can't believe it, I got an A!' " Other girls told us that they hid out in class and never volunteered so classmates wouldn't know how smart they were. One senior explained that she spent years faking intellectual mediocrity. "I never pretended to be a potato, but I didn't want people to think I was a brain, either," she said. "When I qualified as a National Merit Semifinalist, I felt as though I had blown my cover. So I went around saying that I just got lucky on the test; it could never happen again. After I said it often enough, the other kids seemed to believe it."

Today, just as when Coleman wrote *The Adolescent Society,* the most reliable route to popularity for girls is looking pretty. Teenage boys agree that good looks are important for a girl and even claim that pretty girls have better personalities.[13] Our interviews with high schoolers also revealed how adolescents understand the delicate connection between girls' popularity and appearance:

"When you look good, people are envious and give you respect."

"Social status is based a lot on looks."

"Nothing hurts more than being criticized about your style or hair, weight and height."

"Guys think girls always have to be pretty and perfect. Ugh. How tiring is that?"

"Most girls care for their looks on the outside but they should think about what's in the inside, too."

"How can we know who we really are when we are only valued for appearance rather than for thoughts and feelings?"

"Girls face overwhelming pressure to be thin. We have dieting sleepovers where we read about the latest techniques. But always thinking about not eating is tiring."

For today's adolescent girls, *pretty* is synonymous with *thin.* The obsession with being thin takes many forms: girls who skip breakfast or lunch or dinner, or all three; girls who exist on diet drinks and popcorn; girls whose most predictable and reliable daily activity is checking their weight on the scale morning and night; girls who make themselves throw up or pop packages of laxatives; and girls who are addicted to smoking or exercise to control their weight. Sadly, different versions of the following scenes are played out across the country.

> A fifteen-year-old girl looks to the right and left, as if checking for passing cars on a busy street. Seeing that no one is around, she slips outside the dressing room and hurries to look at the prom dress in the large mirror outside. She surveys her appearance critically and pushes the dress down over her hips several times as if to erase them. "I've been starving myself for weeks," she mutters. "I can't believe I'm still so fat." The tag on the dress she is wearing says size three.

> "Allison has such a pretty face," one mother told us after a shopping expedition. "But I can't stand to see her try on clothes. It's pathetic. If only she would lose weight. I don't think I can shop with her anymore. She's so sensitive, and all we do is fight about it."

The obsession with thinness is a recent phenomenon. Before the mass media existed, ideas of beauty were limited to our own communities. Until the advent of photography in 1839, people were not exposed to real-life images of faces and bodies. Most people did not even own mirrors. In earlier times a full figure was thought to be beautiful; ample breasts, belly, and buttocks signified health and fertility. During the 1950s, girls and women worked to achieve the hourglass shape. In that time of "mammary madness," girls bought falsies and stuffed bras with tissue and cotton. Cinch belts and crinoline skirts were also part of the hourglass image. Today the ideal of the curvaceous woman has been replaced by a "tubular" shape, a more linear form that is taller, leaner, and without a noticeable bust or hips. The featured models in fashion and women's magazines have become ever thinner and now weigh a shocking 23–25 percent less than the average woman and maintain a weight 15 to 20 percent below what is considered healthy for her age and weight.[14]

Girls pore over the pictures in fashion magazines, studying the images as a primer for their own appearance. Surrounded by pictures of lithe, lean, long-legged beauty, the adolescent girl confronts a terrible irony. Leg length as a proportion of total height decreases throughout puberty, especially for girls who mature early. To mature normally she gains weight, especially in the bust and hips. The "fat spurt," one of puberty's most dramatic physical changes, is important for reproduction and signals normal development. Yet many fear that the change is permanent and desperately try to take the weight off. They are not aware that once the physical changes during this time cease, their weight will usually stabilize and go to their bodies' natural set point, without the need for dieting. But the shape of the girl *before* puberty, the form left behind during normal maturation, is the image that society says is beautiful.

Advertising companies spend over $200 billion a year teaching Americans what to value.[15] Ads sell a great deal more than products. They sell images, and concepts of success and worth, love and sexuality, popularity and normalcy. They teach us to live in pain because of who we are, versus who we "should" be. More than two out of three adolescent girls say that magazine models influence their idea of what the perfect body is supposed to look like.[16] Magazine editors, in a fierce competition for readers, know that to make a sale, they need only play on doubts or create new ones, making females think they have "problems" that don't really exist. Every part of the female body is picked apart and scrutinized, with most articles describing outright which products women should buy to fix—or at least camouflage—their numerous "flaws." One insightful high schooler shared with us her struggle to resist the demeaning messages in ads:

> I believe that every woman is utterly and completely beautiful. That said, when I find myself faced with produced images of beauty in magazines or billboards, I still can't help but wish I looked like them.

For females of color or those with disabilities, the "image of perfection" presented can be even more disheartening. Disabled women are often portrayed as helpless victims who need protection, or as heroines who have beaten the odds. Rarely is their beauty recognized. The words of one disabled young woman poignantly describe her feelings of isolation.[17]

> Living with a physical disability, I have learned from the dominant messages in society that I am not like other women. In fact, for the most part, I'm actually not considered a woman at all.

Women of color also rarely find themselves in ads and media, and when they do they see models and celebrities who closely follow the white beauty ideal. As one young Hispanic high schooler shared with us,

> As a teenager, I find myself obsessed with achieving the "white girl" look: slim hips, perky breasts, flat stomach. I hate that I don't look like white models in magazines.

It is a devastating dilemma. To mature normally is to become "less attractive" at the very age when beauty is most essential to popularity and self-esteem. For too many girls the course of action is clear: it is estimated that at any given time approximately one-half to three-quarters of adolescent girls and three-quarters of adult women are on a diet.[18]

Studies suggest that reading articles about diet and weight loss can have unhealthy consequences. For five years, researchers from the University of Minnesota surveyed 2,516 middle and high school students about the magazines they read and their dieting behaviors. Forty-four percent of adolescent girls admitted to reading diet articles, and the consequences were staggering. Within five years, these girls were twice as likely to lose weight by skipping meals, fasting, or smoking cigarettes than girls who never read such articles. They were also three times more likely to use measures such as vomiting or taking laxatives. Only 14 percent of boys reported reading diet articles frequently, and they did not report similar extreme dieting behaviors.[19]

Persistent, chronic dieting puts an enormous stress on teenagers, one that takes a toll on physical well-being and the energy needed to learn in school. In one classic study of hunger, a group of men reduced their food intake by half. After six months the men became apathetic, depressed, prone to outbursts of anger, and unable to function well in work or social situations; in some cases their behavior was characterized by psychotic levels of disorganization.[20] Many teenage girls put themselves on equally or even more stringent weight-reduction programs.

The dramatic rise of eating disorders among adolescent and young adult females is alarming: 90 percent of the estimated eleven million Americans struggling with anorexia and bulimia are women between the ages of twelve and twenty-five. For most kids, eating disorders start when they are eleven to thirteen years old. Yet weight concerns can begin at a startlingly young age. Forty-two percent of first- to third-grade girls want to be thinner, and 81 percent of ten-year-olds are afraid of being fat. The number one wish of girls eleven to seventeen years old is to lose weight.[21]

Ironically, in their preteen and adolescent years, most children should be gaining weight. During that critical period, their bones are thickening and lengthening, their hearts are getting stronger in order to pump blood to their growing bodies, and their brains are adding mass, laying down new neurological pathways and pruning others, part of the explosion of mental and emotional development that occurs in those years. When children with eating disorders stop consuming sufficient calories, their bodies begin to conserve energy; heart function slows, blood pressure drops; they have trouble staying warm. The stress hormone cortisol becomes elevated, preventing their bones from hardening. Their hair becomes brittle and falls out in patches. Their bodies begin to consume muscle tissue. The brain, which depends at least in part on dietary fat to grow, begins to atrophy.

While some are troubled by eating disorders as early as elementary school, for most girls it begins at adolescence. Morbidly afraid of being fat, high school and college students suffer from bulimia, episodes of binge eating, vomiting, or abusing laxatives to prevent absorbing food. The self-starvation syndrome of anorexia nervosa plagues adolescents whose images of their bodies are so disturbed that they adamantly refuse to maintain a healthy weight. Anorexia is a lethal disease: one in seven victims of anorexia will die from it.[22]

While many African-American girls and women are comfortable with their bodies, some are now catching up with their white counterparts when it comes to eating disorders, particularly binge eating and the use of laxatives.[23] Like their white peers, many young girls of diverse backgrounds aspire to be like the skinny models and actors they see in the media, a phenomenon psychologists suggest may be a desperate attempt to fit into white middle-class society where "what matters is to be blond, white, and thin." A Harvard Medical School study done on the South Pacific island of Fiji highlights an undeniable connection between the media and eating disorders. Traditionally, weight loss has been perceived in Fijian culture as a sign of illness and deteriorating health. Yet researchers found that three years after television was introduced on the island, teenage girls started to show symptoms of eating disorders for the first time, with 74 percent of girls describing how they feel "too big or fat."[24]

Similarly, plumpness has been accepted in Asian cultures as a sign of prestige and affluence. But that, too, is changing. Consider Eve's story.[25] Eve spent much of her high school years binging and purging during the day, and locked in a closet at night so she couldn't get to the refrigerator. Her mother, a first generation Chinese American, locked her up because she thought her daughter's extra five to ten pounds was a bad reflection on the family. The pressure got so intense that Eve entered the private, painful world of eating disorders. Throughout high school and college, she binged and purged, taking up to thirty laxatives a day and shrinking her five-foot, nine-inch frame to under one hundred pounds. "Being Chinese, the thinking is you can be smarter, you can be better, you can be thinner. Those are very, very high standards. In every aspect, I had to be perfect."

Perfectionism, low self-esteem, and negative body image can set the stage for depression. Increasingly girls are turning to drugs to cope. In fact, teenage girls, having caught up to their male counterparts in illegal drug use and alcohol consumption, now surpass boys in smoking and prescription drug abuse. An astonishing 10 percent of teen girls abuse prescription painkillers, tranquilizers, and stimulants. Girls described smoking and drugs as "convenient" ways to lose weight.[26]

Teachers have told us at workshops that eating disorders are becoming more noticeable and troubling. They described monitoring the high school cafeteria for lunches left uneaten. A business teacher from a rural high school in Ohio described how he walks around the lunchroom to talk to the girls, urging them to eat something. "How do you expect to do well in your schoolwork if you don't eat?" he asks. "You'll never have enough energy to pass the test that's coming up next period." A health teacher said that parents have begun calling her secretly, asking her to check on whether their daughters are eating lunch. "So many of them don't touch anything on their plate," she said. "Maybe they nibble on a few raisins, but that's all." Kristen Golden of the Ms. Foundation for Women put the problem this way: "Suddenly they need diets, even surgery. It's incredible. It's not 'If you study, you can do this.' It's 'If you mutilate yourself, you, too, can look like this.' "[27]

While many teachers are becoming more aware of eating disorders, too often they don't know what to do about them. Naomi Wolf, author of *The Beauty Myth*, described herself when she was a schoolgirl afflicted with anorexia:

> At thirteen I was taking in the caloric equivalent of the food energy available to the famine victims of the siege of Paris. I did my schoolwork diligently and kept quiet in the classroom. I was a wind-up obedience toy. Not a teacher or principal or guidance counselor confronted me with an objection to my evident deportation in stages from the land of the living. . . .
>
> An alien voice took mine over. I have never been so soft-spoken. It lost expression and timbre and sank to a monotone, a dull murmur the opposite of strident. My teachers approved of me. They saw nothing wrong with what I was doing, and I could swear they looked straight at me. My school had stopped dissecting alley cats, since it was considered inhumane. There was no interference in my self-directed science

experiment to find out just how little food could keep a human body alive.[28]

One of the students we interviewed, Nora, struggled with anorexia throughout high school and recalled, "Deep down, I wondered why my teachers never helped me. My body showed my pain, but I needed help to find my voice. Talking and listening to me would have been a first step."[29]

BOYS' BODIES

They exercise for hours, devise rigid rituals surrounding food, obsessively monitor their weight, and yearn to resemble the taut-bodied celebrities whose images grace magazine covers. Most of us probably saw vigilant, model-thin young women in this scenario. Or maybe we envisioned elite athletes competing in gymnastics, cycling, track, or wrestling. But we need to think again.

Long regarded as a female problem, eating disorders—the self-starvation of anorexia, the gorging and purging that characterize bulimia and the uncontrolled consumption of large amounts of food that is binge eating—are increasingly affecting males. Males are about 10 percent of the eleven million Americans struggling with anorexia and bulimia and the twenty-five million suffering from binge eating. But the number of males with an eating disorder may be much higher because males believe that food issues are "female issues" and are likely to deny or fail to recognize their own struggles with eating.[30]

It is not surprising that males participating in sports that demand weight restrictions, such as wrestling, swimming, and weight lifting, are prone to disordered eating. But athletes are not the only ones likely to suffer. Males of any age and body type also appear to be vulnerable to social pressures to achieve the perfect body. But unlike the female ideal, which focuses on overall thinness, males focus on strength and power, on achieving "six-pack" abs. Boys say, "I'm getting into shape," not, "I'm fat and need to go on a diet."[31] Yet the fitness quest can quickly turn life-threatening.

That is what happened to Justin. When he was fourteen years old, his mother had open-heart surgery. During her recovery, the doctor encouraged the entire family to eat healthier and exercise more. Justin's anxiety triggered behaviors that soon developed into anorexia. Within a three-month period, Justin's five-foot, ten-inch frame went from a healthy 155 pounds to a frightening 104 pounds. Justin described the progression of his disease:

> I started to run five or six miles a day. And then I skipped meals, especially breakfast and lunch. I wouldn't eat things that didn't have a label. So if you gave me an orange or homemade bread, I wouldn't eat that because it didn't have the exact nutritional value.

While movies, magazines, and television tell females that being thin is the ticket to success, males receive a different message: the keys to masculinity are body mass, muscle bulge, and definition. For many boys, a muscular body signals superiority. When we asked high school boys what is the best thing about being male, more than 70 percent put sports and being strong at the top of their lists.[32] They want to be buff. They want to be ripped. They want to glisten with six-pack abs and granite pecs.

More than ever, American boys are trying to find these designer bodies not only in a gym but also through steroids. Steroid use has long been widespread among athletes looking for a quick way to add strength or speed, but now boys as young as ten and high school students who do not play team sports are also bulking up with steroids simply because they want to look good. Nearly half a million boys are taking steroids, and risking their lives.[33]

While steroids can guarantee rippling muscles, many of these substances can stifle bone growth and lead to testicular shrinkage, liver tumors, hair loss, acne, and development of male breasts. Some of these effects may be irreversible. Adding steroids to the naturally occurring testosterone in a teenage boy may also lead to violence in the form of a testosterone-driven rage. The quest for the "perfect" body is not a pretty picture.

GO FETCH!

Myra and David wanted to learn more about how students felt they were treated based on their gender. In the mid-1990s they went to talk with students in one of the most elite magnet high schools for mathematics and science in the United States.

"Have you noticed any differences in the ways males and females are treated in this school?" they asked the class of bright, talented students. "Or have you felt any sexism yourself? The question is for males as well as females. Take about ten minutes to describe your experiences, and then we'll talk about them."

Several students begin to write furiously. "Ten minutes," one girl murmurs. "I need days." Others, mainly boys but some girls, stare ahead stone-faced and write nothing. As we walk around the room, we stop by one all-male table. Several boys are slumped at an angle, their legs stretched across the floor and their arms folded.

"Can we help?" we ask.

"I'm thinking," one boy mutters. "I don't have a pencil," says another. We put one on his desk, but he makes no move to pick it up. As we turn to leave, we hear someone whisper, "Just what we need—politically correct BS from liberal Democrats."

"Five more minutes to write," we announce. The hostile male table is still in position—slouched, sprawled, arms folded. But they are the minority and aren't able to set the tone in the room. Most of the students have written something; they look interested and are ready to respond.

A girl sitting toward the front begins to read her statement: "I had a sexist gym teacher last year. He was constantly putting down the girls in my gym class. He would say things like, 'You!' pointing to a girl, 'Get out of the way! Mark actually is trying to make a basket.' He hardly ever called the girls by name, and no matter how hard we tried, he used to say we were lazy."

A white male agrees and adds, "Male gym teachers pick boys to demonstrate things, and they expect more of boys. But P.E. is the only class where I've ever seen anything sexist. I've never experienced any sex discrimination myself."

"I've seen it in computer science and math class," another boy volunteers. "Girls aren't pushed to go to higher levels. It's partly the teacher's fault, but a lot of it is peers. Guys say girls can't do these things, so it discourages them."

Two Hispanic boys are sitting together, and one raises his hand. "Usually boys and girls are treated the same, but some teachers seem to joke more when a girl, usually a blond, does something wrong."

"Yeah," the boy next to him agrees. "Sometimes a male teacher will joke with me or other boys about girls being slow to understand technology. I remember once a teacher made a face behind a girl's back while he explained repeatedly how to do something on a computer."

"I've seen those faces," a serious Asian girl says. "In one of my science classes a certain male teacher made rude remarks about my intelligence. He assaulted me verbally, but there are other science teachers—I've only heard of this, I haven't seen it—who favor girls depending on the length of their skirts."

This comment strikes a chord. Several students begin talking at once:

"I know who you mean. I've heard about him."

"No, it's not true. I had him last year, and he never acted like that."

"Well, my best friend had this particular science teacher last year. She didn't understand the material the entire year, but she wore low-cut blouses and escaped the course with a B."

"A lot of people talk about this," a boy volunteers. "If an attractive girl flirts with a male teacher, he'll let her get away with just about anything."

"Those are just rumors," several students call out.

"It is true! It happened to me," another girl says. "In my chemistry class I felt that if I wore a short skirt or a low-cut blouse—low-cut for a fifteen-year-old—I'd get more attention and help. He massaged girls' shoulders while they were taking tests. Believe me, that massage was anything but relaxing. He looked down their blouses and up their skirts. I heard he had to apologize to one girl."

"I really resent these generalizations," another girl says. "Once a final grade of mine was rounded up to an A. The overwhelming reaction from other students, especially males, was, 'What did you do? Wear a short skirt?' The teacher gave it to me because he knew I was working hard and had come in for tutoring often—not because I'm a girl. I think those short skirt stories are a put-down of my and other girls' intelligence."

Almost everyone in the room has something to say about science teachers and short skirts. But the discussion is becoming a free-for-all, so we intervene and try to paraphrase: "It sounds as though at least some of you think there is a sexist culture here."

"Yes!" "Definitely!" Several girls from the all-female table begin talking at once. "The worst place is the lounge," Betsy, a slight girl with long brown hair, says. "There's usually a group of guys who start talking and making rude comments about girls. I would never go in there alone."

"What do they say?" we ask.

"They usually say things like, 'Go fetch!' " She snaps her fingers. "Get us something to eat. Go fetch a Coke." She snaps her fingers again. "Come do sexual favors for us." She turns beet red but is determined to make her point.

Several boys object: "That's just some guys. Most of us don't act like that."

One boy, the only African-American male in the class, says, "It's mostly people wearing these jerseys." He points to the shirt he and several other boys are wearing that signify they are athletes. "I think it's tough to be a girl here. I don't get to say what I want around certain people. You have to choose your words carefully if you're a minority. And here girls are like a minority."

Another boy, also wearing an athletic jersey, objects. "I think a lot of this is blown out of proportion and there's a double standard. I had a calendar with girls in bathing suits in my locker. I was called a male chauvinist pig. But girls have calendars of guys, and nobody says anything."

Another boy agrees. "You don't dare say anything anymore. You can't even tell a girl she looks good without her getting upset. Girls are so sensitive, and boys are running scared."

A teacher appears at the door. "Where's my geoscience class? The period ended a few minutes ago. You're supposed to go to your next class."

"Geoscience!" several students groan. "We need to stay here and talk," Betsy protests. "Geoscience is forever. This is going on now."

The class begins to gather their books. A few students exit quickly through the rear door, but most walk up front. A group of girls gathers around us, reluctant to go. There is so much more they want to say. Several boys stand just outside the female circle and listen.

"This guy asked his girlfriend to go fetch a soda," Betsy says. "And she did it. That's what annoyed me most. I asked why. She said, 'He can talk to me that way. He's my boyfriend.' "

"Guys say things but they don't mean them," another girl says. "It's just when they're in a group they show off."

"That's true," another girl says. "I see certain guys that are friends of mine going around pinching girls' behinds. Some girls just laugh, other girls tell them to stop, but no one ever really gets mad. But I know that a lot of the girls do not appreciate the advances. When it happens, I don't do anything because I feel it is ultimately up to the other females to tell them to stop."

"It's just testosterone poisoning. It'll go away when they grow up."

"It sure is bad now," a blond girl says. "They say things that make me feel awful."

"What things?" we ask.

Several girls begin talking, clearly upset and angry.

"Get down on your knees and give me a blow job."

"I need sex. Come with me now."

"My balls itch. Come over and scratch them."

"It's a joke, but if you don't brush it off, they'll take you seriously."

"What can you do about the boys who say these things? Is there someone you can go to?"

"Oh, no. We could never tell. They would know it was us. They would make our lives miserable," Betsy says.

The girl standing next to Betsy agrees: "You have to just let it go. Just say, 'Sure, whatever' . . ." She tosses her head as if to show the triviality of the boys' behavior. "But I have a friend who freaked out when those guys said gross things. Now they totally hate her here. She doesn't even want to come to school."

Slowly the students file out, late to geoscience. The last one to leave is a boy from the outer circle. He stands stiffly and awkwardly, looking at us through thick glasses. "I want you to know I would never treat a girl like that. I don't think a lot of boys would. But you have to understand there's a fear of being sexual and a fear of being not sexual. It's a mass of confusion."

As we gather up our books and notes and the essays the students have written, an undergraduate from the university who came with us says, "I didn't know what would happen today, but I never expected this."

"We're shocked, too," we admit. "We expected to talk about textbooks and teaching." As we are about to leave the room, Betsy comes back. She is out of breath, pale, and a little shaken.

"You know that story I told you about the boy who told his girl-friend to fetch and get him things? Well, he heard about what I told you. He and his friends—a group of them—were waiting for me at my next class. They blocked me and said, 'Go fetch, Betsy. Do sexual favors for us, Betsy.' They stood in the hallway in a line in front of me so I couldn't get by."

"That's terrible. What can we do to help?"

"Oh, it doesn't bother me. I just take it as a joke." Betsy manages a faint smile.

"It's not funny, and you look upset."

"Yeah, it kind of hurts. But I can handle it. I have friends who'll help me. Besides, it'll die down. This is Friday. By Monday they'll probably have forgotten all about it. At least I hope so."[34]

In 2005, more than fifteen years after Myra and David talked with these students about the hurt and unfairness they experienced in a leading academic high school, Karen and David visited three Maryland high schools to see if conditions were similar. We asked teachers and students to describe any gender issues students faced at their school. A few teachers expressed concern about the constant need to discipline boys for their disruptive behavior. "Boys are definitely punished more often and publicly," a veteran math teacher told us. "Boys are boys. They talk loudly, interrupt, and push each other around to prove they matter," professed a second-year English teacher. For girls, teachers worried most about sexual harassment. A social studies teacher offered this insight, "Sexual harassment is an unspoken threat to female students. Sadly, I think young males see the verbal and physical harassment of girls as a rite of passage." But what surprised us most was that two-thirds of nearly sixty teachers responded that there were no gender issues in their school. None.[35] Had the gendered world of high school faded into history?

Not according to the students. They described their schools as overwhelmed with gender problems. For boys, unfair discipline and the pressures of the traditional male gender role took center stage.

"Boys get labeled as the 'troublemakers' so even when we do what is right we are suspect."

"Trying to get on the football team. If you don't make it, or don't want to make it, the whole town thinks you are a loser."

"Manhood equals athlete, so it's hard when you don't fit the equation."

"To feel secure and accepted, sometimes a guy has to push others around. I'm not saying it's right, but it is expected."

"We can't take like a music class without being called a fag. So I hide my musical talents, like playing Mozart on the keyboard."

"The male role: Act tough. Case closed."

For girls, students cited friendship issues, popularity, sexual harassment, and academic achievement.

"Being excluded or talked about behind your back. Sometimes we get so obsessed with being 'in' that we forget our friends."
"Catfights. Cruel words crush my spirit more than anything."
"School isn't a place to really learn. It's like a reality-TV show with pressure to look like a designer doll, thin, makeup, and tight fashionable clothes."
"With maturing bodies, girls struggle with feeling confident in their bodies while facing the very real threat of sexual harassment in and out of school."
"Strong females are criticized and silenced by teachers and peers."[36]

Why do teachers miss what is so much a part of student life? It is not because they do not care. But teachers, like many of us, are so immersed in daily tasks that much slips under their radar. Focused on increasing test scores and monitoring 150 students every day, there is little time to focus on other issues, such as gender. Researchers term this "gender blindness."[37] School life for students could improve if teachers were better able to "see" and respond to the gender problems that plague schools.

TOUGH GUYS AND WHISPERING GIRLS

In addition to the one hundred high school students, we also asked more than four hundred middle school students to identify the problems they confront in school: aggression topped the lists for both boys and girls in both middle and high school. For boys, aggression was physical, fighting and bullying. For girls, aggression was relational (the kind of aggression teachers rarely notice).[38]

Boys learn aggression well before they begin school. Society teaches boys to project an outward appearance of strength, confidence, and security even when all are lacking. William Pollack calls this bravado the "boy code" or the "mask of masculinity"—a kind of swaggering posture that boys embrace to hide their fears, suppress dependency and vulnerability, and present a stoic, impervious front.[39] When this "boy code" goes to school, discipline problems erupt. Boys adhering to the "boy code" are more likely to harass and be violent, more likely to see such acts as normal, and less likely to take responsibility for their actions. Typically, boys targeted by such behaviors also respond physically, feeding the cycle of violence while underscoring a pervasive homophobia.[40] It is hardly surprising then that when boys take such behaviors to school, they are targeted for swift and strict discipline. But students report that while the discipline is swift, it often misses the mark. In fact, unfair discipline aimed at boys was a major gender injustice cited by students. Girls and boys both agreed that "innocent boys are targeted unfairly by teachers" while less than innocent girls are rarely criticized, or even noticed.

While boys' misbehavior is legend, girls' misbehavior is subtle. Girls practice relational aggression, such as name-calling, spreading rumors and gossip, mocking clothing or looks, deciding not to play or to speak with certain girls (the silent treatment). Such covert emotional bullying behaviors can be delivered in a whisper, which is more difficult to detect than the public aggression of boys.[41] Here is how girls themselves describe it:

"We gossip too much so I can't trust friends."

"Sometimes you get pushed by in-crowd friends not to like someone else because they don't fit in."

"I was horrified beyond belief when I was called a whore by supposed friends. I stayed away from school for a week I was so embarrassed."

Relationships are central to girls who depend on close, intimate friendships. The trust and support of these relationships provide girls with emotional and psychological safety nets. With their friends behind them, girls will do and say things that are remarkably creative and brave and "out of character." Yet girls can be excruciatingly tough on other girls, particularly at early adolescence. They talk behind each other's backs, they tease and torture one another; they police each other's clothing and body size and fight over real or imagined relationships with boys. In so doing they participate in and help to reproduce largely negative views of female relationships as untrustworthy, deceitful, manipulative, and catty. Unlike boys, girls are not encouraged to act out their anger, so uncomfortable feelings often go underground and come out in unhealthy words.[42]

Why do girls act this way? The need to belong and fear of rejection are high on the list. They want to be part of a sort of club, a club of *innies*.[43] Some girls explain they like the excitement and drama of relational aggression, and evidently there is a wide audience for such behavior. Stories about "cruel and nasty girls" have become the centerpiece for magazines, television shows, and popular books. We are now taught how to tame girls, make them nicer, quieter, easier to deal with, sweeter and more pliable. A decade or two ago we feared girls' loss of voice; now we seem to fear that they have found it. Is this a discussion about "mean girls," or a discussion about society's continuing pattern of defining and demeaning females?

SECRETS IN SCHOOL: SEXUAL HARASSMENT

Is a male student's accidentally bumping into a girl in the hallway an example of sexual harassment? Can teachers hug students? Is hand-holding between students illegal? Although educators wrestle every day with helping students feel safe in school, they themselves are often unfamiliar with what constitutes sexual harassment (and to answer the opening questions, none of these examples qualify). Sexual harassment *is* unwelcome behavior of a sexual nature that interferes with a student's or teacher's ability to learn, study, work, or participate in school activities. It includes name-calling, offensive jokes, intimidation by words and actions, insults, unwanted touching, pressure for sexual activity, and sexual assault or rape.

In a boys' bathroom in Minnesota's Duluth Central High School, vulgar graffiti described sophomore Katy Lyle as having intercourse and oral sex with boys and animals. Anonymous phone calls frequently disturbed Katy's home, and she was tormented by teasing in the school building and on the school bus. When she told the principal, Katy had the feeling he was wondering what she had done to deserve these degrading slurs. Although she had never even had a serious boyfriend, she began to wonder, too. Her behavior changed. She became quiet, withdrawn, and cried often. She dreaded going to school.

When Katy's mother found out what was causing the drastic change in her daughter's behavior, she phoned the school immediately. Eighteen months and fifteen complaints later, the graffiti had not gone away. According to Duluth School District attorney Elizabeth Storaasli, the "graffiti was considered a building maintenance problem at the time." It was only when the Lyles spoke with a representative from the Program for Aid to Victims of Sexual Assault that they realized "building maintenance" was the wrong term. What they were dealing with was sexual harassment. Finally, after a formal complaint was filed with the Minnesota Department of Human Rights, the walls were painted and the ugly words were at last removed. This case was prepared for court and eventually reached a settlement that clarified school sexual harassment policies. In 1989, Katy was awarded fifteen thousand dollars for mental anguish, the first time a high school girl received damages for sexual harassment by male students.[44]

Like businesses, schools are required by federal law to distribute and explain their sexual harassment policies to students. Today, seven in ten students say that their school has a policy on sexual harassment, compared to only 26 percent of students in 1993.[45] But sadly, policies do not always translate into practice. In 1980, the Massachusetts Department of Education conducted the nation's first study of sexual harassment in school, and found that girls experienced sexual harassment in both academic and vocational schools.[46] Twelve years later, conversations with 150 girls and boys in California secondary schools revealed that almost every student had watched, experienced, or participated in some form of sexual harassment.[47] More recently, the American Association of University Women published *Hostile Hallways: Bullying, Teasing, and Sexual Harassment in Schools,* a national survey of 2,064 public school students in eighth through eleventh grades. The conclusion: harassment remains rampant in schools across America, with four out of five students—81 percent of girls and 79 percent of boys—reporting that they have experienced some type of unwanted sexual behavior in school. More than two-thirds of students have been the target of sexual jokes and gestures, and 11 percent report being asked to do something sexual other than kissing. Sixty-five percent of girls and 42 percent of boys say they have been grabbed, touched, or pinched in a sexual way. For many students sexual harassment is an ongoing experience: more than one in four students experience it "often." Sexual harassment knows neither ethnic nor racial barriers. Forty-two percent of African-American and 40 percent of Hispanic females report experiencing sexual harassment by grade six or earlier, as compared to 31 percent of white girls. Thirty-three percent of girls and 12 percent of boys were so troubled after being sexually harassed they did not want to talk in class or even go to school.[48]

Unlike workplace harassment, which is more likely to occur behind closed doors, school harassment is generally in public—in hallways, stairwells, the cafeteria, the gym, on the school bus, and even in classrooms.[49] The public nature of this harassment is yet another sign of the sexist attitudes that thrive in schools. For example, even more than college men, high school boys believe that "women secretly want to get raped," that "only bad girls get raped," and that "girls wear provocative clothing to encourage sexual harassment."[50] Within this accepted culture of harassment, boys, particularly those who do not fit the traditional male stereotype, are also victims.[51]

> Michael is slender and not athletically inclined. In the locker room before gym class, his male peers tease him about his weight and clumsiness. Lately, they have taken to calling him "fag," "sissy," and "girl," and snapping their wet towels on his butt. Several times when Michael has opened his locker, he has found a bra and girls' panties with his name written on them. After another boy, forty pounds heavier than Michael, pounced on him on a wrestling mat and simulated sexual intercourse, Michael began to skip gym class. Michael did complain about these events to his physical education teacher, who replied: "Come on Michael, loosen up and take it like a man."

While peer-to-peer sexual harassment is most prevalent, sometimes the perpetrators are educators who are supposed to be safeguarding the school.[52]

> A high school girl in Maine is the target of daily crude and suggestive remarks by her science teacher. When she complains to her guidance counselor and asks to transfer out of the class, the request is denied. She is told to learn to handle it because it will give her practice in dealing with the real world.

> A student is visibly upset after failing a pop quiz in algebra. Her teacher suggests that she repeat the quiz after school in his office. As the math teacher hands her the quiz, he begins stroking the student's hair and whispering that she should be "nice" to him if she really wanted a good grade.

> A high schooler in Maryland was harassed by two boys for six months. After they backed her into a classroom corner and grabbed her breasts, she told the principal. The principal has a "little chat" with the boys, who emerge from the talk laughing and with no punishment.

Sexual harassment charges hurt a school's reputation, so superintendents and school boards frequently suppress such stories, arranging for accused teachers or administrators to leave quietly. But a committed student can end this cycle. In 1986, Christine Franklin was a sophomore at North Gwinnett High School in Georgia. An economics teacher and sports coach, Andrew Hill, began to make inappropriate remarks, asking her about her sexual experiences with her boyfriend and whether she would consider having intercourse with an older man. Three different times he interrupted classes she was attending and requested that she be excused; he took her to a private office and forced her to have intercourse. Although other students complained to teachers and the principal about Hill's behavior, the school did not take action. In fact, the school's bandleader tried to talk Christine out of pursuing the matter because of negative publicity. Finally, Hill resigned with the understanding that all charges against him would be dropped, and the school closed its investigation. But Christine persisted and filed for damages in federal court under Title IX, the law that prohibits sex discrimination in schools. The case eventually reached the Supreme Court. In February 1992, the Court ruled that compensatory damages were available under Title IX. Many hoped that this decision would significantly enhance the power of Title IX law.[53] Subsequent Court rulings proved otherwise.

In cases from Texas and Georgia, a more conservative Supreme Court placed a high hurdle for anyone trying to hold school districts accountable for sexual harassment: students who are sexually harassed by their teachers or peers can sue school districts for money damages only if a district official actually knows of the abuse and does nothing about it, what the Court termed "deliberate indifference."[54] Crossing this high hurdle is exactly what the Davis family had to do.

LaShonda Davis was in the fifth grade at Hubbard Elementary School in Monroe County, Georgia, when she first complained to her teachers that "G.F.," the classmate assigned to the seat next to her, was sexually harassing her. LaShonda and her parents say they asked that her seat be moved, but for months her teachers did nothing to stop the harassment and wouldn't change her seat. LaShonda was not G.F.'s only alleged victim, and when LaShonda and her peers asked to speak with the principal about G.F.'s behavior, a teacher denied the students' request. For the next five months, the boy repeatedly groped LaShonda's breasts and in her genital area, rubbed against her suggestively, and asked for sex. LaShonda's mother continued to ask her daughter's teachers and school principal for help. None came. LaShonda's grades began to fall, and her father found a suicide note she had written. Desperate for help, LaShonda's parents reported the conduct to the sheriff's office. "G.F." pled guilty to sexual battery.

But school still did not feel like a safe place for LaShonda. She felt that her teachers and school leaders had ignored the harassment, sacrificing not only LaShonda's academic learning but also her physical and emotional well-being. The Davis family filed a sexual harassment lawsuit against the school district. In May 1999, nearly seven years after the harassment began, the U.S. Supreme Court agreed that if it were proven that school leaders had shown "deliberate indifference" in their responsibility of protecting LaShonda from the harassment, she would be entitled to monetary damages.[55] Victims frequently avoid discussing sexual harassment, and few have the courage and stamina of the Davis family's quest. Putting such a high burden on the victims of sexual harassment is unlikely to create safer school climates for girls or boys.

GOOD-BYE GIRLHOOD: HELLO LITTLE HOTTIE

It's a powerful message that starts early: "Little Hottie" T-shirts for female toddlers, bump-and-grind dance routines for middle schoolers, "hookup" workshops for high schoolers. Girls are increasingly exposed to products and images that promote looking and acting sexy. The message plays on television and across the Internet. Youth hear the lyrics on music videos, see it in movies, electronic games, and advertisements. Boys, too, face sexualization. Pubescent-looking males have posed provocatively in Calvin Klein ads, and boys with impossibly sculpted abs hawk teen fashion lines. But females are objectified more often: 85 percent of advertisements that sexualize youth depict girls.[56] The impact is devastating. Sexualization has been linked to three of the most common mental health problems of girls and women: eating disorders, low self-esteem, and depression.

Where did this tidal wave of youth sexualization come from? Diane Levin, Wheelock College education professor, traces much of it to the deregulation of children's television in the mid-1980s. "There became a real awareness of how to use gender and appearance and, increasingly, sex to market to children."[57] Television's influence is incontestable. Nearly a quarter of teens say televised sexual content affects their behavior. And sexual content is growing. In 2005, more than three-quarters of prime-time shows on the major broadcast networks included sexual material, up from two-thirds in 1998. Women and girls were twice as likely as men and boys to have their appearance discussed. They also were three times more likely to appear in sleepwear or underwear than their male counterparts.[58]

Who can blame adolescents—girls and boys—for being confused

about sexuality? On the one hand they see a "green light," as they are bombarded with suggestive advertising, graphic movies, bawdy television shows, and sexualized music lyrics. Contraceptives, including the morning-after pill, offer pregnancy safeguards that did not exist just a few years ago. Then students encounter a "red light" of morality standards preaching abstinence and the looming threat of sexually transmitted diseases (STDs). So how do schools respond to this conflict? The short answer is not well. About one-third of schools preach an "abstinence only until marriage" policy, which discourages sex outside of heterosexual marriage. Other schools embrace comprehensive sex education, which stresses abstinence but also includes contraceptive information. This comprehensive approach has proven more effective. Studies show that teens' sexual behavior, pregnancy rates, and rates of contracting STDs usually remain steady or actually increase following completion of abstinence-only courses. Yet, during the Clinton and Bush administrations, the federal government weighed in on the side of abstinence-only sex education, committing nearly $200 million annually.[59] As this book goes to press, we are waiting to see how the Obama administration responds. The failure of abstinence-only school programs suggests that another direction is needed, and Genevieve's story may offer a clue:

> Genevieve has achieved a rare milestone for high school females: she feels good about her body and her style. For this, she credits her mom, who is "very secure with herself and with being smart and being a woman." She also points to a wellness course at school that made her conscious of how women were depicted. "Seeing a culture of degrading women really influenced me to look at things in a new way and to think how we as high school girls react to that. A lot of girls still hold on to that media ideal. I think I've gotten past it. As I've gotten more comfortable with myself and my body, I'm happy not to be trashy. But most girls are still not completely or even semi-comfortable with themselves physically."[60]

Fortunately, parents and teachers can provide an oasis from such sexual pressure by honestly discussing the role not only of sexuality, but also of sexism in our culture. Exploring and discussing the connection between sexy messages and sexuality happens too rarely, but when it does it may provide a path to a healthier childhood. While some parents and teachers take that burden on, most do not. By the end of high school, nearly half of all students have had sex. Black teens are more likely than Hispanic and white teens to engage in sex: two-thirds of black adolescent boys and more than half of black teen girls have had sex compared to more than half of Latinos, 40 percent of Latinas, about 40 percent of white boys and half of white girls. While teens may initially feel liberated by sexual activity, regret soon follows. Research from the National Campaign to Prevent Teen Pregnancy indicates that two-thirds of teens who have had sex regret the choice and wish they had waited.[61] Girls in particular pay a steep price.

Although national teen pregnancy rates have fallen about 35 percent since 1991, with the steepest decline for black girls, rates of teen pregnancy in this nation remain the highest in the industrialized world. Each year 750,000 teenage girls become pregnant, and about one-third of teenage girls will become pregnant at least once by age twenty.[62] Eighty percent of those pregnancies are unintended, and an astonishing four out of five adolescents who become mothers are single parents.[63] Hispanic women begin families earlier, have fewer abortions, and give birth to almost twice as many children as other girls.[64] Rosie Molinary, author of *Hijas Americanas: Beauty, Body Image, and Growing Up Latina,* explains that her own sex education consisted of her father handing her a quarter before her first date and telling her to keep it between her knees until her wedding night. Not counting quarters, Latinas are less likely than their peers to use birth control. Only 12 percent of Hispanic high school females use the pill, compared to 21 percent of girls overall.[65]

Michelle Fine, a psychology professor at the City University of New York, spent a year observing and interviewing students in a New York City public high school, one that serves predominantly low-income blacks and Hispanics from central Harlem.[66] About six months into her study, new pregnancies became evident in the school. The girls who were going to become mothers held highly traditional notions of what it meant to be female. Fine said those planning to carry the babies to term were not girls "whose bodies, dress, and manner evoked sensuality and experience."[67] Instead, she noticed, they were quiet and passive in their classes. In her research field notes, Fine captured a picture of an eleventh grader, Patricia, who represented these forgotten girls: "She says nothing all day in school. She sits perfectly mute. No need to coerce her into silence. She often wears her coat in class. Sometimes she lays her head on her desk. She never disrupts. Never disobeys. Never speaks. And is never identified as a problem."[68] Two-thirds of the students in the school where Fine observed never made it to graduation. Quiet students like Patricia just slipped through the cracks and disappeared.

THE FEMALE DROPOUT

Over a million students drop out each year, a national problem most associate with boys. In fact, one in three boys, often black, Hispanic, and Native American boys, will fail to graduate from high school in four years. While media attention focuses on such boys, the female dropout is far less visible. Yet, almost half of all dropouts are girls. *When Girls Don't Graduate, We All Fail,* a 2007 report issued by the National Women's Law Center, finds that girls of color are most at risk, with half of Native American girls, and about 40 percent of black and Hispanic girls failing to graduate each year.[69] When girls leave, they rarely return to earn their high school diploma or general equivalency diploma (GED).[70]

There are many reasons that girls and boys drop out—academic failure, boredom, the need to earn money, or to care for family members at home, but one factor unique for girls is pregnancy. Three out of five mothers who have a child before age eighteen will not finish high school.[71] While high school dropouts typically earn less, the costs for girls are especially high. More than 60 percent of single mothers raise their children in poverty.[72] In 2006, women without a high school diploma earned little more than $15,500 for the year, $9,100 less than male dropouts and $6,000 less than women with a high school diploma. A female who drops out of high school will earn sixty-three cents for every dollar earned by a male dropout.[73]

Many girls whose academic options dwindle see a baby as bringing purpose to their lives. Yet adolescent girls searching for their identity are hard-pressed to attend to the daily needs of a young child. As their children grow older, they, too, may exhibit behavior and learning problems. Teens with absent or uninvolved fathers are also likely to engage in earlier sexual activity and become pregnant.[74] By the time their daughters reach adolescence, this next generation of teenage girls is primed to continue the cycle of pregnancy, dropout, and poverty.[75]

FIELD OF BROKEN DREAMS

The principal of an Indiana high school obviously enjoyed showing off his school. He took Myra and David on a tour of the new computer center, the science labs, and a vocational training area. Then he began to smile broadly.

"This is our jewel," he said.

They turned a corner, he opened a door, and they entered the gym. It was enormous. Thousands of seats terraced up all sides, and the ceiling was at least four stories high. The gym was almost as big as the entire rest of the school.

"It's incredible, but why so large?" Myra and David asked.

"Intimidation," the principal responded.

"Intimidation?"

"When the other teams come here, to this small town, they expect a small gym. This place intimidates the hell out of them. The whole town comes out and screams for our boys. This is the town's entertainment center, our sports cathedral."

Studies show that sports is a focal point of school life and growing up male. As we mentioned earlier, when we asked more than four hundred middle and one hundred high school students to describe the best thing about being a boy, they needed only one word: *sports*.[76] A large sign in the hallway of a Maine middle school captures the omnipresence of sports, a visible reminder of the connection between athletics and masculinity:

Feel like being a State Champ—
Join the Boys' Track Team and
Dominate.
Or maybe you would rather sit on the couch and become *fat* and *lazy*. Maybe you don't have the berries to work and win. We're looking for a *few good men*.

Aggression, repressed in the classroom, is harnessed by coaches, put to work on the athletic field, and released against the opposing team. In a middle school study, interviews with students showed how this happens. One football team member who was especially aggressive described how physical violence pleased his coach: "Yeah . . . I really socked that guy. Man, I threw him down on the concrete. Did you hear Coach James yelling 'Way to go, Orville?' " Another boy complained about a teammate who was trying to pick a fight. "Knock his socks off in practice" was the coach's advice.[77] So the playing field becomes a legitimate arena not only for competition, but also for violence.

Boys—and girls—endure pain and suffer through long hours of practice because of the tantalizing awards sports offers: self-esteem, leadership, teamwork, and the satisfaction that comes from playing hard and well.

A select few move from satisfaction to stardom. Even in the elementary grades, talented athletes rise to the top of the popularity charts. But boys who fumble the ball are not so fortunate. A group of researchers observed and interviewed children in two elementary schools for three years. In both schools the most popular boy in each grade was also the best athlete. Those who were clumsy and awkward were picked on, ridiculed, and called "fag" and other names suggesting they were more like girls than boys. Travis, a fifth-grade student, described Wren, an unathletic class-mate, as "a nerd. He's short and his ears stick out." Nikko said about Wren: "When he sits in his chair, he crosses one leg over the other and curls the toe around his calf, so it's double-crossed. . . . It looks so faggy with his 'girly' shoes."[78]

Boys like Wren become school pariahs and isolates. But those who are tough and good at sports achieve social success, sometimes in spite of themselves. According to fifth grader Nick, "Craig is sort of mean, but he's really good at sports, so he's popular." And Ben said, "Everybody wants to be friends with Gabe, even though he makes fun of most of them all the time. But they still all want to pick him for their team and have him be friends with them because he's a good athlete, even though he brags a lot about it. He's popular."[79]

Every boy's dream of being a sports star can turn into a nightmare, especially the least athletic. Men in our workshops remember the humil-iation of failing to measure up:

> I will never forget gym class in high school. I looked down when they picked the teams. I used to imagine I was somewhere else, anywhere but this place of rejection. The teacher picked the two best players to be the captains. Then they picked the members of their teams. The best boys got picked first, then the average, then the worst. By the time they got to the worst players, the ones they picked last, I just wanted the choosing to be over. When they came to me, they would sometimes choose nobody instead. One would say, "You can have him." Then the other would say, "No, I don't want him. You take him." The argument would go on for what seemed like infinity.

Others describe exerting themselves beyond reason and good health to fulfill the male sports role:

> When I was in the eighth grade, I attended a middle school just outside New York City. We all took tests of strength, and almost everyone beat

me, even some girls. I went to a health club and began working out. Weight training became a five-year obsession. I always had to be bigger and stronger than everyone, no matter how much I hurt myself. I'm twenty years old now. I can't lift anymore, I can't play tennis or racquetball anymore. I can't throw a ball, and I have worse joints than most fifty- or sixty-year-olds. But at least I was stronger than those kids in my high school gym class.

For most of this century, schools have struggled to balance academics and athletics. Some high schools and colleges build status and reputation on the backs of teams who climb into the national rankings; and for athletes who might never otherwise see the inside of a college classroom, physical talent becomes the magic key to a college degree. But lack of academic preparation can be the Achilles heel of an otherwise promising athlete. Seduced by their star status, many high school athletes lose touch with reality and dribble away the future.

LEVELING THE PLAYING FIELD

Despite such missteps, high school boys' sports remain the most popular and prestigious of all school-sponsored activities. More than 4.3 million boys engage in a high school sport today.[80] The athletic tradition is that sports builds leadership, courage, self-confidence, and loyalty, not to mention stamina and the ability to handle winning and losing. These are the traits associated with boys; female athletics have often been played in the shadows. Title IX changed that.

As mentioned in chapter 2, Title IX is a federal law that bars sex discrimination in most educational areas, but it is best known for changing the athletic playing field. Title IX requires schools to show that they meet the athletic needs of female students, that they are expanding to meet those needs, or that organized sports roughly reflect the proportions of male and female students in the school. It is the nation's educational promise that the talents of all its citizens—girls and boys—will not be restricted by discrimination.

In a sense, Title IX is like the movie *Field of Dreams*—it is a hope that if you build fields and athletic opportunities, girls will come. And it worked. In 1972, before Title IX, fewer than three hundred thousand high school girls played competitive sports; today, three million girls compete.[81] But where a girl lives exerts a major influence on her athletic opportunities. According to the Women's Sports Foundation, girls at high schools in New Hampshire, Pennsylvania, Maine, Vermont, and Minnesota fare the best. In these states there is less than a 3 percent gap between the number of girls enrolled in school and their athletic participation. At the other end of the spectrum, the gap is over 15 percent in Alabama, Louisiana, the District of Columbia, and Tennessee.[82]

Girls and boys who play sports are more confident and have higher self-esteem and better body images. Female athletes are less likely to be involved in drugs or unwanted pregnancy and are more likely to graduate from high school. One study found that high school female athletes were 73 percent more likely to go on to earn a bachelor's degree compared to nonathletes. Among females from low socioeconomic backgrounds, high school athletes were 40 percent more likely to earn a college degree. More than four out of five executive businesswomen played sports growing up and the vast majority say the lessons learned on the playing field contributed to their success in the boardroom.[83]

Despite these positive results, female athletic programs still lag behind males'. Male high school athletes outnumber female athletes by more than a million, and male athletic participation is now growing at twice the rate of females. Although girls make up 49 percent of the students in the nation's high schools, they receive only 41 percent of the opportunities to play sports.[84] Girls' teams typically have less visibility and status than male teams, and are often denied the same benefits, such as groomed fields, financial support, and publicity. High schools currently are not required to report athletic budgets for boys' and girls' teams, but there is little doubt that boys' programs score big. We frequently receive emails from parents and students concerned about unfair, even dangerous playing conditions for girls' teams. Here are a few of the stories about the uneven playing field:

> In one school district the girls' field hockey team practiced on a poorly maintained field with broken glass, the same field deemed unsafe for the football team.

> Another school constructed a state-of-the-art baseball field for the boys, a field large enough for both the juniors and seniors to practice and play. There were dugouts, generous seating, lockers, a storage room, and a public address system. The girls, on the other hand, had no school field at all. They were told to share a field owned by a local church, without any of the facilities enjoyed by the males.

We are not alone in receiving such stories. The National Women's Law Center has documented the following:

In one western Pennsylvania school, for every dollar the school board spent on sports, girls received only a dime. The district also spent more on the football team than it did to maintain its school buildings.[85]

Shortly before varsity ice hockey tryouts at a Massachusetts high school, boys on the varsity team verbally harassed a girl who had played JV boys' ice hockey and kicked her feet out from under her while she was still on crutches from ankle surgery. The school took no action against the boys on the varsity team.[86]

These are not the stories Americans want to hear. In a 2007 survey of one thousand men and women, eight out of ten supported Title IX and equity in sports, and 9 out of 10 supported taking action in cases of unequal treatment.[87] But schools routinely violate Title IX, and many school administrators are unaware of what the law requires. The federal government does little to enforce the law these days, so it is up to individuals to press for fairness.

Teenager Christine Boehm played field hockey in a Virginia high school for four years. She loved playing the game. But there was a problem.

I saw that the school treated male athletes better, as if they counted more. My teammates and I used faded cotton T-shirts as game jerseys and had no locker room to change in before games. The field was so rough that a referee even questioned the safety of playing a league game on it. Meanwhile, football players and other male athletes had nice jerseys, a newly renovated field, and a nicely equipped locker room with television and space for multiple teams.

It just didn't seem right, so I researched Title IX and contacted the National Women's Law Center. After months of negotiation, my school did the right thing by improving the conditions for female athletes. The school agreed to improve the fields and facilities, ensure that the male and female athletes had equal locker room space, and display girls' trophies and athletic schedules in an equal manner. The process taught me that standing up and demanding what's right not only brings results, but also is very rewarding.[88]

Roderick Jackson also stood up. He coached the girls' basketball team at Ensley High School in Birmingham, Alabama. His players worked hard, won many games, but were forced to play their games in the old gym with wooden backboards, bent rims, and no heat. The boys played in a new gym and rode a bus for travel to away games. The girls had to carpool. The girls' team was denied any of the money the city donated to the school athletics program, and unlike the boys, their team could not keep money earned during games from ticket sales and concession stands.

> [M]y girls had no one else to stand up for them. So I spoke to the school Athletic Director, the Principal, the Athletics Director, the Director of High Schools in Birmingham, and eventually, the Deputy Superintendent of Instruction, who is the second in command of the system. I was shocked that no one seemed to care. Not only did they not fix the problems—instead, they fired me from my coaching job for speaking up.[89]

Jackson went to court to try to get his job back and level the playing field. In 2005, his case made it all the way to the United States Supreme Court. Since Title IX protects people who speak out about gender inequities in school, the Court ruled that Jackson could sue for the retaliation. Coach Jackson got his job back, and the school district promised to create equal opportunities for all its athletes.

SEGREGATED CAREERS

Rebecca's friends nicknamed her "computer whiz" after she installed memory chips and a CD burner into her family's computer. Her high school offers a career education track, and Rebecca decided to explore at Career Day her options as a computer technician. She was disappointed, however, when speakers and materials promoted nursing and child care as good careers for females and computer repair and electrical engineering as male endeavors. She now wonders if her goal is unrealistic.

Forty years ago, girls and women were routinely directed into traditionally female occupations—nurse, secretary, teacher, and homemaker.

While "male only" or "female only" labels are now gone, students get the message even without the labels.

The National Women's Law Center recently examined career education courses in twelve states—Arizona, California, Florida, Illinois, Maryland, Massachusetts, Michigan, Mississippi, Missouri, New Jersey, North Carolina, and Washington. Examining the data was like traveling back in time. In 1977, girls made up 14 percent of students in trade and industrial courses. Today, girls represent 15 percent of students taking classes in traditionally male, higher-paying fields such as carpentry, automotive, masonry, and welding. For example, according to the NWLC report, in 2004, a single girl was studying electrical engineering in a Maryland high school technical program. In New Jersey, girls represented 2 percent of students studying to be automotive technicians. Out of 225 students enrolled in agricultural mechanics in Michigan, only six were female. No girls were enrolled in masonry courses in Missouri or electrician courses in Illinois. Massachusetts's courses in health-care services were 93 percent female. Nationally, the picture is only slightly better: more than 85 percent of females are clustered in traditional courses such as cosmetology, child care, medical assistant, health aide, and nursing. The dollars-and-cents difference is startling. Girls who take up traditionally female occupations can expect to earn half—or less—of what they could make in traditional male fields.[90]

Girls are discouraged from pursuing these lucrative traditionally male fields in a variety of subtle—and not so subtle—ways. A high school student in Pennsylvania was told by her classmates that girls were not supposed to take masonry classes; a young woman in an air-conditioning repair program in Illinois described how she was sexually harassed by her fellow students while her male teachers did nothing to stop them, and sometimes joined in; a counselor in Maine discouraged girls from nontraditional programs because "young ladies don't like to do the dirty or heavy work"; a teacher in Michigan would only allow female students to operate equipment if they had a male student supervising them; and a male student in a computer class in Hawaii created computer-generated, pornographic pictures of a female classmate and circulated them in class.[91]

In recent decades, national emphasis has been put on science, math, engineering, and computer science careers. American students have been encouraged to excel in these subjects to help the United States compete in a global economy. But here, too, the forces of sexism are powerful. For example, in a classic experiment used periodically for about six decades, researchers have been asking students to "draw a scientist." In the 1950s high school students uniformly saw a scientist as a middle-aged or older man wearing glasses and a white coat and working alone in a lab. Sixty years later, little had changed. In a recent "draw-a-scientist" study, the drawings of thirty-nine third graders portrayed thirty-one men and eight women. One boy added a bubble quote for his male scientist that said, "I'm crazy." Another boy wrote, "My scientist makes all kinds of poisons. He is a weird person." Still another caption on the bottom of a drawing said, "Dr. Strangemind," and on the back the student explained, "He does strange things like blow up things and other crazy stuff." Many of the children described their scientist as "blowing things up," "acting crazy" or "goofy," or working with "a lot of potions."[92] These third graders have already internalized the stereotyped image of the mad, male scientist, expressing his frustrations with violence.

As students mature and advance through school, we might expect that such stereotypes would fade away. They don't. A "draw-a-scientist" study of more than 1,500 students in grades K–8 found that students' drawings become *more* stereotypical with age. Students saw scientists as weird, sinister, crazy, nerdy—the very images adolescent girls, worried about appearance and popularity, want to avoid at all costs.[93]

We were curious how today's high schoolers would "draw a scientist." So was Natalie, one of Karen's graduate students teaching in a District of Columbia charter school. She decided to give the assignment to her eleventh graders. Using colored pencils, chalk, and the trusty number 2 pencil, the students diligently made their sketches, and then hung them throughout the room. The twenty-seven drawings creatively captured men with wire-rimmed glasses and white wispy hair working with beakers, Bunsen burners, and long equations. Two scientists were black. One was Asian. Not one was a woman.

> Natalie scanned the walls with surprise. "Who is missing?"
>
> Silence. Perplexed students shifted in their seats and carefully examined the sketches.
>
> A quiet voice suggested, "Women? I thought about Barbara McClintock but she didn't seem real enough."

Natalie saw the invisibility of women as one of those "teachable moments" and challenged students to name as many women scientists as they could.

"Marie Curie."

"The black astronaut, Mae Jemison."

"Barbara McClintock. Oops. We already said her."

Then silence. These eleventh graders could name only three women scientists. (How many of us can name more?)

Sadly, the accomplishments of women in math, science, and technology are largely hidden. Consider Elizabeth Blackwell, who overcame unbelievable pressures to attend and succeed in medical school; or Rachel Carson, an environmentalist who alerted the world to the dangers of pesticides and herbicides; or noted astronomer Maria Mitchell, who explained, "We especially need imagination in science. It is not all mathematics, nor all logic, but is somewhat beauty and poetry." Yet the traditional science stereotype persists. Students who are not white and male struggle to see themselves as scientific, much less understand the cultural barriers that have kept women and minorities out of science.

Like Natalie, a number of teachers encourage girls' participation in math and science classes, often with amazing success. Today girls are the majority in biology, chemistry, algebra, and precalculus courses, an astonishing step forward, although they still lag behind boys in calculus, physics, and computer science. But something happens along the way to undo girls' progress, to derail these careers. The majority of females who took the 2007 SAT said they planned to work in the social sciences, such as psychology, sociology, teaching, political science, and anthropology. In large numbers, they turned away from careers in engineering, the physical or computer sciences.[94] Girls struggle to understand the usefulness of math, science, and technology or they feel uncomfortable with these subjects. Some say these courses make them feel stupid.[95] Clearly, something is going on to short-circuit girls.

Science educator Janice Koch described the subtle process of how girls get turned off science:

> The squeamishness of girls in the science lab is one example of cultural stereotyping that limits the science potential of many females. . . . A former student explained in a familiar story that she loved to dissect frogs in seventh grade, but she screamed the entire time so that the boys would think she was acting like a girl. Herein lies the challenge—to present how acting like a girl means acting scientific.[96]

Math, science, and computer technology, especially at the advanced level, engulf girls in masculine surroundings.[97] "While there is no sign on the computer room door announcing NO GIRLS ALLOWED," says Jo Sanders, coauthor of *The Neuter Computer,* "females place it there mentally themselves." After years of watching the male-computer connection, girls feel they don't belong. But when parents and teachers make special efforts to involve female students, they find converts. "Subtlety does not work," says Sanders. "You have to transmit the message loud and clear that girls and computers belong together." She advocates organizing girls' computer committees and clubs and scheduling special times for girls to use the computer room. In schools where Sanders and her colleagues have intervened, female computer use has skyrocketed, sometimes surpassing that of boys.[98]

Other teachers and researchers are also finding that simple changes can make a world of difference. Girls become more confident when they are allowed to read about and experiment at home before discussing and doing a demonstration in class; this technique puts them on an even footing and lets them catch up with science lessons that males often learn outside school. Collaborative work and "interest enhancers" (puzzles, and mystery and fantasy devices) also involve girls. When teachers bring women who work as scientists into the classroom, the impact is powerful and shows girls that science also belongs to them. And when teachers humanize science, showing that it is relevant and accessible, boys like it better, too.[99]

Although constructive teaching strategies like these are now available, they have reached only a small audience.[100] A major study published in 1990 underscored the prevalence of inequitable instruction. Gail Jones and Jack Wheatley analyzed thirty physical science and thirty chemistry classes, a total of 1,332 students. They found that boys spoke more often and in louder, more confident tones. In contrast, girls received less praise and appeared to be "self-conscious and quiet."[101] Another study published ten years later found that seven out of ten male teachers were more likely to attribute boys' success in technology to talent, while dismissing girls' success as due solely to luck or diligence.[102] Such studies offer us a window into today's classrooms, as do the stories that girls share.

I have a teacher I respect so much because he is smart. When he asks a question, he challenges my mind. I thought he would respect my intelligence, too, but he calls me the class "model" and says things like,

"What music are you listening to? Is there a short circuit up there?" It's like he's trying to make me think I'm an airhead.

People are always surprised to learn I have a 4.0 and I'm a National Merit Finalist. Their image of me is "that *blond* girl who used to go out with Scott." Why can't they understand there's more to me?

The attitudes that keep females from engaging in math, science, and computer technology are the same attitudes that for decades kept women from voting, flying airplanes, playing professional sports, and holding political office. As in countless other activities, women have shown that they are not only capable of pursuing these endeavors, they can excel at them.

Expecting the best from every student means recognizing the unique intellectual energy each boy and girl brings to the world. The questions they ask along the way may open the doors to discoveries that will change all our lives.

SUCCEEDING AT FAIRNESS:
SUGGESTIONS FOR STUDENTS, PARENTS, AND TEACHERS

1. *Media Literacy:* When we think of the curriculum, we think of schools. That's way too limiting. Children learn from magazine ads, television shows, movies, MTV, in short, a pervasive mass media curriculum. This curriculum too often propagates powerful misconceptions about gender, gendered aggression, and sex role stereotypes. Adolescents, in the process of identity formation, are particularly vulnerable to such messages. Teachers and parents should confront these images directly. Schools can offer courses in media literacy. Parents can point out destructive media messages. Students themselves can be taught to analyze and deflect the media's sexist messages, enabling them to distinguish myth from reality, healthy messages from exploitive ones, and to penetrate the subtle and not-so-subtle techniques of an increasingly sophisticated media. (Visit the PBS website for ideas on how to integrate media literacy throughout the curriculum: www.pbs.org/teachersource/media_lit/media_lit.shtm.)

2. *Adults Actually Matter:* Parents and teachers need to realize that although it is sometimes difficult to believe, they actually do influence

adolescents. Adult words and behaviors can go a long way to promote constructive and humane views of the world. Parents who constantly focus on a daughter's looks over her other qualities, who discuss appearance and clothes and weight on a regular basis, are really saying that their daughter's value is on her outside, on appearance rather than substance. Parents who put boys in tight, stereotyped career boxes cut them off from many of life's options such as teaching and nursing. Boys who are artistic rather than athletic need to feel safe at home and at school. Applauding a boy's act of kindness and compassion, or a unique gift or talent, rather than focusing only on stereotypic male areas of achievement, is a way adults can help all boys touch their inner humanity. Parents and teachers who focus on human qualities, on how children treat one another, on how the world can become a better place, on opening all careers to everyone, are saying that each child is unique. Such adult behaviors and comments counter the limiting gender messages that permeate society. And when boys and girls hear the other sex described in terms of their human and individual strengths, instead of by a stereotypical gender yardstick, they learn important lessons that can help undo gender stereotyping.

3. *Healthy Behaviors:* Our society promotes some destructive behaviors for both boys and girls. Males looking at professional athletes might conclude that steroids are the shortcut to manliness and sports success. Girls, emulating fashion models, may be led to believe that thinness is the fast lane to beauty and popularity. Teachers and parents need to do better at monitoring the health habits of children. Are girls and boys not only being served healthy meals, but also eating them—and then digesting them? If an adolescent boy develops highly accentuated and defined muscles, do parents take pride, or look a bit deeper to make certain that steroids are not at the root? Students involved in unhealthy eating and substance abuse sometimes wonder how adults have missed these behaviors. And for too many adults, such behaviors are simply not even on their radar screens.

4. *Careers:* Educators and parents need to take affirmative steps if children are to consider careers without gender blinders. Bringing role models into class or taking field trips for students to visit work sites may be a useful strategy. Parents and teachers should look for biographies that tell about individuals who made a difference and broke gender (or race, ethnic, or other) barriers in their fields. Such biographies may be read to children from picture books for the very young, and then read by chil-

dren as they get older. Librarians can be a great source of information for such books.

Resources

Perfect Girls, Starving Daughters: The Frightening New Normalcy of Hating Your Body, by Courtney E. Martin
    A startling and thought-provoking look at how the latest generation of girls and young women is exhibiting their fear of fat.

Born to Buy: The Commercialized Child and the New Consumer Culture, by Juliet Schor
    Drawing on a significant body of research, including interviews with everyone from advertising executives to the kids themselves, Juliet Schor exposes a well of consumerism and argues that we need to take steps to decommercialize childhood. She lays out several intriguing ideas for how to do so.

Girlfighting, by Lyn Mikel Brown
    Through interviews with more than four hundred girls of diverse racial, economic, and geographic backgrounds, Lyn Mikel Brown chronicles the labyrinthine journey girls take from direct and outspoken children who like and trust other girls, to distrusting and competitive young women. Brown wants us to change things for girls, and suggests ways we can help girls feel strong and supportive of one another.

Skinny Boy: A Young Man's Battle and Triumph over Anorexia, by Gary Grahl
    The author had baseball abilities that attracted the attention of the big leagues, until a shaming inner voice convinced him that he needed to be thinner, leading to an out-of-control compulsion to exercise and starve himself. Challenging the assumption that anorexia is a females-only issue, this book offers therapists, sufferers, and their families powerful tools to help them triumph over this life and death battle.

For additional resources, see *Still Failing at Fairness*'s page on www.simon andschuster.com.

CHAPTER 6

Tests, Grades,
and the Boys' Crisis

Remember test day? Not any test day, the BIG one, the one that kept you up half the night. When morning finally arrived, you found that you had a new companion: fear. Perhaps fear's friends headache and tummy ache arrived as well. You were not alone; everyone seemed frightened, everyone except that know-it-all kid with the annoying smile whose one purpose in life was to make everyone else insecure.

Was your BIG test the one for admission to a selective program, a prestigious college, or perhaps graduate school? Big tests often have CAPITAL letters, such as SAT, ACT or GRE. Are they nameless for a reason, like the witness protection program? Did you remember to bring a handful of sharpened number 2 pencils? (Do number 1 pencils even exist?) Perhaps you anted-up the money for an expensive test-prep book, one that had practice exams for you to do. On test day you discovered that none of the practice tests even remotely resembled the real one. Perhaps you invested in a private test preparation course that all but guaranteed you would earn one hundred more points with tricks like "when clueless, select option C."

For most of us, BIG test day is burned into our memories. For females, it can be a third-degree burn. After years of hard work, girls far more than boys are likely to gasp when they see those test scores. What happened?

Although boys generally, and Asian and white boys in particular, do quite well on these high-pressure tests, boys as a group do not do that well in school. Boys are more likely to get into trouble, more likely not to do their assignments well or on time or at all, and not surprisingly, earn lower school grades. From grade school to graduate school, report cards remind males that they are not doing as well as females. Why do boys score higher on high-stakes tests but receive lower grades? Why do girls receive higher grades but score lower on high-stakes tests?

Grades and test scores highlight a perplexing school paradox: How do we best measure academic performance: by test scores, or school grades? In this chapter, we shall try to unravel this puzzle. Later, we shall take a close and critical look at the claims that boys are in crises, but let's begin by putting test day in perspective.

OUR TEST CULTURE—OR "WHATJAGET?"

Remember that all too familiar nightmare? You go to school in a great mood and wonder why everyone in the class looks glum. And then the teacher starts distributing the test. Test! Oh my, how could you forget the test! And you didn't even study. Guess what? Your test is waiting. Find a sheet of paper, or outline your responses right on the pages below. Take a deep breath, and did we mention?—penmanship counts. Good luck!

Grammar

1. Give nine rules for the use of Capital Letters.
2. Define Verse, Stanza, and Paragraph.
3. What are the Principal Parts of a verb? Give Principal Parts of do, lie, lay, and run.

Arithmetic

1. District No. 33 has a valuation of $35,000. What is the necessary levy to carry on a school seven months at $50 per month, and have $104 for incidentals?
2. What is the cost of a square farm at $15 per acre, the distance around which is 640 rods?

U.S. History

1. Give the epochs into which U.S. History is divided.
2. Tell what you can of the history of Kansas.
3. Describe three of the most prominent battles of the Rebellion.

Orthography

1. What are the following, and give examples of each: Trigraph, sub-vocals, diphthong, cognate letters, linguals?
2. Give four substitutes for caret "u."

3. Mark diacritically and divide into syllables the following, and name the sign that indicates the sound: card, ball, mercy, sir, odd, cell, rise, blood, fare, last.

Geography

1. Name and describe the following: Monrovia, Odessa, Denver, Manitoba, Helena, Yukon, St. Helena, Juan Fernandez, Aspinwall, and Orinoco.
2. Name all the republics of Europe and give capital of each.
3. Describe the movements of the earth. Give inclination of the earth.

Physiology

1. How does nutrition reach the circulation?
2. What is the function of the liver? Of the kidneys?
3. Give some general directions that you think would be beneficial to preserve the human body in a state of health.

How did you do? Ridiculously difficult test, right? Well, if you bombed it, don't feel too badly; few of today's Ph.D.s would pass. Then how do you explain that more than a century ago, on April 13, 1895, to be precise, successfully answering these questions was necessary for students to graduate from school—elementary school?[1] This is an eighth-grade test. Perhaps the critics are right and today's schools are so weak that an eighth grader a century ago knew more than today's college graduates. Or perhaps schools in Salina, Kansas (where this test was required), are tougher than the school you attended.

When we teach our college classes, we use this test. First, we ask our students to try to answer the test questions. They struggle. We tell them that they can work as teams. They struggle. We do not ask our students to memorize these answers, because for most of us, both the questions and answers are pretty irrelevant. We want our students to consider what the test means. Why were these questions and answers considered so important more than a century ago? Why was memorizing this information necessary to graduate from elementary school in Salina, Kansas? This test is a gift, but for none of the reasons many suspect. The test sparks thinking about our current testing culture and begins a discussion of what's worth knowing.

Finally, we tell our students that they can use the Internet, and only then do they begin to answer the questions. Is using the Internet cheating? Some traditionalists might think so, but it is a powerful reminder of what skills are actually needed in the twenty-first century, skills such as retrieving and synthesizing information, and why much of today's memorization in school may not be wise. A century from now, how many people will look back on the tests of today we see as so critical, and wonder "What were they thinking?" Or perhaps, "Were they thinking?" How much of today's "critical" information will one day become a curious, even humorous, footnote to history?

Thanks to No Child Left Behind, the federal law that mandates testing to measure students, teachers, and schools, many Americans now equate test scores with learning. In our "high-stakes tests culture," one test can determine whether a student will graduate, or a school will be closed, or a principal or teacher will be rewarded with extra pay—or terminated. We have placed the nation's children and schools in the hands of a massive testing industry, and assumed that high test scores equal learning. Such tests are little more than a snapshot in time of how a student responds to one test, on one day, in a particular subject. Often the scores confirm what we already know: poor students in poor schools are struggling, and wealthier students in wealthier communities are not. For this we need a test? Thinking No Child Left Behind scores reflect wisdom or insight or predict future contributions to society is just blowing bubbles.

BLOWING BUBBLES

Five-year-old Jessica came home from kindergarten smiling broadly, eager to share her latest achievements. Her mother, an attorney, was curious:

"What did you do in school today?"

"I learned to bubble."

"You blew bubbles? Did you have fun?"

"I didn't blow bubbles. I bubbled. I practiced filling in the little test bubbles with my pencil. You know, not going outside the lines and coloring in the whole bubble."

Jessica attends a school in Washington, D.C., but her lesson could have occurred in almost any school in America. The typical student "bubbles" at least three times every year. Some students undergo as many as twelve standardized tests annually, and each year more states and the federal government require still more tests, with a great deal riding on the results. And when the bubbles burst, the damage can be long lasting.

There is something mesmerizing about a precise test score. "Your score was 618 on the math, and 521 on the verbal. Total score is 1,139." Not 1,138 or 1,140, but just what the test says: 1,139. And that score will be sent to all the schools you apply to and will become part of your life history. Such scores are frighteningly precise, with little room for doubt. Too many of us confuse numbers with objectivity, and obsess over such scores. Our general rule is the higher the score, the greater the obsession. A 700 in the SAT math section is news shared with friends and strangers, an 800 makes a reputation, while a 432 becomes a skeleton in the family closet. If the score is high enough, a club is formed. Really. Ever hear of Mensa, an organization for those scoring in the top 2 percent on IQ tests? (We weren't invited, either.) Test scores create a hierarchy of winners and losers and can reduce learning to a contest.

But tests themselves are neither good nor bad; the key is how they are used. For example, tests can help educators by identifying special needs or gifted students, targeting individual aptitudes and clarifying vocational interests. Tests can also diagnose the skills and information particular students are lacking, helping teachers to repair those deficits as well. Teachers use tests to evaluate their own effectiveness, to see what topics students have, and have not, learned. With this information, a teacher can restructure and reteach the lesson, test again, and make certain the material is mastered. Teacher-made tests along with student projects, classroom participation, portfolios, reports, and the like can offer a more complete picture of a student's academic strengths and weaknesses. These formative tests help shape instruction and improve learning.

There are also standardized tests given to thousands of students across the nation (and sometimes internationally) to compare performance in different schools, states, and countries. Have you ever taken the Iowa Test of Basic Skills, or the National Assessment of Educational Progress, or the California Basic Educational Skills Test? Remember your score? Probably not, since these tests had little or no effect on your life. But these exams offer insights into how well different groups, such as girls and boys, are doing in school.

The best known of these standardized tests is the National Assessment of Educational Progress (NAEP). Often called the "Nation's Report Card," the NAEP has been taking academic snapshots of America's students since 1969. Funded by the federal government, the National Assessment tests are given in the fourth, eighth, and twelfth grades in several subjects, and are significant because the NAEP offers information on a sample of all students, not just those going to college. Students taking this test do not enroll in prep courses, do not buy test-prep books, and do not have teachers "teaching to the test." NAEP scores offer a clearer insight than most tests into just how well American students are doing.

The gender trends on the NAEP have persisted for decades. Girls begin school looking like the favored sex, but as they go through school, they lose ground. Most people are aware of girls' verbal advantage, their reading and writing skills, but few realize that in the early years, girls also surpass boys in math and civics, tie boys in history, but trail them in science. The NAEP results for the twelfth grade tell a different story. Girls still hold a reading and civics advantage, but now boys are ahead in math, science, history, and economics. Girls lose ground and the result is a familiar picture: verbal advantages for girls; the math, science, and social science advantages for boys. Actually, there is more to it than that.[2]

The media pounds the public with stories about gender differences. Gender differences make headlines; similarities do not. In reality, the NAEP reveals more similarities than differences. NAEP is scored on a 300-point system, and the differences between male and female average scores in almost all subjects are 4 points or less, very minor indeed. The one exception is older boys' reading scores which by the twelfth grade lag behind girls by 10–14 points. Reading is an issue for boys, especially older boys, but the differences between the genders in math, science, history, and other subjects is all but nonexistent. The bigger test gaps are elsewhere, imbedded in class, race, and ethnicity. In twelfth-grade reading scores, white students score 14 points higher than Native Americans, 21 points higher than Hispanics, and 26 points higher than African Americans, all greater than the largest gender gap. Between English language learners and English-speaking students, the twelfth-grade reading gap is 41 points, or more than three times greater than the reading gender gap. In mathematics, Asians rise to the top and score 6 points higher than whites, 29 points higher than American Indians, 30 points higher than Hispanics, and 36 points higher than African Americans. These differences are also more dramatic than the gender gap. Even geography trumps gender. Students in the Northeast and Midwest consistently score 5 to 11 points higher than those in the West and South, but this regional achievement gap rarely makes the news.

In terms of gender, the NAEP raises some questions: Why does the public perceive large gender gaps, when the NAEP reports small ones? Why are girls slightly ahead at the beginning of school, yet slightly behind at graduation? Why does a test called "the Nation's Report Card" award boys and girls fairly equal scores, while actual school report cards give girls higher grades? Why do males and females score similarly on the

NAEP, while males outperform females on high-stakes tests, such as the SATs and PSATs, tests that directly impact the lives of students?

HIGH-STAKES TESTS

Not all tests are equal. Some tests, high-stakes tests, are more important to students because admission to a selective program or financial assistance may be riding on the results. The first such test many students encounter is the PSAT. In October of their junior year, college-bound students take a scaled-down version of the SAT called the Preliminary Scholastic Assessment Test, or PSAT. Modeled on the SAT, the PSAT is shorter but serves as a useful dress rehearsal for the SAT test soon to follow. The results of the PSAT are used to select winners of the prestigious National Merit Scholarships, and states, colleges, and others use PSAT scores in awarding their own scholarships: that's where the problems began.

Despite the fact that females and males earn similar NAEP scores, the PSAT tells an expensively different story. For decades, boys scored so much higher than girls that two out of three Merit semifinalists were male. In a typical year, eighteen thousand boys reached the highest PSAT scores, but only eight thousand girls did. This was such a huge and costly gap that for decades, the Educational Testing Service (ETS), which develops many of these tests, counted the verbal scores twice and the math scores only once in order to raise girls' scores. However, "creative scoring" did not work because boys outscored girls on both sections. In the 1990s, court suits halted this practice.[3]

A woman in one of our graduate courses gained enough confidence in her academic ability to share her PSAT secret with her classmates:

> I took the PSAT when I was a sophomore in high school. I scored a 710 combined (out of a possible 1600). My parents had always been proud of how bright I was—until those scores arrived. They never thought I was smart again.
>
> I remember I had a date that weekend with a boy I really liked. He asked me what I got on the PSAT. I told him 710, and he said, "That's great! What did you get on the math?" I was so humiliated, I made up a score.

Poor test performance can be hidden from others but not from the test taker. A low score is a lifelong brand, a never-ending reminder of a hidden intellectual flaw; it is a detour quietly directing students away from prestigious programs and demanding careers, a detour to lower expectations and fewer choices, a detour taken by too many competent girls.

The big test is the SAT (formerly the Scholastic Aptitude Test, and most currently, the SAT Reasoning Test). A high SAT score can mean admission to a prestigious university, perhaps even a free education. In 1967, boys scored 10 points higher than girls in mathematics; by 1987, the boys' lead grew to 24 points; between 1987 and 2006, the boys' math lead grew again, to between 33 and 41 points. As with the PSAT, boys also outscored girls on the verbal section, although by a much smaller margin. Boys outperform girls on both the SAT verbal (now called critical reading) as well as math sections, and have since 1972.[4]

Could the PSAT and SAT scores be on target and the NAEP scores wrong? Fair question, but unlikely. In fact, the SAT has only one purpose. It is not to measure academic accomplishment as the NAEP does. It is not to gauge academic aptitude. Its one purpose: to predict student performance in the first year of college. Colleges use the SAT as a "heads-up," advanced notice as to which students will do well and which will not. That's it. Guess what? Women (remember, those with lower SAT scores) actually get better grades their first year in college (as well as all the other years) than men (who earn higher SAT scores). So the SAT Reasoning Test (and the PSAT) consistently underpredicts female performance while overpredicting male performance. In short, the PSAT and the SAT are broken.

ETS has been under continuing pressure to improve these tests. FairTest, a nonprofit group in Massachusetts, tracks test misuse, adding pressure for change. In 1989, District Judge John Walker noted the gender gap, and how scholarships were given to the highest PSAT scorers in New York. He concluded that "under the most conservative studies presented in evidence, even after removing the effect of [factors such as ethnicity, parental education, high school classes, and proposed college major], at least a 30-point combined differential [out of approximately 60 points] remains unexplained." He barred New York from using only a high-stakes test score to award scholarships, suggesting that school grades and other measures be used as well. As a result of these and other changes, girls' proportion of scholarships has increased over the past decades.[5]

In 2005, both the PSAT and SAT were revised to include three parts: mathematics, critical reading (formerly verbal), and a new section, writing. Since writing is a stronger skill for females, it was anticipated that this new section might eliminate the gender gap. (It did not.) Each of the three new sections is scored on a 200–800 scale, so now the best possible score is 2,400. Females outscore males an average of 11 points on the writing section, which consists of multiple-choice questions and an essay. The new writing section raises female scores across every racial/ethnic group. But boys continue to score a few points higher than girls in critical reading, and more than 30 points higher in mathematics. Even with the new writing section, boys still score 26 points higher on the SAT Reasoning Test, although given the new 2,400-point scale, the gender difference is now smaller.[6]

The SAT is one of life's memorable markers. Twenty or thirty years after the SAT scores arrive in the mail (now more instantaneous via the Internet), people recall the wave of pain or joy or bewilderment the information brought. Many believe that the SAT measures intellect, classifies brain power, making visible the invisible—just how smart someone really is (or isn't). Boys looking into the SAT mirror see a bigger-than-life image; girls see less than is really there. After taking the SAT, girls may wonder if their excellent school grades were given for hard work rather than real intelligence. Or perhaps their higher grades were the teacher's "thank-you" for their quiet, cooperative behavior. After all, report card grades are local and personal: the SAT is objective, scientific, and national.

The SAT sends even more devastating messages to minority and poor students. White, wealthy, and Asian students typically receive the highest scores. In 2006, Asian students outscored white students by 26 points, American Indians by 151, Hispanics by 232 points, and African Americans by 318 points. Class played an equally large role. A student from a family earning less than $10,000 scored 131 points lower than a student whose family earned between $40,000 and $50,000, and 336 points below a student from a family earning more than $100,000. These are staggering gaps.[7] Now consider that within most of these racial and ethnic groups, boys outperform girls. (The one exception is African-American girls, who outscore African-American boys by several points; in 2005, the difference was 7 points.) For most, students who are poor, a minority, and female face a triple penalty.

Although the SAT receives a great deal of publicity, it is not the only college admission test. In some regions, especially the Midwest and South, more than a million students take the ACT, formerly known as the American College Testing Program. ACT is different from the SAT since it focuses directly on what students learn in four school subjects: English, mathematics, science, and reading, with an optional writing test. To create questions, ACT test makers analyze textbooks and interview teachers to record what is taught in class. Because girls get better grades in class, one might expect them to do better on the ACT. (Or maybe by this point, you pretty much know the plot line.) In 2007, the average male score was 21.2, and the average female score was 21.0, a much smaller gap on a much smaller scoring scale, 1–36. Like the SAT, the ACT underpredicts female performance in college; it is the girls who will get better grades. Once again, even larger race, ethnic, and income gaps emerge, with females typically scoring lower than males within each of these groups. But if a girl had a choice of which test to take, she would be wise to choose the ACT.[8]

While most college-bound students engage in an academic duel with either the SAT or the ACT, a smaller group confronts an additional challenge, the subject tests (formerly the SAT IIs or the Achievement Tests). The most selective colleges and universities require students to take three SAT subject tests along with the SAT Reasoning Test. These one-hour, multiple-choice exams gauge accomplishment in specific subjects (e.g. mathematics, science, foreign language, and history) and are scored on the familiar 200 to 800 scale. Do girls lag behind? Probably, but we are not sure. We were unable to get ETS to share these scores.

But we do have some history on these tests. When they were called achievement tests in the 1990s, ETS did share the scores. Boys registered higher scores on 11 of the 14 achievement tests, while girls did better on only 3 (English Comp, German, and Literature). While boys typically overshadowed girls by more than 30 points on 11 tests, girls averaged only 4 points higher on three tests. Back in 1992, the largest gender gap was in physics (62 points), but the year before it had been in European history (60 points). Males had led in almost all fields: the sciences, social sciences, math, and even most languages. The persistence and size of the gender gap on achievement tests was shocking new information back then; it may be shocking information today, if we could only open that secret ETS vault.

While college ends, tests do not. The test most often required for entrance to graduate and doctoral programs is the Graduate Record Examination, or GRE, an older sibling of the SAT and one that bears a remarkable family resemblance in design, content, and scoring. The GRE has three sections: verbal, quantitative, and writing. Like the SATs, the writing section was recently added probably to narrow the gender gap, but without great success. Writing is scored from 0 to 6, and even on this section, males outscore females, but only by a tenth of a point. Women score lower than men in all three sections. Males in the United States score higher on the quantitative and reading sections by over 100 points.[9] When we discuss the gender gap on the GREs with our students, they are in disbelief. After years of higher college grades, few even imagined that female GRE scores lag so far behind. The gender gap is a well-kept secret. Like the SAT subject tests, the GRE also offers in-depth tests in subjects that include biochemistry, psychology, literature, and computer science. We can only speculate as to the gender gap here. Although we made several requests to ETS, these scores evidently are also kept in a tightly sealed vault. As we go to press, there are promises that the GRE will be redesigned, and perhaps the gender gap will be reduced. Putting a spotlight on these tests and any imbedded biases is important since they impact so many lives.

Let's quickly mention a few of the other important graduate school exams. The size of the male scoring advantages varies from test to test, but persists, and few seem to notice. The Graduate Management Admission Test (GMAT) is used by approximately a thousand graduate business schools. On it, women lag behind men by about 40 points on a scale that ranges from 200 to 800. Interested in medical school? On the MCATs, the scale is 3–45, with males typically holding a 2- or 3-point advantage. How about law school? On the LSATs, scores range from 120 to 180, with males holding a 2-point advantage.[10] But seemingly small differences can have a huge impact.

Donna, a woman who attended one of our workshops in New England, wrote how the LSAT rewrote her future plans:

> Ever since I can remember, I wanted to be a lawyer. In high school I joined the prelaw club, and in college I was president of the law and government society. I worked hard in college, and my grades were very good. I felt so lucky. Half my friends didn't know what they wanted to be, while I felt I always knew.
>
> But deep down I had a fear. My SAT scores were not good, and by my second semester in college I had already started to worry about the LSATs.
>
> I first took the LSAT as a junior. It was a disaster. I convinced myself that my score would rise when I retook the test as a senior, but I was still very nervous. I pulled out all the stops. I took dozens of practice tests as well as the Stanley Kaplan preparation program, and I studied all the time. But it wasn't like my courses in college where if I

worked hard enough I could succeed. The more I studied, the more ter-rified I became. On the day of the test I was the first one there, more than an hour early. That only made it worse. I went to the ladies' room, looked in the mirror, and realized I had rushed so much I hadn't even washed all the shampoo out of my hair. That was a bad sign.

My LSATs never improved. My grades were good enough to get me into law school, but my LSAT was bad enough to keep me out of the top schools and eventually the top jobs. The LSAT didn't stop me from becoming a lawyer—I wanted it too much. But I know the test slowed me down and hurt my career. I work as hard as it takes, and I'm sure I could compete with the best students in the best law schools. I just never had the chance.

Like Donna, many women have personal stories of how tests altered their lives. They are bewildered and sometimes resentful. When they went through school, they did what good girls were supposed to: they followed the rules, were conscientious about their studies, finished their homework, and received good grades. Then the standardized test score knocked the wind out of their plans. They attended less prestigious schools, abandoned hopes for a scholarship, decided against further education, and even gave up careers.[11]

We wish there were a widely disseminated *Consumer's Guide to Tests*. Such a guide would tell parents and students how well (or poorly) such tests predict future grades, and what race, class, and gender gaps emerge on these tests. College and professional schools already know the problem; doesn't it make sense that the public know it as well? A grow-ing number of colleges and universities have taken direct action by no longer requiring SAT or ACT for admission, but graduate schools are slow to join the movement. (Visit the FairTest website for an updated list of these schools.)

Unfortunately, rather than a *Consumer's Guide*, we sometimes encounter a *Consumer's Blockade:* test data impossible to find. In 1994, Myra and David discovered this problem as they sought to uncover gen-der data that they were told did not exist. It was clear to them that it did exist. Billion-dollar companies using sophisticated analysis techniques would know the impact of race, class, and gender on their test results. They called FairTest, the Cambridge, Massachusetts, organization that tracks test statistics, and they had the numbers that seem to elude the test makers.

"You were rubber-walled," said Bob Schaeffer of FairTest. "They redirect your calls from one place to another, bouncing you from office to office until you tire out and give up. Of course they have that information. They just hide it. . . . They just run you into walls made of rubber instead of stone."[12]

We encountered fewer rubber walls this time. Testing companies now manage websites that provide the public with some critical research reports, a positive change, although some important statistics, such as subject test scores, are still hidden from public view. Getting such information over the phone is no easy task, but the FairTest website helps. Why the gender gap? Why do those girls with such good grades and strong NAEP scores falter when the tests mean so much?

ARE TESTS BIASED?

While today's SATs have eliminated the blatant race and sex discrimination of the past, many believe subtle bias persists.[13] Here are four ways that our current tests may be lowering girls' scores.

Question Content

Questions can be written in a way that favors one or the other sex. Boys do better on questions with male characters; girls achieve more on questions with female characters or an equal number of males and females. For example, an SAT reading comprehension section mentioned forty-two men but only three women. One of the three women was anthropologist Margaret Mead, whose research was criticized throughout the passage. Such imbalance is not likely to have a positive impact on female test takers.

Many believe that even SAT questions without males or females frequently portray topics more familiar to boys than girls. Studies by ETS researcher Carol Dwyer illustrated how the choice of topics can have a powerful impact on test takers. In the 1960s, when females achieved higher scores on the SAT verbal section, ETS made an effort to help boys by adding questions pertaining to boy-friendly topics: politics, business, and sports. It worked. Males' scores rose and surpassed females on the verbal section. Dwyer noted that no similar effort was made to "balance" the math section to help females. She concludes: "It could be done, but it has not been, and I believe that probably an unconscious form of sexism underlies this pattern. When females show the superior performance, 'balancing' is required; when males show the superior performance, no adjustments are necessary."[14]

As one frustrated gifted high school girl explained:

On the PSAT, the question that was supposed to be easiest on the analogies was a comparison between football and a gridiron. I had no idea what a gridiron was. It shook me that this was supposed to be the easiest question, and I had trouble concentrating on the rest of the test.

Males excel not only on questions dealing with sports but also on test items about measurement, money, science, dates, practical affairs, concrete mental processes, and wars. Girls surpass boys when the questions concern personal relationships, aesthetics, civil rights, women's rights, abstract concepts, and topics traditionally thought to interest women. For example, on one SAT exam, boys were more successful on analogies about finance and war—choice (C) in the first question and (B) in the second:[15]

Dividends: Stockholders

   (A) investments: corporations
   (B) purchases: customers
   (C) royalties: authors
   (D) taxes: workers
   (E) mortgages: homeowners

Mercenary: Soldier

   (A) censor: author
   (B) hack: writer
   (C) agent: performer
   (D) fraud: artist
   (E) critic: soldier

But girls scored better when the questions related to aesthetics—choice (D) in the first question and (B) in the second:

Pendant: Jewelry

   (A) frame: picture
   (B) cue: drama
   (C) violin: music
   (D) mobile: structure
   (E) poetry: prose

Sheen: (Select the antonym)

(A) uneven in length
(B) dull finish
(C) strong flavor
(D) narrow margin
(E) simple shape

Phyllis Rosser, a leading SAT critic, is convinced that the road to scoring equality is paved with questions that avoid gender imbalance. Most test developers claim they are already hard at work filtering out questions friendlier to one gender than the other.[16] But critics claim that more male-friendly items penetrate this filter and remain on the exam.[17] "Standardized tests would be much fairer if items girls do poorly on were eliminated or revised. If boys were scoring lower, they would waste no time rewriting the test."[18]

Multiple Choice and Guessing

While critics and test makers debate content, some studies show that even if the words are right, the format is wrong. While girls perform better on essay questions, a new but small part of some of these exams, boys excel on the multiple-choice questions that dominate the tests. Why? One reason is that males are more likely to take risks, to guess when they do not know the answer. Girls tend to answer only if they are pretty sure they are correct. Test directions warn students that points are subtracted for wrong answers; it is a costly warning that girls are more likely to follow. Contrary to the warning, educated guessing is actually a pretty good testing strategy. If you are able to eliminate one or two of the possible answers on a multiple-choice test, you are often better off guessing among the choices left. Boys guess more than girls, and it probably increases their scores. Some call this guessing "boy bravado"; others, girls' lack of confidence. Either way, it is a clue to something deeper.

When Lyn Mikel Brown and Carol Gilligan interviewed girls at the Laurel School, they discovered that as early as age ten, female students were questioning themselves and relinquishing their opinions.[19] Many girls were responding to questions by saying, "I don't know." This lack of confidence recorded by Brown and Gilligan is sometimes termed as "girls losing their voice." This phenomenon was echoed on an unusual experimental test given by the National Assessment of Educational

Progress. Most multiple-choice tests ask students to select the one correct response from several possibilities, but this experimental test offered an additional option: "I don't know." A student who did not know the answer to a question could guess at a possible answer, leave the question blank, or choose (and admit) "I don't know." If a student was not sure of the answer, guessing at one of the options might garner credit. Choosing "I don't know" clearly would be worth zero points. Significantly more girls than boys raised a white flag, chose "I don't know," and surrendered, abandoning any chance of getting points for the question.[20] Those that chose "I don't know" spoke honestly, but the Educational Testing Service does not award points for honesty. Those who guessed might have been equally clueless but knew even a wild guess could pay dividends. (Unlike the SAT, the ACT does not penalize guessing, perhaps one reason why the gender gap is much smaller on the ACT.) Lack of female confidence to guess could cost girls points on these tests.

Timed Tests

Studies reveal that boys perform better on timed tests such as the SAT, while girls are more likely to succeed when the test is not timed. Females are more likely to work a problem out completely, to consider more than one possible answer, and to check their answers. These desirable traits in school and in life work against females on these exams. Doing work quickly rather than well is not a wonderful predictor of academic thoughtfulness, but it is rewarded by the SAT and the GRE. In fact, when the time constraint is lifted from the test, female scores improve markedly, while male scores remain the same or increase only slightly.[21]

Stereotype Threat

Some forms of test bias are subtle but powerful. Studies undertaken in the late 1990s into the 2000s have uncovered a phenomenon termed *stereotype threat*. Here is a typical experiment. African-American and white college students are asked to take a difficult standardized verbal examination. In one group, the test is presented in a typical way, as a measure of intelligence. In the other, the students are told that ability is not being assessed, but their problem-solving approach is being researched. The two groups were matched so that student abilities, time to take the test, and the tests are similar. In the nonthreatening "research" group, black test takers solved about twice as many problems as they did in the group told that the test would measure their intelligence. White students solved the same number in both groups. What happened? Social context, such as self-image, trust in others, and a sense of belonging, influenced African-American academic performance.[22] Some believe that high-stakes tests are markers not of individuals, but of how school and society treat students differently based on gender, race, and class. Simply asking students to record their race before taking a test can have a negative impact on black test takers.[23] Students who care the most about their academic performance seem most vulnerable to stereotype threat, which may explain in part why African Americans (and others) perform better in college than their SAT scores predict.

Nor are blacks alone. Latinos on English tests, females on math tests, and elderly people on short-term memory tests also fall victim to stereotype threat. In fact, even students with strong test scores can fall prey. White male engineering students with very high SAT scores were told that their performance on a test would help researchers understand the math superiority of Asians. Hearing about the comparison to strong Asian students, the white men's scores tumbled. None of us is immune to stereotype threat, but on high-stakes tests such as the SAT, the threat translates into a lower score for minorities and women.

THE TAINTED HISTORY OF THE TESTING INDUSTRY

The history of the SAT is not pretty. During World War I, the military enlisted the new profession of psychology to identify superior soldiers to form the officer corps, the leaders of the new American army. Psychologists designed a test called the Army Mental Test, which claimed that African Americans, the poor, Jews, and Italians were unfit to be officers. The test showed that wealthy, middle-, and upper-class men, often native-born Protestants whose roots were from northern Europe, were clearly the brightest and the best to lead our army. The test confirmed what most Americans of the day believed: certain races and groups were bright, and others were not. The father of the Army Mental Test, Carl Campbell Brigham, believed that Americans of Nordic ancestry were genetically brighter than others. As one traveled south through Europe, intelligence levels dropped off. According to Brigham, Italians were generally not very bright and by the time Africa was reached, the intellectual gene pool had just about run dry. He viewed the arrival of Africans to the United States as "the most sinister development in the history of the continent." Brigham's insights extended to Jews, whose intelligence he concluded was highly exaggerated. Brigham wrote, "The really important steps are those looking toward the prevention of the continued propagation of defective strains in the present population."[24]

The passage of time has made questions on the Army Mental Test as alien to us today as they must have appeared to the poor Americans and immigrants almost a century ago.[25]

The Percheron is a kind of	goat	horse
	cow	sheep
"There's a reason" is an "ad" for a	drink	revolver
	flour	cleanser
The number of a Kaffir's legs is	two	four
	six	eight
The Pierce Arrow car is made in	Buffalo	Detroit
	Toledo	Flint
Five hundred is played with	rackets	pins
	cards	dice

After the war, Brigham took his racist and anti-Semitic views to Princeton, where he became a professor. He might never have been heard from again if it had not been for the "trouble" at Columbia University. Early in the century almost half the students attending public school in New York City were children of immigrants, many of them Eastern European Jews. By 1915 a substantial portion of those students had found their way to the door of New York's Columbia University. The dean dreaded that Columbia's typical undergraduates—polished students from "homes of refinement"—would be frightened away by the newcomers. Would Columbia be the first Ivy League to go Jewish? Could the alma mater be rescued from this alien threat?

Reenter Professor Brigham of Princeton, who fashioned the Scholastic Aptitude Test from his experience developing the culturally biased Army Mental Test. Not surprisingly, immigrant applicants to Columbia performed miserably on the new SAT. As the "old" Columbia reemerged, Harvard, Yale, Princeton, and others also came to rely on the new test for "discriminating" admissions. Although today's College Board and the Educational Testing Service are quick to disown these unfortunate historical prejudices, this history shows the power of tests to fuel biases.

Given the current emphasis on testing, it is easy to forget that even the best test can offer only a shallow picture of a human being, any human being. Unfortunately, in recent years, No Child Left Behind has intensified the testing culture. These annual tests evaluate school performance in selected subjects. Schools that do not do well (often schools serving the neediest students and most at risk) can be penalized or closed, students transferred elsewhere, and teachers and principals made to suffer the consequences. Today, because of the pressure of No Child Left Behind, many schools have redefined teaching as test preparation. Seventy-nine percent of teachers surveyed by *Education Week* said they spend "a great deal" or "somewhat" of their time instructing students in test-taking skills. As schools struggle to raise student scores, entire subjects such as music, art, social studies, and foreign languages are given little instructional time because they are not part of No Child Left Behind tests. One teacher reported: "At our school, third- and fourth-grade teachers are told not to teach social studies and science until March." Most teachers do not believe that improved test scores reflect more learning; rather, they show better test-taking skills.[26]

Although the testing guidelines issued by the American Psychological Association specifically prohibit basing any consequential decisions about individuals on a single test score, critical decisions based on a single test are common, and for many students, especially minority and female students, such decisions often cause harm.[27] Standardized tests offer easy and simple answers (for example, a single score) to complex issues, and remain popular because they are relatively inexpensive and can be rapidly implemented. But high-stakes standardized tests are plagued with problems and do not serve girls or boys well. Some educators are working to create authentic assessments that more fully and precisely assess learning, encourage students to reflect on their work, and are integrated into students' whole learning process. Such assessments usually require students to actively demonstrate their knowledge through a portfolio, which might include samplings of classroom work, a journal, a formal presentation, an interview, or an experiment they conducted.[28] Most educational measurement experts agree that such multiple assessments are a better gauge of student performance than a standardized test.

Perhaps the biggest concern is that standardized tests fail to measure the most important qualities and skills. These tests do not measure creativity or unique talents, qualities that make each of us special. Nor do these tests assess a child's honesty, integrity, ethics, or compassion. There is a growing chorus of educators who believe we have placed far too much emphasis on standardized multiple-choice tests that report how well a student can solve a quadratic equation, and not enough on more realistic tests that tell us what special gifts a student has, how a student solves problems, how a student responds ethically, or how teachers and parents can best help that student to grow.

THE GRADE GAP

While girls lag on high-stakes tests, school grades tell a different story. From grade school to graduate school, females receive better grades than males. They are more likely to be class valedictorians and to graduate at or near the top of their class. Are girls learning more than boys in school, or are teachers' grades reflecting a bias? We visited a Virginia high school to ask the students.

"Do you think there is any favoritism in the way teachers evaluate and grade boys and girls?" we ask.

This question hits a raw nerve, and several boys are ready to tell their stories. A seventeen-year-old senior says: "In my organic chemistry class, the girls are definitely graded easier than the boys. Last week the teacher returned a lab report with low grades, and some girls were upset and practically in tears. He let them go back and redo it again, and they got the points back. When boys get mad, they get confrontational. I would never have been able to get those points back from my organic chemistry teacher. I think that teachers will bend and cater to the sensitivities of females."

"I agree," another male student says, getting into the discussion. "I think that boys get more attention in class, but they also get checked more closely. When a male and a female student slack off, grading is tougher on the guy."

At both a conscious and an unconscious level, teachers appreciate girls' cooperation, an appreciation that may well be reflected in report card grades. When asked to describe how they assign grades, high school English teachers explain that students receive good grades through hard work, good attendance, handing in assignments on time, classroom tests, quality materials prepared outside of class, positive attitudes, and conforming to prescribed style, including good handwriting. These behaviors describe how girls have broken the code for better classroom grades.[29]

A good grade for good behavior is a compromise worked out in the earliest school years. Linda Grant observed elementary school teachers in midwestern and southern classrooms. Over the course of several years she concentrated on how teachers evaluated girls, and she found they measured female students by blending good behavior with academic achievement. Here's what the teachers in her study said about their high-achieving female students—the ones they rewarded with the best grades.

> I knew about an hour after the year began that [Clarissa] was going to be a top student. She does everything neatly and on time and obeys rules and sets a good example. She reads beautifully, gets along with everybody.

> I have no doubt that [Sheila] will stay in [gifted track classes]. She's always careful and cooperative. She works very hard and is equally strong in reading and math. Pleasant. All the students like her. All the teachers, too.

But Audra was a different story. Although compliance and competence were still connected, it was not a positive association:

> All I can say is that it's good we're living in an era of women's lib. She wants to be a broncobuster, can you imagine that? She wears jeans all the time—always too big—and her hair's a mess. I don't think I could get a comb through it even if she would stand still long enough for me to try. I just don't know what will become of her. On top of everything else, she never seems to listen to what I say.[30]

Author and teacher Raphaela Best has suggested that many girls enter school socialized for docility. Elementary teachers rely on that cadre of dependable female citizens to orient new students, handle chores, and even help the teacher manage discipline problems. "If they talk," one teacher instructed her newly assigned female monitor, "give them one warning, then send them back to their desks."[31] One of our graduate students remembered her own school days when she was sent to the back of the room to sit with the misbehaving boys. "I was devastated," she said, "until the teacher explained that this wasn't for punishment but to quiet the bad boys." In many classrooms female students are made exemplars of appropriate academic and social behavior. And when report cards are sent home, girls are rewarded for their meritorious service.

But this "special treatment" can backfire, as David and Myra uncovered during their talks with the high school students in Virginia:

> A tenth-grade Asian-American girl explained, "I have found that teachers will help girls and tell them the answer. If boys don't know the answer, they will be made to solve it themselves."
>
> Ben, sitting in the back row, raises his hand and says: "That's right. It happened again last week in calculus. I was working on a problem, and I asked the teacher for help. He said, 'You can handle this. Figure it out yourself.' Then a girl asked for help on the same problem. The teacher went over to her desk, took her pencil, set up the problem for her, started the computations, and then let her do the last step. And I was still sitting there trying to figure it out."
>
> "That made you angry?"
>
> "I was burned. I struggled with that problem and never did get the right answer. And that girl not only got help but she got credit for getting it right. She ended up with a higher grade." The other girls and boys in the class quickly agreed. There is a difference in the way teachers interact with girls and boys. Perhaps girls' superior verbal and social skills play a role, or perhaps it is the gender expectations of society that see male toughness and female fragility, but whatever the reason, girls got the better assistance. Or did they? We asked Ben:
>
> "Who got the better education, you or that girl?"
>
> Ben looks startled. This is a new angle on his story, and he takes his time thinking about it. A little less sure but still concerned that he is a victim, Ben responds, "Maybe I did end up learning more about how to do the problem—but my grade sure didn't show it."

There is a cost to the soft bias toward girls, a cost David and Myra wanted Ben to consider. Ben still felt the injustice in his situation, and he was right, it was unfair. But now he had another perspective: the higher grade awarded to that girl had a price tag. The girl's grade improved but her learning was short-circuited. Instead of a vote of confidence that she could find the solution, she was denied an opportunity to try.

Many teachers and parents do not understand the cost of these "learning short-circuits," but those who do can make enormous strides forward. Myra and David found such a mathematics teacher at a prestigious all-girls school just outside Washington, D.C. "Looking at the entering scores of those students, you would not anticipate that one in three would graduate with national honors," she said. "They entered as good students, but they graduated as the best. The difference is that we don't trade passivity for good grades. We expect our students to take calculus and physics and computer science. We expect them to participate actively in class discussion, to take tough courses, and to do well." The results are impressive. One third of the graduates from this school received National Merit recognition, and many went on to top-ranked colleges. For these particular girls, classroom grades reflect genuine academic competence, not rule-following behavior.

Too few schools look beyond gendered expectations to uncover why boys receive lower grades from elementary school through college, and why they are less likely to graduate. Boys are less motivated, less focused on academics, less likely to do their homework, less positive about school, more likely to get into trouble, to be left back a grade, to drop out.[32] In the 1990s, all this was given a name: the *Boy Crisis*.

POLITICIZING BOYS: THE BIRTH OF A "NEW" BOY CRISIS

By the 1990s, the *backlash* (a term coined by Susan Faludi in her best-selling book of the same name) was gaining momentum. Sexism, the backlash declared, was a phony issue pushed by liberals and unsupported by research. Title IX was taking resources from boys and giving them to girls. In fact, if there was any gender bias in school, it was targeting boys. Women were now the majority of college students, outpacing males in biology, medicine, and law. Boys' active, healthy, and natural exuberance was being trampled by feminist teachers who ridiculed masculine activities, physical challenges, and strong male role models, forcing boys to fail, drop out, and forgo college. Schools had become "anti-boy."

While this reaction may sound extreme, it is actually an old refrain. A hundred years ago, at the dawn of the twentieth century, Theodore Roosevelt lamented the arrival of the female teacher and publicly spoke out against her negative impact on boys. Admiral F. E. Chadwick declared that a boy taught by a woman "at his most character-forming age is to render violence to nature [causing] a feminized manhood, emotional, illogical, noncombative." According to the admiral, female teachers endangered national security.[33]

Psychologists joined the fray as G. Stanley Hall explained that a time of rough and uncouth development was necessary so boys could forge their masculine identity. Women as teachers or mothers harmed males by feminizing them, taming them, and transforming them into unnatural "little gentlemen." Denied a "wild period" of toughness and independence, these boys would never mature into "real men." Hall's warnings resonated. A University of Wisconsin professor termed the entry of women into teaching an unwanted "invasion."[34] And an educator from England observed that "the boy in America is not being brought up to punch another boy's head or to stand having his own punched in a healthy and proper manner; that there is a strange and indefinable air coming over the man; a tendency toward a common, if I may call it, sexless tone of thought."[35] (Note the war analogies, the combat, as though the only measure of a true man was physicality, if not brutality.) In 1910, the Boy Scouts were founded to rescue boys from these feminine peacemongers.

But saving boys was too important to be left to the Boy Scouts; schools had a role to play. To develop tougher males while controlling wild ones, some school administrators incorporated the rough-and-tumble games boys played outside of school into the official curriculum. By sponsoring athletic contests, schools not only developed "manly" boys but also subdued unruly ones, exhausting them into compliance. A New York principal observed in 1909 that when "the most troublesome and backward boys" played basketball for an hour each day, miracles were achieved: "An incorrigible class was brought to the gymnasium; a tired but tractable class left it." The administrator also found that sports created school spirit and helped solve discipline problems: "Many instances have come to my notice where big, strong, incorrigible, and stupid boys have been stimulated by the opportunity to represent their schools."[36]

In 1904, the Male Teachers Association of New York City announced to the world that men are "necessary ideals for boys" and are "less mechanical in instruction."[37] Consequently, they concluded, men are more effective teachers and deserve more money. But neither presidents nor professors nor the Boy Scouts nor male teachers could alter one persuasive truth: women worked cheap. By 1920, a school with forty teachers was typically staffed by thirty-four women and six men, saving thousands of tax dollars. The more women teaching, the less money spent on education.

Half a century later, in 1964, Patricia Sexton revived the "anti-boy" issue. Writing in the *Saturday Review,* she explained:

Boys and the schools seem locked in a deadly and ancient conflict that may eventually inflict mortal wounds on both. . . . The problem is not just that teachers are too often women. It is that school is too much a woman's world, governed by women's rules and standards. The school code is that of propriety, obedience, decorum, cleanliness, physical and, too often, mental passivity.[38]

Sexton continued her male distress call in *The Feminized Male,* an influential book published in 1969.[39] She argued that schools emasculated boys by imposing feminine norms that demanded docility, neatness, and silence—all the qualities males lacked. Forcing a boy to go to school was like putting a bull in a china shop. Males who submitted to the feminine school environment added new entries to the school vernacular: "mama's boy," "teacher's pet," and "apple polisher." Those who resisted were punished. Because of female teachers, boys were put in an impossible situation—forced to choose between feminization and failure.

In the 1990s, the backlash reignited this old boy-versus-woman scenario as though it was a new problem created by feminism. The mainstream media, attracted by the audience-building power of controversy, played the story up. Let's face it, a feminist versus a neocon draws a crowd. Network talk shows featured pieces on the boy crisis, as did the Public Broadcasting System (PBS), which aired *The War on Boys,* borrowing the title of the soon-to-be-published *The War Against Boys.* The PBS public affairs program *National Desk* presented a three-part series on "the gender wars" that sought to address "whether the advancement of women in virtually all areas of society can be achieved without a retreat, in some way, on the part of men." An interesting premise, but imagine if it were applied to race: "whether the advancement of blacks in virtually all areas of society can be achieved without a retreat, in some way, on the part of whites."[40]

The *New Republic* included an article attacking schools for their lack of sensitivity as they subjected boys to a "verbally drenched curriculum" that is "leaving boys in the dust." One neurologist described coed classes as antimale, a "biologically disrespectful model of education." A 2006 *Newsweek* story quoted a psychologist who lamented, "Girl behavior becomes the gold standard. Boys are treated like defective girls." The *Atlantic* produced a cover story again promoting the book *The War Against Boys,* but failed to fact-check. On the *Atlantic* cover, smug white girls were portrayed enthusiastically raising their hands and flashing a winning smile as white boys sat glumly cowering at their desks. Girls were academic bullies taunting their prey, defeated white boys.

The media picture of boys is as familiar as it is one-dimensional: boys are antsy and unable to sit for long, often learning disabled or coping with too much Ritalin, "hardwired" differently than girls, unable to read, disliking books, unhappy taking orders from women in school, able to focus on sports, computers, and video games but not academics, a constant source of discipline problems in class, potential grade repeaters and perhaps dropouts, and far less likely to enter a college classroom. Other boys—quiet boys, unathletic boys, thoughtful boys, caring boys, gay boys, boys who liked reading or chess or exploring intellectual ideas, middle- and upper-class boys acing their schoolwork and going on to the Ivy League—these boys disappeared overnight.

Doug Anglin took the boy crisis personally. In 2006, with the help of his lawyer father, the seventeen-year-old senior from a Boston suburb sued his school district for boy-bashing and routinely discriminating against him. Anglin argued that his unimpressive B-minus average was not his fault but the result of sex discrimination: teachers made him follow orders, stay seated, and do what he was told, clearly unnatural and unhealthy behaviors for a boy. It was in a boy's nature to rebel, and schools did not get it. He proposed that all boys' grades should be raised retroactively.[41] A 2006 *Newsweek* cover headline summed it all up: "The Boy Crises. At every level of education they are falling behind. What to do?" Sounds like a national catastrophe.

It is not.

SEPARATING FACT FROM HYPERBOLE: A TALE OF TWO GROUPS

If there were a new, national boy crisis today, boys' school grades, college attendance, and test scores would be tumbling. But none of this is happening. Certainly there are boys struggling in school, but fewer than before. According to the nonpartisan Education Sector and the American Council of Education, most boys are doing better today than they were a decade or two ago. So first we will look at some statistics to honor the progress boys have been making, and then we will turn our attention to those boys who are not doing well. Consider the following:[42]

- *Long-Term Test Trends.* Boys are doing quite well on most tests. We have already described how boys outperform girls on high-stakes tests such as the SATs and GREs. Their performance on the National Assessment of Educational Progress (NAEP) which tests subjects across the curriculum, offers no signs of crises. Fourth- and eighth-grade boys' NAEP scores in reading have actually improved over the past fifteen years. The reading score for twelfth graders is flat and "does not appear to have fallen during the 1990s and early 2000s." In fact, nine-year-old boys did better on reading in 2004 than at any time since the NAEP reading test was first given nearly three decades ago, and in math, boys of all ages also scored higher than ever before. In other subjects, such as geography, science, and history, there have been no dramatic changes in recent years, no evidence of any kind of crises.

- *Test Scores Compared to Girls.* On the NAEP, girls outperform boys in reading at all grade levels, and also are stronger writers. But this is not a new "crisis," since girls have outperformed boys in reading and writing since 1969, when the test was first given. In fact, younger boys have actually reduced the reading gap in recent years, from 13 points to 5 points. In math, boys continue to outperform girls at all levels, and hold a very slight lead in science and geography.

- *College Enrollment.* In 1975, 53 percent of men went from high school directly to college. By the early 2000s (the most recent data available), that number had jumped to 62 percent. A higher percentage of men are enrolled in college today than ever before, although women are now the clear majority. Once college doors opened to women, their jump in attendance was more dramatic, going from 49 percent in 1975 to 68 percent in the early 2000s. Two-thirds of the female increase occurred a quarter of a century ago, between 1970 and 1980. By 2005, women were approximately 57 percent of two-year and four-year college students.

- *Older Students.* Today's college undergraduates are not always what people imagine. Students twenty-five and older make up 40 percent of undergraduates. In this group, women outnumber men by almost two to one as they return to school to increase their income.

- *Race and Class.* Among whites, male undergraduates dropped from 49 percent in 1995–96 to 46 percent in 2003–2004. This change is due to a decline in the number of low-income white students who are male, from 48 percent in 1995–96 to 44 percent in 2003–2004. The share of bachelor's degrees earned by women of color has tripled, from 5 percent in 1976–77 to 15 percent in 2003–2004. The share of degrees earned by minority men also rose, but not as rapidly, from 5 percent in 1976–77 to 9 percent in 2003–2004.

- *Which College?* The term "college enrollment" can be misleading. Men are more likely to make up half or even more of the students at the more prestigious universities. Women become the overwhelming majority at less prestigious and two-year institutions.

- *Degrees.* The *number* of bachelor's degrees awarded to men is on the rise, as it is for women.

- *Special Needs.* More boys than girls are identified as special education students. Improved diagnosis and federal legislation means schools today are required to treat autism, learning disabilities, emotional issues, and attention deficit disorder. These conditions are more likely to impact boys and to disrupt class. However, studies suggest that girls' special needs are more likely to go undiagnosed, in part because they are less likely to disrupt class. It is girls who may actually be losing out.

- *Dropouts.* Most studies agree that more boys than girls drop out of school, with the highest dropout rates among African Americans, Hispanics, and American Indians. The good news is that fewer boys and fewer girls are dropping out today than thirty years ago, but the figure is still way too high. A common government estimate is that 34 percent of boys and 26 percent of girls drop out of high school, a sad statistic for both groups. However, some girls are far more at risk than some boys. More African-American, Hispanic, and American Indian girls drop out than either white or Asian boys. When girls drop out, it is often due to pregnancy, and they are less likely to return and complete their degrees than boys. Dropping out is actually economically far tougher on females, since they are more likely to be unemployed, earn lower wages, and be on public support than male dropouts.

- *Course Enrollments.* More boys than girls continue to enroll in advanced calculus, computer science, and physics classes in high school. About four times as many boys are taking AP courses and tests than were taking them twenty years ago.

- *Income.* When men and women graduate with the same credential (high school diploma, college degree, or graduate degree), men continue to earn significantly higher incomes, beginning as earlier as one year postgraduation. A woman with a college degree earns about the same as a man without a college degree.

There is no new boys' crisis in America, but there continue to be boys who do struggle in school. For boys doing poorly, as well as their parents and teachers, the calamity need not be national to be painful. Some attribute boys' school problems to developmental differences: boys mature more slowly than girls, yet they are expected to perform as well. Others believe that school activities are not responsive to what boys like, a culture clash between sedentary school life and active boys. This boy-school clash echoes the voices of a century ago, although most of today's authors writing on this topic seem unaware of this history. For them, it is all new, and that is how it is often portrayed in the media.

It is important for readers to understand that not all groups advocating for boys are the same. One group that initially received a great deal of media attention about the boys' crisis is political in orientation. They blame feminists and educators for boys' problems and argue that helping girls has hurt boys. This group often suggests "solutions" that herald a return to the traditional classroom practices of the 1950s. They recommend funnier, ruder, and more action-oriented books for boys. Poetry and discussing feelings is out, while strict discipline, competition, and sports are in. They give little consideration to how boys differ, or the impact of their suggestions on girls. They seem intent on convincing Americans that the most entitled citizens in the nation, white males, are now in crisis. They are part of the backlash. Their writings, their sources, their adjectives, their personal attacks on people whose ideas they do not like, and their sarcasm offer insights into their political agenda.

The second group deserves a separate paragraph. This group consists of earnest educators, writers, and parents who recognize that too many boys are struggling in school. They do not blame feminists; on the contrary, they often are feminists suggesting ways that classrooms can be made more responsive to boys. For instance, strict school rules about being quiet and sitting still for long periods of time cause difficulty for many boys (and more than a few girls). Creating more humane classrooms by allowing more movement, more hands-on activities, and less sedentary learning helps many girls as well as boys. Step one is distinguishing between writers with a political agenda and those with an educational agenda. It is not always easy. Step two is seeing which boys are actually in crisis.

THE SOME BOYS' CRISIS

Showing pictures of dejected white boys on the cover of national magazines is a sleight of hand, a magician's misdirect from an authentic problem: Hispanic, African-American, Native American, and poor boys (and girls) are the ones in a major predicament, and there is nothing new about that. Let's take a moment to focus on the difference between males in general and at-risk males.

- The NAEP tests in an array of subjects including math, science, and reading show that a huge gap exists not between boys and girls, but among boys themselves. White and Asian males do well on these exams, but others do not. African-American, Hispanic, and American Indian students lag far behind, a difference far greater than the gender gap. Minority and poor boys' test scores are dreadful, yet catchy phrases like "the boy crisis," rather than highlighting their problems, conceal them.[43]
- Black, Hispanic, and poor boys are far more likely to be grade repeaters than white or Asian boys (or girls from any group).[44]
- The Urban Institute reports that 76 percent of middle- to higher-income students typically graduate from high school, while only 56 percent of poor students do.[45]
- According to UCLA researcher Gary Orfield and the National Women's Law Center, over 70 percent of white and of Asian boys graduate from high school, but only 46 percent of African-American, 45 percent of American Indian, and 52 percent of Hispanic boys graduate.[46]
- Another study reports that only 42 percent of black males entering ninth grade will graduate. Although black students make up 17 percent of all public school students, they make up 41 percent of special education placements, and 85 percent of those students are boys.[47]
- In Boston, for every 100 white males who graduate, 104 white females do. But for every 100 African-American males who graduate, 139 African-American females graduate. Florida's graduation rates are 81 percent for Asians, 60 percent for whites, 48 percent for Hispanics, and 46 percent for blacks, far greater differences than the gender gap. While many in the public and the media blame female teachers for boys' problems, few dare to make a similar comparison

and blame white teachers for the academic problems of blacks and Hispanics. The color and class blindness is everywhere.[48]

- African-American students, mostly boys, are almost sixty times as likely as white students to be expelled for serious school violations in New Jersey.[49]
- In Minnesota, black students are suspended six times more often than whites. Although blacks make up just 5 percent of the public school students in Iowa, they account for 22 percent of the suspensions. No other group is disciplined at such a high rate. Nationally, Hispanic students are suspended and expelled in proportion to their population, while white and Asian students are disciplined far less.[50]

Does African-Americans' behavior warrant such punishments? Not according to Russell Skiba, a professor of educational psychology at Indiana University. His school discipline research shows that African-American students are no more likely to misbehave than other students from the same social and economic class. "In fact, the data indicate that African-American students are punished more severely for the same offense, so clearly something else is going on. We can call it structural inequity or we can call it institutional racism."[51] While most school districts are acutely aware of these racial disparities in discipline, they continue unabated.

For some of these students, being male creates challenges, but institutional racism, the downward pull of poverty, and the hopelessness so many young minority children feel in school are also critical dimensions. For white and Asian boys, school is often hope and upward mobility. For boys of color, it is a reminder of inequity, of under-resourced schools, lower expectation, fewer options, and a white power structure that is alien. Hiding all this under a "boys' crisis" and picturing white boys struggling to be heard in class is not helpful: it is far more complex than that.

The "some boy crisis" becomes the "some man crisis" in adulthood. Nearly half of African Americans born into middle-class homes as children in the 1960s fell into poverty or near poverty as adults. Only 16 percent of whites suffered such reverse mobility.[52] The changing economy plays a part as well. Over the past decades, the culture has sent a clear message to young women that education is critical for their economic security. The educational messages to men have been less clear, in part because they had economic opportunities outside of school. That now is changing. Most jobs today require more education than just a few years ago, and society needs to communicate this message to boys.

A MAGIC MIRROR: WHAT THE BOYS' CRISIS TEACHES US

The boys' crisis provides our nation with a magic mirror that reflects back what each group wants to see. As the nonpartisan Education Sector points out, "The boy crisis offers a perfect opportunity for those seeking an excuse to advance ideological and educational agendas."[53] Traditionalists look in the magic mirror and see feminists heaping school resources on girls and demonizing and feminizing boys. If females are doing better, then males must be doing worse.

Psychologists have joined the fray to offer their own, often conflicting, explanations. Some psychologists argue that girls and boys have different brains and must be taught in different schools, reviving the century-old sexist notions of G. Stanley Hall. The lack of educational significance related to "brain differences" does not slow them down. Hundreds of public schools already have jumped on this bandwagon and now segregate girls and boys. (See chapter 8, "Single-Sex Education.") Still other psychologists argue that such traditional notions of gender roles are the problem, not the solution. They campaign to remove socially imposed gender restrictions that stifle boys, encouraging boys to express their emotional feelings and other qualities that have been shut off by conventional definitions of masculinity. Each camp propagates its own competing views through books, teacher training, websites, and lectures. They have become a new cottage industry, the "boy industry." Welcome to the magic mirror.

While we believe that talk of a new national boys' crisis is not accurate, it is clear that too many boys continue to struggle and could benefit from help. For them, the crisis is personal. Many educators feel a connection to such boys, and work to improve their lives, and there is nothing political about that. One such educator is Rich Weinfeld, one of David's former students, who works with teachers and parents to improve the lives of these boys. He explains: "Most of the parents and teachers to whom I present information don't have a political agenda. They are just looking for ways to help their kids do better. I care about finding strategies and methodology that works for girls and boys." Selfless educators like Rich see students in need and set out to help them.

For us, the boys' crisis makes several stunning points: even middle- and upper-class white males, the group most entitled in school, the group that gets most of the teachers' attention, most of the athletic budget, sees themselves most reflected in the curriculum, aces those high-stakes tests, and will go on to earn the biggest paychecks, even this group feels shortchanged in school. If they feel that schools are not working for them, how should those students further down the pecking order feel?

The boys' crisis is also a reminder that sexism is a two-edged sword, and that boys face their own gender stereotypes. Many educators and psychologists working with boys understand that. We still expect boys to be aggressive, stoic, competitive, and independent extroverts. Society continues to define masculinity in terms that sound anti-intellectual, antifeminine, and antischool. Author Wayne Martino captured boys' view of reading: It is "lame, sitting down and looking at words is pathetic. Most guys who like English are faggots."[54] If that is how we raise our boys to view reading, we need to make some changes.

There is also a dysfunctional clash between the sedentary school culture and the physically active world of many boys (and girls) who attend those schools. We need schools that allow for different learning styles, including more movement and freedom in class for some, more quiet time for others, and more group work for still others. This is not just about boys or just about girls; we need to honor all children who learn in different ways. Many recent boys' crisis books suggest changes the authors believe will help boys but give no consideration as to how these suggestions will impact girls. Many boys' crisis authors consider the girls' problem "fixed," and boys alone need our attention. If that path is taken, we will be back to square one trying to undo the damage done to girls. Many boys' crisis authors fail to discern how race and poverty influence boys (and girls) in school. The result is a set of simplistic suggestions that ignore these looming issues.

Some educators have been working on more comprehensive strategies to help children most at risk. For example, University of Wisconsin professor Gloria Ladson-Billings has done encouraging pioneering work with urban African-American students. She describes how black culture and schools are too often in conflict. Studies of academically successful African-American students reveal that academic success often comes at the expense of cultural and psychosocial well-being. To avoid being labeled "at risk," lazy, or troublemakers, these students separate themselves from other black students. No longer fitting in with their black peers, they are seen as turning their backs on their own kind, as "acting white." They become social isolates.[55]

Can this race-school conflict be resolved? Ladson-Billings believes it can. She studied successful teachers in black communities: What was their secret? It wasn't the race of the teacher, nor was it any particular teaching style. What she found was more basic: successful urban teachers connected the school and the community. These teachers worked to improve the quality of life in the neighborhood, making the school part of, not alien from, the community. Students and teachers worked together to remedy social injustice and poverty in the community, while the school incorporated cultural and historical backgrounds of the students in its curriculum. School success was no longer seen as a form of racial treason, but as a reason for racial pride. Ladson-Billings called this "culturally relevant pedagogy," and it offers a path for improving urban education. Educators like Ladson-Billings help us see beyond sexy terms such as "the boys' crisis" and offer us a direction to help girls and boys most at risk.

The challenge continues in higher education. Poor students who make it to college are more likely to drop out than graduate, and this is especially true of African-American men. A few colleges are rising to the challenge. Florida State University (FSU) initiated a comprehensive program called CARE, which reaches out early to local junior high school students—boys and girls—enrolled in free lunch programs. FSU identifies these poor students, providing them with college information during the summer and after school, and explaining the sometimes baffling route to college admission, how to prepare for the SATs, and even how to unearth financial support. FSU relaxes its regular entrance standards for these poor, first-generation college applicants, but the applicants must agree to participate in the FSU CARE program, which provides them with academic support and counseling before and during their college years. CARE students, about two-thirds of whom are African American, enter FSU with an average SAT score of 940, compared to 1,204 among non-CARE students. This is a huge difference. At a typical university, about 73 percent of the students who enter with an SAT score of 1,204, but only 56 percent of the students who enter with a 940 SAT score, would be expected to graduate. But at FSU, CARE and non-CARE students graduate at the same, higher rate.[56] This is the kind of comprehensive program that is needed to help both males and females at risk. The challenge is so much greater than "a boys' crisis."

Authors lamented boys' struggle with school for much of the nineteenth and twentieth centuries. It has only been a few decades that we have explored the more subtle problems girls encounter in school. Now we are back to the boys. We have done the gender circle. It is time to stop ricocheting from crisis to crisis, from gender to gender, and consider more inclusive visions of school that help all our students.

SUCCEEDING AT FAIRNESS:
SUGGESTIONS FOR STUDENTS, PARENTS, AND TEACHERS

There are many resources that can help both adults and students handle the growing grading and testing pressures, and put school assessments in perspective. We also offer suggestions and resources that take us beyond the testing paradigms of the past two centuries. The boys' crisis offers us a welcome opportunity for considering the nature of all gender roles and how traditional beliefs can limit human potential. Here are a few ideas and resources that may be helpful.

1. Observe classes. Are you seeing behavior—good or bad—impacting a teacher's perception of students' intellectual skills? Are boys being called on in class as a way to teach them—or to keep them from getting into mischief? How are stereotypic expectations for boys and girls reflected in the teacher's comments?

2. How does appearance emerge in evaluating students? Is neatness and attractive design positively influencing girls' grades, while sloppiness detracts from boys' grades? Whose work is publicized in class or posted on bulletin boards: girls' or boys'? How do you view the relationship between appearance of work, and the insights and content of that work?

3. Here is an interesting idea that some have suggested for adolescents, especially those applying to colleges. Pair up girls and boys as teams to learn from one another. For example, girls can explain their approaches to schoolwork and how they manage to achieve good grades. Boys can return the favor by describing their strategies for doing well on high-stakes standardized tests such as the SATs. Perhaps each gender can learn from the other's strengths. (And this can be done in or out of school.)

4. Does the school equate learning with the traditional test scores? Are these tests timed? Are they multiple-choice? Are there cultural and racial assumptions built into the content of these questions? Perhaps you can be an advocate in your school or community for newer and more

diverse assessments. One example would be portfolios that allow for students to be creative (a trait rarely assessed in school) and to demonstrate their strengths in a wide range of fields. Portfolios require students to present samples of their own work, emphasizing their talents over tests that emphasize speed in answering specific questions.

5. Parents and teachers have used a variety of strategies to help students who struggle with high-stakes tests. Most people know of Kaplan and Princeton Review and other companies that offer clues and strategies for enhancing scores. And there is some evidence that such strategies work (which says more about the limits of the test than anything else). But another option is simply to play down the test, even seek out the hundreds of colleges that no longer require such high-stakes entrance exams as the SAT. Visit www.fairtest.org/optinit.htm to find out which colleges no longer require these exams.

6. If girls have an option of which college admission test to take, they should consider the ACT, with its smaller gender gap, over the SAT.

7. One reason that some boys run into grading difficulties in school is the image of the traditional male role. Too often, reading and doing well in school is seen as feminine, and anything feminine is demeaned. Parents and teachers can work to change that image, to define maleness in broader and frankly more humane terms. Art can be honored along with athletics, reading as well as science, and doing well in school applauded. This is a lengthy commitment that runs counter to the cultural current but persistence can pay off.

8. For some interesting reports on the problem with standardized testing, visit the FairTest website at www.fairtest.org or read *Collateral Damage,* cited below.

9. Does your school keep records of who is disciplined, suspended, or expelled? Can you request that your school publish these numbers by gender, race, and ethnicity? These statistics typically reflect the harsher discipline meted out to boys, especially boys of color. You can work to make this information a stepping-off point for staff development of teachers and administrators, and perhaps a more carefully enunciated discipline policy in your school.

10. While you are asking about school records, you might also explore if grades and high-stakes test scores can also be made available by gender, race, ethnicity, and socioeconomic status. This information will not only inform you of how different groups are performing, but may raise the school's awareness of such issues.

11. Many of the barriers boys and girls face are due to poverty, racism, and

lack of school resources. Correcting this is a huge undertaking, a national effort. Are there groups working for social justice that you can join to move this issue forward in your community? Or perhaps you can initiate such a group.

12. Does the school reflect values that promote traditional gender roles, or is there an effort to break down confining restrictions and honor boys and girls who step out of such historical limitations? Adult expectations can reinforce or curtail girls' neatness and boys' troubling behavior. Moving beyond such stereotypes is challenging but essential.

13. Some colleges now have programs and policies more responsive to the needs of students of color, and of first-generation college and poor students. Ask college officials about academic, counseling, and financial resources available for these most at-risk groups. Be sure to ask for admission rates, attendance, and most important, the graduation rates of the different populations that are represented on campus.

Resources

Collateral Damage: How High-Stakes Testing Corrupts America's Schools, by Sharon Nichols and David Berliner

> The authors are noted educational researchers, professionals who believe in the value of some tests. Their background makes the book's thesis all the more powerful: high-stakes tests are threatening American schools, eroding the value of worthwhile testing programs, and corrupting teachers and students in the process.

A Whole New Mind: How Right Brainers Will Rule the Future, by Daniel Pink

> A wonderfully written and thoughtful book that looks into the future to sort out where the economy and the education system—so left brain, logically focused—may be way off course. The author asks for Americans to balance their world, to honor and develop right brain skills from art and storytelling to intuition and creativity. Pink sees this as the best future course for the nation in the new global economy—a very enjoyable and thought-provoking read.

Five Minds for the Future, by Howard Gardner

> Gardner pulls together his decades of research and insights to point to where schools should be headed and the kinds of minds our nation needs. Just as in *A Whole New Mind,* Gardner takes our nation and our school in a new direction, and makes a strong case for why the nation should start focusing on developing other areas of our intellect and humanity, such as the ethical mind.

Manhood in America: A Cultural History, by Michael Kimmel

This is an examination of the meaning of manhood in America over the past few centuries. And that meaning has gone through significant changes. How society defines men is based on society's needs; Kimmel argues it is time for men to define themselves.

Helping Boys in School, by Terry Neu and Rich Weinfeld

This book is geared for boys (their parents and teachers) who are not doing well in school. It is filled with practical suggestions to handle reading problems, bullies, and stereotyping. Parents of girls will find many of these practical suggestions quite helpful as well. Although geared for boys, the book really helps all children who are not doing as well as they might.

For additional resources, see *Still Failing at Fairness*'s page on www.simon andschuster.com.

CHAPTER 7

Higher Education: Peeking Behind the Campus Curtain

When we travel around the country, we sometimes ask older women what college was like before Title IX. Here are some of the stories we have heard.

> During the 1940s I applied for admission to the University of Wisconsin. I never thought I would run into a problem because I had been a good student in high school. A professor told me that my application was incomplete because I had failed to include a letter from my husband giving me permission to attend classes. When I complained to the admissions office that I didn't think a twenty-six-year-old woman needed permission to attend class, they said that requiring permission letters from husbands was a good policy.

> In 1968 my friend Mary and I were education majors at the University of Florida. One evening Mary had to do some research on a legal question for one of her education courses. She returned from the law school library in tears. "What happened?" I asked. She told me that when she walked through the library, all the men sitting at tables shuffled their feet loudly. Laughing, they continued to stomp and shuffle until she left, humiliated. "Mary," I said, "didn't you know that girls aren't supposed to go into the law school library? Whenever a girl enters, it's a tradition for the guys to shuffle their feet until she goes away."

> I registered for a calculus course my first year at DePauw. I was not timid, so on the very first day I raised my hand and asked a question. I still have a vivid memory of the professor rolling his eyes, hitting his head with his hand in frustration, and announcing to everyone, "Why

do they expect me to teach calculus to girls?" I never asked another question. Several weeks later I went to a football game, but I had forgotten to bring my ID. My calculus professor was at the gate checking IDs, so I went up to him and said, "I forgot my ID but you know me, I'm in your class." He looked right at me and said, "I don't remember you in my class." I couldn't believe that someone who changed my life and whom I remember to this day didn't even recognize me.

Patricia Ireland is the student who dropped out of calculus at DePauw. Although she eventually went to law school and became president of the National Organization for Women, to this day she regrets abandoning her studies in mathematics. Patsy Mink, the late U.S. representative from Hawaii, dreamed of becoming a doctor, but none of the twenty medical schools she applied to accepted women. Former congresswoman Edith Green wanted to become an electrical engineer, but her family thought the idea "silly." Bernice Sandler, a part-time teacher at the University of Maryland, expected to become a full-time professor after earning her doctorate, only to be informed that her department colleagues had already decided against her because she was "too strong for a woman." Many of these women translated their pain into action and became the moving force to create a new law, a law called Title IX.[1]

In 2007, *Ms* magazine celebrated the thirty-fifth anniversary of Title IX, taking stock of the accomplishments of the 1972 law. In higher education, it had been one heck of a ride. Before Title IX, women comprised only 40 percent of college students; by 2007 they were 58 percent.[2] In 1970, women were 10 percent of the undergraduate majors in business; by 2005 they were half. In biology, they went from less than 30 percent of the students to more than 60 percent. Such female gains are found in many subjects, although they are not always this dramatic. Female enrollment increases have been boosted in no small part by women of color, who more than doubled their college attendance since 1977. This growth was no less spectacular at the graduate level. Women received only 15 percent of the doctorates in 1970; by 2005 they were earning almost half. Women in medicine and law, less than 10 percent of the students in the early 1970s, were now approaching 50 percent. Dental schools in 1970 enrolled 1 female for every 99 males; by 2005, it was 42 females for every 58 males.

But far more than numbers shape the college experience. College women continue to confront a resilient sexist culture on campus, and a persistent if informal segregation that relegates them to less profitable and prestigious colleges, courses, and careers. For men, the loss of their collegiate monopoly and the emergence of a female majority on campus have raised profound questions about their role and the relevance of higher education in their lives. The new female majority in college has brought the gender issue into a national spotlight, but this chapter is about looking beyond the numbers, peeking behind the campus curtain, and unmasking gender dynamics that are too often overlooked.

WOMEN ARRIVE

During the early history of our nation, women were not allowed a college education, and the pioneering women who first stepped on the male campus were venturing into unmapped terrain. True pioneers who defied conventions to settle in hostile territory, women were not greeted with open arms. After the Civil War, women enrolled at the University of Michigan were prohibited from joining the campus newspaper or college yearbook staffs. Michigauma, the prestigious honor society, closed its doors to females and kept the portals shut throughout the century. Cornell's response to the newcomers was undisguised disgust, and the school excluded them from clubs and social activities. Even speaking to women on campus was an infraction of fraternity rules. At Wesleyan, male students beat other men who talked to women.

Many college administrators were not ecstatic about these new students. At Stanford, 102 men and 98 women graduated in 1901, but it was the women who received more honors and awards. By 1904, Stanford had corrected the problem: quotas were established. For every three males admitted to Stanford, one female would be admitted, a policy maintained until 1933.[3] But the rate of women flooding the nation's colleges could not be halted. In 1870, two out of three postsecondary institutions turned women away; only thirty years later, more than two out of three admitted them. In 1900, 19 percent of college graduates were female. But as their numbers increased, women became more conventional and less courageous.

The early twentieth century witnessed a second generation of college women who were wealthier, less serious, and more conforming. Rather than blaze new career trails, many of these women saw college as a four-year dating game, a prelude to married life. Social activities became central as they formed their own clubs, originally called female fraternities. Barred from leadership positions in the main campus organizations, they created their own newspapers, honor societies, and athletic teams, although these lacked the power and prestige of male clubs and awards.

Women soon understood that their organizations and academic pursuits were not as prestigious as the men's, and they therefore sought to gain prestige by dating the "right" men. Money fueled the dating game: the men financed the cars and entertainment while the women invested in appearance. So much was spent on clothes and makeup that in 1946 one campus reporter observed: "At coeducational colleges the girls generally dress to the teeth . . . [using] all the bait they can for the omnipresent man."[4] College women were judged not by their academic achievements or career goals but by the number and quality of suitors. Wealthy men from the right families and the right fraternities were the most sought-after prizes.

From club to classroom, from social status to postgraduation economics, the signs of a second-class college education for women were everywhere. Some women found their limited higher education intolerable and rebelled. In 1919 a young woman arrived at DePauw College anticipating an "intellectual feast." She wrote: "I looked forward to studying fascinating subjects taught by people who understood what they were talking about. I imagined meeting brilliant students, students who would challenge me to stretch my mind and work. . . . In college, in some way that I devoutly believed in but could not explain, I expected to become a person."[5] Instead she discovered fraternity life and football games. Margaret Mead had come up against her first anthropological insight: the male college culture.

After misspent efforts to join a sorority and fit in, Mead was transformed into a college rebel and transferred to Barnard. There she fought not to get into a sorority but to free Sacco and Vanzetti, two Italian immigrants and anarchists falsely accused of murder. Despite Mead's efforts, they were executed. Mead also worked to destroy the barriers that separated and subjugated women on campus. In the end she provided the college community with the intellectual feast she had so fervently sought.

THE DIVIDED CAMPUS

The trickle of female pioneers fighting for an education in male universities in the 1870s eventually became a tidal wave, although it was not until the 1970s that many Ivy League colleges finally capitulated and admitted women. But admission is not equality; academic majors

became the foundation for a divided campus. Women enrolled in literature, the new social sciences, health courses, and the liberal arts, which
were particularly popular for those preparing to become teachers. The
new field of home economics was created in the late 1800s and grew in
popularity through the early part of the twentieth century. Although
viewed today as the epitome of the status quo, home economics back
then included pioneering courses on the role of women in society, a pre-
cursor of today's women's studies programs, as well as a strong emphasis on the sciences. Science in home economics was in a sense academic
hubris for women, proving that they, too, could master a rigorous science course. But this was the exception. Science really flourished on the
male side of the campus, along with engineering, chemistry, and agriculture. The curricular lines sent men and women into different buildings,
different classrooms, and different parts of the campus.[6]

A century and a half later, academic segregation is still commonplace, channeling women and men into different educations that lead to
separate and unequal futures. Although women have made inroads into
the sciences, particularly biology, most of the "hard" sciences are still
housed on the male side of campus. The majority of physical science
majors are male, and males dominate computer science and engineering
at a ratio of about four to one. Pull back the campus curtain and you realize that ideas and meaning are also viewed as the male domain, with twice
as many men majoring in theology and philosophy than women.[7]

On the other side of the curtain, the "soft" sciences and humanities
are taught to classes populated mostly by women. Females are four
times as likely as males to be studying education, nine times more likely
to be studying family and consumer sciences, and seven times as likely to
be in the health-care professions. Women dominate foreign languages,
consumer science, liberal arts, psychology, and communications.
Although women now earn 60 percent of the master's degrees and
almost half of the doctorates in the United States, the gender channeling
continues. Women dominate graduate degrees in education, communications, health professions, psychology, and library sciences while men earn
far more degrees in business, engineering, and computer science.[8]
Although they pay the same tuition, study in the same libraries, reside in
the same dorms, and receive diplomas with the name of the same college
at the top, female students are less likely to take the courses that lead to
lucrative careers. For them, a college investment does not have the economic payoff that it does for men.

Not that economic return is what college is all about. While women graduates struggle to make ends meet in less lucrative careers, some men struggle to find pleasure and meaning in their academic choices. Lucrative careers in business or law do not necessarily feed the soul, while a less lucrative occupation that a man is taught to shun may be just the one that speaks to his heart. Teaching is one example. The number of male schoolteachers today is at a forty-year low. Like so many fields, teaching has become increasingly gender segregated. Today, three out of four teachers are female, and at the elementary level, 91 percent are female. A man teaching young children not only sacrifices salary, but is at risk of being seen as gay or a pedophile. Steve Weber is a case in point. A preschool teacher in Minnesota, he was falsely accused of molesting a profoundly handicapped female student. Now he insists that his young charges in need of help with their clothes after using the toilet come into the hallway for his assistance. "It's awkward, but I just have to protect myself."[9]

Every now and then the glass wall separating the two campuses becomes visible, as it did for us when we taught at American University. In McKinley Hall, the school of education was on the right side of the building while the physics department was on the left side. Watching college students enter the building brought the divided campus into sharp focus. Almost every male student who entered McKinley turned left, while virtually every female student turned right. A glass wall ran down the building, for all who cared to see.

Sometimes the divided campus actually becomes two campuses: a more esteemed one for males and a less valued one for females. In our hierarchical culture, schools such as Harvard, Yale, Columbia, and Stanford are at the top of the pecking order. These schools either maintain their male student majority or report an even gender ratio, immune from the rising female applicant pool. On the lower end of the prestige spectrum are community colleges. These less esteemed institutions enroll poorer and older students, 60 percent of whom are women. Many who complain about the female majority in college fail to consider these gender differences.

IN A SILENT VOICE

Not all classes or programs are gender segregated, of course, and required courses such as English are taken by all. These integrated classes offer the opportunity to analyze how professors interact with males and females in the same classroom. That's exactly what Myra and

David did in a two-year study. Along with a staff of trained observers, they tracked how teachers interacted with men and women. Their observations revealed how subtle gender differences, rooted in elementary school and exacerbated in high school, emerged full-blown in the college classroom. At the highest educational level, where the instructors are the most credentialed and the students the most capable, teaching may be the most biased. College professors earn a doctorate to win a university position, but effective teaching skills are too rarely on the hiring agenda. Drawn from our research files, the following classroom scene offers more than a discussion of the Constitution; it shows how the subtle sexism begun in elementary classrooms intensifies in college.[10]

The course on the U.S. Constitution is required for graduation, and more than fifty students, approximately half male and half female, file in. The professor begins by asking if there are questions about next week's midterm. Several hands go up.

BERNIE: Do we have to memorize names and dates in the book? Or will the test be more general?

PROFESSOR: You do have to know those critical dates and people. Not every one but the important ones. If I were you, Bernie, I would spend time learning them. Ellen?

ELLEN: What kind of short-answer questions will there be?

PROFESSOR: All multiple choice.

ELLEN: Will we have the whole class time?

PROFESSOR: Yes, we'll have the whole class time. Anyone else?

BEN (calling out): Will there be an extra-credit question?

PROFESSOR: I hadn't planned on it. What do you think?

BEN: I really like them. They take some of the pressure off. You can also see who is doing extra work.

PROFESSOR: I'll take it under advisement. Charles?

CHARLES: How much of our final grade is this?

PROFESSOR: The midterm is 25 percent. But remember, class participation counts as well. Why don't we begin?

The professor lectures on the Constitution for twenty minutes before he asks a question about the electoral college. The electoral college is not as hot a topic as the midterm, so only four hands are raised. The professor calls on Ben.

BEN: The electoral college was created because there was a lack of faith in the people. Rather than have them vote for the president, they voted for the electors.

PROFESSOR: I like the way you think. (He smiles at Ben, and Ben smiles back.) Who could vote? (Five hands go up, five out of fifty.) Angie?

ANGIE: I don't know if this is right, but I thought only men could vote.

BEN (calling out): That was a great idea. We began going downhill when we let women vote. (Angie looks surprised but says nothing. Some of the students laugh, and so does the professor. He calls on Barbara.)

BARBARA: I think you had to be pretty wealthy, own property—

JOSH (not waiting for Barbara to finish, calls out): That's right. There was a distrust of the poor, who could upset the democracy. But if you had property, if you had something at stake, you could be trusted not to do something wild. Only property owners could be trusted.

PROFESSOR: Nice job, Josh. But why do we still have electors today? Mike?

MIKE: Tradition, I guess.

PROFESSOR: Do you think it's tradition? If you walked down the street and asked people their views of the electoral college, what would they say?

MIKE: Probably they'd be clueless. Maybe they would think that it elects the pope. People don't know how it works.

PROFESSOR: Good, Mike. Judy, do you want to say something? (Judy's hand is at "half-mast," raised but just barely. When the professor calls her name, she looks a bit startled.)

JUDY (speaking very softly): Maybe we would need a whole new constitutional convention to change it. And once they get together to change that, they could change anything. That frightens people, doesn't it? (As Judy speaks, a number of students fidget, pass notes, and leaf through their books; a few even begin to whisper.)

The professor in this class did not say anything sexist, and considers himself a fair teacher. We know that because we know him. He is well liked by his students, and is committed to good teaching. But he can do better. He was silent when Ben poked fun at women, at Angie's comment, and at a woman's right to vote. Perhaps it was only Ben's lame attempt at humor, but it did set a tone, a tone that could easily silence women.

When females volunteer, the impact of years of silence and self-devaluation becomes evident. In this scenario, Angie showed this loss. Like many women, she has learned to preface her speech with phrases like "I'm not sure if this is what you want" or "This probably isn't right but . . ." These female preambles of self-deprecation are a predictable part of the college classroom. In our coding system we called them "self-put-downs." In class after class we were disheartened at how many times women compromised superb comments: "I'm not really sure," "This is just a guess," "I don't know, but could the answer be . . ." Or like Judy they spoke in such a soft and tentative manner that their class-mates didn't even bother to listen.

When we asked college women why they neutralized the power of their own speech, they offered revealing explanations:

> I do it to lower expectations. If my answer is wrong, so what? I don't lose anything. I already said it might be wrong.

> I don't want to seem like I'm taking over the class or anything. If I dis-guise that I know the answers, then the other students won't resent me.

> I say I'm not sure because I'm really not sure. I'm not certain that I'm following the professor, and I'm just being honest about it.

> I didn't know I was talking like that.

The last one is the reaction we hear most frequently. Self-doubt has become part of women's public voice, and most are unaware it has happened.[11] This pattern of uncertain speech is reminiscent of the stan-dardized science test taken in elementary and middle school, the exam where many girls selected the "I don't know" option rather than take a guess at the correct response. By the time these schoolgirls become col-lege women, the "I don't know" option, the only one guaranteed not to garner any points, has insinuated itself into speech, a tacit acknowledg-ment of diminished status.

We also found that one-third of the college classrooms that contain both males and females are characterized by informally sex-segregated seating, patterns formed by the students themselves. The salient students, usually male, are well versed in the concept of strategic seating; they choose places where they can be spotted quickly by the professor. Those who want to hide, the silent students, who are more likely to be female, prize the corners, the unobtrusive areas, and the anonymity that grows with distance. It is as if a transparent gender divide was erected within the classroom.

While not as stark, the parallel with the sex segregation of elementary school is obvious. And teachers continue their patterns, too. The subtle bias in teacher reactions that we detected in lower grades resurfaces in college. Professors usually respond to student answers with neutral silence or a vague "okay." But when praise is awarded, when criticism is leveled, or when help is given, the male student is more likely to be on the receiving end. In the class scene we described, Mike was challenged to improve his answer and then rewarded for the correction. In fact, the professor praised three male students: Ben, Josh, and Mike. Women's comments never received the professor's stamp of approval. At best they were merely acknowledged, at worst interrupted or ridiculed. So, like boys in elementary school, men in college receive not only more attention from the professor but better attention as well.

Parents and prospective students do not always visit college classes when they take their tours, and even when they do, they rarely pick up subtle classroom bias. But gender bias is often right before their eyes, if they know how to look. Who is participating, and who is on the sidelines? While 80 percent of pupils in elementary and secondary classes contribute at least one comment in each of their classes, only about half of the college students do. One in two sits through an entire class without ever answering a question, asking one, or making a comment. In college, the percentage of silent women students increases. Considering the rising cost of college tuition, it is sad that the more women pay, the less they say.

At the other end of the college speech spectrum are the salient students who monopolize the discussion. Their hands shoot up for attention even before the professor finishes the question. Others don't bother to wait for recognition; they blurt out answers, sometimes way off the mark, before other students formulate their ideas. As in the class we described, these aggressive, *Jeopardy*-like players are usually male. In our research we have found that men are twice as likely to monopolize class discussions. The college classroom is the finale of a twelve-year rehearsal, the culminating showcase for a manly display of verbal dominance.

Studying classrooms at Harvard, Catherine Krupnick also discovered this gender divide, one where males perform and females watch. Here were some of the most academically talented women in the nation, and even they were silenced. When they did speak, they were more likely to be interrupted. Males talked more often, and they talked longer. When the professor as well as most of the students is male, the stage is set for women to be minor players, a virtual Harvard student underclass (that reflects the faculty underclass we shall discuss later).[12] Harvard is certainly not alone.

Bernice Sandler and Roberta Hall found that professors give males more nonverbal attention as well. They make more eye contact with men, wait longer for them to answer, and are more likely to remember their names. The result, Sandler and Hall concluded, is a "chilly classroom climate," one that silently robs women of knowledge and self-esteem.[13] Many of these studies were done in the 1980s and 1990s, but visits to today's classrooms show little evidence of change. It is sad that federal and other funding resources to study and remediate such chilly classrooms are no longer available.

THE GIRLS NEXT DOOR

While today's campuses reflect strikingly different academic and career paths for men and women, one area actually has become less divided: dorm life.

> When I entered college in North Carolina in the 1960s, I was given my official women's rule book, a thirty-four-page tome filled with guidelines and expectations for all coeds. (Female students were "coeds"; male students were "gentlemen.") The following are some of the rules:
>
> No beer in the dorm, even to use as a hair rinse, as was the custom of the day. Men, of course, could have as much beer in their rooms as they wished.
> No smoking while walking on campus since this was considered "unladylike" conduct.
> No visiting a boy's apartment unless there was another couple present.
> No dates outside the town line unless you were "signed out" to do so.
>   Male students could go wherever they pleased.
>
> The rules went on and on. I don't believe male students had a rule book. To be fair, I should note that by the time I graduated in 1970, the rule book had been shortened to pamphlet length.

In the 1970s students reinvented dorm life, abridging and then discarding the rule book. Almost overnight, single-sex dorms seemed out-of-date and coeducational living became the arrangement of choice. Researchers found both positive and negative sides to these new coed dorms. Men told fewer off-color jokes, drank less, and talked with women more; women became more outgoing and were more likely to attend university events. Cross-sex friendships flourished as residents went to classes, meals, and university activities together. But while men studied more, women in coed dorms took their academic work less seriously, held lower career aspirations, and dropped out of school more often. And stories of unwanted teasing and touching became increasingly frequent.[14]

Stories that first surfaced in the 1970s continue today. A survey of Cornell students found that four out of five women experienced sexist comments and 68 percent received unwanted attention from men. At the Massachusetts Institute of Technology, 92 percent of the women reported receiving unwanted sexual attention. At the University of Rhode Island, seven out of ten women said they were sexually insulted by men. According to the American Association of University Women (2005), nearly two-thirds of college students experience sexual harassment at some point during college, almost one-third during the first year.[15] Sexual harassment can occur anywhere on campus, but students are especially vulnerable when it happens where they live.[16]

My dorm at Stanford is composed of fifty men and women who reside on two coed hallways. We are all freshmen. Last week several of the girls, including me, discovered that the men on the second floor had posted in the men's room a "rating and ranking" sheet of the second-floor women. The ranking was obviously based on the relative physical attractiveness of the girls in the dorm and was accompanied by various and sundry disgusting comments. Naturally, many of the second-floor women were upset by this list. . . . I decided that this was something so fundamentally wrong, I couldn't ignore it.

As the week progressed, I began to discuss "the list" with some of the second-floor men, explaining my objections. I felt that the list was dehumanizing and humiliating . . . immature and childish, a remnant of middle school days. How could these guys whom we'd been living with for eight months think of their closest friends in such superficial terms? How could they degrade us in that way? And most of all, how could they be sitting in front of me and defending themselves instead of apologizing for their actions?

Eventually a male resident adviser decided to hold a house meeting to discuss the problem in a more formal setting. This meeting became a battle between me and the ten to twelve men on the second floor who could find nothing wrong with their "list." Amazingly enough, throughout the entire argument not one of the other second-floor women who had initially been so angered . . . had the strength to help validate my arguments with her support. In fact, several were so afraid to become embroiled in an argument that they pretended they knew nothing about the list. The men who were not part of the ranking and who I knew were opposed to it . . . didn't attack my position, but they certainly were not willing to put themselves on the line to defend it. After this confrontation and for the next few days, however, many of the women in the dorm . . . came to me separately and thanked me for standing up for them and myself, and for trying to explain how disturbing and upsetting the situation was.

In this case, words created a psychological betrayal, shattering the veneer of honest communication. When the betrayal is physical instead of verbal, it is far more threatening:

I was driving home from a bar with five guys who lived in my dorm. Most of them were drunk (I wasn't). I was sitting on the lap of one of my friends. He kept trying to touch me on my inner thighs or my buttocks. I was squirming and telling him to stop, but he ignored me. The other guys kept laughing. One kept grabbing my breasts while another whispered in my ear that I should go to his room tonight. I felt like Jodie Foster in *The Accused*. I was trapped in a car with no way to escape.

The young woman from American University who described this incident said that the "guys were just messing around," and nothing else happened; but she felt "frightened, helpless, and violated." She said, "When I tell people the story, they say that being with five drunk guys is just asking for trouble. But they don't understand. These guys were my *friends*." Another college student also described the frightening transformation of someone she considered a friend, the man who lived next door.

John and I were friends in the same dorm. Just friends. He knew I had a boyfriend and that I saw him as a friend. One day I was in his room talking with him. We were always hanging out in each other's rooms, listening to music and watching TV. When I got up to leave, he blocked the door, grabbed my arms, and forcefully kissed me. I was shocked. I didn't know what to do. I mean, this was a pretty good friend of mine acting like this. He picked me up and threw me down on his bed. . . . He started kissing me and saying how much he wanted to make love to me. I said no. I was completely pinned down. I have never felt so lacking in control in my own life. I realized that something I didn't want to happen could—and I didn't have any say in the situation. He didn't care about my feelings. I must have said no about a thousand times. I kept struggling, and I finally convinced him to stop. . . .

To this day (and I know this for sure because he lives next door to me) he doesn't feel as if he did anything wrong. I still haven't been able to make him understand how he affected me that day. Almost being raped . . . I can only begin to imagine what I would have felt like if a rape had really happened.

Baffled by the way her trusted friend treated her, this young woman keeps playing the incident over and over in her mind, trying to understand why it happened. But these terrifying experiences are not even distant possibilities in the minds of new students as they unload their cars and move into their dorms. And most parents, as they wave good-bye, have no inkling of the alarming extracurricular activities their tuition dollars may be buying.

THE YEARS OF LIVING DANGEROUSLY

For the last several decades, there has been a resurgence of campus fraternities and sororities, but there are dramatic differences between sororities and fraternities. Walk through the typical campus and you may encounter the first physical evidence of gender inequity: there are more fraternity houses than sorority houses. On many campuses, there are no sorority houses at all. If you ask college students why fraternities occupy more campus real estate, you may hear some rendition of the bordello story, which goes something like this: "It's an ancient law here in [the District of Columbia, St. Louis, Boston, or the city of your choice]. When three or four women rent or buy or live in a house together, it's considered a brothel. Back then it was called a bordello. That's why sorority houses are illegal. It has nothing to do with campus inequality; it's just these stupid, outdated bordello laws."

This bordello explanation is so common, it qualifies as campus mythology. But it is off the mark. The longer history of fraternities and their greater wealth and influence, not bordello laws, have created the campus real estate gender gap. Nationally there are more than twice as many fraternities as sororities. And on the typical campus, sorority row is a weak reflection of its male counterpart. On some campuses, the sorority house is big enough only for meetings and parties; no one lives there. On others, there are no sorority houses, just dorm areas where sorority sisters live together. In many cases there is not even dorm space; all that is available is a meeting room in a university building.

Fraternity row is home to an all-male society, one separate from the rest of the world where secret rituals bond new brothers into a surrogate family. Greek life advocates boast improved academics, service to the university, and good deeds done for many charitable causes.[17] We asked students in fraternities and sororities at American University to share their reasons for joining. One of our students, Harris Flax, writes of Alpha Phi Omega, a very different kind of fraternity. It is a national service fraternity that accepts both men and women:

> I joined APO because I lacked a core group of friends at college. In high school, I had a "clique" of seven or eight friends that I could always count on to be by my side. Until APO, college was just several informal acquaintances that I had with other students. APO really helped me find a comfortable place while at school. . . . During one specific service project that I did with APO, I went to a local high school to help ESL students with their homework. After coaching a frustrated Japanese student on the English alphabet, he was so grateful that he would not let me leave without receiving a token of his gratitude; he insisted that I take a piece of gum because this was the only gift that he could offer me.[18]

Sorority members are no less enthusiastic. "Living like sisters creates a lifelong bond. The sorority gave me friendship and support," reports another student. But when things go wrong, the "sisterhood" or the "brotherhood" can go in a very destructive direction.

At DePauw University, the sisters of Delta Zeta seemed to get along well, but were viewed as not very attractive by other students. In 2007, the national officers felt they had to save the chapter from itself. They visited the campus and interviewed the thirty-five DePauw Delta Zeta members. They judged twenty-three of them as insufficiently committed to the sorority, and asked them to vacate the sorority house. The twenty-three members evicted included many sisters who had worked for the sorority, but it also included every sister who was overweight, and the only Korean and Vietnamese members. The twelve allowed to stay were slender and popular, even though some of them did hardly any service for the sorority. A few days after the interviews, the national representatives launched their campaign to recruit new, more attractive members with a party. They asked most of the current members to stay upstairs in their rooms while the party took place downstairs. To welcome prospective members, they assembled a team of slender women members, some brought in from Indiana University.

"They had these unassuming freshman girls downstairs with these plastic women from Indiana University, and twenty-five of my sisters hiding upstairs," one of the banished sisters reported. "It was so fake, so completely dehumanized." Some of the evicted members were so upset that they withdrew from classes. Six of the twelve women asked to stay were so infuriated that they quit. Student protests, letters from alumni and parents, and a statement by DePauw's president about the sorority's insensitivity soon followed. One of the professors sponsoring a faculty petition said, "We were especially troubled that the women they expelled were less about image and more about academic achievement and social service."[19]

What the national officers of Delta Zeta were looking for was a passport to fraternity row, to life's last fling, the "fun time" before work and family responsibilities arrive. Alcohol, parties, good times, and close friendships characterize this dimension of fraternity life. But along with horseplay and harmless fun, there exists a menacing, darker side:

> At UCLA a fraternity manual, forgotten in an apartment, found its way into a campus magazine. The fraternity's history, traditions, and bylaws were included, as well as a series of songs the pledges were supposed to memorize. Many of the lyrics described sexual scenes that were shockingly graphic, unbelievably bizarre, and revoltingly sadistic. For example, one song recounted the life of a Mexican girl named Lupe who performed any sexual act imaginable. She first had intercourse when she was eight years old, and even in death, "while maggots crawl[ed] out of her decomposed womb," the smile on her face signaled that she still wanted more sex.[20]

When fraternity members are involved in these pranks and songs, they create a mind-set that turns women into objects, animals, prey. Then the college campus becomes a setting of very real danger.

The young woman, newly arrived on campus, was seeking acceptance from her classmates. She looked forward to attending the fraternity party, a beginning event in her college social life. At the party she was encouraged to drink, and eventually she passed out. The brothers had a name for this practice: "working a Yes out." She was carried upstairs, stripped, and raped by a number of men. They lined up outside the door and took turns, an approach called "pulling train." Several times she regained consciousness and pleaded for them to stop. The university learned of the incident and punished those involved. Several were required to do community service projects. Some additional reading and writing projects were also assigned for the fraternity members involved. The woman who was gang-raped left without graduating.[21]

Campus rape is more common than college officials care to admit, and they are far less equipped to deal with it than most parents realize.[22] According to national studies, approximately one in four college women says she has been forced into having sex, and one in six reports having been raped.[23] While most people think of rape as an assault by a violent stranger, in nine out of ten college incidents, the sex is forced by a friend or acquaintance. Victims experience a maelstrom of emotions: shock, disbelief, fear, and depression. They also agonize over every nuance of their own behavior and are likely to find themselves at fault: "How could I have been so wrong about him?" "What did I do to lead him on?" When the perpetrator is a "friend," college women are not even sure they have a right to call the ordeal "rape."[24]

While the victim is at a loss to figure out how it happened, the perpetrator fits a predictable profile. Socialized into the aggressive male role, he believes that women tease and lead him on, that they provoke and enjoy sexual encounters and later cry rape falsely. To these men it is not rape at all but part of a game men and women play. More than one in every three college men believes that a woman who says "no" to sex really means "yes," or at least "maybe." According to one study, a shocking 30 percent of men admitted they would rape a woman if they thought they could get away with it.[25]

Drugs and alcohol trigger sexual violence. Intoxicated men are more likely to be violent, and intoxicated women are less able to resist.[26] This dangerous situation is viewed very differently by females and males. When asked, "If a woman is heavily intoxicated, is it okay to have sex with her?" only one in fifty women agreed. But one in four college men said that an intoxicated female was an appropriate target for sex. In addition to alcohol or drugs, location can be a danger, too. Women who find themselves in a man's living quarters, at his party, or even in his car are more vulnerable.[27] So are women who go out with athletes.

Basking in status and popularity, male athletes are like campus nobility. In athletic events and on television, their physical exploits garner glory, network dollars, and alumni contributions. But off the field, physical exploits of a different nature can bring disgrace. The National Institute of Mental Health found athletes involved in one out of every three sexual assaults nationally.

> Meg Davis called them her friends; she "buddied" with them. In the spring semester her "friends," all on the university's football team, sexually assaulted her. For three hours, seven to nine men took turns. She blacked out as she was being sodomized. Back at the dorm, she showered until the hot water ran out. "I felt so dirty. Even so, I didn't call what happened to me rape. These were guys I knew. It wasn't until I went to a women's center in town that someone explained I'd been gang-raped."[28]

Whether called "brotherhood," as in fraternity houses, or "teamwork," as in sports, the male groupthink can suppress independent thought and morality. A director of a rape treatment center described the impact of thoughtless bonding: "There has never been a single case in all the gang rapes we've seen where one man tried to stop it. . . . It's more important to be part of the group than to be the person who does what's right."[29]

At the University of Colorado, sex and football became a toxic mix. Two women attending a recruitment party in 2001 claimed they were gang-raped. They sued. Football coach Gary Barnett defended his team: "These kids are great kids, positive kids. They are not villains, they are not rapists. These kids want to get an education and go to school. That's it. And play football, basketball or whatever else it is."[30] The players returned the favor, describing their coach as a man of high morals and ethics. The athletes' parents joined in, praising the coach and the university, but not everyone agreed. The issue grew as more women came forward to accuse team members of sexual misconduct. One of those was the only woman player on the football team, the kicker. She said that she had been fondled and also raped by her teammates. Barnett responded by saying that she was a terrible player. The university then suspended the coach for reacting to an allegation of rape with an assessment of the accuser's athletic abilities. The issue soon spread beyond Boulder to national talk shows and sports reports.

The campus was divided. Many in the university community defended the coach for giving young athletes a chance at a college education and perhaps even a future in professional football. Many enjoyed the status and publicity that Colorado was receiving for its team's performance on the field. Others called for a thorough investigation. At least one university regent received a death threat if action were taken against the team. The powerful influence of many athletic departments is not unique to CU. "It happens all the time because the athletic department, the football teams and the basketball teams are the cash cows of the university. They're revenue producing. So therefore, university presidents never take control of them. University presidents allow the athletic director and the coaches to call the shots, and in effect, they run the school."[31] When a Colorado district court dismissed the rape charges in 2005 on the grounds that there was insufficient evidence, many thought the controversy would end. It did not.

The young women appealed the court's decision, and in 2007, a higher court found in their favor. The appeals judge wrote that "the assaults were a natural, perhaps inevitable consequence of an officially sanctioned but unsupervised effort to show recruits a 'good time.' " The court concluded that the coach had extensive culpability in creating a climate hostile to women, and the University of Colorado paid the two women $2.85 million to settle the lawsuit. The university also agreed to appoint an independent Title IX adviser to help avoid future misconduct on campus. The *Denver Post* noted that the case ran up an additional $3 million in legal costs. Barnett negotiated his own departure from the university in 2005, receiving a larger payoff than the female victims.[32]

At Carleton College in Northfield, Minnesota, women took matters into their own hands. As one woman said, "I had been on the campus for five weeks when I was raped. The college knew this man was a rapist, and they could have prevented this from happening."[33] After hearing the evidence, Carleton suspended the male offender for less than a year. When he returned to campus, he harassed the woman who had reported the rape. She and others sued the college, and then they did something else. On the wall of the women's bathroom at the university's library, as a warning to other women on campus, they posted an unofficial list of the names of Carleton men who had raped.

Colleges are not always slow to respond. Many institute special programs to sensitize the campus community, but when these programs are evaluated, the results are surprising. Female participants become more sensitive to the problem even before the training begins. Just responding to questions about rape on a survey changes their attitudes, heightens their level of concern, and causes them to become more sympathetic toward rape victims. Once in the program, they place even more importance on stopping college rape. But males respond differently. Traditional educational programs have little impact on their attitudes, and many who continue to believe pro-rape myths also continue to blame the victim. These starkly different reactions to rape prevention reveal not only a profound gender gap in perception but also a fundamental difference in campus entitlement and power.[34]

SEXUAL HARASSMENT: IT IS NOT FOR WOMEN ONLY

Sexual harassment is not limited to the frat house or the athletic field. In one study, more than half of the college men admitted that they had sexually harassed someone on campus, and the excuse they offered most often was "I thought it was funny."[35] College women do not find such behavior amusing, and two-thirds of them take steps to shun the perpetrator, avoid certain places on campus, seek protection, or even drop and skip classes. At Iowa State, 65 percent of female students said they had been the target of sexist comments, and 43 percent said professors flirted with them. At the University of New Hampshire, 10 to 15 percent of students reported receiving repeated email or instant messages that "threatened, insulted, or harassed," and more than half of the students received unwanted pornography.[36]

Joseph Thorpe, a professor at the University of Missouri, knows just how bad it can get. He sent questionnaires to over one thousand women who were recent recipients of psychology doctorates and were members of the American Psychological Association. Thorpe found that many students had been propositioned by their professors. Most of these overtures were turned down, but almost half said they suffered academic penalties for refusing. The survey also revealed that one in every four or five women studying for their psychology doctorates was having sex with the teacher, adviser, or mentor responsible for her academic career.[37]

"These figures seem terribly high," David said in an interview with Thorpe. "Do you think they're inflated?"

"I think they underpredict what's going on," he said. "The study did not interview any of the women who dropped out, the ones who became so emotionally devastated that they never finished their programs. If we knew those numbers, the figures would be higher. In fact, for subgroups in our sample, the numbers were higher. When we looked at the responses from single, separated, or divorced female students, the sex-with-adviser rate climbed to 33 percent."

Senior professors are overwhelmingly male and critically important. These professors distribute funds in the form of assistantships and fellowships. They can offer coauthorships on publications crucial to a fledgling career. With the right phone calls, they can land prestigious jobs for their students. Male students are more likely to be part of this mentoring relationship, but when women are mentored, the dynamics sometimes become sexual.

With grades and professional careers at stake, female students may feel vulnerable and powerless to object.[38] If a professor is a senior faculty member and distinguished in his field, it becomes even more difficult. When one a student at American University told David of harassment she was experiencing in a course, he urged her to bring charges. "It's useless," she said. "This professor is a nationally known scholar. When I said I was going to report him, he laughed. 'No one would believe you,' he said. 'Do you know how many awards I have won? I'm like a god on this campus.' " This young woman did not report the professor; she dropped the course instead.

This story is unfortunately not new. What may be new to many is that men are also victims, and women perpetrators. According to a 2005 national survey by the American Association of University Women (AAUW), college men are as likely as college women to experience sexual harassment. Nearly two-thirds of all respondents—61 percent of men and 62 percent of women—reported being the target of sexual harassment. The study found that nearly a third of female college students admitted to sexually harassing someone. The Men's Center, in Davenport, Iowa, treats male victims of sexual trauma, and its clinical director, Anthony Rodriguez, believes "Women aren't as passive as one would think and males can be victimized."[39] More than one in three male students report that they were targeted for seeming or being homosexual. Offensive jokes and comments pervade college campuses, and more extreme behaviors including groping, shadowing, or forced sexual activity are all too common. Sometimes men were sent unwanted sexual images and messages, either personally or posted electronically.

But men have been socialized into a gender role that inhibits and limits their reactions to such treatment. Many lack the "emotional capital" to articulate their feelings about sexual harassment or abuse. Male targets are half as likely as females to discuss such harassment. "Men compensate with more socially acceptable aggression, or retreat to isolation, or simply focus on working harder. They are in a world of social denial, not a healthy place to be," reports Rodriguez. The authors of the AAUW report believe that these gender differences are tied to today's changing gender roles: How should females assert themselves, and how do men grapple with the image that they, too, can be victims?

One thing both men and women have in common: Few see professors or administrators as a source of help. Only 9 percent of women and 4 percent of men said they told a school employee about their experience. Students do not believe that college administrators or professors offer relief from this problem. Sometimes, they are the source of the problem.

There is another, more familiar way that men can be victimized: false accusations. The Duke University lacrosse team scandal in 2007 is a case in point. An exotic dancer, some termed a stripper, was hired by lacrosse athletes for entertainment at a party off campus. (No one said this was a good idea.) Within a short time, the party was over and the exotic dancer was accusing three players of sodomy and rape. The university, the city of Winston-Salem, and a great majority of the public were sure they were seeing a replay of a familiar story: athletes raping women. This situation was made even more contentious because the female accuser was a black, single mom working her way through a state college, while the players were white men attending an esteemed (and expensive) private university. With a competitive election for Durham County district attorney coming up, the district attorney Mike Nifong wasted no time in indicting the players, a vote-winning move in the community. The university acted swiftly to cancel the remainder of the lacrosse season, and the coach was forced to resign. While waiting for trial, the players were castigated on and off campus, and in the national press. But as months passed, the case unraveled. The accuser's story changed several times; evidence that at least one of the accused players was not even at the party was ignored; Nifong attempted to influence witnesses; and DNA testing revealed no connection between the players and the exotic dancer. Eventually, it was the district attorney who came under scrutiny. The national press reported that the district attorney had violated normal criminal procedures in his rush to indict the athletes while ignoring exculpatory evidence. The charges against the players were dropped. In the end, it was the district attorney who resigned, was disbarred, and was forced to defend himself in a suit for $180 million in damages. This incident is a powerful reminder that it is not only women who are victims of sexual harassment and rape; innocent men can be victimized as well.[40]

OUT OF SIGHT, OUT OF MIND

At the college level, academic freedom means that professors and programs choose their own texts, and many of those texts are compromised by gender omissions and bias. Academic freedom is a precious freedom, but one that puts responsibility on professors and students to analyze their courses and their texts to see what groups are omitted or stereotyped or given short shrift. For college students, it's caveat emptor.

The first grant Myra and David ever received was to investigate sex bias in college textbooks. In the late 1970s, they spent more than a year examining the twenty-four bestselling teacher education books. They read each line, evaluated every photo, and assessed the books from cover to cover—from the table of contents to the index. Twenty-three of the twenty-four texts gave the issue of gender equity less than 1 percent of book space. One-third never mentioned the topic. Those least likely to include girls and women were the books on teaching mathematics and science courses. Not one of the twenty-four texts provided teachers with strategies or resources to eliminate sexism from the classroom.

Using these college texts, new teachers would actually learn to be more sexist. One book offered a lengthy rationale for paying female teachers less than male teachers. Another author advised prospective teachers to stock their classroom libraries with twice as many books about males as females. The author explained that "boys will not read 'girl books' but girls will read 'boy books.' " An educational psychology text offered this helpful tidbit to increase teacher efficiency: "If all the boys in a high school class routinely get distracted when a curvaceous and provocative coed undulates into the room to pick up attendance slips, tape the attendance slips to the outside of the door."[41] Another education text emphasized the impact of technology with a fascinating analogy: if it were not for recent technological breakthroughs, "all women over twenty years of age in the United States would have to be telephone operators to handle all the phone calls." A reading textbook offered recommendations for bringing parent power into the classroom: "Some fathers could help the third-grade boys make birdhouses easier than the teacher could; some mothers could teach sixth-grade girls how to knit; many mothers would be glad to drive a carload of children to the airport, to the museum, or to the public library."[42]

Adding to the stereotyped narrative was the male world presented by the books. From the photographs to the index listings, education was pictured as populated and experienced by boys and men. One text highlighted seventy-three famous educators, seventy-two of whom were male. Another text featured the work of thirty renowned educators, all men. The message to education students, most of whom are women, was clear: even in this female profession, it is the men who deserve to be remembered.

To turn this picture around, Myra and David developed a set of non-sexist guidelines, suggestions for publishers interested in creating fairer college texts. The guidelines suggested including the experiences and contributions of all races and ethnicities, and of both genders. Nonsexist and nonracist words were suggested, and sound references given so authors could broaden their narrative beyond their own experiences, beyond the typical white, male point of view. Several publishers distributed the guidelines to their authors, and it was suggested that they consider "repairing" their work in future editions.

The Sadkers were pleased that their findings were being taken seriously, and they turned their attention to research teacher-student interactions. In 1991, they were jolted back into the world of college books. The second edition of their own teacher education textbook had just been published, and naturally they had taken special care to integrate women and minorities throughout. But no one ever asked them about the outside of the book, the cover. When the new edition arrived, they discovered that the publisher had chosen a vibrant multicultural photograph of children, a beautiful photo with just one problem: there were four times more boys than girls in the photo. A call to the publisher did little to clear up the matter. It was all a "terrible mistake"; the photograph had been chosen to reflect cultural diversity, but the publisher, sensitive to racial representation, had not noticed that girls were left out. The Sadkers felt terrible, and asked,

"What about the nonsexist guidelines?"

"Never saw them. Sorry."

That was a wake-up call. The Sadkers then called other publishers to ask about the guidelines. Here is a typical exchange:

"Guidelines? What guidelines?"

"The nonsexist guidelines you agreed to follow over a decade ago."

"Over a decade ago. That's three editors ago, way before I arrived. I don't remember seeing any nonsexist guidelines."

Time (and editors) march on. So in 2001, Karen and David decided to repeat the study and find out how the newer texts were dealing with gender. We content-analyzed twenty-three leading teacher education texts to determine what they had to say about gender and education.[43] What did we find? These twenty-three teacher education texts devoted only about 3 percent of their space to gender. That is a bit more than the Sadkers found in the 1970s, but still quite minimal. Despite decades of research documenting gender bias in education, and the creation of resources to respond to such bias, these texts continue the old patterns of offering little if any help to future teachers.

Let's take reading as an example. For boys, reading problems are central: boys lag behind girls in reading and writing performance, and have for decades. Many boys consider reading and writing as "feminine," and may feel that it is okay, natural, for boys to do poorly. What can be done to make reading and writing more appealing to boys? What can teachers do to improve boys' reading and writing skills? The typical reading text does not even mention the problem boys face. Little wonder that reading and writing issues continue to short-circuit boys. For girls, the problem is stereotyping. There is a great deal of research documenting that male characters dominate children's books, while females are presented as passive observers, often in stereotypic roles. But those studying to be teachers would learn little about such stereotypes from their education textbooks, much less the strategies that could respond to such negative stereotypes.

Back in 1978, Mary Budd Rowe's science methods book announced that being female was "A Special Handicap" in science. Her text informed readers that girls "know less, do less, explore less, and are prone to be more superstitious than boys." Twenty years later, science and math methods texts avoid such blatant stereotypes, yet give only minimal coverage to gender bias or gender in general (1.1 percent in science, and 0.6 percent in math). None of the science texts we analyzed even mentioned a female scientist. Only one math text included a female pioneer, whose contribution was given passing mention: "*Incidentally* [italics added], the first woman mathematician we hear of in ancient time is Hypatia (ca. 410), who wrote commentaries on the work of Diophantus." This one-line acknowledgment is prefaced by a detailed analysis of the work of seventeen male mathematicians.

The lack of information is not the only problem; sometimes these texts offer confusing, even contradictory information. A 2008 introduction to an education text opens a section about gender by emphasizing "research that has uncovered some important differences" between girls and boys, such as boys preferring "rough and tumble" activity and girls being less assertive, more extroverted, anxious, trusting, and suffering from slightly lower self-esteem. (The text omits the research that points out the overwhelming number of similarities between the genders.) Future teachers are left to believe that the genders are far more different than similar.[44] After several pages emphasizing the different strengths and deficits that males and females bring to the classroom, the authors offer a practical suggestion for teachers: generally treat boys and girls equally and similarly. The advice is sound; the discussion preceding it is illogical.

Teacher education is not alone. The stories female students read in their other courses also reflect gender bias. As one student remarked, "In history we never talked about what women did; in geography it was always what was important to men; it was the same in our English class—we hardly ever studied women authors. I won't even talk about math and science. . . . I always felt as though I didn't belong. . . . Now I just deaden myself against it so I don't hear it anymore. But I really feel alienated."[45]

Sometimes language can take a toll as well. Texts often use generic male pronouns and nouns such as *man* or *he* to refer to both males and females. Many of us have grown comfortable with this, but not everybody. Do words such as *he* and *mankind* mean everyone, or do they exclude females, or are we to analyze the context to determine if females are meant to be included? Some studies show that using such male generic words does take a toll. For instance, if you say that the policemen arrived, are you surprised if one of them turns out to be a woman? When we say that cavemen used fire, were they men or women? We do know that if you describe a career or job using male pronouns, females find the job less appealing than when it is described in neutral terms. Not surprisingly, a job applicant referred to as a "girl" instead of a "woman" is seen as less tough, less dignified, and of course, is less well paid.[46] Sensitive authors struggle with the imbedded bias in our language, and some have devised creative responses. More than one book opens with a request to readers, a request that they imagine that inclusive language has been used (as if saying makes it so). One author puts it this way:

Note that we have not made a distinction between the sexes. The theory is intended to apply to adolescent boys as well as adolescent girls.

> We have used the masculine gender in this report for convenience; it
> should be considered a neutral, general usage.[47]

Imagine if the author had written:

> Note that we have not made a distinction between the sexes. The the-
> ory is intended to apply to adolescent boys as well as adolescent girls.
> We have used the *feminine gender* in this report for convenience; it
> should be considered a neutral, general usage.

Teachers who have tried this in their classrooms, using *she* or *her* to refer
to both genders, report immediate results: male hostility. Boys simply
refuse to use the feminine form of words to refer to themselves. Evidently,
male words can subsume female words, but not the other way around.

While textbooks frequently make women invisible, some women
have developed creative responses. Years ago, when Myra was discussing sexism in the language with her class, one of her students, Paul,
showed us a copy of *Everyone Wins: A Citizen's Guide to Development,*
a book about protecting the environment.[48] "This book belongs to my
friend Connie at Portland State," he told her. "I want you to see what
she did." As she leafed through the text, Myra saw how Connie had
laboriously crossed out all the *he* and *him* pronouns and replaced them
with *she* and *her.* "Connie felt as though the book was talking to someone else," Paul said, "so as she read through it, she included herself."

While Connie used her inspired pen to insert her gender into her
text, others use their feet to walk across the divided campus and enroll
in one or more courses offered by the feminist studies program. Here
they can take refuge with instructors and books that teach them about
themselves, about the missing chapters. Not everyone is a fan of feminist
studies, and some view such programs not as prowomen but as antimale.
Some campuses have responded by replacing feminist studies with gender studies, a more inclusive exploration of both female and male socialization and experiences. Other pioneering universities are looking at the
nature of masculinity, and have established men's studies programs.
(Visit the website at the end of this chapter.) But such courses are new
territory. David teaches a gender course for future teachers at American
University: "Gender and Cultural Diversity." In any given semester,
twenty women may enroll, but only two or three men. The women are
seeking gender information and skills not offered in their other college
courses. The men are realizing that gender is not synonymous with

women, that they, too, are a gender. Gender touches all our lives in very profound ways, but few students are learning that from the college textbooks they read.

FEMALE MAJORITY ON A MALE CAMPUS

Back in the 1980s, female students became a majority, and by 2007 they made up 57 percent of college students. The media reported this not as a positive development for women, but as a threatening one for men. The usually staid *New York Times* declared: "At college, women are leaving men in the dust." In a *New York Times* column in 2006, the dean of admissions at Kenyon College offered an amazing confession: she regularly admits less qualified males while rejecting more qualified females. Her comments sparked an exchange among readers as to whether this was a good idea or not. Though clearly pained by the college's practices, she stood her ground: "The reality is that because young men are rarer, they're more valued applicants."[49] She is probably not alone in revealing how colleges are returning to the biased admissions practices of the past. It does not seem to matter much if men are the majority as they had been for centuries, or the minority, as they are now; colleges find their own reasons for favoring male applicants.

Another sign of male preference rolls around at student elections. Even with a female student majority, male students often dominate student leadership positions. Nicole Capp, for example, was the first female student in eight years to serve as president of the student government of George Washington University in Washington, D.C., and only the second female president to be elected in three decades, a story repeated on campuses across the nation.[50] Why do males dominate student leadership? Perhaps women sense that the power structure, both on and beyond campus, is male.

Females may be the majority of students, but it is not their campus. In 2006, men were 86 percent of the presidents in major research universities, and 77 percent of all college presidents. Three of every four full professors are men. Men are 62 percent of associate professors and 54 percent of assistant professors. Only in the lowest ranks do females become a slight majority, comprising 52 percent of instructors but only 47 percent of lecturers. Women are more likely to be teaching at a two-year commuter school than a four-year residential campus, at the less prestigious schools, and in the lowest faculty ranks.[51]

Research shows that females and minority students are more likely to succeed with mentors and counselors who can relate to them, who are females and minorities themselves.[52] Yet such mentors are still rare. Students who are both minority and female receive an even stronger negative signal of their place on campus. Lacking role models and missing the mentoring connection, college women are less likely to pursue graduate work. The process becomes a continuing cycle: mainly male professors prepare men to become the faculty of the future, and the campus remains divided and unequal. In the nation's top twenty philosophy departments, for example, women hold fewer than 20 percent of the tenure-track positions. In two of those departments, they are fewer than 10 percent. History does better, but not well, with females comprising 18 percent of full professors and 39 percent of assistant professors.[53] In more traditional male fields, the gaps are even more striking. In the top fifty science and engineering departments, men constitute between 85 and 97 percent of the full professors, while the highest percentage of female faculty is usually at the assistant professor level, the lowest rank. None of these tenure-track women in these top fifty schools is black, Hispanic, or Native American. None. In some areas, it is likely that a woman can earn a bachelor of science degree without being taught by a female professor, or attain a Ph.D. in science or engineering without having access to a woman faculty member in her field. Although a growing number of women are completing their Ph.D.s, clearly few are becoming professors of science or engineering.[54]

Some universities continue to pursue affirmative action practices to recruit and retain minority and female faculty, but with limited success. David has served on a number of new faculty search committees at American University and is no longer surprised by their inability to attract and retain people of color. Despite extra effort and paperwork tracking and categorizing female and minority candidates, in the end few applicants of color get offered a position, choose to accept a position, or if hired, win tenure. In the past two decades, David can remember only three blacks and no Hispanics being hired in his school of education. To date, two of the black candidates were denied tenure and left. The third has not yet come up for tenure review. His experiences mirror the national picture. There are few minority faculty on the nation's campuses, and the vast majority of academic departments have none. While fields such as education do better in hiring and promoting females, other departments struggle.

A colleague at a Midwestern university recently lamented that despite the attention given to affirmative action on her campus, personal connections and the mysterious ways of the university still rule. She writes, "On our campus, all but one of our visiting professors is female. We have one male who was visiting for one year and was secretly 'upgraded' to tenure track status. The message is loud and clear." It is unlikely that this situation will improve any time soon, given court decisions limiting affirmative action and public opinion against the practice. In California, for example, the percent of women faculty hired in the university system plummeted 30 percent in the three years following the state's new anti-affirmative-action policies.[55]

The (Un)Changing Face of the Ivy League, a report examining diversity issues at the elite Ivy League schools, confirmed two distinct cultures: a top tier of overwhelmingly white, male professors working in secure, well-compensated, high-status tenured and tenure-track positions, and a second tier of females and people of color working largely in poorly paid, part-time, and impermanent jobs.[56] The relatively few women and people of color who manage to climb onto the first tier are paid less than their male colleagues at every faculty rank. For example, the small number of women who were promoted to full professors earned 93 percent of what men earn at the same rank, 91 percent of men's earnings at the associate and assistant professor rank, and 77 percent of male earnings across all faculty ranks.[57] No surprise then that a survey of almost seven thousand tenure-track faculty at seventy-seven four-year colleges and universities revealed that white and male junior faculty members continue to experience greater satisfaction with their careers than their minority and female counterparts do. Women and minority faculty report alienation in academe, view their superiors as less fair, and their colleagues as less cooperative. White men report that they "fit in" to the department fairly well.[58]

This male culture can lead to hubris, with former Harvard University president Lawrence H. Summers a case in point. In 2005, Summers was already at odds with the faculty on a number of issues when he volunteered his view on the reason for so few female professors in math and science: he speculated that women lacked the "innate" math and science abilities of men. His comment was in conflict with Harvard's public statements, recruitment efforts, and research findings, sparking angry reactions that hastened his departure. His replacement was a surprise: Drew Gilpin Faust, the first woman president at Harvard since its founding in 1636. In fact, by 2008, half the presidents of Ivy League schools were women, a remarkable sign of progress. But even these highly talented female leaders may not be able to change the white, male campus culture.

One of the challenges these presidents face is a shrinking faculty: adjunct, ad hoc, and temporary employees are replacing full-time faculty, and fewer tenured teaching positions mean fewer opportunities for minorities and women. Temporary appointments are not only short-term, but pay less, provide few or no health care or other benefits, offer no security, and may even carry higher teaching loads.[59] In 2003 in Ivy League schools, white Ph.D.s were twice as likely, but black and Hispanic Ph.D.s four times as likely, to find themselves in such nonladder, poorly paid, nontenure positions. Men were more than twice as likely and women more than three times as likely to be hired into this growing faculty underclass. Temporary positions have made university employment less secure and desirable for all academics, but the burden is greater for women and people of color.[60] The white, male dominance of administration and faculty seems to be in no immediate danger.

THE STUDENT REALITY GAP

We are at a critical juncture in the history of women and men in higher education. Some see gender bias against women as a vestige of the past, while others argue that men are the new victims of gender discrimination. Both views are off the mark. Let's take a closer look at the men and women who arrive on campus.

We can start by briefly considering the persistent and frightening media story about the disappearing male student. While it is true that more females than males are attending college today, it is also true that more men are earning college degrees than at any time in history. Both genders have increased their college enrollments, a good news story, but females have done it at a faster rate. If you envision a "typical" college student as an eighteen-year-old graduating from high school and going directly on to college, you can pretty much forget the gender gap altogether. This group consists of 66 percent females and 65.5 percent males.[61] As reports by the American Council on Education and the Education Sector have shown, it is not white, middle-class, or wealthy males who are missing from the college ranks. Race plays a big role in the gender gap: minority men are less likely than minority women to be attending college. Economics plays a role: as family income rises, the gender gap disappears across all racial and ethnic groups. Wealthy families send their sons and daughters to college at relatively equal rates.[62] Age matters: to increase their earning power, about twice as many older women than older men return to college.[63] The gender gap in college enrollments is due primarily to the underenrollment of African-American, Hispanic, poor, and older men.

Why are older women and those from poor and minority groups more likely to enroll in college? One obvious reason is—they can. The legal, economic, and social restrictions that made college an impossible dream for many are now gone.[64] A second reason: women *need* college more than men. For women, it is Economics 101. A college degree is a woman's insurance policy, a step up to greater economic security. Although a woman with a college education still earns less than a man with the same education, she earns more than a man (and much more than a woman) with only a high school diploma. The same is true at the master's and doctoral levels: a woman with a graduate degree earns less than a male with the same graduate degree, but more than a man with only a bachelor's degree. For women, one more degree translates into a higher standard of living for herself and her family.[65]

Women and men come to college with high hopes. A 2007 survey of nearly one hundred thousand incoming freshmen at 292 public and private two- and four-year colleges found that most students believe they will earn their degree "no matter what obstacles get in my way." But men are even more confident. When asked to rate their intellectual self-confidence, nearly two-thirds of male first-year college students put themselves in the top two categories—"above average" or "highest 10 percent." Less than half of the women put themselves in these categories.[66] But men have this all wrong: it is the women who are more likely to graduate.

One reason is how women and men spend their time in college. Men arrive at college with great self-assurance, but that is not enough. They have fewer intellectual interests and poorer study habits. Men enjoy reading books less than women do and invest less effort in taking careful notes in class or in studying hard. Men do spend more time in leisurely activities than women.[67] Despite their lower effort, lower grades, and lower likelihood of completing a college degree, men evaluate their academic abilities higher than women.

Women spend more time studying, meeting with instructors, participating in student groups, doing volunteer work, and performing household or family chores. Women work harder and attain a higher GPA but they, too, pay a price. Women enter college with higher levels of stress and depression than men, and rate their emotional and physical health lower than men. While men's choices cause academic setbacks, they relieve stress. These gender differences in work, study habits, and depression persist throughout the college years.[68]

Males feeling entitlement on college campuses is not new. In the 1800s, college had become the place where rich young men acquired social polish while having a rollicking good time. Informal sporting events and athletic competitions were harbingers of today's lucrative college football and basketball seasons. Fraternities created a world without adult rules, a haven for males in their late teens and early twenties who drank, gambled, and talked about loose women. While a few focused on academics, most worked at fitting in and getting along, the marks of a successful student. In the vernacular of the 1800s, working to win the approval of the professor by class participation was ridiculed as "sticking your neck out" or "fishing." Cheaters were shielded by fraternities and secret societies, and peer loyalty was the measure of integrity.[69]

So while men arrive on campus confident in their entitlements, women arrive with a sense of vulnerability. Women worry if they are good enough. Despite their stronger college performance, their better study habits, their higher grades, and their greater likelihood of graduating from college, today's college women see themselves as less than they are, and less than males.[70]

Does it matter? After all, what's wrong with men having great confidence in themselves? Isn't confidence a good thing? And even if women have self-doubts, they still do well in their studies. Isn't modesty a good thing? In fact, we believe such differences are symbols of deeper concerns. Men's unrealistic perceptions inhibit them from self-improvement. Men spend more time playing video games and sports, partying, and watching television than women do. Certainly, male humor, athletics, and fun can be a great gift, but balance is key; endless hours with PlayStation or watching ESPN may not be a great idea. How can colleges help males balance their leisurely interests with academic pursuits? How can we help men understand that reading and studying are important activities? What are the lifelong consequences of men believing that they can do less and expect more?

For women, low confidence in academic abilities leads to self selection out of academic pursuits. Dorothy Holland and Margaret Eisenhart spent four years interviewing college women as they progressed from their freshman year through their senior year. Some of the women attended a predominantly white institution while others were enrolled in a historically black college. At first the researchers were surprised that so many arrived on campus with clear and ambitious career goals, but after a while the researchers found a gradual but persistent drop in professional aspirations.

Paula, for example, was a straight-A high school student who planned to major in biology en route to becoming a doctor. But as her grades dropped, she switched majors, first to nursing and then to education. By her sophomore year Paula was less sure of her professional future than when she had first set foot on campus. Her social goals, on the other hand, were coming into sharp focus. "Since I've been here, I've changed my mind about a thousand times. . . . And, like right now, I feel like . . . just not working would be the greatest thing in the world—just taking care of children and not studying." Paula eventually majored in the social sciences, enrolled in a management training program at a department store, and got married. A few years after graduation, she viewed the world of work this way: "[My husband and I] want to have successful careers . . . his is a career, where I feel mine is a job. So my career goals are for his career more than mine. . . . I'm trying to be there to help [him] when I can."[71]

Even today, when the Cinderella myth is supposedly shattered, many women experience a campus climate reminiscent of an earlier time when courtship was more important than careers. Thursday, Friday, and Saturday night dates, bars, and parties are campus events that often conflict with and eventually become more important than demanding academic majors and high grade point averages. As the social world replaces the academic one, many women willingly revise and scale down their career goals. They plan for future employment that they think will mesh more comfortably with the demands of wife and mother.

While black colleges show impressive academic results, females in these schools are caught in the same disturbing undertow. African-American women may actually lose assertiveness in college as heightened social pressure pushes them toward sex-stereotyped careers. Just as these women are increasing their academic capability, they are being "romanced" away from lucrative future professions.[72]

Self-doubt afflicts even the most intellectually talented young women. Karen Arnold studied students graduating at the top of their class. She has tracked high school valedictorians and salutatorians, forty-six women and thirty-five men selected from schools throughout Illinois. When these students graduated, they reported equal estimations of their own intelligence. But by their sophomore year of college the women had lowered their opinions of their own intellect while the men had not. By the time these top students were college seniors, not a single female valedictorian still thought her intelligence was "far above average" even though most were planning to enter graduate and professional schools. But 23 percent of the male valedictorians still put themselves in this top category. Although the women continued to earn high grades in college—slightly higher than the men, in fact—they saw themselves as less competent.[73]

Fewer women than men in this valedictorian study found their way into prestigious professions. In increasing numbers they abandoned careers in science, mathematics, and medicine. A decade of interviews revealed that even top-graded high school women harbor deep-rooted questions about their intellectual ability, and this uncertainty affects their future.

Women's self-doubt and family concerns may be exacerbated by finances. In their first year of college, both females and males worry that they may not have enough money to complete their educations, this despite the fact that the median family income for college students is actually on the rise. But because poorer and older women are now attending college, women's family income has fallen further and further behind men's. Today women are more likely than men to need and have jobs while in college.[74]

The combination of financial need and family responsibilities weighs heavily on many female students, yet few colleges make an active effort to respond. Princeton is an exception, and has made its graduate program more family friendly by providing:

- Three months of paid maternity leave, along with extensions of academic deadlines and fellowships, so leave time does not count against any limits on time to receive financial support or finish degrees.
- Child-care support of up to five thousand dollars a year per child (for up to two children).
- Additional funds to pay for child care—either at home or on-site— when graduate students need to travel for academic conferences or other events related to degree programs.
- Additional funds to pay for backup child care when regular child care is not available.
- Mortgage assistance, which can be used anywhere in the country,

that can reduce both points and closing costs for graduate students purchasing real estate.[75]

Not every university has the resources of Princeton, but most can do far more than they are doing now. Effective and targeted counseling strategies to help males, particularly minority males, succeed academically are woefully lacking. Programs to help women strengthen their self-confidence and relieve family and financial stress are also rare. How strange that women and men have complementary skills and face complementary challenges. One can only wonder if they can help each other find a healthier balance. Can males help females develop greater self-confidence? Can females help males develop stronger academic skills? Can colleges find creative avenues to facilitate such cooperation and to mend the divided campus? There are so many possibilities, and so few imaginative responses.

SUCCEEDING AT FAIRNESS:
SUGGESTIONS FOR STUDENTS, PARENTS, AND TEACHERS

For most families, the college decision is big. For some families, it is historical: the first family member to go on to college, opening up a new family chapter of the American Dream. For others, it is not just college, but the "right college." The college decision is a pressure-filled experience of seeking acceptance to a high-prestige college, perhaps the Ivy League, to win an academic trophy in our ever-so-competitive culture. After all those years of high school effort, of extracurricular activities, of AP courses and A grades, of earning those high SAT or ACT scores, families wait anxiously for that April letter that will say it has all been worth it. Americans can be pretty hyper about college. The truth is there are many wonderful choices available, many potential colleges to attend, or many paths to pursue outside of the four-year campus experience. But if college seems to be the next right step, then consideration of gender issues should be part of the decision making. Here are some suggestions with a gender focus that may be helpful in choosing a college.

1. What do the college brochures and literature tell you about the role of gender on campus? What is the male-female gender ratio on campus?

Are genders presented in stereotyped roles, or are they exploring a variety of career and activity options? What do the photographs tell you? What does the commentary teach you?

2. Look at the gender focus in the student newspaper. Are male and female sports teams given reasonable coverage? How many stories are about women? How many about men? Analyze the adjectives used to describe males and females. What other gender-related insights do you detect?

3. Now go beyond the glossy material and request the number of majors in different fields, from engineering to education. How many women, men, or students of color are majoring in each of these fields? If, like many institutions, there is hypersegregation in physics, teaching, the health fields, computer science, and engineering, ask the college representatives what is being done to break down these gender barriers. If there are few students of color on campus, it is fair to ask the college what steps it is taking to attract the underrepresented groups (and men of color may be particularly underrepresented).

4. If you or your child has an interest in a particular field, ask for the percentage of male and female students majoring in that field. Do the same for the faculty. Are there generally equal numbers of men and women, or does one gender dominate? You might also want to consider faculty ranks: How many women and people of color are full professors, associate professors, assistant professors, instructors, and lecturers? (If you never broke that university code before, we just gave you the key to faculty rankings and salary levels. How many women and people of color are at the top [professor] versus near the bottom? How many of them are in temporary appointments?) Truth is, a student of color or a female student can often relate better to faculty members who share their experiences, and this can translate into academic success. This is particularly important when students are studying in nontraditional fields. How many women faculty in the sciences? How many male faculty in education? How many faculty of color on campus?

5. Talk to the students and ask them what they like about the school, and what they would like to change. Ask them about fraternities and sororities on campus, and what the social life is like. Ask them if they feel safe and honored, or at risk. Are student-to-student conversations characterized by caring? The more students you ask, the better your information will be.

6. If the college has a Greek life, take a stroll down fraternity and sorority row. Do these cultures look relatively equal, or is fraternity row more elaborate? Are fraternities male only—or are they opened to women?

7. Observe classes. Are students gender-segregated in different parts of the room or lab? Is one gender dominating classroom discourse while the other is silent? Are a few students carrying the load and the majority simply passively listening—or perhaps with their attention on email or other laptop distractions?

8. Check out the bookstore. Are books providing various viewpoints and representing both genders and different races and ethnicities?

9. Is there a gender, or men's, or women's studies program on campus? The presence of such a program is a good sign. Visit their offices and ask those professors and students how they see gender issues on campus. Is there awareness of sexism, and of men's and women's gender issues on campus? Is the campus safe for gay and lesbian as well as heterosexual and transgendered students? Warning: you may be the only one asking these people for information, but that is to your advantage.

10. Are there programs to promote gender harmony and reduce sexual harassment?

11. While you are exploring the campus culture, ask security—the campus police—for a copy of crime figures on campus. They are required to share statistics related to serious crimes, including rape, with the public. In some cases, these figures are underreported because off-campus crimes involving students are not included. You might inquire about that as well.

12. Does the college recognize different learning styles, and offer learning options that appeal to these different styles (which would help girls and boys)? Or are the courses mostly lecture and question oriented? (Students might be a good source of information on this.)

13. Males even more than females must deal with poor study habits. How does the college respond to this need? Is it successful? What are the graduation rates for males and females?

14. Learning disabilities are yet another challenge confronting many students, particularly males. How does the college respond to learning challenges? Even more to the point, how does the college help students (more often boys) move through their studies successfully?

15. It is particularly important for graduate students to study in an institution that recognizes family pressures and responsibilities. Does the campus have child-care facilities? Does it offer time off or even financial assistance for students caring for younger (or older) relatives? Is maternity/paternity leave in place?

Resources

Men's Lives by Michael S. Kimmel and Michael A. Messner

This is one of the most current collections of articles on masculinity. This book offers many of the missing chapters on how men, too, are gendered, and shows how race, class, age, and sexuality influence our conceptions of masculinity.

Fraternity Gang Rape: Sex, Brotherhood, and Privilege on Campus, by Peggy Reeves Sanday

Sanday is a leading expert on rape and the dark side of fraternity life. The book is a primer to students and parents of the risks posed by some fraternities on some campuses.

Three Magic Letters: Getting to Ph.D., by Michael Nettles and Catherine M. Millett

Since the establishment of graduate work at Johns Hopkins in 1876, gender, race, and class have played an extraordinary role in graduate education. This book reviews the research on the experiences of graduate school students pursuing doctoral degrees in the United States.

Two-Year Colleges for Women and Minorities, by Barbara Townsend (Kindle edition)

You will need a special format for this Kindle (online) edition, but if you are looking for a two-year, nonprofit college with a student body that is entirely female or at least 25 percent black, Hispanic, or Native American, this is your resource. Many of the schools described serve as shining examples of academic access and achievement for female students of color.

For additional resources, see *Still Failing at Fairness*'s page on www.simon andschuster.com.

CHAPTER 8

Single-Sex Education: A Good Idea?

Ever been in a single-sex school? Most of us haven't, yet we often hold some pretty strong images of what these schools are like: tony and exclusive schools for the wealthy; artificial and disconnected from the real world; a preppy path for the Ivy League bound; a religious school determined to postpone social interactions between girls and boys for as long as biologically possible. Do any of these images match reality? To offer readers a glimpse behind the doors of such schools, Myra and David visited several private single-sex schools and described them in the first edition of *Failing at Fairness*. They interviewed students and teachers, watched classes in action, and reported it all, capturing the experience of learning in an all-boys and all-girls school. In the early 1990s, it seemed important because single-sex schools were going the way of the dinosaur. The Sadkers wrote: "Today, single-sex schools are an endangered species; they are [often] illegal in the public system and vanishing rapidly from the private sector."[1] Would they be around another decade, or would they be gone?

As they visited these schools and reviewed the available research and narratives, they discovered that some of these single-sex schools were quite impressive: dedicated teachers and students working on rigorous academics. For girls especially, they offered an academic refuge, a place to free voices too often silenced in coeducational schools. Many girls in single-sex schools reported higher self-esteem, more interest in nontraditional subjects such as science and math, and were less likely to pursue stereotypical jobs and careers. Robert Johnson, a male English teacher in a girls' school, believed that all-female education provided "an atmosphere these girls may well never find again in their lives: an island in our culture that is about women . . . one where their major responsibility is to learn and to be themselves."[2] Alumnae reported that single-sex schools helped them develop self-confidence, assertiveness, and a strong sense of identity.[3]

According to Jadwiga Sebrechts, former executive director of the Women's College Coalition, "Single-sex schools are a unique place where women are valued and supported; they offer the kind of environment available to men at coed schools and in society. The single-sex high school can help girls make it through low self-esteem during adolescence. And the single-sex college develops women professionally, helping them realize they can be experts and authorities." In fact, the research of the 1990s emphasized that graduates from women's colleges attain more degrees in nontraditional fields such as economics, life science, physical science, and mathematics than women who attended coed colleges. They were also more likely than their coeducational peers to enter medical school; and, as advocates of women's colleges are quick to point out, their graduates are well represented in Fortune 500 companies and at the highest levels of government.[4]

The success of girls' schools and the women's colleges is often attributed to role models and mentors. Typically, women's colleges have more women in the science and math faculty than coed institutions. Writer Mary Conroy remembers female role models and leaders in the Catholic girls' school she attended in Chicago:

> Almost by osmosis we learned one very basic assumption: that girls could achieve, that there was nothing unusual about girls being leaders. Everywhere we looked we saw girls as star athletes, class officers, and editors of the school publications. We also saw role models among the faculty: Since there were only two male teachers at our school, we learned that women could run the business office, enforce school rules, and take the lead as a school principal. After four years of this environment, it never occurred to us that women couldn't lead.[5]

David and Myra were encouraged by these accounts, although it was clear even then that boys' schools were fewer in number and had less evidence of success. But they, too, had their advocates who argued that boys benefited from a gender island. Free of gender role expectations and less concerned with impressing girls, boys were more willing to enroll in nontraditional courses such as languages and the arts without fear of ridicule. Many male alums recall that sexual stereotypes seem to fade into the background in these boys' schools.

So when David and Myra wrote about single-sex schools in *Failing at Fairness* in the mid-1990s, they tried to capture these benefits, hoping that coed public schools would adopt such practices. The Sadkers illustrated how girls in single-sex schools spoke freely and often in class. Why couldn't girls in coed classes do that as well? The girls' school curriculum and wall displays reflected the lives and contributions not just of men, but of women as well. Why couldn't coed schools do that? Single-sex schools had much smaller classes, a strong academic focus, a willingness to experiment, and teachers who worked with students in a collegial and personal way. Why couldn't coed schools do that? In single-sex schools, students, teachers, and parents believed that students would not only "go on to college," but more important, lead meaningful lives. As actor Tom Hanks, father of a daughter at the all-girls Archer School explained, these girls would "one day rule our City–State and the world."[6] Why couldn't coed schools create such exuberance? Pleased that some single-sex schools were doing such wonderful things, the Sadkers' point was not to promote gender-segregated schooling but rather to disseminate their good practices to coed schools whenever possible, to create safe spaces for girls and boys to learn.

Let's be practical here: segregating children by sex is not a long-term solution to gender bias in school or in society. In fact, when the Sadkers wrote about these private single-sex schools in the first edition, they thought they were capturing the flavor of an educational practice that might soon be gone. Events have rewritten this chapter, single-sex schools and classes are back in force, and that's not necessarily good news. Today, hundreds of public schools are scrambling to open their own single-sex classes, but ignoring the educational practices that make private single-sex schools (especially for girls) effective. Rather than improving schools, they are inviting a whole new set of problems (which we will describe in more detail later in this chapter).

Why are they back? Are single-sex schools and classrooms better than coeducation? What does the research say? In this chapter we will explore what we know, and do not know, about the effectiveness of single-sex education. We will also try to bring these schools to life, going behind classroom doors to give you firsthand accounts from students who learn and teachers who work in single-sex environments. At the end of the chapter, we will offer some practical advice about the merits and pitfalls of single-sex education for educators, parents, and students to consider. Let's begin by taking a brief look at the roots of single-sex education in America.

A BRIEF LOOK BACK

America has been slow to educate its female citizens, and many decades passed before girls were even admitted to any Colonial school (and even then it was usually in the evenings or summers when boys were elsewhere).[7] By the mid-1800s, Horace Mann was championing free *common schools* as a birthright for all American children. He saw the potential of a common school as a "great equalizer" between rich and poor, uniting Americans from diverse backgrounds (although for African Americans, integration was still a century and a half in the future). As the idea of free public schooling spread, it was not only the poor who benefited, but girls as well. Few records remain detailing any controversy that may have accompanied girls as Mann and others opened the schoolhouse door for them, but historians David Tyack and Elisabeth Hansot believe their admission "was arguably the most important event in the gender history of American public education."[8]

"Mixed instruction," as it was called then, seemed to work with young children, but for adolescent boys and girls in the throes of puberty it was far dicier. Unless a girl lived in one of the few cities or large towns with an all-female secondary school, elementary school was the end of the line. Coeducation in high school gained acceptance only slowly, and the increasing numbers of girls in coed schools was seen as a real test of our nation's democratic principles. One writer in 1853 described it as "the question of the day."[9] As one educator wrote in the *New York Teacher,* "The whole human race, and true civilization, progress, and religion, depended upon the settlement."[10] And so the dispute between single-sex and coeducation took root.

Advocates of single-sex schools believed that the sexes were different by nature, and that those differences were honored and nurtured only in single-sex schools. To mingle the sexes was to dabble with nature and threaten the very fabric of social life and family structure. The sacred institution of marriage was also at risk: Could a man "love and esteem a wife that was in her mind, feeling, and disposition the exact replica of himself?"[11]

Supporters of coeducation believed that a man educated alongside a woman could indeed still love her, and that coeducation should mirror life. They viewed single-sex schools as unhealthy, and described boys from all-male schools as "sailors and soldiers in foreign lands" who felt free to "engage in all kinds of immorality," including obscenity, drinking, and midnight debauchery.[12] As one writer to the *Common School Journal* urged, "Let boys and girls be trained together in the schoolroom as they are in families. This is Nature's way, God's way, and the more closely we follow it, the better."[13] Advocates asked, "If the sexes must be segregated at school, why not be uniform and carry the separation into the very streets themselves?"[14]

Over time it became clear that coeducation was winning the battle, in no small part because it was cheaper. It was difficult to persuade taxpayers to pay for two high schools, one for boys and the other for girls, when a single high school with mixed instruction could do the job. Even the 1873 publication of Dr. Edward Clarke's notorious book, *Sex and Education,* could not halt the coeducation trend. Clarke, a Harvard physician, argued that coeducation was at odds with female biology and caused illness. He explained that females needed a good blood flow for menstruation, but education was diverting the blood from the sexual organs to the brain. Women were now simultaneously at risk of sterility and insanity. Any girl who tried to attend school with boys and compete with them could do herself irreparable harm.[15] Many girls and women undoubtedly were deterred from education by popular press reports about these health hazards. But many others persisted, enrolling in high schools in record numbers.

In 1905, psychologist G. Stanley Hall resuscitated Clarke's biological boogey-women in his book *Adolescence.* Hall claimed that sex differences were large and crucial, and that schools should recognize and build upon them.[16] He recommended separate schools, especially during adolescence, with male teachers for boys and female teachers for girls. According to Hall, education for girls should "keep the purely mental back and by every method . . . bring the intuitions to the front."[17] In these single-sex schools, a botany course for boys could stress scientific aspects while one for girls could emphasize aesthetics.

Some noted educators found Hall's ideas outrageous. Writing in the *Ladies' Home Journal* in 1911, John Dewey scoffed at " 'female botany,' 'female algebra,' and for all I know a 'female multiplication table' adapted to the 'female mind.' " He went on to say, "Upon no subject has there been so much dogmatic assertion based on so little scientific evidence, as upon male and female types of mind."[18] And as late as 1923, Columbia University professor Willystine Goodsell, still fighting Hall's influence, charged that his approach "could thrust girls with eager minds and widening vision back into the exclusively domestic circle from which they have but recently emerged."[19]

Throughout most of the twentieth century, although males and females studied in the same building, they were divided by "curricular glass walls" as they pursued different courses in different classrooms en route to different life paths. Girls studied home economics, typing, and shorthand, while boys took manual training and courses in the trades. A 1966 article in the *National Elementary Principal* lauded different curricula for girls and boys. The author enthusiastically described how teachers used more science materials and experiments with boys' classes. "Mold," he suggested, "can be studied from a medical standpoint by boys and in terms of cooking by girls." In the girls' classes, teachers played games that "emphasize activities such as sewing and housekeeping." In the boys' classes the games involved "noise and muscle movement and are based on a transportation theme."[20] Into the 1960s and '70s, sex segregation sliced the curriculum.

In 1972, Title IX became law and prohibited many forms of sex discrimination in public schools. The gendered curriculum slowly began to change. By the 1980s, girls were enrolling not only in advanced science and math, but in shop courses as well. Boys were allowed to enroll in cooking, typing, and shorthand, though fewer chose to do so. The male curriculum was seen as far more enticing and valuable than the female curriculum, so girls crossed the gender line far more frequently than boys. While Title IX shook up the curriculum, it did not eliminate single-sex schools, most of which were private. Market forces did that.

With boys and girls now enrolled in the same classes, single-sex schools seemed a relic of a Victorian past, and began a decades-long decline. While public schools could still legally separate girls and boys for specific purposes (teaching human reproduction, for example), most public single-sex schools and programs were disappearing. Single-sex colleges and universities also joined the endangered list. Although segregated for centuries, many became coed, or closed their doors for lack of students. Hundreds of women's colleges disappeared between the 1960s and the 1990s, with fewer than eighty remaining by the end of the century. During the 1970s, prestigious Ivy League universities such as Harvard and Yale went coed, and in 1980 Columbia became the last Ivy to admit women, ending three centuries of discrimination. Here, too, market forces played a major role. Competition for the more valued male students became intense and single-sex Ivy League schools such as Princeton were learning that many of their most desirable male applicants were choosing to go elsewhere, to places like Stanford. Coed universities had a special draw: women. For Princeton to compete, women on campus became a necessity.[21] And clearly simply finding families who could afford the very expensive tuition at these exclusive universities was a major challenge. Admitting women from wealthy families eased this financial challenge by doubling the applicant pool.

Not every college joined the trend. State-supported military schools, such as the Citadel and Virginia Military Institute (VMI), could not see beyond a "male only" corps of cadets. The fact that major military academies like West Point and Annapolis had admitted women was not argument enough for these schools to change their male-only traditions. But the law was clear: public funds supported both the Citadel and VMI, and sex discrimination was illegal. In the mid-1990s, the Citadel and VMI lost their last court battle, raised the white flag, and admitted female cadets. Coeducation had triumphed over single-sex education. Or had it?

THE PERFECT STORM: THE REBIRTH OF SINGLE-SEX EDUCATION

Class Divide: Single-Sex Schoolrooms Take Off
Hartford Courant, June 12, 2007

Austin Explores All-boys Academy
Austin American-Statesman, April 9, 2007

District wants to provide options
San Diego Union Tribune, April 12, 2007

Boys can make the grade, if they're not bored
Detroit Free Press, May 21, 2007

Nashville to test single-sex classes;
Parent interest to play a part in picking schools
Tennessean.com, April 4, 2007

More public schools dividing boys, girls
Houston Chronicle, January 25, 2007

While only five public single-sex high schools were still operating in 1996, a decade later that number had jumped to more than thirty.[22] News stories reported that public schools were creating hundreds of single-sex schools and classrooms.[23] Why was the clock now running backward to educating girls and boys separately? America's schools were being drawn into a "perfect storm" fueled by political and social trends—let's call them *edutrends*—that were reviving single-sex education.

Edutrend 1: Broken Coeducation

By 2001, American students' low scores on international tests, high dropout rates, and episodes of school violence fed a public perception that the nation's schools were "failing." The schools were also failing the gender fairness test as teachers continued to give boys more attention, to help them more, praise them more, and even criticize them more.[24] Feminists argued that a fair education for females could only be achieved in a nonsexist environment, and a nonsexist environment could only be achieved in single-sex schools.

Edutrend 2: The Backlash

By the mid-1990s, gender equity and feminism were fair game in a more politically conservative America, and a backlash, described in chapter 2, was in full swing. Backlash critics contended that schools needed to change to fit boys' learning styles: stronger discipline, more competitions, greater emphasis on physicality, and a curriculum that would feature male characters and war poetry.[25] The backlash was also an attack on progressive education and a call for more traditional classrooms. The backlash arguments were often funded by far-right political foundations and fraught with factual errors, for example, blaming the feminist movement for boys' academic problems that existed long before the feminist movement even began. But the notion that schools were not serving boys gained traction. Like the feminists, backlash critics were arguing for a return to single-sex schooling, although the visions these groups held for these single-sex schools could not have been more different.[26]

Edutrend 3: Brain Differences and Biology

Books and articles proclaimed that female and male biology, especially brain differences, required separate schools, separate classes, and different teaching strategies. Leonard Sax, a physician and a psychologist, argues that boys should learn through physical games, tough competition, harsh discipline, and shorter lessons. Applying medical and science research to the classroom, Sax explains that boys' hearing is not as good as girls', and thus boys should be placed closer to the teacher. Teachers are advised that yelling at boys could be quite effective since boys need very clear direction and boundaries, but teachers should not ". . . hold an eye-to-eye stare with a boy unless you're trying to discipline him or reprimand him. Don't smile."[27] Sax believes that boys who like to read, do not enjoy contact sports, and lack close male friends are "anomalous males." He suggests that "anomalous males" would benefit from firm discipline, competitive sports, a strong male environment, and a reevaluation of the parenting techniques that have led to this situation.[28]

Michael Gurian, also a psychologist advocating sex-different educations, believes that male superiority in math is a result of daily surges of testosterone, and that boys are born with the skills to excel in philosophy and engineering. He explains that girls are born to be concrete thinkers and are stuck in their menstrual cycles, able to compete with boys in math only when they have an estrogen surge. Sax writes that girls are genetically more placid and conforming, relational and collaborative in nature, and prefer a calmer learning atmosphere. Girls should not be given stressful time limits on tests and should be encouraged to take their shoes off in class to help them relax.[29] Both Sax and Gurian are active in training teachers and speaking to educators although those who disagree with their recommendations point out that neither is an educator.

Edutrend 4: Distraction-Free Learning

Others believed that single-sex schooling was needed to manage adolescent hormones that were out of control in the classroom. Teachers and parents voiced their fears that dating, social status, and thoughts about sex preoccupy adolescents' attention and derail their academic focus. Puberty and hormones can also spark sexual harassment, another common hormonal distraction in coed school life. Removing the opposite sex from the classroom would redirect the adolescent sex drive to an off-ramp, and academic focus would return to the classroom.

Edutrend 5: The Testing Culture

No Child Left Behind spurred a testing culture that put many schools, particularly under-resourced urban schools, at risk of being penalized and even closed if test scores lagged. Pressured principals and teachers, not to mention students and parents, focused on survival and test preparation programs, but when that did not raise the scores, other strategies were needed. Some schools saw the single-sex movement as an inexpensive way to reestablish discipline and improve test scores, a magic bullet that could transform the school.

Edutrend 6: An Educational Civil Right

America has some of the best—and some of the worst—schools in the world. Unfortunately, poor families are dealt weak schools while wealthy families send their children to elite schools, sometimes private and sometimes single-sex. Why not give poor parents the same educational choices enjoyed by the wealthy? Creating public single-sex schools would do just that, offer another educational opportunity for poor families. Think of school choice as a civil right, and single-sex classes and schools as one of the options poor parents should enjoy.

Edutrend 7: Making It Legal

To allow public schools to segregate students by race or sex was illegal, so in order to separate children by sex, a civil rights law needed to be changed. In 2004, the Bush administration proposed changing Title IX to make it quite simple for coed public schools to separate girls and boys into different classes within a school. A school administrator only needed to provide a reason (such as to increase parental choice), invite parents to enroll their children in these new single-sex options, and the segregation would be legal. Under the new law, a school could also create single-sex classes for one gender, and not the other. The law no longer guaranteed "equal treatment" between the sexes.

In 2004, David was one of the guests invited to talk about the proposed changes on National Public Radio's *Talk of the Nation*. He expressed dismay and concern at what seemed more a political decision than an educational one. Ken Marcus of the Office for Civil Rights at the U.S. Department of Education was also a guest on that show, and he assured the audience that the Bush administration invited the public to respond on the proposed changes. "We do take public comments very seriously," the Bush appointee said.[30] Almost six thousand citizens did respond. Approximately one hundred people supported the changes, and well over five thousand opposed them.[31] Despite the public comments, in

2007 the civil rights law was changed: today, segregating the sexes in public schools became legal.[32]

Edutrend 8: The Wonders of Single-Sex Education

High-profile graduates of single-sex education joined the fray to extol the benefits they enjoyed attending such schools. Wellesley's Hillary Clinton and Trinity College's Nancy Pelosi added luster to the pro-single-sex-school arguments, as did reports and books lauding many single-sex education practices (including the Sadkers' 1994 *Failing at Fairness*). In the 1990s, Myra and David had great enthusiasm about these schools, and hopes for the promise they offered. Let's retrieve the flavor of this optimism through the eyes of teachers and students, descriptions that the Sadkers captured as they visited and described life in an all-girls and an all-boys school. First, we will visit a highly selective all-girls secondary school.

SPEAKING THEIR MINDS

Thirteen girls in uniform gray sweatshirts and plaid skirts sat in a semicircle and talked quietly. The teacher walked over to the side of the room where we were watching and handed us the book the class was using. "It's officially called *Essays Old and New*," she said with a smile, "but the students call it *Essays Old and Older*." She began the class with a series of questions: "Why are the lower classes more willing to be passionate?" "Do you agree with Emerson that 'a foolish consistency is the hobgoblin of little minds'?" "Emerson says that to be great is to be misunderstood. Do you agree?" After she offered each question, there was a short silence, and then several girls responded at once, their answers overlapping. There was no wild hand waving or grandstanding, but the girls spoke freely as though in a conversation. This was a startling difference from the coeducational classroom where boys called out and girls waited to be recognized. When some of the quieter girls apologized for answers they felt were inadequate, the teacher did not let them. "No, no, it's fine," she urged. "Say it again."

The more outspoken girls didn't just call out answers, they pushed the teacher with questions of their own. "Emerson says you should follow what you believe. What if you're a racist? Is it okay to follow what you believe then?" The teacher offered an explanation, but the students were not convinced; they pressed on with more questions. "Doesn't this justify bad things and evil people, like Hitler?" The girls in this class demanded answers that satisfied them. If they didn't get them, they persisted, asking again and again in a display of female assertiveness we had rarely seen in coeducational settings.

Eighth-grade algebra, the next class we visited, made the English class seem subdued. As math problems were put on the board, the students bombarded the teacher with questions: "I have a question about that." "Wait, go back and do that again. It doesn't make sense." "I don't get it. Can you explain it again?"

We had rarely seen girls admit their confusion so openly, not with any sense of defeat or self-put-down but with a tenacity to understand. Sometimes the teacher answered the questions, and sometimes she threw them back at the class, encouraging the girls to help one another. At the end of the period we asked a group of students who had formerly attended a coeducational school if they acted differently there.

"I don't think it matters whether it's single-sex or coed," said one of the girls who talked most often in class. "I'm not afraid to talk wherever I am."

But another girl, one who had been much quieter in class, had a different opinion: "I was a lot more nervous when I went to a coeducational school. I was afraid I would be made fun of, so I just got quiet."

"Did boys make fun of you?" we asked.

"Only sometimes, but once it happened, I was afraid it would happen again, so I stopped talking."

"Won't girls here make fun of you?"

"No, they won't." She spoke softly. "They take me seriously here." In Advanced Placement biology, the next class on our schedule, the barrage of student questions began again, even heavier than in the math class we had just left. We began to wonder if the girls were trying to give the science teacher a hard time, literally burying her under an avalanche of interrogation, but as we watched, we become convinced they were driven by genuine curiosity and a desire to understand. As the teacher chose one question to answer, side conversations broke out with girls helping one another. After class we caught up with one of the students.

"Do the students in your class always ask so many questions?" we asked.

"Of course," she said. "This stuff is hard to understand, so when we don't get it, we ask questions. What else would you do? How else could you run a class anyway?" The girl began to question us.

"We've seen lots of classes where students didn't ask many questions. For example, the teacher gave a lecture and then asked the students questions."

The girl looked thoughtful. "I guess it could be done that way," she said. "Our English and history classes are a little more like that. But math and science are really hard, so the way we learn here is, we ask."

In twelfth-grade history we saw what she meant. Ten students and a male teacher were discussing Thomas Friedman's book *From Beirut to Jerusalem*. The dynamic here was more traditional: the teacher asked and the students answered. Sometimes raising their hands and sometimes calling out, they handled a very sophisticated level of discussion, and the tone, as in the morning English class, was that of a quiet and serious conversation. But occasionally questions broke out here, too. When one girl asked a question, a "tipping" effect occurred, with several students questioning in quick succession. Then the pattern reversed, and the teacher once again became the authority figure, the one questioning.

When we interviewed teachers in this school, they expressed a sense of mission about educating girls. A math teacher talked about how male students diverted attention from females: "When I taught in a coed school," she said, "I found the boys were so much more demanding of my attention. In my classes here, if I forget a paper, I can leave the class, walk to the office, and copy something, and the girls would just chat among themselves. If I did that with boys, I'd come back to find them running around the room and hitting one another over the head."

A science teacher said, "I used to teach in a coed school, too. I had to be constantly vigilant. The boys were so verbally aggressive; they demanded that you focus in on them. I found I had to establish a personal relationship with girls before they would talk or take risks. Now I'm the parent of a daughter who's in a coed school. I watch as her aggressiveness, her spirit, diminishes with age. It's as if she's learning by osmosis not to speak out. I can't wait until she's old enough to come here."

The history teacher had taught in several cross-registration classes, those admitting male students from the coordinate boys' school. He said, "When it's all female, the girls take chances. But when guys are in the class, the girls stop asking questions the way they do now. They begin to say things like, 'I'm not sure if this is the right answer, but . . .'"

"How do the boys act?"

"They take wild risks. They make comments even when they haven't read the material. They're right out there with a nerve, a spontaneity, a courageousness that's almost athletic. And there's a one-upmanship that I rarely see among the girls."

When we talked with students, their comments echoed the perceptions of their teachers. Most liked going to school without being distracted or intimidated by boys. An all-girls school "lets you be yourself without worrying about how you look or being pressured and embarrassed by guys," one girl said. Another added, "It's a place where you can concentrate on academics rather than that 'social popularity thing.' "

While most girls offered endorsements, others had their doubts. One flatly admitted, "After being here for ten years, I just don't know how to deal with boys." Another told us, "I have trouble thinking of boys as actual people with ideas. I get intimidated by them easily and don't know how to be myself around them. I think a single-sex school prepares students poorly for a double-sex world."

SEXISM REARS ITS HEAD

Several girls had pointed to the eleventh- and twelfth-grade cross-registration program as one way to get used to boys, so we organized a group interview. Many single-sex schools allow limited cross-registration, and this elite girls' school had such a coordinate program with a neighboring, and also exclusive, boys' school.

"What's it like attending classes at the boys' school?" we asked.

"The guys fool around more," a dark-haired girl said, smiling at the others as if remembering a private joke. Then several chimed in:

"They throw erasers and pencils in class."

"They call one another names and make fun of one another. That would never happen in our school."

"It's not that they're stupid, they're witty and smart and all, but they just joke around."

"Do you enjoy that?" we asked. There was a pause. The girls looked at one another and then started talking at once, at first all positively: "Yeah, I think it's fun." "It makes going to class more interesting." "One guy used to come to class with his telephone number written on his jacket, and he kept flashing it at us. I thought he was funny."

But then came the negatives: "Sometimes the jokes made me feel uncomfortable. I felt different, like I was there but never really accepted." Another girl, one who looked as if she was remembering something painful, agreed and added, "It was worse than that. I was the only girl in an English class. It took me two weeks before I said anything. I felt really intimidated. Every time I said something, they all turned around and looked at me. And if you said something, they began to talk, and you wondered what they were saying about you."

"I didn't feel that way in my Spanish class," said another, joining in. "But there were four of us. The teacher loved having girls. The first day we walked in he said, 'It's so nice having roses among the thorns.' " The girls laughed.

"Did you like being treated like roses?"

"It wasn't always like that. Just sometimes—like when it was cold and the teacher turned the heat up. He said the boys could take it, but he was making it warmer for the girls."

Another girl shook her head. "Our French class was completely different. I thought it was sexist."

"What do you mean, sexist?" We prompted her to be specific.

"We had this vocabulary contest. The teacher gave us a word, and if you knew the synonym in French, you banged your hand down on the table. Well, the girls were the only ones who had studied, so we were way ahead. And the teacher kept saying to the boys, 'C'mon! You can't let girls get ahead of you.' "

Another girl added to the story: "And Natalie"—she pointed to the girl who had described the contest—"had the most points of all. When the teacher couldn't get the boys to do better, he drew a funny little face with glasses on the board, wrote Natalie's name by it, and said, 'Here we call people like this nerds.' "

"How did you feel when that happened?"

"That wasn't so bad," Natalie said. "The play was worse. It was so sexist, about the Trojan War. The girls had to read the part of Helen. We wanted to read the guys' parts because there were more of them. Over here in the girls' school you get to read all the parts, and a lot of the time the men's roles are better."

Other girls from the French class joined in. "There was this woman standing naked in water."

"I guess it was Helen. And these guys came along and captured her."

"And her big line throughout the play was, 'I live to obey you.' "

Several of the girls were laughing now, repeating the line in a parody that almost became a chant: 'I live to obey you. I live to obey you.' " Then Natalie stopped laughing. "I hated that play," she said.

"It really bothered you to read that line."

She turned beet red. "I refused. I wouldn't do it. I would rather not have a part than read a line like that."

Jeanna, a vivacious girl who had been laughing through much of the discussion, now also looked thoughtful and serious. "There was some-thing else that bothered me at the boys' school. It was the stuff they had on the wall."

"You mean the pictures?"

"In our class there were two big pictures. One was really a poster and the other a picture of the poster. They were both of the same woman, just her torso. She was blond, of course, and tan. She had the tiniest waist." Jeanna gestured with her hands as if pushing her own waist in eight inches. "And she had Perrier bottle caps over her." The girl gestured again, this time covering her breasts. "And there was this corkscrew right next to her, pointing right at her. And it was so suggestive, even of vio-lence. The guys really liked it, but a few of them said it was disgusting. I talked to the teacher and told her I didn't like it, that it made me feel uncomfortable. She said I could take it down if I wanted to."

"Did you?"

"Well, no."

"Why not?"

"It's not my school. Everyone would have been mad at me. I wanted the teacher to take it down. I thought it was her place to do it. I still can't believe a teacher—a woman teacher—would have a picture like that in her room."

"But eventually the picture did come down." Natalie said. "One day when we went to class it was gone. We don't know how it happened, but it just wasn't there anymore."

LOST IN THE PAST

To find out more about the boys' schools, we visited and observed in two of them. On our first visit, we walked into a room to talk with boys who were wearing ties and jackets as they sprawled over chairs during their free period, their books open but mainly unread as they talked to one another. We are introduced to the group by the assistant headmaster and then left on our own.

"We're trying to find out how coeducation compares with single-sex schools," we say. The students regard us with curiosity and caution. "Has anyone here been in coed classrooms or those that have cross-registration with girls?"

Several boys laugh and point to others as potential subjects for inter-view. "Go talk to Jerry, he's a woman. He's been in classes in the girls' school." "Talk to Ed. He can tell you all about going to school with girls." Finally Tony is identified as one who is taking Advanced Placement biology at the girls' school. As we approach him, he sits up and looks serious.

"It's pretty much the same whether there are girls in the class or it's all boys" is Tony's response to our question.

"Do you think boys and girls behave the same in class, or do they act differently?"

"Pretty much the same." He pauses. "Well, I guess the girls aren't as rowdy."

"What happens here that's rowdy?" The question generates interest from the others who have been bystanders. They join the conversation and describe rowdy behavior with obvious relish.

"We kick balls around."

"We have snowball fights."

We try to clarify their remarks: "You mean outside?"

"No, we do it inside. In the hallways." Several boys laugh and playfully punch one another. Then they continue with more examples:

"Boys give teachers more of a hard time."

"We throw spitballs. And we play dumb jokes in class."

"What kind of dumb jokes?" A circle of boys has now officially joined the interview.

"If someone says something dumb in class, we make cracks."

"We're sarcastic."

"We tear him apart."

"When someone does something stupid, we laugh."

"When guys make jokes and laugh, does that make you feel bad or keep you from answering questions?" The circle widens as more boys try to help us understand how one-upmanship works in their classes.

"No, we all know one another, and we expect it."

"We wouldn't do it as much to strangers."

"Yeah, and if someone was really in trouble in class, we wouldn't do it. We only go for someone when he makes a *humorous* mistake."

"When girls are in your classes, how do they feel when you make cracks and jokes and put each other down?"

The boys look puzzled, and then one says, "You've got to talk to Ed. He's in this calculus class, and there's one girl in it from another school. He gave her a rose on Valentine's Day." Several boys are now pointing to the other side of the room. "He's over there."

When we arrive at the table, Ed is staring intently at his book as though we would go away if he doesn't look up. "We hear you're in a cross-registered calculus class. Can you tell us what it's like?"

Flushing, he points to other boys at the table. "Ask them, too," he says. "They're in the class." We open the question up to involve the other boys. Karen, the lone girl in the class, has obviously been the subject of prior discussion.

"She's a ditz!" one boy says vehemently. "She's a Valley Girl, but she's got the highest average in the class." He shakes his head as if in disbelief.

"Yeah," another boy agrees. "I can't figure out how she does it."

Others around the table offer their opinions:

"She's book smart, but she has no common sense."

"She can't find her way around the school. She's been here for months now, and she still can't get around the building."

"She can't even drive right. She keeps getting into accidents."

"I bet she studies nonstop. There's no other way she could get those grades."

"Come to our class. Fourth period."

Fourteen students, thirteen boys and one girl, are sitting in rows. The room is immaculate, except for graffiti on the desks: "Henderson's face looks like a Pap smear." "Henderson needs a penile prosthesis." Posters of famous sports figures and all-male teams are on the walls. The class proceeds at a brisk, businesslike pace as the teacher puts examples on the board and asks questions. Occasionally students request clarification, but mostly the teacher directs, a pattern similar to the coeducational classes we have spent years observing.

But one dynamic is clearly different—the level of showmanship. If observing classes in the girls' school is like listening in on a conversation, watching the classes in this boys' school is like sitting in on a performance, one with very public peer evaluation. For example, a boy in the front of the room answers a tough question correctly, and the class groans. The boy turns around to his classmates, holds his arms up in a mock shrug, and smiles. "What can I say? I'm just on today." This pattern of showmanship continues throughout the period, and the teacher eventually turns to us and says with a smile, "They're showing off for you." Then his gaze turns back to the class. "I'll get them tomorrow," he says, but his tone is friendly rather than threatening.

"What's it like to teach an advanced math class of all boys and only one girl?" we ask the teacher after the students have left.

"This class is not a problem," he says. "One reason it works is that

Karen is the top student. She has the highest grades in the class. The boys here respect academic achievement, so no matter how much they might like to, they can't put her down."

Next on our schedule is eleventh-grade English. We arrive early to watch the eleven boys enter the room, and they cause a commotion. The teacher enters and surveys the class seriously. "I want to make sure you know how to do the footnotes for your research paper." He speaks softly, but the class quiets down. "Tune in, Josh"—the tone is calm but firm. As the teacher explains how he wants the footnotes, it is as if there has been a magical change: boys who were loud and boisterous are now intent, earnest, and serious. And then the showmanship begins. One boy makes a clever comment; the teacher responds with a quiet, appraising look. "Wow, are you sharp," he says softly. "Whooo!" the other boys chorus. "I'm all fired up today," the boy acknowledges.

After class we talk with the teacher about the pattern of putting each other down. "The boys do a lot of hazing," he says, "jockeying for place, trying to establish where they are in the pack. I think it goes along with sports. It's how they behave on the athletic field."

"What happens to the class atmosphere when there are girls?"

"It depends on who they are. One year I had a group of girls who were strong both academically and personally. They just gave the boys a look or even hazed back. That group of strong girls really helped the class. They were so smart and focused, and the boys were determined not to be shown up. There were some crude jocks in that class, and I think the girls had a healing influence. But another year I had six girls who were very weak academically. Those girls had a terrible time."

Linguist Deborah Tannen said that a source of inspiration for her book *You Just Don't Understand* was a research project in which she observed videotapes of pairs of friends on different age levels as they communicated with each other.[33] Instructed to "find something serious to talk about," elementary and secondary school girls on the videotapes faced each other directly and quietly discussed personal events. But the boys behaved differently. More accustomed to playing games and doing things, elementary school boys on the videotapes had trouble complying with the instructions. Restless, they pretended to fight, teased each other, and told jokes. While topics of conversation differed by age, the communication behavior Tannen saw parallels the interaction we observed in the boys' school: joking and teasing, sometimes offensively; performing;

defying authority; putting each other down; and jockeying for place within the pack.

But among the videotaped conversations of male friends, Tannen listened to one that was very different, one where the discussion was intensely personal. In this dialogue one boy, Todd, revealed how alienated he felt, how he was left out at parties and was ill at ease with girls and even his own close friends. He spoke haltingly and wistfully of a time when he could really communicate with others. The conversation, Tannen said, was the most "intimate talk" she heard on all the research videotapes.

Amid all the joking and performing and putting down we observed at the boys' school, we also heard this kind of intimate and personal discussion. A psychology class with eleven boys and a female teacher (the only one we saw in the school) talked about gender roles.

"Those of you who have been reading your book have come across the terms 'animus' and 'anima,' a male side and a female side," the teacher says to begin the class.

"You mean enema!" a boy calls out. Others laugh, but the teacher ignores the outburst. "This could show up in a lot of simple things like colors. Look at the suits you're wearing. You're all in dark blue and brown and gray, but I'm allowed to express myself through colors. I can wear pink—"

"Excuse me," a boy says, interrupting. "I'm in pink. I wear pink boxers."

"But they're not showing." The teacher grins. "I guess that side of you is repressed." The students laugh, but the teacher persists with her point. "Now I want you to be serious. Do you think men can be gentle and nurturing? Or do they have to be macho?"

Almost magically the class becomes serious. "I think we act macho now," a tall, thin boy says, "and it feels awkward to be gentle. But I think gentleness develops with age. Once you have resolved your own personality, then artificial walls break down. It's society that limits you."

"Actually," says the teacher, "we have some experts on this very subject." She introduces us. Pulled into the discussion, we ask the boys how all-boy classes compare to coeducation.

"We're much more open here," a redhead called Danny says. "When I was fourteen, I hated going to school with girls. I felt awkward. So I came here. I think you get a much better education when you're with guys. We feel comfortable with each other. If I were trying to get a date with some girl in the class, I wouldn't feel free to say whatever I wanted. In a coed class you look at the girl and then you gauge your answers and say what you think the girl wants to hear."

"But what if the girl isn't sexually attractive to you?" another boy asks. "Couldn't you say what you wanted to then? It's just that girls are different. Like if there were black students in this class, there would be a difference."

"No," Danny says vehemently. "I don't think girls can be just friends. The issue isn't difference. It's *sex*."

"Do you think women reinforce your macho qualities?" the teacher asks, joining the conversation.

"Some do and some don't. From my experience, which is admittedly limited"—the tall, thin boy shrugs and smiles—"some women want you to be a hunter, and some women want you to wear a tutu and cry."

"Which kind of girl do you like better?" the teacher asks.

"I like the one who lets me wear a tutu and cry."

"How many of you would like the other kind of girl?" the teacher asks.

Several boys, including Danny, raise their hands. "I like it when a girl makes me feel like a man," Danny says.

"I like the kind of girl who lets me be myself," another boy says. "I like it when I can be comfortable and I don't have to pretend."

Throughout the latter part of this discussion there has been no teasing, insulting, or putting down. These boys have been remarkably open and very vulnerable, but nobody has taken advantage. After class the teacher talks about "her boys": "The joking around is a veneer they have. In a way they've just learned to mask their feelings, but they have such intense feelings. Go look in the art room. They do such beautiful, expressive work."

"What happens when there are girls in your class?" we ask.

"I have to work harder at involving them, getting them to talk. And when girls are there, boys don't share their feelings as much. The males make the analytical comments while the girls do the expressive work."

"Do you think an all-male environment is good for these boys?"

The teacher pauses and then says thoughtfully, "Not really. Maybe during junior high school. Otherwise, I don't. I think interaction with girls is healthy. Girls today are testing every frontier of their psyche, but these boys are feeling left out and left behind. They're lost in the past, and someone needs to bring them out."

Generally, teachers at boys' schools expressed a wide spectrum of opinions about the value of all-male education. Some said males were better off in single-sex schools with men as teachers and role models. They thought boys concentrated more on their studies and were freer to express themselves honestly when girls were not in the room. But others considered coeducation a healthier environment, one where boys benefited from interaction with girls.

IS SINGLE-SEX EDUCATION BETTER THAN COEDUCATION?

These descriptions from students and teachers underscore some of the advantages and some of the problems in single-sex schools. They remind us that when girls feel safe, they are more likely to speak up in class, engage the teacher rather than "play dumb," or stay silent for fear of becoming a "target." For boys, safety means exploring topics and emotions typically avoided in coed school. Many have relied on such positive descriptions to make a number of claims for the superiority of single-sex schooling. Let's first look at a few of these claims and then turn our attention to what the research says. The claims below are phrased as questions because they really are questions to be explored. Under each question we shall briefly describe some of the conflicting research, and why these claims must be taken with more than just a grain of salt.[34]

Does Single-Sex Education Increase Girls' Self-Esteem and Academic Achievement?

Here is an example of how cautious we must be with the research. A decade or more ago, advocates of single-sex education were encouraged by studies suggesting that females in single-sex schools demonstrate increased academic achievement, self-esteem, and career salience, as well as a decrease in sex-role stereotyping.[35] One study found that female students in girls' schools in the United States expressed greater interest in both mathematics and English, took more mathematics courses, did more homework, and had more positive attitudes toward academic achievement than girls attending coeducational institutions.[36] Others found that girls in single-sex schools showed more interest in the feminist movement and were less sex-role stereotyped than were their peers in coeducational schools.[37] But before you jump to any conclusions, it is not at all clear if these results are due to single-sex schooling. Perhaps these schools attracted these students with high achievement goals, or perhaps students did well because they were attending wonderful schools that happened to be single-sex. Was single-sex schooling responsible, or were small class sizes, skilled teachers, strong academics, involved parents, and a selective admission process?[38]

Other studies were less positive.[39] Paul LePore and John Warren (1997) found no significant academic differences between girls in all-girls Catholic schools and girls in coeducational Catholic schools. Valerie Lee analyzed a national sample of private (not Catholic) secondary schools, and found "no consistent pattern of effects for attending either single-sex or coeducational independent schools for either girls or boys."[40]

Few reverse the question: Is coeducation more effective than single-sex schooling? Some studies indicate this may be true. Carole Shmurak examined records of nearly thirteen thousand graduates from thirteen private schools recording the number of women pursuing careers in ten fields, from medicine to architecture. She found that women graduating from coeducational schools were more likely to be in law, computers, scientific research, and psychology. There was no significant difference in other fields, and surprisingly, none of the graduates from girls' schools had a higher proportion of graduates in any of these fields.[41]

Do Boys Focus on Academics Better in a Single-Sex Environment?

There is a popular belief that all-boys schools provide the motivation and discipline boys need to become strong students, and it is certainly true that there are some wonderful boys' schools. Hollywood is somewhat taken with this concept and has produced several films about preppy boys' schools where a little dose of Latin and a bigger dose of character building paves a path to Harvard or Yale. But those images are best left on the DVD; few studies support the idea that all single-sex schools work for boys in the United States.

Several comprehensive studies of single-sex schooling were done by University of Michigan researcher Valerie Lee, with her colleagues Helen Marks and Tina Byrd, in the 1980s and 1990s. In one study, they undertook site visits to a random sample of twenty-one nonreligious independent schools: seven male, seven female, and seven coeducational. In coed schools they found boys dominating discussions, and sexist incidents were particularly prevalent in the chemistry classes they observed. In all-male classrooms, Lee reports that teachers encouraged boys to be aggressive, to "give 'em hell"; one even addressed his students as "studs." Boys' schools also can harbor sexism and promote some shocking forms of misogyny.[42] The worst culprits in Lee's observations were English classes where discussions of sexual scenes in literature sometimes degenerated into the treatment of girls as sex objects. In one English class, a male teacher encouraged boys to use specific examples in their writing. Then he gave an example of his own, suggesting body measurements as a relevant detail in describing female characters. Sexual depictions of women decorated the walls in several all-boys schools. In a room where boys were studying French, there was a large picture of a woman's lips without her face, and a bikini-clad woman with her arms raised was displayed in a calculus classroom. Other researchers have concluded that boys in single-sex schools actually achieve less well than boys in coeducational classrooms, or find no performance difference between single-sex and coeducational settings.[43]

Other studies paint a more positive picture. For example, one found that boys disadvantaged in the elementary years felt more comfortable in a single-sex environment.[44] Cornelius Riordan found that many anti-academic elements in the youth culture (such as peer group pressures) can be overcome in a boys' school, especially for poorer boys.[45] The boys in his study had higher test scores, greater leadership skills, better homework habits, and higher academic expectations. But Riordan also found that single-sex schools had little or no effect on middle-class or wealthier children of either gender, and his work, mostly in Catholic schools, may not apply to public schools. Given such ambiguous results, the jury is still out when it comes to all-male education.

Do Single-Sex Schools and Classes Respond Better to Male/Female Brain Differences?

Research suggests that there are differences in brain development between girls and boys that influence some areas of cognition and behavior, including memory and vision, hearing and stress hormones.[46] Some advocates of single-sex schools see these differences as central and immutable, concluding that boys and girls are best educated separately and differently.[47] Leonard Sax, a biology-is-educational-destiny advocate, writes: "Human nature is gendered to the core"[48] and "in the ways that matter, single-sex schools may provide better preparation for the real world than coed schools do."[49] Michael Gurian writes that boys are deductive thinkers, prefer to work silently, enjoy jargon, and are easily bored, so teachers must keep stimulating them. Girls, on the other hand, are inductive and concrete thinkers, actually enjoy details, and focus more on group dynamics.[50]

Such gender generalizations, despite their scientific-sounding aura, quickly become problematic. For example, Gurian's training materials inform teachers, "Pursuit of power is a universal male trait. Pursuit of a comfortable environment is a universal female trait."[51] Really? These pseudoscientific pronouncements by those promoting "hardwired" gender brain differences have been criticized by educators for using incomplete and misleading data, cherry-picking findings, making claims that far outpace the research, and "romanticizing" conclusions.[52] The brain consists of two hemispheres designed to work together, not apart. They are complementary and creative partners. Our children should learn how to use all their brain. Our knowledge of the educational implications of brain functioning on learning, and the role that sex may or not play in all this, remains far more rudimentary than these advocates claim.

The most recent and perhaps most thorough review of this topic was undertaken by Janet Hyde at the University of Wisconsin, Madison. She used a sophisticated meta-analysis technique as she considered all studies on gender differences working to uncover persistent and prominent findings. Are boys more aggressive than girls? Are they better at math and science? Do girls have stronger verbal and fine motor skills? Are they more nurturing than boys?

Hyde's review was startling for those constantly hearing the "Men are from Mars and women are from Venus" chorus: "The evidence, often based on meta-analysis, indicates generally small gender differences for most abilities and behaviors, even those commonly said to show large differences."[53] In some cases, her findings were counterconventional: males exhibited slightly more helping behaviors than females; self-esteem levels for adult men and women are actually quite similar. It seems that men and women are both from earth, and more alike than our culture reveals. Hyde did find some educationally relevant differences: males demonstrated greater aggression and activity level, had stronger math problem-solving skills beginning in high school, and a better ability to rotate objects mentally. Yet it is not clear which, if any, of these differences are due to biology, or to culture, or to a combination of the two. After an exhaustive review, Hyde settled on a "gender similarities hypothesis": males and females are more alike than different.[54]

Also at the University of Wisconsin, Richard Davidson, research professor of psychology and psychiatry, has used functional magnetic resonance imaging (fMRI) and electroencephalograms (EEG) to demonstrate how Buddhist monks can alter brain activities through meditation, which may indicate that they have created new neural pathways. Researchers have coined the term *neuroplasticity* to describe the ability of the brain to reorganize itself by incorporating neural connections based on experience.[55] We have so much to learn about the brain.

The preponderance of studies on gender differences to date find that boys differ from other boys, and girls differ from other girls more than the average boy differs from the average girl.[56] To group students by sex ignores the great diversity within each sex. The research actually makes a strong case for individualizing instruction, not "genderizing" instruction.

Do Single-Sex Schools and Classes Provide Distraction-Free Learning?

Anyone who has attended school knows that boys can attract attention, acting out and even "showboating" for the opposite sex. Girls may take the opposite path, limiting their words and actions in front of boys so as not to draw attention, or appear stupid—or too smart. So it is not surprising that girls in all-girls private schools and math and science classes may feel less distracted and have more positive attitudes toward math and science than those in coed settings.[57] Similarly, some research suggests that boys in single-sex schools seem freer to value and enjoy nontraditional subjects such as literature and art when girls are not present.[58]

Yet removing the "other sex" is far from a guarantee of eliminating distractions or "sexual tension" from the classroom. Teachers report that all-boys classes can have far more distractions and be far more difficult to manage than coed classes. A British study found that in all-boys classes, boys distract one another with a "macho, male culture."[59] Others find that same-sex bullying may be as prevalent in single-sex schools as sexual harassment is in coed schools.[60] In fact some teachers report that the presence of girls in class actually reduces male misbehavior and increases the boys' academic performance. In single-sex classes, girls have been known to "show off" and try to impress one another in an effort to raise their own social standing.[61] Let's face it: no matter where they are, students can be quite inventive in their ability to distract one another. The lesson may be less about segregating the sexes and more about the importance of effective classroom management techniques.

In another study, Valerie Lee investigated sixty independent secondary schools (twenty girls' schools, twenty boys' schools, twenty coed schools). David and Myra asked her if she had reached a decision about the merits of single-sex education. She said:

> Right now I'm equivocal [a word Dr. Lee repeated throughout the interview]. I can't conclude that all you need to do is send your girls to an all-female school and your problems will be solved. It really depends on the school. You have to sit in on the classes and find out what's going on there. Even in the best girls' schools we saw sexism. For example, we saw a history teacher give a research paper to a class of very capable girls. She said, "This is a difficult assignment, so there will be major hand-holding available." I think that's overly supportive; I can't imagine a teacher offering "major hand-holding" to boys.
>
> I'm also equivocal because when we saw really outlandish behavior, it was most likely to happen in single-sex schools. In a few girls' schools we saw male bashing, which I think is entirely inappropriate. And in boys' schools we saw incidents that went beyond the pale. When I see a class of boys talking about women as a collection of body parts hooked together, I think it's a scandal.

A more recent review of single-sex schooling research, undertaken by the U.S. Department of Education in 2005, also relied on the word *equivocal,* although in this case, the government concluded "equivocal" results favored single-sex schools. The federal government contracted a multiyear literature review to see if "single-sex schools are more or less effective than coeducational schools" in classroom treatment of students, gender equity, and how people see the school climate. The vast majority of the studies available did not meet rigorous research standards, so most were rejected. Of the remaining, few dealt with boys' schools, or considered critical variables such as the socioeconomic status of students. In short, "equivocal" was an optimistic assessment from an administration strongly pushing for single-sex schooling.[62]

As you have probably figured out for yourself by now, the research is not helpful. We do not know if single-sex schools are more or less effective than coeducational schools. (Sorry for those of you looking for a quick and easy resolution to this question.) Many of the studies that do exist were done overseas, at the college level, or in Catholic schools, and may not apply to most U.S. public schools. Worse yet, most studies were poorly designed, comparing single-sex schools with coeducational schools but ignoring such critical differences as teacher qualifications, curriculum studied, classroom methodology, socioeconomic class, and parental involvement. Even fewer studies looked at single-sex classes, where little evidence shows any long-term benefits for either boys or girls. Yet all around America, such schools and classes are springing up. Many educators, drawn in by the excitement surrounding single-sex education, have turned a blind eye to the research and to the emerging warning signs.

PUBLIC SCHOOLS EXPERIMENTING WITH SINGLE-SEX EDUCATION

A number of public schools have set sail into the perfect storm, and it is not always a smooth sail.[63] The largest study of public single-sex schools to date was done in California. In the 1990s, California created twelve "dual academies," each containing a boys' school and a girls' school. They served low-income and minority students and were primarily designed to increase school choice.[64] A team of researchers observed these academies and conducted more than three hundred interviews. What they found was frightening: "traditional gender stereotypes were often reinforced. Boys tended to be taught in more regimented, traditional, and individualistic fashion, and girls in more nurturing, cooperative and open environments." Also, "students received mixed messages about gender from their teachers." One of the findings peculiar to this situation is that "the creation of separate academies for boys and girls on the same campus led to a dichotomous understanding of gender, where girls were seen as 'good' and boys were seen as 'bad.' " Although the intent was to focus on sex segregation, little attention was paid to teaching methods and gender-related learning strategies. California started with twelve such schools; within a few years, eleven had closed.[65]

Despite the less-than-impressive results, California proved to be a trendsetter. By 2008, almost three hundred single-sex classes and schools were started by public school systems around the nation. Many of them were in urban settings, serving at-risk populations, and facing major challenges. Why was single-sex instruction popular there? We talked to teachers and principals in these schools to find out.

Emily, a bright, new teacher, was eager to make a change in a challenging Washington, D.C., inner-city school. She came from the Midwest with energy and commitment, and through an alternative teacher certification program was placed in a single-sex school. Two years later, she found herself frustrated by many aspects of the single-sex model.

My middle school went single-sex mainly to deal with discipline problems. There was no rationale related to gender equitable teaching practices. We are a school plagued by low test scores and serious discipline challenges, and going single-sex seems to be used as a tracking system to deal with some of this. I believe this model, however, is hurting both the boys and the girls in my classes, just in different ways. More often than not, girls' classes gain a reputation as easier to manage, and as a result we are more open to expanding them. During my first year, we split the eighth grade into two girls' sections and three boys' sections. This meant that the girls' sections numbered thirty students or more and the boys' sections had only fifteen students in each class. If a teacher was out, we always combined the girls' classes, making them grow even larger.

A few aspects of the single-sex model in my school worked out well. Because the boys and girls were separate, I and other teachers often designed our lessons differently, attempting to cater to the interests of the boys' and girls' classes (English teachers often had the classes read different books). I also believe girls participate more actively in my math classes than they might otherwise. While most of these were sound practices, other times I was not sure that I was doing the right thing. Because girls are seen as having fewer behavioral problems, I found myself being more casual with them. I think I did a better job fostering independent thinking for the girls. I tended to have the girls work in small groups, creating posters and projects to learn certain math concepts. The very next period, when the boys entered my room, I would teach the same concept through direct instruction. Instead of creating posters, the boys were taking notes and raising their hands to answer questions. I was fearful that the boys' classes were too wild to handle work that was more independent. Overall, I am more authoritarian and harsher when I manage and instruct the boys sections. We never had training, and I think I and many other teachers in the school are doing a lot of stereotyping.

If my school is going to maintain a single-sex environment, it must be related more to gender equitable instruction and less to managing behavior challenges. Also, there must be a safe space structured into the day in which girls and boys are given an opportunity to interact with one another. Right now this does not exist and as a result, when girls and boys pass each other in the hallways, behavior is sometimes violent, and play-fighting is age-inappropriate. Students need an environment in which they learn how to maturely converse with the other sex. Right now we are not confronting the real issues of gender differences and academic performance.

Another D.C. teacher was also introspective about single-sex education.

> At first, I felt there were some real advantages to separating the girls and boys. There was certainly less teasing, which had gotten out-of-hand the year before. So I saw the separation as having marginal advantages. But over time, each gender developed other discipline issues. Cliques of girls began teasing each other. They replaced the boys as the discipline problem. Boys really began acting out. They actually got goofier. Then there was a second problem: boys struggling with their sexual identity really lost out. Some of these boys had girls as their best friends, and when the separate classes began, they literally lost their best friends. They were now isolated in an alpha male environment. They were treated harshly and ridiculed. The third problem was sheer numbers: there were more girls in these classes than boys. The girls' classes got much bigger. The girls got less individualized attention. So what I thought at first would be a help for girls really failed them. It was not a good idea.
>
> I pride myself in not being an ideologue. I do not like it when people get stuck in one camp or the other. Show me something that works, and I want to find out why and how we can use it. But this did not work.

Such experiences have not deterred urban school principals from initiating single-sex classes and schools in their search for the silver bullet to calm troubled waters and raise test scores. One such principal explained, "Our test scores were low and we had real problems, so they (central office) decided to move the sixth grade to another school. Our school was losing parent support and students. So we tried single-sex classes and the parents thought it was a great idea. They stopped transferring; we were told that we could keep our sixth grade. Now I am a big fan. It works wonders with our discussion of male and female hygiene, and with social graces. The students bond more with their teachers now."

David asked the principal if we could visit the school and see the changes. She said she would have to check with the central office. Three months and several telephone calls later, we were still not allowed to visit.

In another urban school experimenting with single-sex classes, the principal was excited to receive David's telephone call. David was excited, too, thinking perhaps we would be able to visit the school and see these classes in action. But there was a misunderstanding: the principal thought that David was volunteering to train her teachers. Although David offered to discuss that possibility, other issues soon took priority and she also never called back. While many private single-sex schools put out the welcome mat for us, the public single-sex schools did not.

In May 2006, the principal of a junior high school in Livingston Parish, Louisiana, told students and parents that the school would soon be divided by gender due to the research on brain differences. Girls would be taught "good character" and boys taught about "heroic" behavior and what it means to be a man. When the American Civil Liberties Union threatened legal action, the Louisiana school district abandoned its sex-segregation plan. Perhaps the school district recognized that the proposed scheme was illegal under Title IX. However, only two months later, the new Title IX regulations were issued, encouraging public schools across the country to institute sex segregation, just as this Louisiana school system originally intended.[66] (One rule we have learned when it comes to detecting gender bias is to replace the word *gender* or *sex* with *race* or *religion,* forms of discrimination that are more obvious to Americans. Imagine if a new civil rights regulation were changed to read that schools can separate students for ethnic reasons, or based on race, or can establish Islamic, Christian, and Jewish schools, because they gave parents choice. We dare say there would be some outrage. As a nation we are less aware that sex segregation can also be damaging.)

LESSONS LEARNED

Single-sex education has taught us some valuable lessons, if we choose to learn them. Women's experiences, in fact all of our experiences, need to be recognized and respected in (and beyond) schools. Too often that is not the case as we are taught the "right way" to see and do things, typically through the eyes of the dominant culture and gender. Too often it is not only girls who are silenced in school, it is the shy boys, those new to English, those who feel less safe, and those who do not "fit in." It is not just *women's ways of knowing,* it is each one of us that has a way of knowing, of learning, of seeing the world. The feminist emphasis on connection, of learning from each other and not simply from an authority figure or in a competitive climate, offers a powerful lesson for schools. We learn from each other, and when classrooms include only one race, one socioeconomic class, one religion, or one gender, we are all the poorer.

Remember the D.C. teacher who takes pride in not being an ideologue? We, too, disdain the ideologue tag. In the mid-1990s, in the original *Failing at Fairness,* Myra and David were optimistic about single-sex schools; they often liked what they saw, in part because they often created safe spaces for females and honored individual differences. Today there is less cause for optimism and more for caution.

We believe that the success of many private single-sex schools (and here we are typically talking about girls' schools, both more prevalent and more studied) is not their single-sexness, but their educational practices, and that is the lesson they should be teaching us. These schools have what many other schools lack: students competing to attend; adequate, sometimes abundant resources; small classes; involved parents; well-trained teachers; a coherent curriculum that looks beyond high-stakes tests to more meaningful learning. Let's be honest: if all of these elite, private single-sex schools went coed tomorrow, they would all still be elite, private schools. Plainly put, many of them are simply terrific schools. We are not ready to dismiss the potential of single-sex education entirely, for there may be boys who excel in an all-male environment; there may be girls who excel in an all-female environment. But for right now, the evidence is lacking, and the stampede to single-sex classes is causing a dust storm of confusion—and maybe more than a little damage.

Most teachers have zero experience as a student or a teacher in a single-sex school, but there is no shortage of opinions. When David spoke on the subject at a National Education Association conference in 2007, he asked teachers for their views of single-sex education. The teacher comments were mixed, and no clear consensus emerged. Some were supportive, such as the Wyoming teacher who explained: "I never attended one, but it may encourage girls to excel and students to focus on academics rather than personal issues." An Ohio teacher agreed: "I watch how girls retreat to themselves when boys are constantly running the class." But others described themselves as "skeptical." A teacher from Hawaii feared that "it does not teach tolerance, interpersonal relations with the other sex." A kindergarten teacher from Vermont explained, "I am the father of two daughters. Last year my kindergarten class was ten boys and zero girls. I felt a lot was missing for these students' first year."

This teacher realizes that sometimes the familiar hides gifts. Could coeducation be such a gift?

Andre Boyd, a South Carolina middle school teacher, writes:

Our students have much to contribute to each other, and students of all ages benefit from being engaged in activities and learning in the company of the opposite sex. In the classroom, learning experiences need to resemble real-world life experiences. How can we prepare students for future families, homes, and workplaces without exposing them to members of the opposite sex? How can we expect them to learn to respect and appreciate gender differences as adults if we do not teach them to form healthy relationships and have positive interactions and appropriate dialogues now?

I also believe that female classmates encourage many unmotivated male students. In my middle school classroom, I see my female students try to motivate my male students who seem to be less interested.

As educators, our efforts should not be driven by how we can separate students to minimize distractions but by how we can bring all students together to maximize learning. In my experience, students tend to learn better when teachers learn to teach better—regardless of the gender of the students.[67]

That is not to say that all of today's coed schools are working well for our students; they are not. Too many fail to provide safe spaces for girls or boys, and struggle with too few resources and too much indifference. Are there lessons to be learned from single-sex education that can be used to improve coed schools? Probably. Are we learning them? We doubt it. Lessons to be learned from single-sex education might come through reflective and objective research, but educational researcher and author Gerald Bracey reminds us that a coherent strategy of selecting single-sex schools and comparing them to coed in a thoughtful, systematic way has yet to occur. To date, we have more than enough emotions and opinions, but a dearth of reflective research. What might such research explore? Here are a few questions that we would like to see investigated. (Do you have some to add to the list?)

- How do boys' schools differ from girls' schools?
- Are girls' schools more or less effective than boys' schools?
- What should be done if single-sex schooling works for one sex, and not the other?
- Are there types of students who benefit in single-sex settings? And if so, how do we identify them?

- Is single-sex education more or less effective at certain levels of schooling (elementary, middle, high school, or even college)?
- Do girls and boys develop stronger self-esteem in single-sex schools?
- How do coed and single-sex schools influence how girls and boys perceive each other?
- What is lost or gained when boys and girls are educated separately?
- How do single-sex schools and single-sex classes compare? Is one more or less effective than the other?
- Are there single-sex school practices that should be transferred to coed public schools?
- Are there single-sex practices that should be avoided in coed settings?
- Historically, the more valued group has received greater resources. How do we ensure that girls' classes and schools do not lose resources over time?
- How are the civil rights protections of Title IX affected by public single-sex classes and schools?

Public coeducation is a democratic promise to educate all, but public schools are breaking that promise. Schools in wealthy communities offer better teachers, better programs, and better futures while poorer schools are literally falling apart, a situation author Jonathan Kozol termed *savage inequalities*. Whites and blacks are more segregated today than they have been in decades, and recent Supreme Court rulings are likely to widen that racial divide. Now new voices advocate dividing our children yet again, this time by sex. What lessons are we teaching our children?

SUCCEEDING AT FAIRNESS:
SUGGESTIONS FOR STUDENTS, PARENTS, AND TEACHERS

There are some exceptional single-sex schools, and for some children, these schools might be an excellent match. A good school is a good school. There may even be special circumstances or preferences that suggest single-sex schooling as a good choice. But what are those special circumstances? Perhaps a particularly quiet girl who may blossom in a single-sex climate? Or a boy who connects with friends and teachers and the culture of an all-boys school? The truth is, we do not yet know what, if any, special draw a single-sex school has for certain students. Parents and students are left to sort out which schools work best for them.

Whether single-sex or coed, in choosing a school, parents and students typically inquire about course offerings, extracurricular activities, the percentage of students going on to college (and what colleges they attend). But other characteristics may be even more revealing, including the quality and equality of the educational experience. Here are some suggestions that may be helpful.

1. Does the school honor each student's learning style and experiences, or does it assume that all members of a group learn and behave in the same way?
2. Observe classes. Whether single-sex or coed, are some students dominating and others silent? Are there different teaching and learning styles? Does the classroom feel like a safe space for all students?
3. Are student-to-student conversations characterized by caring, indifference, or teasing?
4. Talk to the students and ask them what they like about the school, and what they would like to change. That may be your best source of information.
5. Ask the children if there are cliques in the school, and have them describe those cliques.
6. Look at the bulletin boards, the hallways, and classrooms. Are both genders represented and honored in a wide array of roles and accomplishments? Is there stereotyping?
7. Look at the curriculum. Are both genders and a multiracial world represented?
8. Does the school reflect values that are congruent with your own? For example, if you value social justice, is the school working with—or against—your beliefs?
9. What advanced or special courses and programs are offered? Do all students benefit—or only a few?
10. If you are considering a single-sex school, is it because it is a good school that happens to be single-sex, or specifically because it is single-sex? If the latter, why do you think this is important? What about you or the student makes this single-sex aspect important?
11. Be cautious of those who promote single-sex schools based on hardwired

differences between the sexes, or on research that proves single-sex schools or classes are better. The research does not support such claims.

Resources

Gender in Policy and Practice: Perspectives on Single-Sex and Coeducational Schooling, edited by Amanda Datnow and Lea Hubbard

The editors have collected a wide array of views about single-sex schooling, many of them from researchers working in this arena. Rather than persuade the reader, the book informs the reader about the potential benefits and pitfalls of single-sex schooling. While definitive answers are not forthcoming, an honest and balanced consideration of the issue is well worth the read.

Learning Together: A History of Coeducation in American Public Schools, by David Tyack and Elisabeth Hansot

Two talented historians review the history of coeducation in the United States. In this well-written and objective book, the reader learns how practical considerations can create national policy.

Achieving Gender Equity Through Education, edited by Susan Klein

For those looking for a comprehensive review of the research on single-sex education, we recommend Emily Arms's chapter "Gender Equity in Coeducational and Single-sex Environments" and Janet Hyde's chapter "Facts and Assumptions about the Nature of Gender Differences and the Implications for Gender Equity," both in this well-researched book.

Taking the Field: Women, Men, and Sports, by Michael A. Messner

Messner is a master at showing the interplay between sports and gender construction, especially for boys. Sports culture begins to shape our boys and girls from very young ages, whether in coed or single-sex schools. Sports influences how we see ourselves, and each other.

For additional resources, see *Still Failing at Fairness*'s page on www.simonandschuster.com.

CHAPTER 9

Possibilities, Such Possibilities

We are teachers who love teaching, but not everything about teaching is wonderful. In the past, schools were places for wealthy, white males, and teachers were often looked upon as little more than indentured servants. Well into the twentieth century, teachers were often considered second-class citizens, pressured to conform to strict moral and social codes while being paid meager wages. Today teaching and education are center stage, a common topic in the media and in political debates. But teachers themselves are rarely invited to the table to sort out how to reform schools—and that is sad.

In this chapter, we will invite ourselves to the table and share not only some ideas for school reform but also some of the disturbing facts that we need to consider if we are to improve the lives of all our children. Statistics remind us how slow change can be.

- College men have fewer intellectual interests and poorer study habits than college women. They enjoy reading books less, take fewer notes, study less, and play more. Despite their lower effort, lower grades, and lower likelihood of completing a college degree, men evaluate their academic abilities higher than women.[1]
- More than twenty nations, including Sri Lanka and Moldova, have smaller gender gaps in education, politics, and health than the United States. We are sixty-eighth in the world in women's participation in national legislatures. Women hold 98 percent of the low-paying "women's" jobs and fewer than 15 percent of the board seats at major corporations.[2]
- A majority of both men (74 percent) and women (83 percent) say they would choose a job that had lower pay but provided benefits such as family leave, flexible hours, and help with family care. Among college-educated adults, men are still more likely to have

flex-time options at their workplace than women (55.5 percent to 39.7 percent).[3]

- Education can help women close—but not eliminate—the wage gap. Female physicians and surgeons earn 38 percent less than their male counterparts, female college and university teachers earn 25 percent less than men, and female lawyers earn 30 percent less than male lawyers.[4]

In 2008 the Supreme Court unraveled decades of pay equity guarantees in *Ledbetter v. Goodyear Tire & Rubber Co.* Lilly Ledbetter had worked as a manager at Goodyear for nineteen years. Although her performance evaluations were strong, she was always paid less than the males she worked alongside—but she never knew. It took nineteen years before someone broke the code of silence (the company had rules prohibiting employees from discussing their salaries) and told her that despite her excellent performance, she was being paid less than the male managers. The sex discrimination in pay was not subtle. Lilly sued, and the lower courts awarded her significant damages. But the Supreme Court overturned their rulings. In a 5–4 decision, the Court ruled that an employee who is discriminated against must file a lawsuit within 180 days after the first discriminatory pay decision, even if the employee did not know that discrimination was happening. Companies that hide their discrimination for at least 180 days are home free, and employees who are victims of discrimination, like Lilly, are just out of luck. This was a radical departure from precedent (some might say it was legislating from the bench). For Lilly Ledbetter, the decision not only meant almost two decades of lost pay but a future of lower retirement and Social Security benefits; it is an injustice that keeps on taking money out of her pocket. Justice Ruth Bader Ginsburg, speaking for those who dissented, wrote: "In our view, the court does not comprehend, or is indifferent to, the insidious way in which women can be victims of pay discrimination. . . ."[5]

In 2009, the Senate rewrote pay equity legislation so that Lilly Ledbetter and others in her position can receive justice. There will be future opportunities for each of us to let our voices be heard and to promote positive change. Gandhi advised us to be the change we want to see. This chapter is about following his advice.

LESSONS WE ARE LEARNING

The struggle for gender equality has taught us several useful lessons, and we would like to share a few with you. Myra and David learned some of these lessons in the 1980s and '90s, and with the publication of *Failing at Fairness*. After that book came out, there were more lessons to learn, and David and Karen continue to work on them.

Not that long ago, most people saw schools as pretty fair places. Blatant racism was no longer acceptable, and people missed the more subtle race and gender bias that characterized school life. In 1994, *Failing at Fairness* offered some insights into how sex bias operated in schools. At first it was difficult convincing adults that sitting in the same classrooms, listening to the same teachers, reading the same textbooks, girls and boys were getting two very different educations. It was especially challenging because many believed that girls were doing well in school. After all, girls earned higher report card grades, the gratitude of their teachers for their patience and good behavior, the appreciation of their parents for generally avoiding trouble and for being helpful at home, and girls were attending college in growing numbers. What was the problem?

The first lesson: Some inequities, including gender bias, simply fly below people's radar. To make progress, people have to learn how to "see" subtle bias.

In the 1980s, videotapes came to the rescue. The Sadkers showed tapes of classroom scenes to teachers and parents, and they saw these taped scenes as not particularly biased. "That teacher was pretty good!" was a typical remark. Then they taught people how to code or count the teacher-student exchanges, to evaluate verbal interactions objectively and detect if bias is present. The second showing of those classroom videotapes brought dramatically different results. "How did we miss that boys were getting so much more instructional time?" "The teacher questioned the boys more than twice as much as girls, and I thought it was equal!" The rapid pace of classroom interaction hides these micro inequities, and many simply do not see them, including teachers. (The quick pace of the adult workplace also masks many subtle inequities!) But the educational impact is anything but invisible. Over time, girls are transformed into spectators in their own classrooms; they became quieter and more passive, problems not reflected on report card grades or in college attendance. Without training, without learning how to see bias, it is all missed.

This is the reason that the initial *Failing at Fairness* devoted more pages to having people "see" gender bias impacting those seemingly successful female students. This was the more difficult bias to detect.

The second lesson we learned was that change frightens many, and fear not only erects huge blockades, but can stampede the press.

In the 1980s and '90s, the Sadkers' research and writing were an appeal to unravel gender stereotyping in school, a reminder that our nation's promise of fairness for all was still not a reality. Myra and David thought, perhaps naïvely, that once Americans see such injustice, they would call for change. Many people did, but some found change too threatening. After all, traditional male and female gender roles have been the foundation of so much in our culture. The Sadkers, the American Association of University Women, Carol Gilligan, and others were soon attacked for their efforts. Pundits on the right declared that the hundreds of studies illustrating gender bias were poorly done, that any bias against girls was a thing of the past, and that the efforts to create fair classrooms resulted in a "war on boys" (as though the United States needed more wars). Many false and misleading charges were published and weaved into a movement that became known as the *backlash*. The backlash crowd not only accused educators of waging war on boys, but crusaded for a return to traditional gender roles, and used the occasion to launch an attack on progressive education, convinced that boys were suffering because of educational practices they considered too liberal and too feminine. They called for more "boy-friendly" schools that emphasized conventional lectures, more testing, reading war poetry to boys, harsh discipline, and more competition.[6] During this time, Title IX civil rights enforcement was weakened, but few complained. People understood that boys struggled in school, and now they believed they had identified the cause: the attention being "lavished" on girls. After David gives an interview about gender research in schools to a reporter, he is sometimes asked to recommend someone "on the other side of the issue, someone who supports the boys." The press seems to thrive on framing two conflicting sides to every story, even if there is only one side—or many sides. Lacking the time or expertise to actually read the research or check the backgrounds of those they interview, the media simply identify two opposing points of view. The resulting stories can be misleading.

In this book, you have read that the problems boys face in school are significant—and far from new. Blaming women and teachers for boys' problems is an old ploy, but one that still resonates with the public.

(How ironic that female teachers led the fight for more humane class-rooms and an end to corporal punishment, great benefits for boys.) It also reminds us that the male stereotype is far more entrenched in our culture than the female stereotype. Gender bias is not now, nor ever was, a competition between boys and girls. Gender bias is a two-edged sword: it curtails the futures and the happiness of both males and females. We have forgotten Margaret Mead's insight: "Every time we liberate a woman, we liberate a man."

The third lesson we learned is that gender issues are dramatically impacted by race, ethnicity, and class. We need more precision when we discuss gender.

Gender roles vary dramatically from community to community. Too often we forget this point, and this omission leads to confusion. While many middle-class and white parents imagine their sons in new jeopardy, in reality it is poor, African-American, Native American, and Hispanic boys who lag behind, as they have for decades. Ironically, claiming that all boys are at risk masks those in real need.

How do gender, race, class, and ethnicity intersect? How can a generally white feminist movement become more inclusive? How is being a man or a woman in an African-American culture different from being a man or a woman in white, Hispanic, Asian, or American Indian communities? Why are traditional gender roles so entrenched in poorer communities? What strategies can be used within each group to help girls and boys reach their full potential? Bias based on race, class, gender, ethnicity, or sexuality limits our citizens' futures, and we need to learn more about how these biases interact with each other. As Audre Lorde reminds us, "There is no hierarchy of oppressions."

The fourth lesson we want to share is that each of us has enormous power, if we choose to use it.

When David taught history in a high school, he would spend some time teaching his students the Bill of Rights. When the unit ended, he would ask "Which of these rights is guaranteed?" "All," the students would say, puzzled at the question. "None," David would answer, "unless you are willing to stand up for them. They are yours if you fight for them." In the past few years, we have been reminded of that lesson as Title IX was weakened and few have spoken out. We were reminded again in the Lilly Ledbetter injustice. But at least in these injustices, voices of protest were heard. If more citizens work to right these wrongs, justice will reign.

We can create the kind of world we want. Yes, we are sermonizing a bit, but we think it is called for. Alice Walker summarizes the fourth lesson for us: "We are the change we have been waiting for."

OUR INVISIBLE POWER

Even our thoughts can bring about change. In the classic study and book *Pygmalion in the Classroom,* the researchers introduce us to some of our hidden clout. Children in an elementary school were given a special assessment, one designed to identify "intellectual bloomers," those pupils most likely to show remarkable academic gains during the school year. Researchers told the teacher the names of the students who were ready to spurt ahead. Eight months later the accuracy of the special assessment was confirmed. When the "intellectual bloomers" were given an IQ test, they scored much higher than they had on previous exams. Apparently the new test was an educational breakthrough because it could predict students poised for academic acceleration.

But Robert Rosenthal and Lenore Jacobson, the researchers conducting the study, had tricked the teachers. The special assessment was phony; it was not really a harbinger of intellectual readiness but rather a standard intelligence test. And the student names given to the teachers were not carefully selected from test scores but simply picked at random. According to the researchers, teacher expectations caused the students to make exceptional gains. When the teacher thought children were ready to spurt ahead intellectually, she did little things to encourage them—a smile, perhaps, or an extra question or a few minutes of additional attention or praise. Through these nuances, the teacher conveyed the message "You are talented and capable. I have faith in you." While the methodology of this research was sometimes criticized, follow-up studies confirmed the results: adult expectations can influence reality.[7]

In the same way, children are influenced by the gendered expectations of adults. Studies show that both mothers and fathers express more warmth, use more emotional words, and are more likely to talk about sad events and feelings with their daughters.[8]

A parent described how his children react directly when they see gender bias in his behavior:

My kids say I reprimand them differently. They tell me that when I'm working at home and my son comes into the study and pesters me, I shout, "Get out of here!" When my daughter does the same thing, I say, "Young lady, would you please leave." When we talked it over, my two alert kids told me about other differences. My daughter claims I compliment her for wearing a new dress or looking pretty, but I praise my son for achievement, especially in sports. We're still talking, and I'm still trying.

The mirror held up to this father by his own children is echoed in studies of parenting behaviors. Males are likely to encourage sex-typed behavior, by protecting their daughters, complimenting them on appearance, and showing them affection. Meanwhile, they roughhouse with sons, encourage athletic participation, and punish them more harshly. Many fathers come down particularly hard on boys for playing with dolls or other cuddly toys.[9]

Parents who pay close attention to children's playthings understand that toys shape personality traits, interests, and even physical and academic skills. In the first edition of *Failing at Fairness,* we described a 1990 study done by a team of Canadian researchers. They visited young children's homes and found boys' rooms filled with sports equipment, toy vehicles, tools, and building kits. The girls' rooms contained children's furniture, kitchen utensils, and lots of dolls. Girls slept in multicolored beds with sheets of pink and yellow. For boys the bedding was mostly blue. The research team concluded that parents are still raising girls and boys in environments that are "globally different"; they are still encouraging "sex-typed play by selecting different toys for female and male children, even before the child can express her or his own preferences."[10]

For this edition, *Still Failing at Fairness,* we revisited the color issue. In 2008, Grandma Licia bought a travel suitcase over the Internet for her two-year-old grandson, Bimi; but when it arrived, the red color online became pink in real life. Although Bimi loved the suitcase—pink wheels, pink polka dots, and all—Grandma Licia decided to return it. Bimi's mom (and our friend) Audra sees herself as a feminist, but she agreed with grandma's decision. She explains:

> I am okay with it, and Bimi loved it, but I know that Bimi will face ridicule from his friends down the line. They will tease him for his girlie suitcase. I wish I could be more open, but he will end up not using it.

Audra's feminist friends share similar concerns. One mom proudly dressed her daughter in blue, but would not put anything pink on her son. Another mom explained to Audra that she, Audra, was lucky that she had a son first, because her second child, whether a girl or boy, could inherit his wardrobe with no problems. Had the first child been a girl, this would not be possible. Clearly, different standards for sons and daughters are still all too common.

A father describes how arbitrary but powerful the pinks and blues can be. On a visit to Costco, he and his young daughter came upon two stacks of Fisher-Price children's digital cameras: one set of pink cameras, and another stack of blue ones. His daughter explained that the blue cameras were for the boys, and the pink for girls. "No baby, anybody can have any color camera they want. . . . A boy can have a pink one and a girl can have a blue one if they want." The daughter did not buy that line, and the father thought, "It was a digital camera, of all things. . . . Did there really need to be a 'boy' camera and a 'girl' camera?"[11]

Since toy companies continue to promote the purchase of strongly stereotyped playthings, parents must consciously swim against the tide to avoid rigidly channeling children's play.[12] In Texas, a researcher spent months observing parent and child interactions in toy stores. She observed at two types of stores, a boutique toy store and a large discount store. At both stores, there were distinct boys' and girls' sections. The researcher explained: "In 300 hours of toy selling, I only witnessed two occasions of customers resisting the typical gender categories." At these stores, women employees were working in the doll and stuffed-animal sections, while men staffed the electronics departments. In both stores, white men were in charge, and mostly white or light-skinned females worked as cashiers. The stockers, cleaning staff, and other behind-the-scenes workers were predominantly minorities. The researcher noticed that white customers were treated better than black or Hispanic customers and that white employees were treated with greater respect by customers, particularly white customers.[13] The staffing patterns and toy selection taught children all about gender role stereotypes and racism, although many of these lessons probably went unnoticed by parents.

But choosing toys is only the beginning. One father described how he learned there was more to be done:

After attending your workshop, I went home to check my daughters' toy box. There was one Barbie after another, most of them without heads. I couldn't believe it. I know I bought chemistry sets and science kits, but they were nowhere to be found. I couldn't understand how they had disappeared until I asked the kids.

"We swapped them," the girls explained.

"Swapped them?" I was flabbergasted.

"We didn't know why you bought us those things. We didn't like some of them, and we didn't know how to work the science things. So we gave them away and got Barbies instead. We never told you because we didn't want to hurt your feelings."

This father had taken the first step—he had provided a range of toys—and thought the job was done, but he had not made the extra effort to engage his daughters in the chemistry and science kits. Without adults showing the way, the science kits or sports equipment may be unused, discarded, or swapped. Promoting gender equity is also about parents modeling nonsexist attitudes and actively engaging their children with those toys. A mother who looks at slides through a microscope becomes a role model for her daughter, and also teaches her son an important lesson about women and science. When a father plays sports or constructs log houses and Lego projects with his daughter, he sends an important message: girls do not lose their appeal to males when they are athletes or engineers. In one study, as fathers' gender stereotyping increased, their sons' interest in math also increased—but their daughters' interest in math decreased. That study also found that both moms and dads spend more time on math and science activities with their sons, and buy their sons more math and science toys. These behaviors send sexist messages to their daughters.[14] Nonsexist behavior broadens options; sexist behaviors limit them.

Breaking gender stereotypes for boys is often a greater challenge than for girls. Our culture holds male-gendered values as a priority: competition, success, earning a huge paycheck, toughness, athleticism, math and science skills, and keeping cool rather than sharing emotions are culturally honored behaviors. Toys reinforce this narrow male path. Dolls do not exist to teach boys about parenting; action figures take their place and teach boys to control the world through force and physical prowess. Wrestlers, Superman, Batman, Iron Man, Spider-Man, and athletic figures are all about physical dominance, violence, pain, and even superhuman power. But thoughtful, attentive boys, peaceful boys intuitively understand that controlling the world and superhuman powers are unhealthy fantasies. These boys do not connect with action figures.

Unathletic boys also do not see themselves reflected in such action figures. These nontraditional boys may feel like interlopers and become targets of derision in the current narrow and unforgiving boy culture.

We have all seen little boys play war games with the ever popular G.I. Joe, using toy guns and rifles to "kill" each other. When they grow a bit older, this theme is reinforced by violent video games. When they grow older still, they fight real wars where death is permanent. While few doubt the need for a capable military, preparing two-year-old boys for war and death is unseemly. G.I. Joe is a plaything with grave consequences.

More than war scenarios are available on video games. The popular Grand Theft Auto IV welcomes you to Liberty City with advertising that announces that "gardens are for wimps." In Liberty City, killing on the streets is commonplace, and if sex with a prostitute does not work out, simply beat her up and take back your money. What is the public's reaction to such misogyny and violence? Rave reviews and billions of sales dollars. Why do we tolerate and promote such violence? Do we believe that such violence will not impact our culture? Do we lack the imagination to create toys and games that teach boys and men to resolve conflicts in peaceful ways? How might teaching conflict resolution strategies to young boys offer a brighter future for our nation? Could Gandhi or Nelson Mandela or Albert Schweitzer ever replace Hulk Hogan?

Change is more than possible, it is necessary. Parents and teachers can introduce boys to other options. Adults can encourage boys to explore a variety of nontraditional fields, from the caring professions to parenting skills, from dance to the theater, from humanitarian work to peacemakers. An artist kit might be a good addition to that chemistry or erector set a parent buys. A teacher who incorporates dance and music in the curriculum helps boys move beyond gender role restrictions. Parents who take their sons to the theater and other creative venues are opening up doors that many boys may find enriching, and some even enticing. Adults who encourage boys to think about parenting skills and the joys of fatherhood, who teach their sons to honor differences, to connect with others, to explore their feelings, and to move beyond the harsh borders of boyness are offering their sons wider life choices.

SHOW AND TELL

A California woman shared the following story:

> I walked by the room of our two sons, ages ten and five. Noticing the late hour, I asked them to turn out their light and go to sleep.
>
> "Dad said we could have the lights on for five minutes," my older son answered.
>
> "I'd like the lights off now."
>
> "Well, Dad's the boss," said my son. "You're just the assistant."

If children see business offices where men, for the most part, are managers and women are secretaries; if they see hospitals where males are mainly doctors and females are nurses; and if in their schools they watch male principals giving directions to mostly female teachers, they reach an inescapable conclusion: men are bosses and women work for them. Once crystallized, these assumptions may seem unshakable. Children's early contact with the world of medicine creates some of the staunchest stereotypes. A kindergarten teacher told this story:

> Six-year-old Sarah initiated a heated class discussion by announcing that only boys could be doctors and only girls could be nurses. Surprised by the girl's adamant conclusion, I arranged for a field trip to the local hospital. There my class met both male and female nurses and doctors. I was proud of nipping sexism in the bud—until I asked the students their reaction to the man who was a nurse and the woman who was a doctor. Sarah had only one question: "Why did they lie?"

Even parents who work in nontraditional roles cannot assume their children see them as role models. They, too, need to make extra efforts to stop stereotypes from forming.

In 2008, Sarah, a mother in Washington, D.C., described the following scene:

> I was getting dressed up a bit and my daughter asked, "Where are you going?"
>
> "To work," I replied.
>
> "You don't work. You are a mom."
>
> "But you've seen me dress up before and go to work."

"You go to meetings, not to work."

Sarah used the opportunity to teach: "But moms can be doctors and lawyers and many things."

"Not lawyers," her daughter explained, "Dad's a lawyer."

I couldn't believe it. I'm a lawyer. But because I am here for her when she comes home from school, she thinks I don't work. As soon as she's old enough, I'm taking her to my office.

The Ms. Foundation wanted all parents to understand that girls need to see firsthand the range of work that women do, so they created "Take Our Daughters to Work Day." On the first day of this national initiative, almost a million girls ages nine to fifteen went to work with parents, relatives, and friends to see women in every imaginable place of employment: hospitals, police and fire stations, business offices, media studios, courts, and Congress. Taking daughters into the workplace presents them with important role models and introduces them to potential careers. For example, studies have shown that girls who meet scientists and watch them at work are more likely to consider becoming scientists, too.

Leaving boys at home or at school during "Take Our Daughters to Work Day" proved to be a bad idea, and the title soon became "Take Our Sons and Daughters to Work Day." Nothing wrong with having all children learn about work, but if we were constructing that day, girls and boys would learn more than job options. Boys lag behind girls in understanding that their gender role has limitations, but "Take a Son to Work" misses the boat. The traditional male role often overemphasizes work and salary as a measure of one's value while underemphasizing family life and parenting. Perhaps boys could benefit from insights into how to balance work and family life, how to resolve problems peacefully, how to honor their emotions, nurture their children, and care for the welfare of others. Parents who want to offer healthier life options for their sons have too few resources, organizations, and websites to assist. When writing this book, we struggled to find good resources for boys. Although there are some fine books available on boy rearing, there are also some pretty regressive books on the market, books that take boys back to constricted views of what it means to be a male. We are only just beginning to understand the limiting nature of the male stereotype, and we are years away from taming this tiger.

While real-life role models influence children, so do characters in books. "Read it again," children plead. At a young and impressionable age girls listen repeatedly to classic sexist themes: Cinderella finds success in beauty and marriage to the prince. Snow White and Sleeping Beauty are so passive they literally sleep until a man saves them. Although there are folktale females who rely on brains to save themselves, most parents and teachers don't know these stories exist.

One mother, a former teacher, told us how she conscientiously collected the best literature, the Caldecott winners and Honor books decorated by the American Library Association with gold and silver medals as the finest picture books of the year. The night after attending one of our workshops, she looked through her daughter's bookshelf to count the number of stories about active, resourceful girls and was amazed to find only one book with a female main character:

> There was Max and the Wild Things and Sylvester, the donkey, with his magic pebble. And all those Dr. Seuss books—so many imaginative characters and so few females. Did you ever read *And to Think That I Saw It on Mulberry Street*? This boy comes home from school and imagines meeting hundreds of zany characters. But there's not a single girl on Mulberry Street. My daughter loves that book. We read it over and over and over. I hate to think how I've been programming her for invisibility. Thank heavens for *Madeline*! Without her there would have been no girls at all in my daughter's book collection.

Studies of children's literature confirm these insights. Between 1967 and 1971, for every girl drawn in a Caldecott winner, eleven boys were pictured. When female characters were included, they were inconspicuous: a girl playing quietly in the corner, a silent woman carrying wood, a princess whose hand is given in marriage, a mother who packs lunch and waves good-bye. Jobs for adult women were limited to mother, mermaid, and fairy. In contrast, men were main characters and were shown as house builders, storekeepers, kings, farmers, judges, preachers, fathers, adventurers, soldiers, policemen, fishermen, monks, fighters, gods, and storytellers.[15]

As we explored in chapter 3, studies of newer children's books continue to be populated mostly by male figures and reinforce a skewed world, portraying competitive, creative, aggressive, and active boys with dependent, submissive, and passive girls.[16] Few fathers are portrayed, and they are most often stoic, working dads who rarely outwardly nurture their children.[17]

As with toys and games, parents and other adults need to become involved. From movies to magazines, from picture books to real life, parents and teachers can point out sexism when they see it and clearly explain to their children the problems with restricted gender roles for girls and boys. They also should be frank about obstacles, discussing openly and honestly specific steps that girls and boys can take to surmount them.

BOYS AND GIRLS, YOU'RE AMAZING

All the work done at home by thoughtful parents and teachers can be undone by school officials. *And Tango Makes Three* by Justin Richardson and Peter Parnell is a children's book about two male penguins that hatch and parent a chick. In 2008 it was pulled from an elementary school's library shelves in Loudoun County, Virginia, after a parent complained that it promoted a gay agenda. The penguin story is actually true, and based on the lives of two chinstrap penguins at the Central Park Zoo in New York. The publisher, Simon & Schuster, sponsors a website about the book that explains: "Tango has two fathers instead of the traditional mother and father. Do you have a nontraditional family, or do you know someone who does?"[18] But none of that was enough to stop the superintendent from censoring the book. Loudoun County is not alone. The penguins flew to the top of the American Library Association's list of banned or challenged books in 2006.

When books that look beyond traditional gender expectations are banned at school, resourceful parents can read such books and educate their children at home, helping them learn about wise and resourceful women and girls and caring and thoughtful boys and men. Here are a few "peeks" at some of the amazing books out there. In *Henry's Baby,* by Mary Hoffman and Susan Winter, Henry is a grade-schooler who wants to be part of the in-group. (Like, who doesn't?) Unfortunately he is not clever or athletic or tough, and he doubts the other guys will like him. Worse yet, he cares for his baby brother. But that same baby brother opens the hearts of Henry's peers, and voilà, Henry is seen as "cool." In *Daddy Makes the Best Spaghetti,* Anna Grossnickle Hines shares the story of an engaged and playful father, a figure too often missing in children's books. In *Boy, You're Amazing,* Virginia L. Kroll and Sachiko Yoshikawa honor traditional male values such as athletics and physical activity, as well as other male qualities such as nurturing, courage, and generosity. If you like that one, then check out *Girl, You're Amazing,* a book that honors girl's capabilities. The Judy Blume books are always popular (and often banned by schools). One of our favorites is *Are You There God? It's Me, Margaret,* about an eleven-year-old who moves to a new town, needs to make new friends, and turns to God for some answers. Today there are wonderful books like these, but parents will need to seek them out. Librarians are a great source for nonsexist books, as is the Internet—but be prepared for resistance. Some of the best books by critical standards have been banned or hidden behind the librarian's desk.

"If you are putting something behind a desk, you are saying something is wrong with it," said Judith Krug, director of the office for intellectual freedom at the American Library Association. "It's a degree of censorship, because they are making access to information extremely difficult."[19] Other commonly banned, but wonderful books, include *The Chocolate War* by Robert Cormier, Mark Twain's *The Adventures of Huckleberry Finn, The Color Purple* by Alice Walker, and *I Know Why the Caged Bird Sings* by Maya Angelou.

Can traditional folktales and stories be changed to remove historic barriers? People disagree, but one of David and Myra's former students, Paul, did just that. His class had been reading books about boys, and the new story he was about to introduce, a Celtic legend, also featured male main characters. He was considering making one of the boys in the story a girl, but he felt uncomfortable about changing literature. Myra and David suggested that he talk the problem over with his students and then decide what to do.

We are sitting in the back of Paul's fifth-grade class to observe his lesson. He enters the room carrying a mysterious box with the words BEWARE: BRITTLE PAPER written prominently on the cover. Puzzled, the students look at one another. Without saying a word, the teacher holds the box in front of him and tips it slightly. Sand slides from the crevices and falls to the classroom floor. He has the students' attention; their curiosity is obvious: What could be inside? Slowly the teacher opens the box, removes an ancient-looking book, and carefully holds it up to show the class. As he blows dust off the jacket, the title becomes clear: *The Celtic Dragon Myth.* All eyes are on the teacher as he introduces the array of characters in the story—giants, lions, blacksmiths, falcons, magic fish, kings, fishermen, dragons, and princesses.

"Would you like to read this book?" the teacher asks the class. The students are united in enthusiasm, their excitement almost palpable.

"First, I have something to ask you," Paul continues. "The three main characters in this book are boys. Do you think it's fair to read and listen to books in which all the main characters are male?"

The students are clearly taken aback. This is a question no teacher has ever asked them before. Boys respond first.

"I think it's fair to read a myth about boys. What's wrong with that?"

"I don't care if it's a book about girls or boys or half and half. I just want it to be a good story."

"What's the big deal? You said there are princesses, so there's some girls in it."

"Let's get the female point of view," the teacher intervenes.

"I agree with Mark," one girl says matter-of-factly. "I don't care if it's about boys or girls as long as it's a good story. That's what matters."

But a girl sitting on the other side of the room objects:

"Why should we have to listen to it if there are no girls? Why does it always have to be about boys?"

"It doesn't really bother me, but I think the author must be a little sexist," a girl in the front says. "Who wrote it anyway?"

As the students try to figure out if a legend has an author, a girl raises her hand and asks, "It says it's Celtic, so could the Celtic people have been sexist?"

"I don't think you can say that a whole group of people are sexist," another girl from the front says thoughtfully. "Maybe it's because the story was written so long ago. All women did then was stay home and clean the house."

"Why are you getting upset about this?" One of the boys is back in the discussion. "It's no big deal, just a few characters in a story."

"Well, I think it is important." The girl speaking now is angry. "I get really bored when I read only about boys. I'm tired of hearing 'he, he, he' all the time! Why can't it be 'he, he, *she*' once in a while? Didn't those brothers have any sisters?"

Based on the discussion, the teacher reaches a decision. "I didn't understand that some of you felt so strongly about this," he says. "I'm beginning to think these brothers do need a sister, so I'm going to make one of the characters a girl."

In reading and language arts classes, teachers can find books about resourceful girls or they can change the names, but in history they have an additional burden: relearning the past and finding out about the women they never studied in school. More and more teachers are making that effort, and they are also discovering the books and posters developed by the National Women's History Project. This California-based group has created awareness of multicultural women's history in school systems across America. Their efforts have already been far-reaching, providing the impetus for National Women's History Week, which was later expanded from seven days to the month of March.

"Students who read our books and see our displays say they can't believe how badly they've been cheated out of their own history," said Molly MacGregor, one of the project's founders. And historian Sara Evans wrote, "Having a history is a prerequisite to claiming a right to shape the future." When children read books that portray women in traditional jobs, their perceptions become more stereotyped. But when they read about females who accomplish outstanding deeds, both girls and boys believe that women are capable of great achievement.[20]

BELIEVING IS SEEING

David was invited by the State Department in 2006 to give a series of workshops and lectures in half a dozen large cities across India. The Indian audiences were mostly high school and college faculties and students, and each school marked the lecture with some sort of elaborate ceremony, including special dinners, gift exchanges, and even military honor guards. David was struck by the kindness and openness of the Indians toward gender equity. But in each school he was reminded how deep the gender divisions are in cultures around the world. When David turned to the audience, the story was always the same: he was looking at hundreds of people in the auditorium, hundreds of sex-segregated people with males on one side and females on the other. Indian audiences were always gender-segregated as they awaited the talk on gender equity.

But such blatant sexism offers an easy way to point out the issue. Rarely do we walk into public places in the United States where all the males are sitting on one side of the room, and all the females on the other. In the states, gender bias is often far more subtle. An anthropologist once said that if a fish were an anthropologist, the last thing it would discover would be water. Our eyes have grown accustomed to everyday bias, and like the fish missing the water, we no longer see it. We must be fitted with a new set of glasses.

Given the hectic pace of classroom life, clocked at several hundred to a thousand interactions daily, most teachers cannot monitor accurately who receives their attention. They, too, are teaching in a sea of subtle bias. But tallying how many times a teacher calls on or responds to boys and girls, blacks and whites, quiet children or more active ones, provides clear information on who is benefiting from teacher attention, and who is not. In a fair classroom, each child interacts with the teacher and no child dominates or is ignored.

The number of girls and boys in a class also matters. A seventh-grade teacher told what happened the first time she asked a colleague to come in and count the questions going to each gender.

"Girls definitely talked half the time in your class," the colleague reported when the class was over and the check marks had been tallied.

"That's great," the conscientious teacher said with relief. "Thanks for letting me know it was fair."

"Well," the observer said with a smile, "I didn't say it was fair. I just said girls talked half the time. More than three-quarters of your students are female, but they're only talking half the time. In terms of their representation in the class, boys, who are 25 percent of the students, are getting 50 percent of your time."

An observer can offer even more specific information by drawing a class seating plan that indicates where each boy or girl is located in the room. Every time a teacher speaks to a student, the observer makes a check on the chart, tracking each individual's participation. Then a teacher who studies the chart has a visible record of otherwise elusive patterns: Is one gender receiving more attention? Is one race or ethnic group dominating? Who is being left out? Which areas of the room are attention rich, and where are the dead zones, those places students can hide unnoticed? The observer can even record who is praised or criticized and who gets instruction on how to improve.

Using an objective record is what teachers need and deserve to recognize their own patterns, but looking at the evidence is only the first step on a long journey. When teachers participate in effective training, they can eradicate gender bias from their instruction.

The Sadkers analyzed the classrooms of elementary, secondary, and college teachers who participated in faculty development workshops. When college professors who received training were compared with a control group who had not, striking differences emerged. In the control group, typically half the class did not speak, and most of the silent students were women. But in the classrooms of professors who had been trained for gender equity, only 7 percent of students were silent, and females and males were equally active in discussion.

In elementary and secondary schools, boys typically dominated discussions and called out comments. But an eye-opening change occurred in the classrooms of trained teachers: Girls no longer waited to be selected by the teacher; they became much more assertive, and the gender gap in calling out almost disappeared. The ratio of males to females calling out, which had been significant, became almost even. When the classroom climate was warm and accepting, girls left the spectator role and joined the boys in the interaction.[21]

Teachers from around the country have told us their own creative strategies to equalize the gender gap in classroom attention, such as the one devised by a Wisconsin teacher who attended a workshop:

"I read about your research before I came," she said, "and I tried an idea in my own classroom that really got quiet girls involved. I discovered poker chips. Several times a week at the beginning of my class, I gave each student two chips. Whenever they wanted to ask or answer a question, they had to spend a chip. And everybody had to spend their chips before the class was over."

We congratulated the teacher on her innovative technique to involve silent students, who were more likely to be girls.

"But it's better than that," she said. "The students who usually dominate the classroom receive a wonderful lesson, too. Because they can talk only twice, they must choose which comments to say. Now noisy students are doing something they never did before: They think before they speak."

Almost all teachers we have talked with made it clear that relying on noisy students, the ones who volunteer, is a direct path to a classroom controlled by boys. Girls who know the answer are more likely to wait to be called on, while males are more apt to shout out.

Many teachers have also said that using wait time works well. Wait time is the silent time between a teacher's question and a student's answer. Often it is less than a second. When teachers consciously extend their wait time to three to five seconds, especially where a thoughtful response is warranted, more girls, more minorities, more English language learners, and more shy children are pulled into the discussion.

Leveling with students is one of our favorite strategies. Since gender equity should not be a secret goal but one shared with students, we give a handout to classes. Called "Education Is Not a Spectator Sport," it describes research on gender differences in classroom discussion and asks students to consider whether girls or boys talk more in their own classrooms. And when we encounter situations where boys are dominating and demanding more of our attention, we point this out and talk it over with the students.

David recalls a unique student gathering in an auditorium in a midwestern high school. More than a hundred school newspaper reporters were gathered for a gender equity "press conference" to ask David and others about their research. At first the students seemed reluctant, but then the comments came quickly, an avalanche of questions.

"Hold it a minute," David said, halting the rapid-fire pace of the press conference. "Do you notice anything ironic going on here?" The room of reporters looked around blankly. Then a girl from the back, where most of the females were clustered, said, "The boys are asking all the questions." There was an audible gasp as the students realized they had become living proof of the story they were supposed to report.

"Here we are, talking about boys dominating discussions, and it's happening right in front of us. How can we change this?"

The students looked at one another uncomfortably, and then the girls began asking questions, some even more assertively than the boys. But after ten minutes the burst was over, and the original pattern reemerged with the boys dominating the discussion. Again David stopped to call the students' attention to the imbalance, but this time he gave specific suggestions to change the pattern. He recommended that students write down good questions instead of shouting out anything that came to mind, and then suggested that the students move their seats so that the girls were no longer clustered in the back. David also asked the boys to do something they were rarely asked to do—be mindful about sharing time. We wonder how many boys and girls remembered the lesson from the news conference, or did they return to old patterns when they went back to their classrooms?

A private school teacher in Chicago understands the challenge. She said, "One day I noticed how inevitably a girl's head turned toward a boy as he approached, even if she and I were discussing her current piece of writing. Next I realized with a jolt that my head invariably turned toward him, too."

Learning not to hear boys more than girls became a daily act of personal resistance for this teacher, one that played out like this:

TEACHER: Well, Patricia, how do you think you can convince your reader that—(Steven approaches, waving his paper. Patricia turns toward him.) No, Patricia. I'm talking with *you*. Keep watching me. (The teacher takes Patricia's chin in her hand and forces eye contact.) Don't look at Steven. You are the important one right now.

This teacher also needed to keep her own attention focused, using her hand "like a horse's blinder" to keep Steven and other boys from pulling her attention away from Patricia. She said, "As my focus on the girls has grown sharper, I find it easier to attend to their concerns and not set them aside when a boy fills the horizon. It's a daily challenge because most boys haven't set aside their feeling that they come first. I still haven't trained my ears not to turn toward Steven's insistent questions from halfway across the room."[22]

This need for watchful intentionality is echoed in research findings. A study of a university-based preschool class showed again how male students take over and teachers unintentionally let it happen. During snack time two girls, two boys, and one teacher sat at each table, and researchers analyzed their conversations. The teachers were scrupulously fair in how food was given out, but they never considered how they distributed the invisible staples of time and attention. During their conversations, the teachers frequently interrupted female students. And the boys, secure in their right to be heard, freely interrupted their female teachers. The lessons were insidious but devastating: If you are a young male, you are entitled to talk; and if you are female, no matter your age, your words are worth less and can be cut short. This preschool study is similar to research on interaction in families that show fathers talk more with male children and both parents interrupt daughters more than sons.[23]

After describing this preschool study at a workshop in Missouri, we received a note from a teacher who was also a parent of young children:

We have two daughters and two sons, and when you talked about that study, our family dinner table at home flashed into my mind. As I began to think about it, it seemed as though our sons were usually talking and our daughters were waiting to speak. So I counted the interruptions. Our house is like the preschool, with the boys talking, laughing, interrupting their sisters, and vying for their father's attention, and the girls trying to get a word in edgewise. Last night my sons had a lesson on letting girls talk, too.

While some parents are teaching their sons not to interrupt, others are working with their daughters and developing strategies to help them speak up. A lawyer from Indiana, who is also the parent of two children, wrote us this letter:

> When I returned home after your symposium, I asked my daughter who got called on the most in her class. I did not specify whether I wanted a name or a group. She said, "The boys." I then asked her if she ever gave an answer before the teacher called on her. She said, "No, the teacher wouldn't like that." I asked if anyone gave answers before being called on, and she said, "Sure. The boys do all the time."
>
> Elementary teachings, perhaps, but I had no idea. I may not be able to change the schools, but I can change how I help my daughter, and I can help my son and husband understand.

A woman from Illinois, one with an unusually sophisticated awareness of gender bias, told us about the successful strategies she and her husband used to help their gifted daughter shatter the barrier of silence and speak her mind at school:

> When our daughter Lara was in high school, she was extremely reluctant to speak out in class. In fact, she refused to wear red (a color that accentuates her dark hair and coloring) to school because it made her too noticeable. . . . One history teacher notified the students that they could not receive a grade of A if they did not participate in class. This teacher was also notorious for "pushing" students when they gave an answer. Many students were not used to this type of give-and-take and would not answer in class. Our daughter, with her reticent nature, would have been quite content to sit back and listen. . . .
>
> She was in tears at home. "I can't talk in there. All those debaters know everything. ['All those debaters' were boys.] I'll feel like an idiot if I'm wrong." We asked her if she would rather get a B even though she knew the material perfectly. She decided she wanted to try to participate. We helped her set goals. At first she had to volunteer a certain number of times per week. Then it was a set number of times per day. We told her we didn't care if she got wrong answers, all she had to do was talk, and we would pay her the magnificent sum of five cents for each interaction. She laughed at our cheap reward but was sufficiently motivated to try the scheme.
>
> There were many days when she came home in tears because she

just couldn't make herself raise her hand. Finally she forced herself to take the plunge on a regular basis, and by the end of the semester she was participating freely and even received a comment on her report card that she "participates well in class"; this was next to her grade—an A.

Lara's academic career was one of extraordinary accomplishment. After graduating as valedictorian of her high school class, she attended Harvard/Radcliffe, was a member of Phi Beta Kappa, graduated magna cum laude as a physics major, and won a fellowship for graduate work in biophysics at the University of California at Berkeley. But without vigilance and the willingness to intervene, her mother suspects that Lara's story might not have had such a happy ending.

Like Lara's mother and father, parents need to keep an eye on the curriculum and protest sexism when they see it. And they must offer support from the home, refusing to let their daughters or their sons receive second-class treatment.

EMAILS

For the original *Failing at Fairness* in 1994, Myra and David collected stories at each workshop they led, at each school they visited. Now the Internet brings the stories instantly to our screens—isn't technology grand? David and Karen received emails that ask all kinds of Title IX questions. Here is a sample: A businessman wondered if he gave money to the boys' football team, would he also need to contribute to a girls' team? Many emails questioned the blatant discrepancies between female and male athletic facilities, with boys having state-of-the-art athletic fields, while girls play on inferior, sometimes dangerous fields. A boy complained that he was not allowed to play on the field hockey team. A teacher asked us if requiring boys to do twenty push-ups and girls to do ten violates the law. A pregnant student worried about her due date, which was also the date for the final exam. The professor warned her that if she did not take the final exam on that specific date, she would be given a zero.

Do you struggle with these questions, wondering which if any violated Title IX? Most people would, including school administrators. Fortunately, there are resources for you to learn more about Title IX. Our website for the Myra Sadker Foundation, www.sadker.org, includes articles and information about Title IX. So do "Title IX: Exercise Your Rights," at www.titleix.info, the National Women's Law Center at www.nwlc.org, and the Women Sports Foundation at www.womens sportsfoundation.org.

When we visit schools, we see Title IX violations everywhere. Girls and boys divided by gender for all kinds of strange purposes, including eating lunch. We see children in the schoolyard lining up to enter the building—by sex. We hear of boys versus girls academic competitions. We have yet to hear of spelling bees where it is the Jews against the Christians, or school officials who ask white children to enter the building before the black children do. But few question the educational thinking behind requests that pit one gender against another. We wonder what our inbox would look like if parents and teachers knew that Title IX covered far more than athletics.

Since the connection between Title IX and athletics is most often in the media, it is not surprising that most of the emails we receive are about athletics, and most detail illegal actions. Coaches and parents write us for help, but it is the Office for Civil Rights (OCR) in the U.S. Department of Education to which they should be writing to correct these violations. The problem is that too few schools inform parents or teachers about Title IX, the complaint procedure, or about the responsibilities of OCR to enforce Title IX. (If you are wondering, not sharing this information is in itself a violation of the law.) The ardor of OCR does vary with the federal government administration in power, and parents and teachers should be conscious of that. But make no mistake about it, a committed teacher or parent can make an extraordinary difference. Herb Dempsey is a case in point.

We never met Herb, who lives in Washington State, but we read online about his exploits, and we reached out to him to learn his story. Herb was a teacher for more than thirty years, and a union activist. He also trained police officers for more than a decade. When he retired in 1992, he wondered how he would spend his time. He soon found out. His epiphany came while he and an air force colonel watched their daughters turn blue as they played soccer in lightweight summer uniforms in 29-degree sleet: "This just is not fair," he remembers thinking, and his retirement was over: he had a cause.

Not that gender bias was new to Herb. He remembered the unfairness years earlier when his female colleagues lost their jobs and medical coverage when they became pregnant. He also recalled the fight he took on as union president to save a woman's track coaching job. The school administration had decided to supplement a male football coach's salary by making him the track coach in the "off season." To make room for him, they fired the female coach. It did not matter to the school officials that the male coach was not as competent in track, but it did matter to Herb. He fought the firing. He won that battle, and the female coach was reinstated with back pay. But watching his daughter play soccer in the cold, he was no longer a teacher or union president; he was a dad. His concern for young girls was growing, and the everyday injustices were becoming more intolerable.

He began examining the gaps between the boys' and girls' teams, and used a "fairness scorecard." Each team was rated in different categories: quality of coaches, practice and competition schedules, equipment, training, medical treatment, travel reimbursements, and how many teams are available for each gender. The scorecard is not complicated to use, but few take the time to do it. Herb scored the boys' and the girls' teams; his goal was not to have a winner, but for the girls and boys to tie. It did not work out that way. The differences usually favored boys who benefited from better fields, schedules, and equipment. Herb began lodging complaints with OCR, often confronting resistant administrators. Herb was making waves.

Herb now gets emails and calls from parents across the country asking how to file complaints, and how to make change happen. In one case, a father in the Northwest called Herb about the boys' terrible baseball field. The school officials had told him that they did not have to worry about boys' athletics. But of course, they do. Title IX covers all students. Herb helped the father with the complaint and the school district was forced to improve the boys' baseball field, to make it as good as the girls' softball field. Although the changes happened too late for the father to see his son play on the new field, other boys have benefited from his efforts.

During the second Bush administration, compliance with Title IX noticeably slowed. Herb called it "Delay, Deny, and Defend" (descriptors borrowed from McKinsey & Company consulting firm). Schools dragged their feet on responding to complaints, trying to run out the clock until the affected students graduated. When that happens, the complaint is mooted and thrown out. But Herb is not mooted, nor need we be. Each parent, each teacher, each student can make a difference. Here are just two of those stories.[24]

In Rockland County, New York, Bruce Cloer felt fortunate that his flexible work schedule enabled him to attend his daughter's school activities. But Bruce noticed that his daughter's teams rarely got to play on the best fields or at the best times. The parents who voiced concern were told that girls don't take sports as seriously as boys and the school saw no need to schedule the girls on the better fields. When his daughter was a teenager, he was told by league officials that Title IX was a bad thing because it forced schools to take programs away from boys. But his call to the Women's Sports Foundation taught him otherwise. Bruce began attending school board meetings, informed them of Title IX violations, and was pleased to discover that the school administration wanted to correct these problems. To spread awareness, he handed out SAVE TITLE IX bracelets, Title IX T-shirts, and posters. He called all local area schools only to discover that very few had a Title IX coordinator. In conjunction with 2007 National Girls and Women in Sports Day, Bruce hosted a Title IX workshop and panel and invited fifty administrators. WNBA basketball great Teresa Weatherspoon and Olympic soccer star Carla Overbeck spoke at the event about their Title IX experiences. A committed parent and a responsive school district turned things around.

Gina Wesley-Hunt could not believe that in this day and age she'd get fired for having a baby. Gina was at the Smithsonian Institution as a postdoctoral researcher, a temporary academic position between graduate school and a professorship. She told her boss about her pregnancy and asked to discuss schedules and research priorities during her twelve weeks leave (without pay). Instead she was told that she would be let go. She could not believe it, and after a month of speaking to anyone who would listen, Smithsonian lawyers finally convinced her managers to reinstate her. However, because of the hostile work climate, she decided to resign and left for a permanent academic position elsewhere. But she did not give up her fight, and eventually prevailed when a new nondiscrimination policy covering everyone at the Smithsonian was created. The new policy recognizes pregnancy discrimination as a form of sex discrimination.

I DREAM OF THINGS THAT NEVER WERE, AND ASK "WHY NOT?"

Parent, teacher, and student efforts foreshadow a growing movement for gender equity in schools—and in our culture. As Margaret Mead and these stories remind us, we should never doubt that even "a small group of thoughtful people could change the world. Indeed, it's the only thing that ever has."

The American Association of University Women (AAUW) has been one organization working to change the world. From their groundbreaking report *How Schools Shortchange Girls* (1992) to *Where the Girls Are* (2008), the AAUW has sponsored research that documents bias, discrimination, and harassment in our nation's schools. The National Women's Law Center (NWLC) remains a beacon of hope for those who find themselves the target of discrimination. We are constantly referring parents, educators, and students to the NWLC for legal assistance. They provide free legal advice and have fought against gender discrimination even to the Supreme Court. The Myra Sadker Foundation provides scholarships and awards to students and teachers researching gender issues and promoting gender equity. The National Coalition for Women and Girls in Education consists of these and other like-minded organizations joined together in a common cause. Its reports, *Title IX at 30* and *Title IX at 35,* offer a running scorecard on progress and problems.

The organizations, readings, and the book's website offer resources you can use in your effort to create a better, fairer world. Ellen Bravo also offers a strategy. In *Taking on the Big Boys,* she outlines a multistep action plan that she calls DREAM.[25] We will paraphrase it here:

Dare to imagine the world you want, a world of justice and caring. Imagine it. Meditate on it. Create that reality first in your mind. Envisioning your goal will bring the vision closer to reality. Victor Hugo once said: "There is nothing like a dream to create *future.*"

Reach out. There are others out there who will support you, who may feel just as strong as you do about social justice. You can pool the skills and insights of colleagues, community members, students, parents, friends, and strangers as you pursue gender equity, begin to implement Title IX, or move to create more positive environments for girls and boys.

Educate yourself. This has multiple dimensions. Researching the issue is one part. We are astonished at how many citizens, parents, and educators are unaware of basic educational research, such as the lack of evidence supporting major gender differences between girls and boys, or the lack of support of the effectiveness of single-sex schools. When decision makers are uninformed or misinformed, bad decisions are guaranteed. The second part of educating yourself is learning about the politics of it all. What are the most urgent issues you face? Who are the allies that you can count on? Who in government can help you? Where are your best opportunities to succeed?

Act. There are many levels of action, and all of them make a difference.

Simply sharing information about gender equity with friends and colleagues is a great start. Finding your voice and speaking up for fairness in public and social settings and supporting others who agree with you are all important. You can write a piece for the newspaper, join a group working for better schools or promoting social justice, contact public officials, vote for progressive candidates, attend rallies, join organizations, or start your own group working to improve our lives. You need to find what works best for you—but apathy, silence, and inaction are not the answers.

Multiply. This is all about joining a group and persevering. Those who persist and work with others over the long haul are those who multiply their numbers and eventually win. Be prepared for setbacks, but stay focused on the long-term goal. As Lao Tzu reminds us: An ant on the move does more than a dozing ox.

RIGHT BRAIN RISING

We hope we have you thinking about your own contributions in moving the world forward. Your energy can lead not only to a more equitable society, but to a more creative one as well, like the one described by Daniel Pink in his book *A Whole New Mind: Why Right-Brainers Will Rule the Future*.[26] Pink contends that American society, businesses, and certainly schools, are stuck in an old and predictable vision of society, but one that will undergo profound changes in the near future. The United States continues to focus on what Pink terms left directional thinking, thinking that emanates from the left side of the brain and is logical and linear. For example, our society promotes math, science, and technology (all left-brain activities) in an effort to compete economically in the world. But Pink argues that is the wrong approach because we will never be able to compete with talented and cheap Asian workers and outsourcing will grow in the years ahead. Equally problematic are the advances in computer technology that continue to make human workers obsolete. Pink explains that we think that we are in the information age, but we are already moving beyond that, into what he calls a conceptual age where other capabilities, such as creativity, are paramount. If we are to compete in the twenty-first century, the United States will need to focus more on right-brain skills: intuition, aesthetics, nonlinear thinking, emotions, pattern detecting, and nonverbal communication; in short, many of the skills we currently neglect. Here are some examples of the right-brain skills Pink believes will be most valuable in the coming years:

Boundary Crossers: These are creative people comfortable working in different disciplines, cultures, and languages. A physician using both Western and Eastern medicine to heal patients, a business person helping American companies work more effectively with Indian computer experts, and an elementary teacher working with students to improve the environment, all of these are boundary crossers.

Design: We have lots of quality products that work well, from laptops to automobiles, so the question is which of these products do people choose? The companies that will profit in the years ahead will be those whose designs appeal to the consumer. Business may need fewer MBAs, and more MFAs, people with fine arts skills to design alluring and pleasing products. Most people do not buy Apple computers because they believe they are more reliable than a PC. People are drawn to the design. Apple offers a user-friendly screen, a glowing apple logo, and appealing all white or black colors. Perhaps if we push our right brain a bit further, we can hire talented designers who are also boundary crossers, creating innovative school buildings made of sustainable materials that honor the earth.

Joy: "People rarely succeed at anything unless they are having fun" is a Southwest Airline motto. More and more companies are realizing that strict adherence to the Protestant work ethic may be less productive than they once believed. Happiness, yes happiness, is an important goal. Incorporating games, humor, laughing, and play into our businesses and schools may increase learning, productivity, satisfaction, and health.

Materialism versus Meaning: Americans may lead the world in material wealth, but many remain discontented; clearly, material wealth is no guarantee of happiness. Pink believes that in the future, Americans will seek other paths to lead more meaningful lives. He cites increased interest in meditation, yoga, public service, and spirituality as examples of our search for meaning, a search for purpose attributed to the right side of our brains.

Intuition: Albert Einstein, arguably one of our greatest scientists, had it right when he wrote: "The intuitive mind is a sacred gift; the rational mind, its servant." Why do schools honor the servant (rational thinking) and disregard the sacred (intuition)? How can schools help people develop and honor their intuition?

In fact, how might schools teach these new skills? How will these new priorities change our world and our schools? And what is the gender connection to all this?

Some people are prone to "genderize" the brain, to create a sexist anatomy where the left side, the logical, linear, more honored side, is male, while the right side, the intuitive and emotional side, is female. But this is a case of myopia, of not seeing the world as it could be. There is far more to the story than that. The brain is not two organs, but one, and it works best when all of its parts are used. When the brains of meditating Buddhist monks are scanned, this gender divide is not seen. In fact, when monks meditate, they engage not one side, but the entire brain. Like muscles, our brains can grow and develop. This is termed *neuroplasticity.*[27] We train people who suffered strokes how to teach healthy parts of the brain to do what the injured parts once did. If we teach our students to engage both sides of the brain, they will be more creative, more balanced, and we will all benefit. As one researcher put it, "creativity generally involves crossing boundaries of domains."[28]

We wrote this book to cross boundaries, in this case gender boundaries. Biased teaching patterns, one-sided curricular materials, the superficiality of test scores, and society's powerful gender stereotypes limit both girls and boys. We need to move beyond ill-conceived "gender wars" and "boys versus girls" to a new, more humane, and inclusive way of seeing the genders. There are only two genders on our planet. Surely that is not too many for our brains to consider simultaneously and treat fairly.

Our culture puts great emphasis—too much emphasis—on outside appearances. Our gender, race, religion, economic class, body type, dress—all our outside packaging—provide physical markers that influence how we treat each other. It becomes easy to forget that we are not our outside packaging; we are unique souls inside those packages. The Hindu greeting *Namaste* is said with hands together in a prayerful position. It may be translated as *the sacredness within me recognizes and honors the sacredness within you.* Each of us is sacred and irreplaceable. We must protect ourselves, our children, and each other from sexist and racist behaviors that diminish our sacredness.

SUCCEEDING AT FAIRNESS:
SUGGESTIONS FOR STUDENTS, PARENTS, AND TEACHERS

1. Visit a toy store and do your own analysis of gender issues. How are the aisles labeled? How can you tell the boy and girl sections apart? Which sections are larger? List the types and specific examples of toys found in

each section. Compare the colors, lettering, and packaging of the toys in the two sections. Compare the language used, words such as *create* and *destroy*. What behaviors do the toys in each section promote—violence, communication, friendship, competition, learning, and parenting? What careers are associated with the toys? How would you characterize the salaries associated with these careers?

2. All politics is local. Fairness, while part of our national creed, could sometimes use a citizen's help. Parents, teachers, and students can work to ensure that our government representatives are responsive to gender equity through advocacy, campaigning, and involvement. As history teaches us, gender equity depends on the support of our elected local, state, and federal officials. How do your representatives vote on issues of gender fairness? What have your representatives done to move this issue forward and to open up options for all our children? Are they working to ensure that Title IX is being implemented—or are they road-blocks to equity? When is the last time you communicated with them?

3. Adults can also select nonbiased movies and films for their children. The Geena Davis Institute on Gender in Media is a good place to start. And if you see things that you find offensive, take action. If you see things that you like, tell theater owners and film companies that as well. Writing Hollywood about films and television shows you like and dislike can make a difference, especially when public approval and profits are at stake.

4. You, too, can check on whether Title IX is being implemented. The book's website will help. Asking your school district for the name of the Title IX compliance officer or for a copy of the grievance procedure will get the ball rolling. Information about Title IX and the compliance officer needs to be posted or distributed for all to see. Is it? You get the idea. If the school is resistant, the Office for Civil Rights at the U.S. Department of Education is your next stop. You could also check with the National Women's Law Center through their free website at www.nwlc.org, or with "Exercise Your Rights" at www.titleix.info.

5. While visiting these websites, feel free to visit the National Coalition of Women and Girls in Education at www.ncwge.org/affiliates.html. You will find a list of participating organizations all working to eliminate gender bias. Read through the list and check out the websites of those organizations. Find one or more that speak to your heart and volunteer time or money to that cause.

6. Resources focused on boys are too rare. So consider this an open invitation to initiate a group in your community to confront male violence,

traditional career paths, lack of male family time, and other aspects of the male role that are distasteful, limiting, harmful—or all three. It is also an invitation for those interested in boys' issues to create a destination website for all of us. We have been unable to find a satisfactory one in the research for this book, and would be pleased indeed if male gender role resources could grow in the years ahead.

Resources

The Courage to Raise Good Men, by Olga Silverstein and Beth Rashbaum
Olga Silverstein and Beth Rashbaum cast a highly critical eye on how we raise boys. With rich examples from myths to movies, from Freud to Bly, the authors show how society works to convince us that only a father can make a boy a man and sanctions the emotional shutdown of males.

Taking on the Big Boys: Or Why Feminism Is Good for Families, Business, and the Nation, by Ellen Bravo
Ellen Bravo provides a clear and convincing case for the nation to consider how feminist ideas are practical rather than radical, how fair pay enhances families and the nation. (The "Big Boys" are those men who profit from gender bias, exploit the misunderstandings about feminism, and ridicule and reject feminists.)

200 Ways to Raise a Boy's Self-Esteem: An Indispensable Guide for Parents, Teachers & Other Concerned Caregivers, by Will Glennon
This guide offers practical tools for raising emotionally healthy boys in a culture that represses emotional awareness in males. The book suggests activities for both home and school.

Backlash: The Undeclared War Against American Women, by Susan Faludi
Pulitzer Prize–winning author Susan Faludi finds evidence of antifeminist backlash in Hollywood movies, TV shows, politics, and 1980s fashion ads. It is a classic.

For additional resources, see *Still Failing at Fairness*'s page on www.simon andschuster.com.

Notes

Chapter 1. Didn't We Solve This Problem Years Ago?

1. Williamson, Marianne. *A Return to Love: Reflections on the Principles of a Course in Miracles*. New York: HarperCollins, 1994.
2. The Sadkers' first study, which analyzed gender bias in elementary and secondary classrooms, lasted more than three years and was funded by the National Institute of Education. The report submitted to the government was Sadker, Myra, and David Sadker, *Year 3: Final Report: Promoting Effectiveness in Classroom Instruction*. Washington, DC: National Institute of Education, 1984.

   Sadker, Myra, and David Sadker. "Sexism in the Schoolroom of the Eighties." *Psychology Today* (March 1985), pp. 54–57.

   Sadker, Myra, and David Sadker. "Sexism in the Classroom: From Grade School to Graduate School." *Phi Delta Kappan* 67:7 (March 1986), pp. 512–15.

   We also reported this study as one of the contributing authors to Wellesley College Center for Research on Women. *How Schools Shortchange Girls: The AAUW Report*. Washington, DC: American Association of University Women Educational Foundation, 1992.

   Since the Sadkers' original studies, others have updated the classroom interaction research:

   Altermatt, Ellen, Jasna Jovanovic, and Michelle Perry. "Bias or Responsivity? Sex and Achievement-Level Effects on Teachers' Classroom Questioning Practices." *Journal of Educational Psychology* 90 (1998), pp. 516–27.

   Beaman, Robyn, Kevin Wheldall, and Coral Kemp. "Differential teacher attention to boys and girls in the classroom." *Educational Review* 58:3 (2006), pp. 339–66.

   Duffy, Jim, Kelly Warren, and Margaret Walsh. "Classroom interactions: Gender of teacher, gender of student, and classroom subject." *Sex Roles* 45:9/10 (2001), pp. 579–93.

   Montague, Marjorie, and Christine Rinaldi. "Classroom Dynamics and Children at Risk." *Learning Disability Quarterly* 24 (2001), pp. 75–83.
3. Kidder, Tracy. *Among Schoolchildren*. Boston: Houghton Mifflin, 1989, p. 3.
4. Kidder, *Among Schoolchildren*, p. 262.
5. These episodes are drawn primarily from our three-year study of sex bias in ele-

321

mentary and secondary classrooms. They are also taken from classroom observations conducted as we supervised student teachers at American University and as we consulted with schools around the country and assessed their classrooms for gender bias.

6. Trecker, Janice Law. "Women in U.S. History High School Textbooks." *Social Education* 35 (1971), pp. 249–60.

7. Roberts, Cokie. *Founding Mothers: The Women Who Raised Our Nation.* New York: Perennial, 2005.

8. Weitzman, Lenore, and Diane Rizzo. *Biased Textbooks: Images of Males and Females in Elementary School Textbooks.* Washington, DC: Resource Center on Sex Roles in Education, 1976.

   Saario, Terry, Carol Jacklin, and Carol Tittle. "Sex Role Stereotyping in the Public Schools," *Harvard Educational Review* 43 (1973), pp. 386–416.

   Women on Words and Images. *Dick and Jane as Victims: Sex Stereotyping in Children's Readers.* Princeton, NJ: Carolingian Press, 1972.

9. Hodes, Carol L. "Gender Representations in Mathematics Software," *Journal of Educational Technology Systems* 24 (1995–96), pp. 67–73.

10. For more than a decade we have offered workshops on gender bias for educators and parents around the country. At these workshops we have collected anecdotes and stories from students, teachers, and parents about sex bias that they faced at school.

11. "This Is What You Thought: Were Any of Your Teachers Biased Against Females?" *Glamour* (August 1992), p. 157.

12. American Association of University Women. *Tech-Savvy: Educating Girls in the New Computer Age.* Washington, DC: AAUW, 2000.

13. Li, Q. "Teachers' Beliefs and Gender Differences in Mathematics: A Review." *Educational Research* 41 (1999), p. 63.

14. *The Super Girl Dilemma: Girls Feel the Pressure to be Perfect, Accomplished, Thin and Accommodating.* October 2006, www.girlsinc.org/ic/page.php?is=2.1.36.

15. Margolis, Jane, and Allan Fisher. *Unlocking the Clubhouse: Women in Computing.* Cambridge, MA: MIT Press, 2003, pp. 35–36.

16. Carlson, Scott. "Wanted: Female Computer-Science Students: Colleges work to attract and support women in technology majors." *Chronicle of Higher Education* (January 13, 2006), http://chronicle.com/free/v52/i19/19a03501.htm.

17. Zittleman, Karen. "Title IX and Gender: A Study of the Knowledge, Perceptions, and Experiences of Middle and Junior High School Teachers and Students." *Dissertation Abstracts International* 66:11 (2005) (UMI No. 3194815).

18. Ibid.; See also Zittleman, Karen. "Gender Perceptions of Middle Schoolers: The Good and the Bad." *Middle Grades Research Journal* 2:2 (Fall 2007), pp. 65–97.

19. Following the Sadkers' three-year study of elementary and secondary classrooms, the Sadkers conducted a two-year study of college classrooms and were sponsored by the Fund for the Improvement of Postsecondary Education. The project report submitted to the government was Sadker, Myra, and David Sadker. *Final Report: Project Effect (Effectiveness and Equity in College Teaching).* Washington, DC: Fund for the Improvement of Postsecondary Education, 1986.

   Sadker, Myra, and David Sadker. "Confronting Sexism in the College

Classroom." In Gabriel, Susan, and Isaiah Smithson, eds., *Gender in the Classroom: Power and Pedagogy*. Urbana: University of Illinois Press, 1990, pp. 176–87.

20. Office for Sex Equity in Education, Michigan Department of Education. "The Influence of Gender-Role Socialization on Student Perceptions: A Report Based on Data Collected from Michigan Public School Students" (revised June 1990).

21. Stepp, Laura Sessions. "Book Smarts Lacking on Gender Equality." *Washington Post*. January 15, 2008, pp. F1, F6.

22. Eisler, Riane. "How Feminist-Caring Economics Can Empower Women." *Clearinghouse on Women's Issues* (January 2008), p. 2. See also Eisler, Riane. *The Real Wealth of Nations: Creating a Caring Economics*. San Francisco: Berrett-Koehler, 2007.

23. Berkowitz, Marvin W. "The Complete Moral Person: Anatomy and Formation." In J. M. DuBois, ed., *Moral Issues in Psychology: Personalist Contributions to Selected Problems*. Lanham, MD: University Press of America, 1997, pp. 11–42; Berkowitz, Marvin W. "The Science of Character Education." In William Damon, ed., *Bringing in a New Era in Character Education*. Palo Alto, CA: Hoover Institution, 2002, pp. 43–63.

24. *Title IX at 35*. Washington, DC: National Coalition for Women and Girls in Education, 2007; Reichert, Michael C., and Richard A. Hawley, "Confronting the 'Boy Problem': A Self-Study Approach to Deepen Schools' Moral Stance." *Teachers College Record*, October 25, 2006.

25. *The Supergirl Dilemma: Girls Grapple with the Mounting Pressure of Expectations*. New York: Girls Incorporated, October 2006, http://www.girlsinc.org/supergirldilemma.

26. Data documenting the loss of academic achievement were obtained from reports, tables, news releases, and studies issued by test publishers, including American College Testing in Iowa City, Iowa, and the Educational Testing Service in Princeton, New Jersey. For example, the Medical College Admission Test (MCAT) is developed by ACT in Iowa City. Other sources include the Association of American Medical Colleges, the Graduate Management Admissions Council, and the Law School Data Assembly Service. FairTest in Cambridge, Massachusetts is a good source for testing issues. For some additional analysis of testing problems, see articles and books published by researchers such as David Berliner and Gerald Bracey.

27. Sadker and Sadker, *Year 3: Final Report*; Sadker and Sadker, *Final Report: Project Effect*; Altermatt, Jovanovic, and Perry, "Bias or Responsivity?"; Beaman, Wheldall, and Kemp, "Differential teacher attention"; Duffy, Warren, and Walsh, "Classroom interactions"; Montague and Rinaldi, "Classroom Dynamics."

28. *Title IX at 35*.

29. *Harassment-Free Hallways: How to Stop Harassment in School*. Washington, DC: American Association of University Women Educational Foundation, 2004, p. 10, http://www.aauw.org/ef/harass/index.cfm; Zittleman, "Title IX and Gender."

30. The Eating Disorders Coalition (www.aedweb.org) and the Renfrew Center (http://www.renfrewcenter.com) are excellent sources of information and statistics on eating disorders. A vast body of research documents girls' declining self-esteem at adolescence:

    Allgood-Merten, Betty, Peter Lewinsohn, and Hyman Hops. "Sex Differences and Adolescent Depression." *Journal of Abnormal Psychology* 99:1 (February 1990), pp. 55–63; Brutsaert, Herman. "Changing Sources of Self-Esteem Among Girls and Boys in Secondary Schools." *Urban Education* 24:4 (January 1990), pp. 432–39; Kelly, Kevin, and LaVerne Jordan. "Effects of Academic Achievement and Gender on Academic and Social Self-Concept: A Replication Study." *Journal of Counseling and Development* 69 (November–December 1990), pp. 173–77; Widaman, Keith, et al. "Differences in Adolescents' Self-Concept as a Function of Academic Level, Ethnicity, and Gender." *American Journal of Mental Retardation* 96:4 (1992), pp. 387–404; Williams, Sheila, and Rob McGee. "Adolescents' Self-Perceptions of Their Strengths." *Journal of Youth and Adolescence* 20:3 (June 1991), pp. 325–37; Nagel, K. L., and Karen H. Jones. "Sociological Factors in the Development of Eating Disorders," *Adolescence* 27 (Spring 1992), pp. 107–13; Wiseman, Claire, James Gray, James Mosimann, and Anthony Ahrens. "Cultural Expectations of Thinness in Women: An Update." *International Journal of Eating Disorders* 11:1 (1992), pp. 85–89; Button, Eric. "Self-Esteem in Girls Aged 11–12: Baseline Findings from a Planned Prospective Study of Vulnerability to Eating Disorders." *Journal of Adolescence* 13 (1990), pp. 407–13.

31. American Association of University Women. "Pay Gap Exists as Early as One Year out of College, New Research Says." http://www.aauw.org/newsroom/pressreleases/042307_PayGap.cfm.

32. Bravo, Ellen. *Taking on the Big Boys, or Why Feminism is Good for Families, Business and the Nation.* New York: Feminist Press of the City University of New York, 2007; U.S. Department of Commerce, Census Bureau, "Educational Attainment in the United States: 2006 Detailed Tables," Table 9, http://www.census.gov/population/www/socdemo/education/cps2006.html; Institute for Women's Policy Research. "Wage Gap Persists in 2006: New Government Data Show No Progress in Closing the Gender Wage Gap." April 24, 2007. www.iwpr.org/pdf/c350.pdf.

33. *AFL-CIO, Department of Professional Employees.* "Professional Women: Vital Statistics *Fact Sheet 2007.*" January 21, 2008. http://www.dpeaflcio.org/programs/factsheets/fs_2008_Professional_Women.htm.

34. Organisation for Economic Co-operation and Development. "Can Parents Afford to Work? Childcare costs, tax-benefit policies and work incentives." January 2006. http://www.oecd.org/dataoecd/35/43/35969537.pdf; U.S. Department of Agriculture, Center for Nutrition Policy and Promotion. "Expenditure on Children by Families, 2004." http://www.usda.gov/cnpp/Crc/crc2004.pdf.

35. U.S. Department of Labor, Bureau of Labor Statistics. "Perspectives on Working Women: A Databook." Bulletin 2080, 1980; "Perspectives on Working Women: A Databook," 2008. http://www.bls.gov/cps/wlf-databook2008.htm.

36. Inter-Parliamentary Union. "Women in Parliaments: World Classification." www.ipu.org/wmn-e/classif.htm.

Chapter 2: Opening the Schoolhouse Door

1. Frazier, Nancy, and Myra Sadker. *Sexism in School and Society.* New York: Harper & Row, 1973, p. 122.

2. Woody, Thomas. *A History of Women's Education in the United States,* vols. 1 and 2. New York: Octagon, 1966, p. 273.

3. Greene, Maxine. *Landscapes of Learning*. New York: Teachers College Press, 1978, pp. 225–43.

Tannenbaum Deutsch, David. "The Polite Lady: Portraits of American Schoolgirls and Their Accomplishments, 1725–1830." *Antiques* 135 (March 1980), pp. 742–53.

4. Tyack, David, and Elisabeth Hansot. *Learning Together: A History of Coeducation in American Schools*. New Haven, CT: Yale University Press, 1990, pp. 13–27.

Bailyn, Bernard. *Education in the Forming of American Society*. Chapel Hill: University of North Carolina Press, 1960.

Cremin, Lawrence. *American Education: The Colonial Experience, 1607–1783*. New York: Harper & Row, 1970.

5. Axtell, James. *The School Upon a Hill: Education and Society in Colonial New England*. New Haven, CT: Yale University Press, 1974.

6. Messerli, Jonathan. *Horace Mann: A Biography*. New York: Knopf, 1972.

Tyack, David, and Elisabeth Hansot. *Learning Together: A History of Coeducation in American Schools*. New Haven, CT: Yale University Press, 1990.

7. Higginson, J. *Common Sense About Women*. Quoted in Woody, *A History of Women's Education*, vol. 2, pp. 200–1.

Krug, Edward A. *The Shaping of the American High School*. New York: Harper & Row, 1964.

Cremin, Lawrence A. *The Transformation of the School: Progressivism in American Education, 1876–1957*. New York: Knopf, 1961.

8. Tyack and Hansot, *Learning Together*. A comprehensive discussion of coeducation is provided in Keller, Arnold Jack. *A Historical Analysis of the Arguments for and Against Coeducational Public High Schools in the United States*. Ph.D. diss., Columbia University, 1971.

9. Curti, Merle. *The Social Ideas of American Educators*. Totowa, NJ: Littlefield, 1959, p. 185.

10. Clark, Alice. *Working Life of Women in the Seventeenth Century*. London: Routledge & Kegan Paul, 1982 (1919), pp. 259–63.

11. Salomone, Rosemary. *Equal Education Under the Law: Legal Rights and Federal Policy in the Post-Brown Era*. New York: St. Martin's, 1986.

12. Pearson, Carol, Judith Touchton, and Donna Shavlik. *Educating the Majority: Women Challenge Tradition in Higher Education*. New York: Macmillan, 1989, pp. 48–49.

Solomon, Barbara. *In the Company of Educated Women*. New Haven, CT: Yale University Press, 1985, p. 152.

13. Mann, Horace. *A Few Thoughts on the Powers and Duties of Women*. Syracuse, NY: Hall, Mills, 1853, p. 82.

14. Blount, Jackie. "Spinsters, Bachelors and Other Gender Transgressors in School Employment, 1850–1990." *Review of Educational Research* 70, no. 1 (Spring 2000), pp. 83–101.

15. Blount, "Spinsters, Bachelors and Other Gender Transgressors."

16. Marcus, Eric. *Making History: The Struggle for Gay and Lesbian Equal Rights, 1945–1990, An Oral History*. New York: HarperCollins, 1992.

17. Griffin, Gail. "Women's Education and the American Midwest." *Change* (January–February 1984), p. 36.

18. "A Satire on a College for Women in Kentucky." *Springfield* [Massachusetts] *Republican and Journal.* March 14, 1835.

19. Gordon, Lynn Dorothy. *Gender and Higher Education in the Progressive Era.* New Haven, CT: Yale University Press, 1990, pp. 22–23.

20. Griffin, "Women's Education and the American Midwest," p. 37.

21. Gordon, J. E. H. "The After Careers of University-Educated Women." *Nineteenth Century* 37 (June 1895), pp. 955–60. Quoted in Woody, *A History of Women's Education,* vol. 2, p. 206.

22. Woody, *A History of Women's Education,* vol. 2, p. 319.

23. Lucy Downing, quoted in Woody, *A History of Women's Education,* vol. 2, p. 137.

24. Jewett, Milo. "Origin of Vassar College." March 1879, typed copy, p. 5, Vassar College Library, Poughkeepsie, NY. Quoted in Helen Lefkowitz Horowitz, *Alma Mater.* New York: Knopf, 1984, p. 29.

25. Quoted in Horowitz, *Alma Mater,* pp. 74–75.

26. Howe, Julia Ward. "Introduction." In Annie Nathan Meyer, *Woman's Work in America.* New York: Henry Holt, 1891.

27. Quoted in Patricia Smith Butcher, *Education for Equality: Women's Rights Periodicals and Women's Higher Education, 1849–1920.* New York: Greenwood, 1989, p. 89.

28. Clarke, Edward H. *Sex in Education: Or, A Fair Chance for Girls.* Boston: Houghton Mifflin, 1873, pp. 120–28.

29. A good discussion of Edward Clarke's beliefs and impact is provided in Tyack and Hansot, *Learning Together,* pp. 146–54.

30. Thomas, M. Carey. "Present Tendencies in Women's Education." *Education Review* 25 (1908), pp. 64–85. Quoted in Tyack and Hansot, *Learning Together,* p. 68.

31. Faludi, Susan. *Backlash: The Undeclared War Against American Women.* New York: Crown, 1991, pp. 259–63.

    Gurian, Michael, and Kathy Stevens. *The Minds of Boys: Saving Our Sons from Falling Behind in School and Life.* San Francisco: Jossey-Bass, 2005.

    Sommers, Christina. *The War Against Boys: How Misguided Feminism Is Harming Our Young Men.* New York: Simon & Schuster, 2000.

32. Faludi, *Backlash,* pp. 259–63.

    Zittleman, Karen. "Title IX and Gender: A Study of the Knowledge, Perceptions, and Experiences of Middle and Junior High School Teachers and Students." *Dissertation Abstracts International* 66:11 (UMI No. 3194815) (2005).

33. Bravo, Ellen. *Taking on the Big Boys: Or Why Feminism is Good for Families, Business, and the Nation.* New York: Feminist Press, 2007.

34. Faludi, *Backlash,* p. xix.

35. Susan Klein. Personal communication, January 2009.

36. *Brown v. Board of Education,* 347 U.S. 483, 495 (1954).

37. United States Department of Education. "Secretary Spellings Announces More Choices in Single Sex Education Amended Regulations Give Communities." October 24, 2006. http://www.ed.gov/news/pressreleases/2006/10/10242006 .html.

38. National Women's Law Center. *New Single-Sex Regulations: Endangering Equal Opportunity for Girls.* March 11, 2004. http://www.nwlc.org/pdf/Single SexRegsEditMemo31104.pdf.

39. National Women's Law Center, *New Single-Sex Regulations.*
40. Arms, Emily. "Gender Equity in Coeducational and Single-Sex Environments." In Susan Klein, ed., *Handbook for Achieving Gender Equity through Education.* Mahwah, NJ: Lawrence Erlbaum, 2007, pp. 171–90.
41. Hogshead-Makar, Nancy. "Nancy Hogshead-Makar's Response to House Committee's Questions: Responses to Committee Members' Questions at the First Tee Hearing on Positive Impact of Participation in Athletics in Building Character, Leadership Skills, and Health of All Children on June 28, 2006." http://www.womenssportsfoundation.org/Content/Articles/Issues/Title-IX/N/ Nancy-HogsheadMakars-Response-to-House-Committees-Questions.aspx.
42. National Women's Law Center. *Barriers to Fair Play.* June 2007. http://www.nwlc.org/pdf/BarriersToFairPlay.pdf.
    Vincente, Roberto. *1981-82-2004-05 Sports Sponsorship and Participation Report.* Indianapolis, IN: National Collegiate Athletics Association, 2006.
    Women's Sports Foundation. *2007 Statistics—Gender Equity in High School and College Athletics: Most Recent Participation & Budget Statistics.* http://www.womenssportsfoundation.org/Content/Articles/Issues/General/123/ 2008-Statistics--Gender-Equity-in-High-School-and-College-Athletics-Most-Recent-Participation--Budge.aspx.
43. *National Wrestling Coaches Association v. United States Department of Education,* Civ.No. 02–0072, US. District Court, 2003.
44. United States Department of Education, Office for Civil Rights. *Additional Clarification of Intercollegiate Athletics Policy: Three Part Test—Part Three.* March 17, 2005. http://www.ed.gov/about/offices/list/ocr/docs/title9guidance additional.html.
45. Zittleman, "Title IX and Gender."
46. Ibid.
    Zittleman, Karen. Unpublished dissertation data from interviews and surveys of one hundred high school students and seventeen teachers in three Maryland public high schools. 2005.
47. Zittleman, "Title IX and Gender."
    Women's Sports Foundation, *2007 Statistics.*

Chapter 3: The Beginning of the Classroom Compromise:
The Elementary School Years

1. Sadker, Myra, and David Sadker. *Year 3: Final Report: Promoting Effectiveness in Classroom Instruction.* Washington, DC: National Institute of Education, 1984.
    Sadker, Myra, and David Sadker. "Sexism in the Classroom: From Grade School to Graduate School." *Phi Delta Kappan* 67:7 (March 1986), pp. 512–15.
    Wellesley College Center for Research on Women. *How Schools Shortchange Girls: The AAUW Report.* Washington, DC: American Association of University Women Educational Foundation, 1992.
    Sadker, Myra, David Sadker, and Lisa Stulberg. "Fair and Square? Creating a Nonsexist Classroom." *Instructor* 102:7 (March 1993), pp. 45–46, 67.
2. Meehan, Diana. *Learning Like A Girl: Educating Our Daughters in Schools of Their Own.* New York: PublicAffairs, 2007.
3. Sadker and Sadker, *Year 3: Final Report;* Sadker and Sadker, "Sexism in the

Classroom"; Wellesley College Center for Research on Women, *How Schools Shortchange Girls*; Sadker, Sadker, and Stulberg, "Fair and Square?"

4. Ibid.

5. Altermatt, Ellen, Jasna Jovanovic, and Michelle Perry. "Bias or Responsivity? Sex and Achievement-Level Effects on Teachers' Classroom Questioning Practices." *Journal of Educational Psychology* 90 (1998), pp. 516–27.

   Beaman, Robyn, Kevin Wheldall, and Coral Kemp. "Differential teacher attention to boys and girls in the classroom." *Educational Review* 58:3 (2006), pp. 339–66.

   Duffy, Jim, Kelly Warren, and Margaret Walsh. "Classroom interactions: Gender of teacher, gender of student, and classroom subject." *Sex Roles* 45:9–10 (2001), pp. 579–93.

   Montague, Marjorie, and Christine Rinaldi. "Classroom Dynamics and Children at Risk." *Learning Disability Quarterly* 24 (2001), pp. 75–83.

6. Feldhusen, John F., and Colleen Willard-Holt. "Gender Differences in Classroom Interactions and Career Aspirations of Gifted Students." *Contemporary Educational Psychology* 18:3 (July 1993), pp. 355–62.

   Fox, Lynn, and Janet Soller. "Gender Equity for Gifted Students." In Susan S. Klein, ed., *Handbook for Achieving Gender Equity through Education*, 2nd ed. New York: Lawrence Erlbaum, Taylor & Francis, (2007), pp. 573–82.

   Jones, Gail M., and Thomas M. Gerig. "Silent Sixth-Grade Students: Characteristics, Achievement, and Teacher Expectations." *Elementary School Journal* 95 (1994), pp. 169–82.

   Siegle, Don. *Teacher Bias in Identifying Gifted and Talented Students.* Paper presented at the Annual Meeting of the Council for Exceptional Children, Kansas City, MO, April 18–21, 2001.

7. Irvine, Jacqueline Jordan. "Teacher-Student Interactions: Effects of Student Race, Sex, and Grade Level." *Journal of Educational Psychology* 78:1 (1986), pp. 14–21.

   Irvine, Jacqueline Jordan. *In Search of Wholeness: African American Teachers and Their Culturally Specific Classroom Practices.* New York: Palgrave/St. Martin's, 2002.

8. Grant, Linda. "Helpers, Enforcers, and Go-Betweens: Black Females in Elementary School Classrooms." In Maxine Baca Zinn and Bonnie Thornton Dill, eds., *Women of Color in U.S. Society.* Philadelphia: University of Pennsylvania Press, 1994.

9. Altermatt, Jovanovic, and Perry, "Bias or Responsivity?"

   Jones, Susanne M., and Kathryn Dindia. "A Meta-Analytic Perspective on Sex Equity in the Classroom." *Review of Educational Research* 74:4 (Winter 2004), pp. 443–71.

   Spencer, Renee, Michelle Porche, and Deborah Tolman. "We've come a long way—maybe: New challenges for gender equity education." *Teachers College Record* 105:9 (2003), pp. 1774–1807.

   See also Sadker, Sadker, and Stulberg, "Fair and Square?"

10. Irvine, "Teacher-Student Interactions"; Irvine, *In Search of Wholeness.*

11. Rowe, Mary Budd. "Wait Time: Slowing Down May Be a Way of Speeding Up!" *Journal of Teacher Education* 37:1 (1986), pp. 43–50.

    Black, Susan. "Ask Me a Question." *American School Board Journal* 188:5 (May 2001).

12. Black, "Ask Me a Question."

    Dolle-Willemsen, Dora, and Theodora Elisabeth. "Making the gender dimension in classroom interaction visible by using gender as a lens in primary teacher education." *Proquest Dissertations and Theses 1997. Section 0687, Part 0524.* Netherlands: Katholieke Universiteit Brabant; Publication AAT C684929, 1997.

    Gore, Dolores, and Daniel Roumagoux. "Wait-Time as a Variable in Sex-Related Differences During Fourth-Grade Mathematics Instruction." *Journal of Educational Research* 76:5 (1983), pp. 273–75.

13. Dweck, Carol, William Davidson, Sharon Nelson, and Bradley Enna. "Sex Differences in Learned Helplessness: II. The Contingencies of Evaluative Feedback in the Classroom, III. An Experimental Analysis." *Developmental Psychology* 14:3 (1978), pp. 268–76.

    Koch, Janice. "Gender issues in the classroom." In W. R. Reynolds and G. E. Miller, eds., *Educational Psychology,* vol. 6 of the *Comprehensive Handbook of Psychology,* ed. I. B. Weiner. New York: Wiley, 2002.

14. Zittleman, Karen. "Gender Perceptions of Middle Schoolers: The Good and the Bad." *Middle Grades Research Journal* 2:2 (Fall 2007), pp. 65–97.

    Zittleman, Karen. "Title IX and Gender: A Study of the Knowledge, Perceptions, and Experiences of Middle and Junior High School Teachers and Students." *Dissertation Abstracts International* 66:11 (2005) (UMI No. 3194815).

15. Best, Raphaela. *We've All Got Scars: What Boys and Girls Learn in Elementary School.* Bloomington, IN: Indiana University Press, 1983.

16. Zittleman, "Gender Perceptions of Middle Schoolers"; Zittleman, "Title IX and Gender."

17. Mahaffey, Foyne. "An Elementary School Teacher Reflects on Harassment: Are We Accepting Too Much?" *Rethinking Schools* (May–June 1992), p. 6.

18. Sadker and Sadker, *Year 3: Final Report.*

19. Safir, Marilyn, Rachel Hertz-Lazarowitz, Shoshana BenTsvi-Mayer, and Haggai Kupermintz. "Prominence of Girls and Boys in the Classroom: Schoolchildren's Perceptions." *Sex Roles* 27:9–10 (1992), pp. 439–53.

    BenTsvi-Mayer, Shoshana, Rachel Hertz-Lazarowitz, and Marilyn P. Safir. "Teachers' Selections of Boys and Girls as Prominent Pupils." *Sex Roles* 21:3–4 (1989), pp. 231–45.

    See also Zittleman, "Gender Perceptions of Middle Schoolers" and Zittleman, "Title IX and Gender."

20. Adler, Patricia, Steven Kless, and Peter Adler. "Socialization to Gender Roles: Popularity Among Elementary School Boys and Girls." *Sociology of Education* 65:3 (July 1992), pp.169–87.

21. Ferguson, Ann. *Bad Boys: Public Schools in the Making of Black Masculinity.* Ann Arbor: University of Michigan Press, 2001.

    See also Grant, "Helpers, Enforcers, and Go-Betweens."

22. Ferguson, *Bad Boys,* p. 10.

23. Ibid., p. 85.

24. Ibid., p. 91.

25. Ibid., p. 92.

26. Women on Words and Images. *Dick and Jane as Victims: Sex Stereotyping in Children's Readers.* Princeton, NJ: Women on Words and Images, 1975.

27. Weitzman, Lenore, et al. "Sex Role Socialization in Picture Books for Preschool Children." *American Journal of Sociology* 77:6 (1972), pp. 1125–50.

28. McCracken, Glenn, and Charles Walcutt, eds. *Lippincott Basic Reading Series,*
    Book H, 1970.
    O'Donnell, Mabel. *Around the Corner.* New York: Harper & Row, 1966.
    Robinson, Helen, et al., eds. *Ventures,* Book 4. Upper Saddle River, NJ: Scott
    Foresman, 1965.
    Handforth, Thomas. *Mei Li.* New York: Doubleday, 1938.
29. During the 1970s publishers developed and disseminated the following guide-
    lines for the preparation of nonsexist materials:
    Avoiding Stereotypes. College Division, Houghton Mifflin. Boston:
    Houghton Mifflin, 1975.
    *Guidelines for Creating Positive Sexual and Racial Images in Educational
    Materials.* New York: Macmillan, 1975.
    *Guidelines for the Development of Elementary and Secondary Instructional
    Materials.* New York: Holt, Rinehart & Winston, 1975.
    *Guidelines for Eliminating Stereotypes from Instructional Materials, Grades
    K–12.* School Department, Harper & Row. New York: Harper & Row, 1976.
    *Guidelines for Equal Treatment of the Sexes in McGraw-Hill Book Com-
    pany Publications.* New York: McGraw-Hill, 1979.
    Guidelines for Improving the Image of Women in Textbooks. Glenview, IL:
    Scott Foresman, 1972.
    Statement on Bias-Free Materials. School Division, Association of American
    Publishers. New York: Association of American Publishers, 1976.
30. Fan, Lianghuo, and Gurcharn S. Kaeley. "The influence of textbooks on teach-
    ing strategies." *Mid-Western Educational Researcher* 13:4 (2000), pp. 2–9.
    Starnes, Bobby Ann. "Textbooks, School Reform, and the Silver Lining." *Phi
    Delta Kappan* 86:2 (2004), pp. 170–71.
    Woodward, Arthur, and David. L. Elliot. "Textbook Use and Teacher Profes-
    sionalism." In D. L. Elliot and A. Woodward, eds., *Textbooks and Schooling in
    the United States,* 89th Yearbook of the National Society for the Study of
    Education. Chicago: University of Chicago Press, 1990, pp. 178–93.
31. Children's Book Council. *Industry Sales Surveys for the Years 1999–2001.*
    New York: Children's Book Council, 2002.
32. Hodes, Carol L. "Gender Representations in Mathematics Software." *Journal
    of Educational Technology Systems* 24 (1995–96), pp. 67–73.
33. Chick, Kay. "Gender Balance in K–12 American History Textbooks." *Social
    Studies Research and Practice* 1:3 (Winter 2006). www.socstrp.org.
34. Beck, Roger, Linda Black, Phyllis Naylor, and Dahlia Ibo Shabaka. *World His-
    tory: Patterns of Interaction.* Evanston, IL: McDougal Littell, 2005.
35. Dacquino, V. T. *Sybil Ludington: The Call to Arms.* Layfette, LA: Purple
    Mountain, 2000.
36. Vare, Ethlie Ann, and Greg Ptacek. *Mothers of Invention.* New York: William
    Morrow, 1988.
37. Evans, Lorraine, and Kimberly Davies. "No sissy boys here: A content analysis
    of the representation of masculinity in elementary school reading textbooks."
    Sex Roles 42 (2000), pp. 255–70.
38. Hamilton, Mykol, David A. Anderson, Michelle Broaddus, and Kate Young.
    "Gender stereotyping and under-representation of female characters in 200
    popular children's picture books: A twenty-first century update." *Sex Roles* 55
    (2006), pp. 757–65.

39. Anderson, David A., and Mykol Hamilton. "Gender Role Stereotyping of Fathers in Children's Picture Books: The Invisible Father." *Sex Roles* 52:3/4 (February 2005), pp. 145–51.
40. Hamilton, Anderson, Broaddus, and Young, "Gender stereotyping and under-representation."
41. Weitzman, Lenore, Deborah Eifler, Elizabeth Hokada, and Catherine Ross. "Sex role socialization in picture books for preschool children." *American Journal of Sociology* 77 (1972), pp. 1125–30.
42. Gurian, Michael, Patricia Henley, and Terry Trueman. *Boys and Girls Learn Differently! A Guide for Teachers and Parents.* San Francisco: Jossey-Bass, 2001.

Sax, Leonard. *Why Gender Matters: What Parents and Teachers Need to Know about the Emerging Science of Sex Differences.* New York: Doubleday, 2005.

Sommers, Christina Hoff. *The War Against Boys: How Misguided Feminism Is Harming Our Young Men.* New York: Simon & Schuster, 2000.

Tyre, Peg. *The Trouble with Boys: A Surprising Report Card on Our Sons, Their Problems at School and What Parents and Educators Must Do.* New York: Crown, 2008.
43. Henry K. Kaiser Family Foundation, "Generation M: Media in the Lives of 8–18 Year-Olds," March 2005. www.kff.org/entmedia/entmedia030905pkg .cfm.

Chapter 4: Self-Esteem Slides: The Middle Years

1. Kerr, Barbara. *Smart Girls, Gifted Women.* Columbus: Ohio Psychology Publishing Co., 1985, p. 87.
2. Disch, Estelle, *Reconstructing Gender: A Multicultural Anthology.* 4th ed. New York: McGraw-Hill, 2006.

Ladson-Billings, Gloria. "Culturally Relevant Teaching: Theory and Practice." In James Banks and Cherry A. McGee Banks, eds., *Multicultural Education: Issues and Perspectives.* 6th ed. Hoboken, NJ: Wiley, 2007, pp. 221–45.

Ladson-Billings, Gloria. "It's Not the Culture of Poverty, It's the Poverty of Culture: The Problem with Teacher Education." *Anthropology and Education Quarterly* 37:2 (June 2006), pp. 104–9.

Klein, Susan S. *Handbook for Achieving Gender Equity through Education.* 2nd ed. New York: Lawrence Erlbaum Associates, Taylor & Francis Group, 2007.

Pollack, William. *Real Boys: Rescuing Our Sons from the Myths of Boyhood.* New York: Random House, 1998.
3. Brutsaert, Herman. "Changing Sources of Self-Esteem Among Girls and Boys in Secondary Schools." *Urban Education* 24:4 (January 1990), pp. 432–39.

Carlson, Cindy, Sarika Uppal, and Ellie C. Prosser. "Ethnic Differences in Processes Contributing to the Self-Esteem of Early Adolescent Girls." *Journal of Early Adolescence* 20 (2000), pp. 44–67.

See also Disch, *Reconstructing Gender*; Klein, *Handbook for Achieving Gender Equity through Education*; Ladson-Billings, "It's Not the Culture of Poverty, It's the Poverty of Culture."
4. Juvonen, Jaana. *Focus on the Wonder Years: Challenges Facing the American*

Middle School (Santa Monica, CA: RAND Corporations, 2004). www.rand
.org/pubs/monographs/2004/RAND_MG139.pdf.

5. Zittleman, Karen. "Gender Perceptions of Middle Schoolers: The Good and the
Bad," *Middle Grades Research Journal* 2:2 (Fall 2007), pp. 65–97.

    Zittleman, Karen. "Title IX and Gender: A Study of the Knowledge, Percep-
tions, and Experiences of Middle and Junior High School Teachers and Students." *Dissertation Abstracts International* 66:11 (2005) (UMI No. 3194815).

6. American Association of University Women. *How schools shortchange girls.*
Washington, DC: AAUW, 1992.

    A vast body of research documents girls' declining self-esteem at adolescence:

    Allgood-Merten, Betty, Peter Lewinsohn, and Hyman Hops. "Sex Differ-
ences and Adolescent Depression." *Journal of Abnormal Psychology* 99:1
(1990), pp. 55–63.

    Brutsaert, Herman. "Changing Sources of Self-Esteem Among Girls and Boys
in Secondary Schools." *Urban Education* 24:4 (January 1990), pp. 432–39.

    Carlson, Cindy, Sarika Uppal, and Ellie C. Prosser. "Ethnic Differences in
Processes Contributing to the Self-Esteem of Early Adolescent Girls." *Journal of
Early Adolescence* 20 (2000), pp. 44–67.

    Disch, Estelle. *Reconstructing Gender: A Multicultural Anthology.* 4th ed.
New York: McGraw-Hill, 2006.

    Klein, Susan S. *Handbook for Achieving Gender Equity through Education.*
2nd ed. New York: Lawrence Erlbaum Associates, Taylor & Francis Group,
2007.

    Tolman, Deborah L., Emily A. Impett, Allison J. Tracy, and Alice Michael.
"Looking Good, Sounding Good: Femininity Ideology and Adolescent Girls'
Mental Health." *Psychology of Women Quarterly* 30 (March 2006),
pp. 85–95.

    Williams, Sheila, and Rob McGee. "Adolescents' Self-Perceptions of Their
Strengths." *Journal of Youth and Adolescence* 20:3 (1991), pp. 325–37.

7. Kerr, Barbara. *Smart Girls: A New Psychology of Girls, Women, and Gifted-
ness.* Phoenix: Gifted Psychology, 1997.

8. Petersen, Anne, Pamela Sarigiani, and Robert Kennedy. "Adolescent Depression: Why More Girls?" *Journal of Youth and Adolescence* 20:2 (1991), pp.
247–71.

    Whitehead, D. B., and T. Ooms. *Goodbye to Girlhood: What's Troubling
Girls and What We Can Do About It.* Washington, DC: National Campaign to
Prevent Teen Pregnancy, 1999.

9. American Association of University Women. *How Schools Shortchange Girls.*
Washington, DC: AAUW, 1992.

10. Kerr, *Smart Girls.*

11. Hesse-Biber, Sharlene Nagy, Stephanie A. Howling, Patricia Leavy, and Meg
Lovejoy. "Racial Identity and the Development of Body Image Issues among
African American Adolescent Girls." *Qualitative Report* 9 (March 2004),
pp. 49–79.

12. American Association of University Women, *How Schools Shortchange Girls.*

13. Zittleman, "Gender Perceptions of Middle Schoolers"; Zittleman, "Title IX and
Gender."

14. Serbin, Lisa, and Daniel O'Leary. "How Nursery Schools Teach Girls to Shut
Up." *Psychology Today* (July 1975), pp. 56–58, 102–3.

15. Cruz-Janzen, Marta. "A Case Study of Gender Interactions in a Bilingual Early Childhood Education Classroom." Paper presented at the American Educational Research Association, San Francisco, 1992.

16. National Center for Education Statistics. *Elementary and Secondary Education: An International Perspective.* 2000. http://nces.ed.gov/pubsearch/pubsinfo.asp ?pubid=2000033.

17. Zittleman, "Gender Perceptions of Middle Schoolers"; Zittleman, "Title IX and Gender."

18. These examples are drawn from field notes in Myra and David Sadker's three-year study of classroom interaction, *Year 3: Final Report: Promoting Effectiveness in Classroom Instruction.* Washington, DC: National Institute of Education, 1984, and from Karen Zittleman's dissertation, "Title IX and Gender."

19. Zittleman, "Gender Perceptions of Middle Schoolers"; Zittleman, "Title IX and Gender."

20. Office for Sex Equity in Education, Michigan Department of Education. "The Influence of Gender-Role Socialization on Student Perceptions: A Report Based on Data Collected from Michigan Public School Students" (revised June 1992).

21. As we consult with schools around the country to help them eliminate sex bias, we often visit classrooms to talk with students. We have found one of the best ways to elicit reactions about gender quickly is to ask them to write essays about waking up as a member of the other sex. The quotes in this chapter were drawn from essays written by upper-elementary and middle school students from twenty-nine classrooms in Maryland, Virginia, Wisconsin, and Washington, DC.

22. Zittleman, "Gender Perceptions of Middle Schoolers"; Zittleman, "Title IX and Gender."

23. Ibid.

24. American Association of University Women, *How Schools Shortchange Girls.*

25. Erickson, Sarah J., and Melissa Gerstle. "Investigation of ethnic differences in body image between Hispanic/biethnic-Hispanic and non-Hispanic White preadolescent girls." *Body Image* 4 (March 2007), pp. 69–78.

    Hesse-Biber, Sharlene Nagy, Stephanie A. Howling, Patricia Leavy, and Meg Lovejoy. "Racial Identity and the Development of Body Image Issues among African American Adolescent Girls." *Qualitative Report* 9 (March 2004), pp. 49–79.

26. Hesse-Biber et al. "Racial Identity and the Development of Body Image Issues."

27. Kemer, B. J. "A Study of the Relationship Between the Sex of Students and the Assignment of Marks by Secondary School Teachers." Cited in Nancy Frazier and Myra Sadker, *Sexism in School and Society.* New York: Harper & Row, 1973, pp. 139–40.

28. Girls Inc. *The SuperGirl Dilemma: Girls Feel the Pressure to Be Perfect, Accomplished, Thin, and Accommodating.* New York: Girls Inc., 2006.

29. American Association of University Women, *How Schools Shortchange Girls.*

    Jones, Gail M., and Thomas M. Gerig. "Silent sixth-grade students: Characteristics, achievement, and teacher expectations." *Elementary School Journal* 95 (1994), pp. 169–82; Jones, Susanne, and Kathryn Dindia. "A meta-analytic perspective of sex equity in the classroom." *Review of Educational Research* 74:4 (2004), pp. 443–71.

    See also Zittleman, "Gender Perceptions of Middle Schoolers"; Zittleman, "Title IX and Gender."

30. American Association of University Women, *How Schools Shortchange Girls.*

31. Zittleman, "Gender Perceptions of Middle Schoolers"; Zittleman, "Title IX and Gender."

32. Brown, Lyn Mikel, and Carol Gilligan. *Meeting at the Crossroads: Women's Psychology and Girls' Development.* Cambridge, MA: Harvard University Press, 1992.

33. Brown and Gilligan, *Meeting at the Crossroads,* p. 56.

34. Ibid., p. 126.

35. Ibid., p. 135.

36. Ibid., p. 40.

37. Kramer, *Gifted Adolescent Girls,* p. 113.

38. Ibid., p. 127.

39. Ibid., p. 109.

40. Fang, Zhihui. "A review of research on teacher beliefs and practices." *Educational Research* 38:1 (1996), pp. 47–65.

   Shepardson, Daniel, and Edward Pizzini. "Gender Bias in Female Elementary Teachers' Perceptions of the Scientific Ability of Students." *Science Education* 76:2 (1992), pp. 147–53.

   See also Zittleman, "Gender Perceptions of Middle Schoolers"; Zittleman, "Title IX and Gender."

41. American Association of University Women. *Tech-Savvy: Educating Girls in the New Computer Age.* Washington, DC: AAUW, 2000.

42. Hyde, Janet, Sara Lindberg, Marcia Linn, Amy Ellis, and Caroline Williams. "Gender Similarities Characterize Math Performance." *Science* 321:5888 (July 2008), pp. 494–95.

   National Center for Education Statistics. *Trends in Educational Equity for Girls and Women.* 2004. http://nces.ed.gov/pubsearch/pubsinfo.asp?pubid =2005016.

43. Dalton, Ben, Steven J. Ingels, Jane Downing, and Robert Bozick. *Advanced Mathematics and Science Coursetaking in the Spring High School Senior Classes of 1982, 1992, and 2004* (NCES 2007-312). Washington, DC: National Center for Education Statistics, Institute of Education Sciences, U.S. Department of Education, 2007.

   Burger, Carol, Gypsy Abbott, Sheila Tobias, Janice Koch, and Christina Vogt. "Gender Equity in Science, Engineering, and Technology." In Susan S. Klein, ed., *Handbook for Achieving Gender Equity through Education.* 2nd ed. New York: Lawrence Erlbaum Associates, Taylor & Francis Group, 2007, pp. 255–79.

   Lacampagne, Carole, Patricia A. Campbell, Suzanne Damarin, Abbe Herzig, and Christina Vogt. "Gender Equity in Mathematics." In Klein, ed., *Handbook for Achieving Gender Equity through Education,* pp. 235–53.

44. Dalton et al., *Advanced Mathematics and Science Coursetaking.*

45. Mau, Wei-Cheng. "Factors that Influence Persistence in Science and Engineering Career Aspirations." *Career Development Quarterly* 51 (2003), pp. 234–43.

   Phillips, Katherine, Lloyd Barrow, and Meera Chandresekhar. "Science career interest among high school girls one year after participation in summer science programs." *Journal of Women and Minorities in Science and Engineering* 8 (2002), pp. 235–47.

46. Roach, Ronald. *Survey: Americans Aren't Interested in STEM Careers.* Chicago: Women's Society of Engineers, 2006.

47. Davis-Kean, Pamela. "Dads influence daughters' interest in mathematics." Paper presented at Educating a STEM Workforce: New Strategies for U-M and the State of Michigan. Ann Arbor, MI, 2007.

48. Zittleman, "Gender Perceptions of Middle Schoolers"; Zittleman, "Title IX and Gender."

49. Centers for Disease Control and Prevention, National Center for Injury Prevention and Control, *Suicide Data Page, 2004.* http://www.cdc.gov/ncipc/factsheets/suifacts.htm.

   Kimmel, Michael. " 'What about the boys?' What the current debates tell us—and don't tell us—about boys in school." In Disch, ed., *Reconstructing Gender,* pp. 361–75.

   National Center for Education Statistics. *The Nation's Report Card.* http://nces.ed.gov/nationsreportcard/.

   National Dropout Prevention Center Network. *Effective Strategies.* Clemson University, South Carolina, 2006.

   Swanson, Christopher B. *The Real Truth about Low Graduation Rates: An Evidence-Based Commentary.* Washington, DC: Urban Institute, 2004. http://www.urban.org/publications/411050.html.

   United States Department of Education, Office of Special Education Programs, 26th Annual Report to Congress, 2004. http://www.ed.gov/about/reports/annual/osep/2004/index.html.

50. Ibid.

   National Women's Law Center. *When Girls Don't Graduate We All Fail: A Call to Improve the Graduation Rates of Girls.* Washington, DC: National Women's Law Center, 2007. http://www.nwlc.org/pdf/DropoutReport.pdf.

   Witt, Howard. "Discipline Tougher on African Americans." *Chicago Tribune,* September 25, 2007.

51. Gilligan, Carol. *In a Different Voice: Psychological Theory and Women's Development.* Cambridge, MA: Harvard University Press, 1992.

   Pollack, William. *Real Boys: Rescuing Our Sons from the Myths of Boyhood.* New York: Random House, 1998.

52. Brannon, Robert, and Deborah David. *The Forty-Nine Percent Majority.* Reading, PA: Addison Wesley, 1976.

53. American Association of University Women. *Hostile Hallways: Bullying, Teasing, and Sexual Harassment in School.* Washington, DC: AAUW, 2004.

54. Campenni, C. Estelle. "Gender Stereotyping of Children's Toys: A Comparison of Parents and Nonparents." *Sex Roles* 40: 1–2 (1999), pp. 121–38.

   Golombok, Susan, and Robyn Fivush. *Gender Development.* New York: Cambridge University Press, 1994.

   Hort, Barbara, Beverly I. Faggot, and Mary Driver Leinbach. "Are People's Notions of Maleness More Stereotypically Framed Than Their Notions of Femaleness?" *Sex Roles* 23:3–4 (August 1990), pp. 197–212.

   Martin, Carol Lynn. "Attitudes and Expectations About Children with Nontraditional and Traditional Gender Roles." *Sex Roles* 22:3–4 (1990), pp. 151–65.

   Sandnabba, N. Kenneth, and Christian Ahlberg. "Parents' Attitudes and

Expectations about Children's Cross-gender Behavior." *Sex Roles* 40:3–4 (1999), pp. 249–63.

55. Kimmel, " 'What about the boys?' " p. 366.

56. Goffman, Erving. *Stigma: Notes on the Management of Spoiled Identity.* Englewood Cliffs, NJ: Prentice Hall, 1963.

57. Kimmel, " 'What about the boys?' " pp. 361–75.

58. Harris Interactive and GLSEN. *From Teasing to Torment: School Climate in America. A Survey of Students and Teachers.* (New York: GLSEN), 2005. http://www.glsen.org/cgi-bin/iowa/all/news/record/1859.html. Kimmel, " 'What about the boys?' " pp. 361–75.

   Tarshis, Thomas, and Lynne Huffman. "Psychometric Properties of the Peer Interactions in Primary School Questionnaire." *Journal of Developmental and Behavioral Pediatrics* 28 (April 2007).

59. Tillman, Linda, Linda McDonald, Renee Brickner, and C. Jeffrey Dykhuizen. "The world of young boys." *Independent School* (Fall 1992), pp. 29–32.

60. Tavris, Carol. *The Mismeasure of Woman.* New York: Simon & Schuster, 1992, pp. 63, 261–62.

61. Goleman, Daniel. *Emotional Intelligence. 10th Anniversary Edition: Why It Can Matter More than IQ.* New York: Bantam, 2006.

62. "University of Illinois at Urbana–Champaign 10 Years On, High-school Social Skills Predict Better Earnings Than Test Scores." *ScienceDaily* (October 16, 2008). http://www.sciencedaily.com /releases/2008/10/081015120749.htm.

63. Berman, Phyllis. "Young Children's Responses to Babies: Do They Foreshadow Differences Between Maternal and Paternal Styles?" In Alan Fogel and Gail F. Melson, eds., *Origins of Nurturance: Developmental, Biological, and Cultural Perspectives on Caregiving.* Hillsdale, NJ: Lawrence Erlbaum Associates, 1986.

64. Rotundo, E. Anthony. *American Manhood.* New York: Basic Books, 1993, p. 291.

65. Kindlon, Dan, and Michael Thompson. *Raising Cain: Protecting the Emotional Life of Boys.* New York: Ballantine, 2000.

   Osborne, R. W. "Men and intimacy: An empirical review." Paper presented at the American Psychological Association, San Francisco, 1991.

   Pollack, William. *Real Boys: Rescuing Our Sons from the Myths of Boyhood.* New York: Random House, 1998.

   Thompson, Michael, and Catherine O'Neill Grace. *Best Friends, Worst Enemies: Understanding the Social Lives of Children.* New York: Ballantine, 2001.

Chapter 5: Life in High School

1. Keyes, Ralph. *Is There Life After High School?* Boston: Little, Brown, 1976.

2. Boyer, Ernest L. *High Schools: A Report on Secondary Education in America.* New York: Harper & Row, 1983, p. 202.

3. Pierce, K. M. "Posing, Pretending, Waiting for the Bell: Life in High School Classrooms." *High School Journal* 89:2 (December–January 2005–2006), pp. 1–15.

4. Hersch, Patricia. *A Tribe Apart: A Journey Into the Heart of American Adolescence.* New York: Random House, 1999.

5. Cooley, Charles Horton. *Human Nature and the Social Order.* New York: Charles Scribner & Sons, 1902.

6. Ibid.

    Shaffer, Leigh. "From Mirror Self-Recognition to the Looking-Glass Self: Exploring the Justification Hypothesis." *Journal of Clinical Psychology* 61 (Special Issue) (January 2005), pp. 47–65.

    Yeung, King-To, and John Levi Martin. "The Looking Glass Self: An Empirical Test and Elaboration." *Social Forces* 81 (March 2003), pp. 843–79.

7. Coleman, James. *The Adolescent Society.* New York: Free Press, 1961.

8. Ibid., p. 37.

9. Keyes, *Is There Life After High School?*

10. Ibid.

11. Ephron quoted in Keyes, *Is There Life After High School?*, p. 106.

12. Ephron quoted in Keyes, *Is There Life After High School?*, p. 107.

13. Zittleman, Karen. "Title IX and Gender: A Study of the Knowledge, Perceptions, and Experiences of Middle and Junior High School Teachers and Students." *Dissertation Abstracts International* 66:11 (2005) (UMI No. 3194815).

    Zittleman, Karen. Unpublished dissertation data from interviews and surveys of one hundred high school students in three Maryland public high schools, 2005.

    Downs, A. C., and Garry R. Abshier. "Conceptions of Physical Appearance Among Young Adolescents: The Interrelationships Among Self-Judged Appearance, Attractiveness, Stereotyping, and Sex-Typed Characteristics." *Journal of Early Adolescence* 2 (1982), pp. 255–65.

14. Maine, Margo, and Joe Kelly. *The Body Myth.* New York: Wiley, 2005.

    Social Issues Research Center. *Can You Really Never Be Too Rich or Too Thin?* (December 30, 2006). http://www.sirc.org/news/sirc_in_the_news_2006.html.

15. Boston Women's Health Book Collective. *Our Bodies, Ourselves: A New Edition for a New Era.* New York: Touchstone, 2005.

16. Ibid.

17. Ibid.

18. Greenfield, Lauren, and Joan Jacobs Brumberg. *Thin.* San Francisco: Chronicle Books, 2006.

    National Eating Disorders Coalition. *Statistics and Study Findings.* http://www.eatingdisorderscoalition.org/reports/statistics.html.

19. Van den Berg, Patricia, Dianne Neumark-Sztainer, Peter J. Hannan, and Jess Haines. "Is Dieting Advice From Magazines Helpful or Harmful? Five-Year Associations With Weight-Control Behaviors and Psychological Outcomes in Adolescents." *Journal of Pediatrics* 119:2 (January 2007), pp. 30–37.

20. Keys, Ancel, et al. *The Biology of Human Starvation.* Minneapolis: University of Minnesota Press, 1950.

21. Greenfield and Brumberg, *Thin*; National Eating Disorders Coalition, *Statistics and Study Findings*; Maine and Kelly, *The Body Myth*.

22. National Eating Disorders Association. "Information and Resources." Retrieved on January 28, 2009 from http://www.nationaleatingdisorders.org; Greenfield and Brumberg, *Thin*; National Eating Disorders Coalition, *Statistics and Study Findings*.

23. Bisaga, Katarzyna, Agnes Whitaker, Mark Davies, Shirley Chuang, Judith Feldman, and B. Timothy Walsh. "Eating disorders and depressive symptoms in urban high school girls from different ethnic backgrounds." *Journal of Developmental Behavioral Pediatrics* 26:4 (August 2005), pp. 257–66.

Hesse-Biber, Sharlene Nagy, Stephanie A. Howling, Patricia Leavy, and Meg Lovejoy. "Racial Identity and the Development of Body Image Issues among African American Adolescent Girls." *Qualitative Report* 9 (March 2004), pp. 49–79.

24. Ibid.

25. Bunch, Kathy. "Culture Shock: Fitting In, Losing Out." *MedicineNet.com,* January 15, 2001. http://www.medicinenet.com/script/main/art.asp?article key=51270.

26. Substance Abuse and Mental Health Services Administration. Results from the 2006 *National Survey on Drug Use and Health: National Findings* (Office of Applied Studies, NSDUH Series H-32, DHHS Publication No. SMA 07–4293), Rockville, MD, 2007.

27. Golden is quoted in Nancy Perry. "Why It's So Tough to Be a Girl," *Fortune* (August 10, 1992), p. 82.

28. Naomi Wolf. *The Beauty Myth*. New York: Anchor, p. 202.

29. Zittleman, unpublished dissertation data.

30. "Anorexia Nervosa and Related Eating Disorders," *Eating Disorders Statistics*; Greenfield and Brumberg, *Thin*.

31. "Anorexia Nervosa and Related Eating Disorders," *Eating Disorders Statistics*.

32. Zittleman, unpublished dissertation data.

33. National Institute on Drug Abuse. *Anabolic Steroid Abuse*. NIH Publication Number 06–3721, August 2006. http://www.nida.nih.gov/PDF/RRSteroids.pdf.

34. The classroom scenes in this chapter are based on Myra and David Sadker's discussions with classes of high school students; however, the names of individual students have been changed.

35. Zittleman, unpublished dissertation data.

36. Ibid.

37. Bailey, Bambi, Kathryn Scantlebury, and William Letts. "It's not my style: Using disclaimers to ignore issues in science." *Journal of Teacher Education* 48:1 (1997), pp. 29–35.

38. Zittleman, "Title IX and Gender"; Zittleman, unpublished dissertation data.

39. Pollack, William. *Real Boys: Rescuing Our Sons from the Myths of Boyhood*. New York: Random House, 1998.

40. Ibid.

Perry, Elissa. L., James M. Schmidtke, and Carol T. Kulik. "Propensity to sexually harass: An exploration of gender differences." *Sex Roles* 38:5–6 (1998), pp. 443–60.

41. Brown, Lynn Mikel. *Girlfighting: Betrayal and Rejection Among Girls*. New York: New York University Press, 2003.

Merten, Don. "The meaning of meanness: Popularity, competition, and conflict among junior high school girls." *Sociology of Education* 70 (1997), pp. 175–91.

42. Brown, *Girlfighting*.

Crick, Nicki R., and Jennifer K. Grotpeter. "Relational aggression, gender and social psychological adjustment." *Child Development* 66 (1995), pp. 710–22.

43. Brown, *Girlfighting*.

Zittleman, Karen. "Gender Perceptions of Middle Schoolers: The Good and the Bad." *Middle Grades Research Journal* 2:2 (Fall 2007), pp. 65–97.

See also Zittleman, unpublished dissertation data.

44. Researched by Louis Harris and Associates. *Hostile Hallways: The AAUW Survey on Sexual Harassment in America's Schools.* Washington, DC: American Association of University Women, 1993.
45. American Association of University Women. *Hostile Hallways: Bullying, Teasing, and Sexual Harassment in School.* Washington, DC: AAUW, 2001.
46. Stein, Nan. "It Happens Here, Too: Sexual Harassment in the Schools." *Education Week* (November 27, 1991), p. 37.
47. Conversations with California students reported in Jane Gross, "Schools, the Newest Arena for Sex-Harassment Cases." *New York Times* (March 11, 1992), p. B8.
48. American Association of University Women, *Hostile Hallways.*
49. Ibid.
    LeBlanc, Adrian Nicole. "Harassment in the Hall." *Seventeen* (September 1992), pp. 163–65, 170; quote from p. 163.
    See also Zittleman, "Gender Perceptions of Middle Schoolers."
50. Blumberg, Michelle, and David Lester. "High School and College Students' Attitudes Toward Rape." *Adolescence* 26:103 (Fall 1991), pp. 727–29.
    Feltey, Kathryn, Julie Ainslie, and Aleta Geib. "Sexual Coercion Attitudes Among High School Students." *Youth and Society* 23:2 (December 1991), pp. 229–50.
    See also Zittleman, unpublished dissertation data.
51. Zittleman, "Gender Perceptions of Middle Schoolers"; Zittleman, unpublished dissertation data.
52. These incidents have been told to us by teachers and administrators at our workshops.
53. Zirkel, Perry. "Damages for Sexual Harassment," *Phi Delta Kappan* 73:10 (June 1992), pp. 812–13.
54. *Davis v. Monroe County Board of Education,* 97 U.S. 843 (1999).
    Gebser v. Lago Vista Independent School District, 96 U.S. 1866 (1998).
55. *Davis v. Monroe County Board of Education,* 97 U.S. 843 (1999).
56. American Psychological Association, Task Force on the Sexualization of Girls. *Report of the APA Task Force on the Sexualization of Girls.* Washington, DC: American Psychological Association, 2007. www.apa.org/pi/wpo/sexualization.html.
    Weiner, Stacey. "Goodbye to Girlhood: As Pop Culture Targets Ever Younger Girls, Psychologists Worry About a Premature Focus on Sex and Appearance." *Washington Post.* February 20, 2007, p. HE01.
57. Quoted in Weiner, "Goodbye to Girlhood."
58. Rideout, Victoria. *Parents, Children, and Media: A Kaiser Family Foundation Study,* June 2007. http://www.kff.org/entmedia/7638.cfm; Weiner, "Goodbye to Girlhood."
59. "Familiar Reality Requires Common-Sense Sex Ed." *New York Times,* September 3, 2008, p. 14A.
    Stepps, Laura Sessions. "Study Casts Doubt on Abstinence-Only Programs." *Washington Post,* April 14, 2007, p. A02.
60. Weiner, "Goodbye to Girlhood."
61. National Campaign to Prevent and End Unplanned Pregnancy. *Teen Sexual Activity, Pregnancy, and Childbearing Fact Sheets,* 2007. http://www.teenpregnancy.org/resources/reading/fact_sheets/default.asp.

"Vital Statistics. Teenagers Changing Sexual Behavior." *New York Times,* August 26, 2008, p. D7.

62. Ibid.

63. Ibid.

64. Molinary, Rosie. *Hijas Americanas: Beauty, Body Image, and Growing Up Latina.* Emeryville, CA: Seal Press, 2007.

65. Ibid.

66. Fine, Michelle. "Sexuality, Schooling, and Adolescent Females: The Missing Discourse of Desire." *Harvard Educational Review* 58:1 (February 1988), pp. 29–53.

67. Ibid., p. 49.

68. Fine, Michelle. "Silencing in Public Schools." *Language Arts* 64:2 (February 1987), p. 172.

69. National Women's Law Center. *When Girls Don't Graduate We All Fail: A Call to Improve the Graduation Rates of Girls.* Washington, DC: National Women's Law Center, 2007. http://www.nwlc.org/pdf/DropoutReport.pdf.

70. American Council on Education. *GED Testing Program Participation Rises Slightly in Fourth Year of New Exam Series,* 2006. http://www.acenet.edu/AM/Template.cfm?Section=20062&TEMPLATE=/CM/ContentDisplay.cfm&CONTENTID=19595.

71. Bridgeland, John, John J. Dilulio, Jr., and Karen Burke Morison. *The Silent Epidemic: Perspectives of High School Dropouts.* Washington, DC: Civic Enterprises, 2006. www.civicenterprises.net.

72. National Campaign to Prevent and End Unplanned Pregnancy. *Why It Matters: Teen Pregnancy, Poverty, and Income Disparity.* http://www.teenpregnancy.org/wim/pdf/poverty.pdf.

73. National Women's Law Center, *When Girls Don't Graduate We All Fail.*

74. Ellis, Bruce J. "Does father absence place daughters at special risk for early sexual activity and teen pregnancy?" *Child Development* 74:3 (May/June 2003), pp. 801–21.

75. National Campaign to Prevent and End Unplanned Pregnancy, *Why It Matters.*

76. Zittleman, "Gender Perceptions of Middle Schoolers"; Zittleman, unpublished dissertation data.

77. Eder, Donna, and Stephen Parker. "The Cultural Production and Reproduction of Gender: The Effect of Extracurricular Activities on Peer-Group Culture." *Sociology of Education* 60:3 (July 1987), pp. 200–13; quote from p. 206.

78. Adler, Patricia, Stephen Kless, and Peter Adler. "Socialization to Gender Roles: Popularity Among Elementary School Boys and Girls." *Sociology of Education* 65:3 (July 1992), pp. 169–87; quote from p. 174.

79. Ibid., p. 172.

80. National Federation of State High School Associations. "High School Sports Participation Increases Again; Boys, Girls and Overall Participation Reach All-time Highs." September 2008. http://www.nfhs.org/web/2008/09/high_school_sports_participation.aspx.

81. Ibid.

82. Women's Sports Foundation. *2007 Statistics—Gender Equity in High School and College Athletics: Most Recent Participation and Budget Statistics.* http://www.womenssportsfoundation.org.

83. National Federation of State High School Associations. *The Case for High School Activities.* http://www.nfhs.org/web/2004/01/the_case_for_high_school _activities.aspx.

  National Women's Law Center. *The Battle for Gender Equity in Athletics in Elementary and Secondary Schools,* 2007. http://www.nwlc.org/pdf/ Battle%202007.pdf.

84. National Women's Law Center. *Barriers to Fair Play,* June 2007. http://www .nwlc.org/pdf/BarriersToFairPlay.pdf.

  See also Women's Sports Foundation, *2007 Statistics.*

85. National Women's Law Center, *The Battle for Gender Equity in Athletics.*

86. *Keeping Score: Girls Participation in High School Athletics in Massachusetts.* A joint report by the National Women's Law Center and Harvard Prevention Research Center on Nutrition and Physical Activity, Harvard School of Public Health, February 2004. www.nwlc.org.

87. National Women's Law Center. Poll conducted by the Mellman Group, 2007. http://www.fairplaynow.org/TitleIXpollresults.pdf.

88. Speech given at American University, Washington, DC, for Myra Sadker Day Awards, March 2005.

89. Jackson, Roderick. Statement of Roderick Jackson, Plaintiff in "Jackson v. Birmingham Board of Education" on Title IX Case Before the Supreme Court, June 10, 2004. http://www.nwlc.org/details.cfm?id=1905&section=newsroom.

  National Women's Law Center. *Level the Playing Field: Get Girls in the Game,* 2007. http://www.fairplaynow.org/jackson.html.

90. National Women's Law Center. *Tools of the Trade: Using the Law to Address Sex Segregation in High School Career and Technical Education,* 2005. http://www.nwlc.org/pdf/NWLCToolsoftheTrade05.pdf.

91. Ibid.

92. Koch, Janice. "A Gender Inclusive Approach to Science Education." In David Sadker and Ellen Silber, eds., *Gender in the Classroom: Foundations, Skills, Methods and Strategies across the Curriculum.* Mahwah, NJ: Lawrence Erlbaum, 2007, pp. 205–23.

93. Ibid.

94. Hodgman, John. "The Commonwealth's STEM Talent Pipeline: Update for 2007." *Massachusetts STEM Initiative,* 2007. http://www.massachusetts.edu/ stem/stem_talent_pipeline.html.

95. Mau, Wei-Cheng. "Factors that Influence Persistence in Science and Engineering Career Aspirations." *Career Development Quarterly* 51 (2003), pp. 234–43.

  Phillips, Kathryn, Lloyd Barrow, and Meera Chandresekhar. "Science career interest among high school girls one year after participation in summer science programs." *Journal of Women and Minorities in Science and Engineering* 8 (2002), pp. 235–47.

  See also Zittleman, unpublished dissertation data.

96. Koch, "A Gender Inclusive Approach," pp. 207–8.

97. American Association of University Women. *Tech-Savvy: Educating Girls in the New Computer Age.* Washington, DC: AAUW, 2000.

  Koch, "A Gender Inclusive Approach," pp. 205–23.

  Sanders, Jo, Janice Koch, and Josephine Urso. *Gender Equity Right from the Start: Instructional Activities for Teacher Educators in Math, Science, and Technology.* Mahwah, NJ: Lawrence Erlbaum, 1997.

98. Fish, Marian, Alan Gross, and Jo Sanders. "The Effect of Equity Strategies on Girls' Computer Usage in School." *Computers in Human Behavior* 2:2 (1986), pp. 127–84.

See also Sanders, Koch, and Urso, *Gender Equity Right from the Start.*

99. The discussion of successful strategies for teaching science was drawn from the following sources:

American Association of University Women, *Tech-Savvy.*

Koch, "A Gender Inclusive Approach," pp. 205–23.

Martinez, Michael. "Interest Enhancements to Science Experiments: Interactions with Student Gender." *Journal of Research in Science Teaching* 29:2 (1992), pp. 167–77.

Mason, Cheryl, and Jane Butler Kahle. "Student Attitudes Toward Science and Science-Related Careers: A Program Designed to Promote a Stimulating Gender-Free Learning Environment." *Journal of Research in Science Teaching* 26:1 (1988), pp. 25–39.

Sanders, Jo. "Gender and Technology in Education: A Research Review." In Christine Skelton, Becky Francis, and Lisa Smulyan, eds., *The SAGE Handbook of Gender and Education.* Thousand Oaks, CA: SAGE, 2007.

Sanders, Koch, and Urso, *Gender Equity Right from the Start.*

Smith, Walter, and Thomas Owen Erb. "Effect of Women Science Career Role Models on Early Adolescents' Attitudes Toward Scientists and Women in Science." *Journal of Research in Science Teaching* 23:8 (1986), pp. 664–76.

Zittleman, Karen. *Making Public Schools Great for Every Girl and Boy: Gender Equity in the Mathematics and Science Classroom: Confronting the Barriers that Remain.* Washington, DC: National Education Association, 2004.

100. Koch, "A Gender Inclusive Approach," pp. 205–23.

101. Jones, M. Gail, and Jack Wheatley. "Gender Differences in Teacher-Student Interactions in Science Classrooms." *Journal of Research in Science Teaching* 27:9 (1990), pp. 861–74.

Jones, M. Gail. "Action Zone Theory, Target Students and Science Classroom Interactions." *Journal of Research in Science Teaching* 27:7 (1990), pp. 651–60.

102. American Association of University Women, *Tech-Savvy.*

Chapter 6: Tests, Grades, and the Boys' Crisis

1. Smoky Valley Genealogical Society and Library in Salina, Kansas, and reprinted by the *Salina Journal,* http://skyways.lib.ks.us/genweb/saline/society/exam.html.

2. National Assessment of Educational Progress. *Most Current Report Card Releases.* http://nationsreportcard.gov/.

3. Dorsher, Mike. "Are Biased Tests Hurting Girls?" *Wall Street Journal,* September 17, 1992.

Davidoff, Judith. "Are Girls Getting Cheated?" *Isthmus* (September 3, 1992), p. 6; Reid, Alexander. "Ruling Seen Changing How Scholarships Are Won," *Boston Globe,* February 10, 1989.

4. College Board. *Mean SAT Scores of College-Bound Seniors 1967–2007.* http://www.collegeboard.com/prod_downloads/about/news_info/cbsenior/yr 2007/tables/2.pdf.

5. FairTest *Examiner.* "SAT Score Decline Damages College Board Credibility, Helps Rival ACT." October 2006. http://www.fairtest.org/sat-score-decline-damages-college-board-credibility-helps-rival-act; FairTest, "The SAT: Questions and Answers," http://www.fairtest.org/facts/satfact.htm.

6. College Board. Press Releases. College Board Announces Scores for New SAT with Writing Section. August 29, 2006. http://www.collegeboard.com/press/releases/150054.html.

7. A chart of 2007 college-bound seniors average SAT scores retrieved from the FairTest website, http://www.fairtest.org/files/SATScores2007Chart.pdf .

   See also FairTest *Examiner,* "SAT Score Decline Damages College Board Credibility"; FairTest, "The SAT: Questions and Answers."

8. FairTest, "The ACT: Biased, Inaccurate, Coachable, and Misused." http://www.fairtest.org/facts/act.html; FairTest, "ACT 'Smokescreen' focuses on small annual Score Changes but Hides Strong Link Between Test Results and Family Income, a Major Reason Why 740+ Colleges are Now ACT/SAT Optional." August 15, 2007. http://www.fairtest.org.

9. *Graduate Record Examinations: Factors that Can Influence Performance on the GRE General Test, 2004–2005.* Princeton, NJ: Educational Testing Service, 2007.

10. *Profile of Graduate Management Admission Test Candidates, 2001–2006, Five Year Study.* McLean, VA: Graduate Management Admission Council, 2006. www.gmac.com.

    Dalessandro, Susan P., Lisa A. Stilwell, and Lynda M. Reese. *LSAT Performance with Regional, Gender, and Racial/Ethnic Breakdowns: 1997–1998 Through 2003–2004 Testing Years.* LSAC RESEARCH REPORT SERIES, Law School Admission Council, LSAT Technical Report 04-01. October 2004.

    Telephone conversation with Lauren Richards at MCAT, October 16, 2007.

11. Rosser, Phyllis. "Gender and Testing." Paper commissioned by the National Commission on Testing and Public Policy, Graduate School of Education, University of California at Berkeley, 1989.

12. Telephone conversation with Bob Schaeffer at FairTest, September 30, 1992.

13. Reed, Dianne, Lynn Fox, Mary Lou Andrews, Nancy Betz, Jan Perry Evenstad, Anthony Harris, Carol Hightower-Parker, Judy Johnson, Shirley Johnson, Barbara Polnick, and Phyllis Rosser. "Gender Equity in Testing and Assessment." In Susan S. Klein, ed., *Handbook for Achieving Gender Equity through Education.* 2nd ed. New York: Lawrence Erlbaum Associates, Taylor & Francis Group, 2007, pp. 155–69.

    Bridgeman, Brent, and Cathy Wendler. *Prediction of Grades in College Mathematical Courses as a Component of SAT-M Placement Validity.* New York: College Entrance Examination Board, 1990.

    McCornack, Robert, and Mary McLeod. "Gender Bias in the Prediction of College Course Performance." *Journal of Educational Measurement* 25:4 (1988), pp. 321–32.

    Wainer, Howard, and Linda Steinberg. "Sex Differences in Performance on the Mathematics Section of the Scholastic Aptitude Test: A Bidirectional Validity Study." Princeton, NJ: Educational Testing Service, 1990.

    Horner, Blair, and Joe Sammons, with FairTest staff. *Rolling Loaded Dice: Use of the Scholastic Aptitude Test (SAT) for Higher Education Admissions in New York State.* New York: Public Interest Research Group, 1989.

14. Carol Dwyer, quoted by FairTest at http://www.fairtest.org/facts/genderbias .htm.

15. Items from the PSAT and SAT are taken from Rosser, *The SAT Gender Gap*, pp. 141–42.

16. Alaimo, Kara. "New SAT Could Shrink the Test's Gender Gap." WeNews. March 15, 2005. http://www.womensenews.org/article.cfm/dyn/aid/2220.

17. Eckstrom, Ruth B., Marlaine E. Lockheed, and Thomas F. Donlon. "Sex Differences and Sex Bias in Test Content." *Educational Horizons* 58:1 (Fall 1979), pp. 47–52.

Becker, Betsy Jane. "Item Characteristics and Gender Differences on the SAT-M for Mathematically Able Youths." *American Educational Research Journal* 27:1 (Spring 1990), pp. 65–87.

Loewen, James, Phyllis Rosser, and J. Katzman. "Gender Bias in SAT Items." Paper presented at the Annual Meeting of the American Educational Research Association, New Orleans, LA, April 5–9, 1988.

Chipman, Susan. "Word Problems Where Test Bias Creeps In." Paper presented at the Annual Meeting of the American Educational Research Association, New Orleans, LA, April 5–9, 1988.

Pearlman, M. "Trends in Women's Total Score and Item Performance on Verbal Measures." Paper presented at the Annual Meeting of the American Educational Research Association, Washington, DC, April 1987.

Zwick, Rebecca, and Erickan Kadriye. "Analysis of Differential Item Functioning in the NAEP History Assessment." *Journal of Educational Measurement* 26:1 (Spring 1989), pp. 55–66.

Wendler, Cathy L. W., and Sydell T. Carlton. "An Examination of SAT Verbal Items for Differential Performance by Women and Men: An Exploratory Study." Paper presented at the Annual Meeting of the American Educational Research Association, Washington, DC, April 1987.

Sappington, John, Chris Larsen, James Martin, and Kari Murphy. "Sex Differences in Math Problem Solving as a Function of Gender-Specific Item Content." *Educational and Psychological Measurement* 51 (1991), pp. 1041–48.

Murphy, Laura, and Steven Ross. "Protagonist Gender as a Design Variable in Adapting Mathematics Story Problems to Learner Interests." *Educational Technology Research and Development* 38:3 (1990), pp. 27–37.

18. Telephone interview with Phyllis Rosser, September 1992.

19. Brown, Lyn Mikel, and Carol Gilligan. *Meeting at the Crossroads*. Cambridge, MA: Harvard University Press, 1992.

20. Linn, Marcia et al. "Gender Differences in National Assessment of Educational Progress Science Items: What Does 'I Don't Know' Really Mean?" *Journal of Research in Science Teaching* 24:3 (1987), pp. 267–78.

21. Mazzeo, John, Alicia P. Schmitt, and Carole A. Bleistein. "Do Women Perform Better, Relative to Men, on Constructed-Response Tests or Multiple-Choice Tests? Evidence from the Advanced Placement Examinations." Paper presented at the Annual Meeting of the National Council of Measurement in Education, Chicago, April 1991.

Gallagher, Shelagh, and Edward S. Johnson. "The Effect of Time Limits on Performance of Mental Rotations by Gifted Adolescents." *Gifted Child Quarterly* 36:1 (Winter 1992), pp. 19–22.

See also http://www.fairtest.org/facts/genderbias.htm.

22. Zwick, Rebecca. *Fair Game? The Use of Standardized Admissions Tests in Higher Education.* New York: RoutledgeFalmer, 2002; Wilder, Gita Z., and K. Powell. *Sex Differences in Test Performance: A Survey of the Literature.* College Board Research Report No. 1989-3. New York: College Board, 1989.

23. Aronson, Joshua, and Claude M. Steele. "Stereotypes and the Fragility of Human Competence, Motivation, and Self Concept." In Carol Dweck and Andrew Elliot, eds., *Handbook of Competence and Motivation.* New York: Guilford, 2005.

   Aronson, Joshua, "The Threat of Stereotype." *Educational Leadership* 62:3 (November 2004), pp. 14–19.

   Aronson, Joshua. "The Effects of Conceiving Ability as Fixed or Improvable on Responses to Stereotype Threat." Unpublished manuscript, New York University, 2004.

24. Crouse, James, and Dale Trusheim. *The Case Against the SAT.* Chicago: University of Chicago Press, 1988, pp. 19, 23.

25. Owen, David. *None of the Above: Behind the Myth of Scholastic Aptitude.* Boston: Houghton Mifflin, 1985, pp. 181, 183.

   Hoffman, Banesh. *The Tyranny of Testing.* New York: Crowell-Collier, 1962.

26. Hoffman, James, Assaf Czop, Lori Paris, and Scott Paris. "High-Stakes Testing in Reading: Today in Texas, Tomorrow?" *Reading Teacher* 54:5 (February 2001), pp. 482–92.

   Kingsbury, Alex. "Schools Cut Other Subjects to Teach Reading and Math," *U.S. News & World Report,* July 25, 2007. http://www.usnews.com/usnews/edu/articles/070725/25nclb.htm.

   Perrin, Stephanie. "Why Arts Education Matters." *Education Week.* January 30, 2008, pp. 26–27.

27. Elmore, Richard. "Testing Trap." Adapted from *Education Next* 105 (September–October 2002), p. 35.

   Gleason, Barbara. "ASCD Adopts Positions in High-Stakes Testing and the Achievement Gap." *ASCD Conference News.* March 20–22, 2004.

28. Wiggins, Grant. "Teaching to the (Authentic) Test." *Educational Leadership* 46:7 (April 1989), pp. 41–47.

   See also Gene I. Maeroff. "Assessing Alternative Assessment." *Phi Delta Kappan* 73:4 (December 1991), pp. 272–81.

   Zessoules, Rieneke, and Howard Gardner. "Authentic Assessment: Beyond the Buzzword and into the Classroom." In Vito Perrone, ed., *Expanding Student Assessment.* Alexandria, VA: Association for Supervision and Curriculum Development, 1991.

29. Lewis, W., and W. Smith. "Marks, Grades and Their Meaning." Draft report, School of Education, University of Missouri, Kansas City. Cited in Ruth B. Ekstrom. "Gender Differences in High School Grades: An Exploratory Study." College Board Report No. 94-3. Princeton, NJ: Educational Testing Service, 1994.

   See also Qing Li. "Teachers' Belief and Gender Differences in Mathematics: A Review." *Educational Research* 41:1 (Spring 1999), pp. 63–77.

   Gold, Dolores, Gail Crombie, and Sally Noble. "Relations Between Teachers' Judgments of Girls' and Boys' Compliance and Intellectual Competence." *Sex Roles* 16:7–8 (April 1987), pp. 351–58.

   Kornblau, Barbara. "The Teachable Pupil Survey: A Technique for Assessing

Teachers' Perceptions of Pupil Attributes." *Psychology in the Schools* 19 (1982), pp. 170–74.

    While girls receive higher GPAs than boys, the gender difference may be less than many believe. See U.S. Department of Education, National Center for Education Statistics, *The Nation's Report Card: America's High School Graduates: Results From the 2005 NAEP High School Transcript Study,* by Carolyn Shettle, Shep Roey, Joy Mordica, Robert Perkins, Christine Nord, Jelena Teodorovic, Janis Brown, Marsha Lyons, Chris Averett, and David Kastberg. NCES 2007-467. Washington, DC: U.S. Government Printing Office, 2007.

30. Grant, Linda. "Race and the Schooling of Young Girls." In Julia Wrigley, ed., *Education and Gender Equality.* London: Falmer, 1992, pp. 91–114.

31. Best, Raphaela. *We've All Got Scars: What Boys and Girls Learn in Elementary School.* Bloomington: Indiana University Press, 1983, p. 90.

32. Van Houtte, Mieke. "Why Boys Achieve Less at School than Girls; The Difference Between Boys' and Girls' Academic Culture." *Educational Studies* 30:2 (June 2004), pp. 159–73.

33. Tyack, David, and Elisabeth Hansot. *Learning Together: A History of Coeducation in American Schools.* New Haven, CT: Yale University Press, 1990, pp. 155, 157.

34. Keller, Arnold Jack. *A Historical Analysis of the Arguments for and Against Coeducational Public High Schools in the United States.* Ph.D. diss., Columbia University, 1971, pp. 323–24.

35. Tyack and Hansot, *Learning Together,* p. 157.

36. New York City Report for 1909, p. 475. Quoted in Tyack and Hansot, *Learning Together,* p. 193.

37. Male Teachers' Association of New York City. "Are There Too Many Women Teachers?" *Educational Review* 28 (1904), pp. 98–105. Quoted in Tyack and Hansot, *Learning Together,* p. 159.

38. Sexton, Patricia. "Are Schools Emasculating Our Boys?" *Saturday Review* (June 19, 1965), p. 57.

39. Sexton, Patricia. *The Feminized Male: Classrooms, White Collars and the Decline of Manliness.* New York: Random House, 1969.

40. Pozner, Jennifer. "Rally 'Round the Boys: PBS's National Desk enlists in the 'Gender Wars.' " Fairness and Accuracy in Reporting, September/October 1999. http://www.fair.org/extra/9909/national-desk.html.

41. Jan, Tracy. "Schoolboy's bias suit." *Boston Globe,* January 26, 2006. http://www.boston.com/news/local/articles/2006/01/26/schoolboys_bias_suit/.

42. The statistics for this section come from the following sources:

    American Council on Education. *College Enrollment Gender Gap Widens for White and Hispanic Students, but Race and Income Disparities Still Most Significant New ACE Report Finds.* July 11, 2006. Washington, DC: ACE. http://www.acenet.edu/AM/Template.cfm?Section=HENA&TEMPLATE=/CM/ContentDisplay.cfm&CONTENTID=17251.

    Mead, Sara. *The Evidence Suggests Otherwise: The Truth about Boys and Girls.* Washington, DC: Education Sector, June 2006. http://www.education sector.org.

    Mertens, Donna M., Amy Wilson, and Judith Mounty. "Gender Equity for People with Disabilities." In Susan S. Klein, ed., *Handbook for Achieving*

Gender Equity through Education. 2nd ed. New York: Lawrence Erlbaum Associates, Taylor & Francis Group, 2007, pp. 583–604.

See also Carey, Kevin. *A Matter of Degrees: Improving Graduation Rates in Four Year Colleges and Universities.* Washington, DC: Education Trust, 2004. http://www2.edtrust.org/NR/rdonlyres/11B4283F-104E-4511-B0CA-1D3023 231157/0/highered.pdf.

Kimmel, Michael. "A War Against Boys?" *Dissent* (Fall 2006), pp. 65–70.

National Women's Law Center. *When Girls Don't Graduate, We All Fail: A Call to Improve High School Graduation Rates for Girls.* Washington, DC: NWLC, 2007. http://www.nwlc.org/pdf/DropoutReport.pdf.

Perie, Marianne, Wendy S. Grigg, and Patricia L. Donahue. *The Nation's Report Card: Reading 2005.* Washington, DC: U.S. Department of Education, Institute of Education Sciences, National Center for Education Statistics, 2005. http://nces.ed.gov/nationsreportcard/reading/.

Orfield, Gary. *Losing Our Future: Being Left Behind by the Graduation Rate Crises.* Urban Institute, 2004. www.urban.org.

43. Perie, Marianne, Rebbeca Moran, and Anthony D. Lukas. *NAEP 2004 Trends in Academic Progress: Three Decades of Student Performance in Reading and Mathematics.* Washington, DC: U.S. Department of Education, July 2005; see also http://www.fairtest.org/facts/genderbias.htm.

44. Mead, *The Evidence Suggests Otherwise.*

Rivers, Caryl, and Rosalind Chait Barnett. "The Myth of 'The Boy Crisis.'" *Washington Post,* April 9, 2006, p. B01.

45. Orfield, *Losing Our Future.*

46. National Women's Law Center, *When Girls Don't Graduate, We All Fail*; Orfield, *Losing Our Future.*

47. Chew, Cassie M. "Current News: Five Men, Five Different Views on Educating Black Males." *Diverse,* October 15, 2007, pp. 21–41.

48. Rivers, and Barnett, "The Myth of 'The Boy Crisis.'"

49. Witt, Howard. "School discipline tougher on African Americans." *Chicago Tribune,* September 25, 2007. http://www.chicagotribune.com/news/nationworld/chi-070924discipline,1,6597576.story?ctrack=1&cset=truc.

50. Ibid.

51. Ibid.

52. Fletcher, Michael. "Middle-Class Dreams Elude African American Families." *Washington Post,* November 13, 2007, p. A1, A6.

53. Mead, *The Evidence Suggests Otherwise,* p. 14, 17.

54. Kimmel, Michael. "A War Against Boys?" *On Campus with Women* 35:3. Washington, DC: Association of American Colleges and Universities, 2007. http://www.aacu.org/ocww/volume35_3/feature.cfm?section=1.

55. Ladson-Billings, Gloria. "Culturally Relevant Teaching: Theory and Practice." In James Banks and Cherry A. McGee Banks, eds., *Multicultural Education: Issues and Perspectives.* 6th ed. Hoboken, NJ: Wiley, 2007, pp. 221–45.

56. Carey, Kevin. *Graduation Rate Watch: Making Minority Student Success a Priority.* Washington, DC: Education Sector, 2008. http://www.educationsector.org/usr_doc/Graduation_Rate_Watch.pdf.

Chapter 7: Higher Education: Peeking
Behind the Campus Curtain

1. "The Triumphs of Title IX." *Ms.* (Fall 2007), p. 42.
2. Musil, Caryn McTighe. "Scaling the Ivory Towers." *Ms.* (Fall 2007), pp. 43–45; U.S. Department of Education, National Center for Education Statistics, *Biennial Survey of Education in the United States; Opening Fall Enrollment in Higher Education,* 1963 through 1965; Higher Education General Information Survey (HEGIS), "Fall Enrollment in Colleges and Universities," surveys, 1966–1985, 1986–2005 Integrated Postsecondary Education Data System, "Fall Enrollment Survey" (IPEDS-EF:86-99), and Spring 2001–Spring 2006. This table was prepared August 2006. See also *The Digest of Educational Statistics.* National Center for Educational Statistics, 2007. http://nces.ed.gov/programs/digest/d07/index.asp.
3. Chamberlain, Miriam K., ed. *Women in Academe: Progress and Prospects.* New York: Russell Sage Foundation, 1988, p. 4.
4. Blake, Patricia. "Why College Girls Dress That Way." *New York Times Magazine* (April 7, 1946), p. 23. Quoted in Helen Lefkowitz Horowitz, *Campus Life: Undergraduate Cultures from the End of the Eighteenth Century to the Present.* New York: Knopf, 1987, p. 212.
5. Quoted in Horowitz, *Campus Life,* p. 92.
6. Solomon, Barbara Miller. *In the Company of Educated Women: A History of Women and Higher Education in America.* New Haven, CT: Yale University Press, 1985, pp. 78–93.
7. U.S. Department of Education, National Center for Education Statistics, *Biennial Survey of Education in the United States; Opening Fall Enrollment in Higher Education,* 1963 through 1965; Higher Education General Information Survey (HEGIS), "Fall Enrollment in Colleges and Universities" surveys, 1966–1985; 1986–2005 Integrated Postsecondary Education Data System, "Fall Enrollment Survey" (IPEDS-EF:86-99), and Spring 2001–Spring 2006. This table was prepared August 2006.
8. Ibid.
9. Scelfo, Julie. "Come Back, Mr. Chips." *Newsweek* (September 17, 2007), p. 44.
10. Following our three-year study of elementary and secondary classrooms, we conducted a two-year study of college classrooms and were sponsored by the Fund for the Improvement of Postsecondary Education. The project report submitted to the government was Sadker, Myra, and David Sadker. *Final Report: Project Effect (Effectiveness and Equity in College Teaching).* Washington, DC: Fund for the Improvement of Postsecondary Education, 1986.
    Sadker, Myra, and David Sadker. "Confronting Sexism in the College Classroom." In Susan Gabriel and Isaiah Smithson, eds., *Gender in the Classroom: Power and Pedagogy.* Urbana: University of Illinois Press, 1990, pp. 176–87.
11. For a discussion of how classroom communication is more compatible with male communication training, see Tannen, Deborah. "Teachers' Classroom Strategies Should Recognize That Men and Women Use Language Differently." *Chronicle of Higher Education* 37 (June 19, 1991), pp. B1–B3.
12. Krupnick, Catherine. "Unlearning Gender Roles." In Kenneth Winston and Mary Jo Bane, eds., *Gender and Public Policy: Cases and Comments.* Boulder, CO: Westview, 1992.

Krupnick, Catherine. "Women and Men in the Classroom: Inequality and Its Remedies." *Teaching and Learning: Journal of the Harvard Danforth Center* 1:1 (May 1985), pp. 18–25.

13. Hall, Roberta, and Bernice Sandler. *The Classroom Climate: A Chilly One for Women?* Washington, DC: Project on the Status and Education of Women, Association of American Colleges, 1982.

For a summary of differences in women's and men's views of Harvard, see Light, Richard. *The Harvard Assessment Seminars, First Report.* Cambridge, MA: Harvard University Press, 1990.

14. Corbett, Judith, and Robert Sommer. "Anatomy of a Coed Residence Hall." *Journal of College Student Personnel* 13:3 (May 1972), pp. 215–17.

Moos, Rudolf H., and Jean Otto. "The Impact of Coed Living on Males and Females." *Journal of College Student Personnel* 16:6 (November 1975), pp. 459–67.

Brown, Robert, John Winkworth, and Larry Brakskamp. "Student Development in a Coed Residence Hall: Promiscuity, Prophylactic, or Panacea?" *Journal of College Student Personnel* 14:2 (March 1973), pp. 98–104.

Schroeder, Charles C., and Morris LeMay. "The Impact of Coed Residence Halls on Self-Actualization." *Journal of College Student Personnel* 14:2 (March 1973), pp. 105–10.

15. Hill, Catherine, and Elena Silva. *Drawing the Line: Sexual Harassment on Campus.* Washington, DC: American Association of University Women, 2005.

16. "Harassing Women Becomes a Sick College Sport." *Utne Reader* (May–June 1990), pp. 70–71.

Rubin, Linda J., and Sherry B. Borgers. "Sexual Harassment in Universities During the 1980s." *Sex Roles* 23:7–8 (1990), pp. 397–411.

17. *Phi Kappa Theta.* http://www.phikaps.org/join/parentguide.html.

18. Interview with Harris Flax, student at American University.

19. Dillon, Sam. "Sorority Evictions Raise Issue of Looks and Bias." *New York Times,* February 25, 2007.

20. For additional examples and analyses of these activities, see Hughes, Jean O'Gorman, and Bernice Sandler. *Peer Harassment: Hassles for Women on Campus.* Washington, DC: Project on the Status and Education of Women, Association of American Colleges, 1988.

21. McMillen, Lis. "An Anthropologist's Disturbing Picture of Gang Rape on Campus." *Chronicle of Higher Education* 37 (September 19, 1990), p. A3.

Sanday, Peggy Reeves. *Fraternity Gang Rape: Sex, Brotherhood, and Privilege on Campus.* New York: New York University Press, 2007.

22. Sanday, *Fraternity Gang Rape.*

23. Koss, Mary P., Christine A. Gidycz, and Nadine Wisniewski. "The Scope of Rape: Incidence and Prevalence of Sexual Aggression and Victimization in a National Sample of Higher Education Students." *Journal of Consulting and Clinical Psychology* 55:2 (1987), pp. 162–70.

24. Adams, Aileen, and Gail Abarbanel. *Sexual Assault on Campus: What Colleges Can Do.* Santa Monica, CA: Rape Treatment Center, 1988.

Russell, Diana E. H. *Sexual Exploitation: Rape, Child Sexual Assault, and Workplace Harassment.* Beverly Hills, CA: Sage, 1984.

25. Berkowitz, Alan. "College Men as Perpetrators of Acquaintance Rape and

Sexual Assault: A Review of Recent Research." *College Health* 40 (January 1992), pp. 175–81.

Koss, Mary, Thomas E. Dinero, Cynthia Seibel, and Susan Cox. "Stranger and Acquaintance Rape: Are There Differences in the Victim's Experience?" *Psychology of Women Quarterly* 12 (March 1988), pp. 1–24.

Ménard, Kim S., Gordon C. Nagayama Hall, Amber H. Phung, Marian F. Erian Ghebrial, and Lynette Martin. "Gender Differences in Sexual Harassment and Coercion in College Students: Developmental, Individual, and Situational Determinants." *Journal of Interpersonal Violence* 18 (2003), pp. 1222–39. http://jiv.sagepub.com/cgi/content/abstract/18/10/1222.

See also Sanday, *Fraternity Gang Rape.*

26. Desimone, Jeffrey S. "Fraternity Membership and Binge Drinking." University of Texas at Arlington, Department of Economics; National Bureau of Economic Research, August 2006.

27. Muehlenhard, Charlene, and Melaney Linton. "Date Rape and Sexual Aggression in Dating Situations: Incidence and Risk Factors." *Journal of Counseling Psychology* 34:2 (1987), pp. 186–96.

Naylor, Kelly Elizabeth. *Gender Role Strain: A Contributing Factor to Acquaintance Rape in a College Population at Risk.* Ph.D. diss., DePaul University, 1991.

Jackson, Thomas. "A University Athletic Department's Rape and Assault Experiences." *Journal of College Student Development* 32 (January 1991), pp. 77–78.

Melnick, Merrill. "Male Athletes and Sexual Assault." *Journal of Physical Education, Recreation and Dance* 63 (May–June 1992), pp. 32–35.

28. Neimark, Jill. "Out of Bounds: The Truth About Athletes and Rape." *Mademoiselle* (May 1991), pp. 198, 244.

29. Gail Abarbanel quoted in Neimark, "The Truth About Athletes and Rape," p. 198.

30. "Sixth rape allegation surfaces at CU," CNN.com, February 20, 2004, http://www.cnn.com/2004/US/Central/02/19/colorado.football/.

31. "Offensive Behavior," *OnLine NewsHour,* February 26, 2004, http://www.pbs.org/newshour/bb/sports/jan-june04/offensive_02-26.html.

Jania, Rebecca. "Presentation Connects Sports and Rape." *Western Courier,* April 11, 2005. http://media.www.westerncourier.com/media/storage/paper650/news/2005/04/11/News/Presentation.Connects.Sports.And.Rape-919832.shtml.

32. Oh-Willeke, Andrew. "Dust Settles In CU Rape Case," *Colorado Confidential,* December 7, 2007. http://www.coloradoconfidential.com/showDiary.do?diaryId=3197.

Pankratz, Howard. "$2.8 million deal in CU rape case." *Denver Post,* December 5, 2007. http://www.denverpost.com/snowsports/ci_7640880.

Plati, David. "Barnett Steps Down As CU Football Coach." *Colorado Buffaloes,* December 9, 2005. http://www.cubuffs.com/ViewArticle.dbml?DB_OEM_ID=600&ATCLID=219912.

33. Collison, Michelle. "Increase in Reports of Sexual Assaults Strains Campus Disciplinary Systems." *Chronicle of Higher Education* (May 15, 1991), pp. A29–A30.

34. Lenihan, Genie O., et al. "Gender Differences in Rape Supportive Attitudes

Before and After Date Rape Education Intervention." *Journal of College Student Development* 33:4 (July 1992), pp. 331–38.

Martin, Patricia Yancey, and Robert A. Hummer. "Fraternities and Rape on Campus." *Gender and Society* 3:4 (December 1989), pp. 457–73.

Ellis, David. "Setting New Goals for the Greek System," *Educational Record* 70:3–4 (Summer–Fall 1989), pp. 48–53.

Status of the College Fraternity and Sorority, 1990. Bloomington, IN: Center for the Study of the College Fraternity, 1990.

Harrison, Patrick J., Jeanette Downes, and Michael D. Williams. "Date and Acquaintance Rape: Perceptions and Attitude Change Strategies." *Journal of College Student Development* 32 (March 1991), pp. 131–39.

35. Hill and Silva, *Drawing the Line.*
36. Finn, Jerry. "A Survey of Online Harassment at a University Campus." *Journal of Interpersonal Violence* 19:4 (2004), pp. 468–83.
37. Glaser, Robert D., and Joseph S. Thorpe. "Unethical Intimacy: A Survey of Sexual Contact and Advances Between Psychology Educators and Female Graduate Students." *American Psychologist* 40 (January 1986), pp. 43–51.

Dziech, Billie Wright, and Linda Weiner. *The Lecherous Professor: Sexual Harassment on Campus.* Boston: Beacon, 1984, pp. 13, 115–16.

Dreifus, Claudia. "Sex with Professors." *Glamour* (August 1986), pp. 264–65, 308–9, 311.
38. Bask, Patricia L., Joanne L. Jensen, and Jami Price. "Women's Graduate School Experiences, Professional Career Expectations and Their Relationship." Paper presented at the American Educational Research Association, Chicago, April 1991.

Jenkins, S. Y. *Gender Differences in Graduate Student Relationships with Their Major Faculty Advisor.* Ph.D. diss., University of Oregon, 1985.

Pope, Kenneth S., Hanna Levinson, and L. R. Schover. "Sexual Relationships in Psychology Training: Results and Implications of a National Survey." *American Psychologist* 34 (1979), pp. 682–89.

Ethington, Corinna A., and Rita Bode. "Differences in the Graduate Experience for Males and Females." Paper presented at the American Educational Research Association, San Francisco, April 1991.
39. Stevens, Allison. "Study: Both Sexes on Campus Are Harassed." *Women's eNews,* January 25, 2006, http://www.themenscenter.net/press/Womens ENews_25Jan06.php.
40. Baker, Mike. "Duke Lax Players Sue School, City." Associated Press. February 22, 2008. http://www.usatoday.com/news/nation/2008-02-21-2722365523 _x.htm.
41. Sadker, Myra, and David Sadker. *Beyond Pictures and Pronouns: Sexism in Teacher Education Textbooks.* Washington, DC: Office of Education, 1980, pp. 8, 38.
42. Ibid., pp. 38, 39.
43. Zittleman, Karen, and David Sadker. "Teacher Education Textbooks: The Unfinished Gender Revolution." *Educational Leadership* 60:4 (December 2002/January 2003), pp. 59–63.
44. Kauchak, Donald, and Paul Eggen. *Introduction to Teaching: Becoming a Professional.* Saddle River, NJ: Pearson Education, 2008, pp. 87–90.

45. Lewis, Magda. "Interrupting Patriarchy: Politics, Resistance, and Transformation in the Feminist Classroom." *Harvard Educational Review* 60:4 (November 1990), pp. 467–88.

46. Eakins, Barbara Westbrook, and R. Gene Eakins. *Sex Differences in Human Communication.* Boston: Houghton Mifflin, 1978.

    Schneider, Joseph, and Sally Hacker. "Sex Role Imagery and the Use of Generic 'Man' in Introductory Texts: A Case in the Sociology of Sociology." *American Sociologist* 8 (February 1973), pp. 12–18.

    Kramer, Cheris, Barrie Thorne, and Nancy Henley. "Perspectives on Language and Communication." *Signs: Journal of Women in Culture and Society* 3:3 (1978), pp. 638–51.

    Brannon, Robert. "The Consequences of Sexist Language." Paper presented at the American Psychological Association, Toronto, August 1978.

47. Gold, Martin, and David Mann. *Expelled to a Friendlier Place: A Study of Effective Alternative Schools.* Ann Arbor: University of Michigan Press, 1984, p. 6.

48. Klein, Richard. *Everyone Wins! A Citizen's Guide to Development.* Chicago: Planners Press, 1990.

49. Britz, Jennifer C. "To All the Girls I've Rejected." *New York Times,* March 23, 2006.

50. Schiff, Jaclyn. "Students Attest to 'Hillary Effect' on Campus." *Women's eNews,* October, 5, 2007. http://www.womensenews.org/article.cfm/dyn/aid/3338/context/archive.

51. See U.S. Department of Education, National Center for Education Statistics, in note 2 on p. 348, including the *Digest of Educational Statistics,* 2007. http://nces.ed.gov/programs/digest/d07/index.asp.

52. Nettles, Michael, and Catherine M. Millet. *Three Magic Letters: Getting to Ph.D.* Baltimore: Johns Hopkins University Press, 2006.

53. Jaschik, Scott. "Philosophy and Sexism." *Inside Higher Ed,* September 10, 2007. http://insidehighered.com/news/2007/09/10/philos.

    Musil, Caryn McTighe. "Harvard Isn't Enough; Women in Academia Still Face Hurdles to Equity—Including the 'Baby Gap,' " *Ms.* (Spring 2007).

54. Nelson, Donna J., and Diana C. Rogers. *A National Analysis of Diversity in Science and Engineering Faculties at Research Universities.* Revised 2007. http://cheminfo.ou.edu/~djn/diversity/briefings/Diversity%20Report%20Final.pdf.

55. Musil, Caryn McTighe, "Scaling the Ivory Towers." *Ms.* (Fall 2007), pp. 43–45.

56. Reed, Adolph. "The (Un)Changing Face of the Ivy League." Joint Report of GESO, GSEU, GET-UP. February 2005. http://www.yaleunions.org/geso/reports/Ivy.pdf.

57. Ibid., p. 5.

58. Jaschik, Scott. "The Satisfaction Gap." *Inside Higher Ed,* August 2, 2007. http://insidehighered.com/news/2007/08/02/coache.

59. Elaine McArdle. "The Adjunct Explosion." *University Business* (December 2002).

    FACE=Faculty and College Excellence. http://face.aft.org/index.cfm?action=cat&categoryID=0da5e79b-6bf7-4366-8ffe-609500d5fca9.

    Reed, "The (Un)Changing Face," p. 1.

60. Reed, "The (Un)Changing Face," p. 4.

61. U.S. Department of Labor, Bureau of Labor Statistics. "College Enrollment and Work Activity of 2006 High School Graduates" (USDL 07-0604). Washington, DC, April 26, 2007. http://www.bls.gov/news.release/hsgec.nr0.htm.

62. King, Jacqueline. *Gender Equity in Higher Education*. Washington, DC: American Council on Education, 2006.

   Goldin, Claudia, Lawrence F. Katz, and Ilyana Kuziemko. "The Homecoming of American College Women: The Reversal of the College Gender Gap." NBER Working Paper No. 12139. Cambridge, MA: National Bureau of Economic Research, 2006.

63. Corbett, Christianne, Catherine Hill, and Andresse St. Rose. *Where the Girls Are: The Facts About Gender Education*. Washington, DC: American Association of University Women, 2008.

64. Goldin, Katz, and Kuziemko, "The Homecoming of American College Women."

65. Dougherty, Christopher. "Why Are the Returns to Schooling Higher for Women than for Men?" *Journal of Human Resources* 40:4 (2005), pp. 969–88.

   DiPrete, Thomas A., and Claudia Buchmann. "Gender-Specific Trends in the Value of Education and the Emerging Gender Gap in College Completion." *Demography* 43:1 (February 2006), pp. 1–24.

66. Sax, Linda J. "College Women Still Face Many Obstacles in Reaching Their Full Potential." *Chronicle of Higher Education* (September 28, 2007), p. B46.

67. Lederman, Doug. "Clues About the Gender Gap." *Inside Higher Ed*. January 15, 2006. http://insidehighered.com/news/2007/01/15/freshmen.

68. Sax, "College Women Still Face."

69. An interesting and lively discussion of this period is provided in Horowitz, *Campus Life*.

70. Sax, "College Women Still Face."

71. Holland, Dorothy C., and Margaret A. Eisenhart. *Educated in Romance: Women, Achievement and College Culture*. Chicago: University of Chicago Press, 1990.

72. Fleming, Jacqueline. *Blacks in College*. San Francisco: Jossey-Bass, 1984.

73. Arnold, Karen D. "The Illinois Valedictorian Project: Academically Talented Women Ten Years After High School Graduation." Paper presented at the Annual Meeting of the American Educational Research Association, San Francisco, April 24, 1992.

   Arnold, Karen. "Values and Vocations: The Career Aspirations of Academically Gifted Females in the First Five Years After High School." Paper presented at the Annual Meeting of the American Educational Research Association, Washington, DC, April 24, 1987.

   Arnold, Karen, and Terry Denny. "The Lives of Academic Achievers: The Career Aspirations of Male and Female High School Valedictorians and Salutatorians." Paper presented at the Annual Meeting of the American Educational Research Association, Chicago, April 1985.

74. Sax, "College Women Still Face."

75. Cliatt, Cass. "University Expands Family-friendly Policies for Graduate Students," *News at Princeton*, April 3, 2007. http://www.princeton.edu/main/news/archive/S17/52/12A01/index.xml?section=topstories.

Chapter 8: Single-Sex Education: A Good Idea?

1. Sadker, Myra, and David Sadker. *Failing at Fairness: How Our Schools Cheat Girls*. New York: Touchstone, 1995, p. 232.
2. Johnson, Robert. "A Brave New World." *Independent School* 52:1 (Fall 1992), pp. 57–58; quote from p. 58.
3. Yankelovich, Shulman. *Girls' School Alumnae: Accomplished, Distinguished, Community-Minded*. Concord, MA: National Coalition of Girls Schools, 1990.
4. Sebrechts, Jadwiga. "The Cultivation of Scientists at Women's Colleges." *Journal of NIH Research* 4 (June 1992), pp. 22–26.
5. Conroy, Mary. "Single-Sex Schools." *New Woman* (September 1990), p. 146.
6. Hanks, Tom. Introduction in Diana Meehan, *Learning Like a Girl: Educating Our Daughters in Schools of Their Own*. New York: PublicAffairs, 2007.
7. Keller, Arnold Jack. *A Historical Analysis of the Arguments for and Against Coeducational Public High Schools in the United States*. Ph.D. diss., Columbia University, 1971.
8. Tyack, David, and Elisabeth Hansot. *Learning Together: A History of Coeducation in American Schools*. New Haven, CT: Yale University Press, 1990, p. 46.
9. Fairchild, James. "The Joint Education of the Sexes." *Pennsylvania School Journal* 1 (January 1853), p. 314.
10. "Female Education." *New York Teacher* 2 (January 1854), p. 97.
11. Brown, J. H. "Remarks on the Coeducation of the Sexes." *Pennsylvania School Journal* 3 (September 1854), pp. 120–22.
12. Thompson, James, and James Wickersham. "The Coeducation of the Sexes." *Pennsylvania School Journal* 3 (July 1854), p. 89. Quoted in Keller, *A Historical Analysis*, p. 137.
13. "Description of a Good School." *Common School Journal* 8 (December 1, 1846), p. 357. Quoted in Keller, *A Historical Analysis*, p. 156.
14. Charlestown, Massachusetts. *Reports Made to the School Committee of the City of Charlestown, Massachusetts, for a Separation of the Sexes in the Howard School*. Boston: Tuttle & Dennett, 1848. Quoted in Keller, *A Historical Analysis*, p. 160.
15. Clarke, Edward. *Sex in Education; Or, A Fair Chance for Girls*. Boston: Houghton Mifflin, 1874.
16. Hall, Stanley G. *Adolescence: Its Psychology and Its Relations to Physiology, Anthropology, Sociology, Sex, Crime, Religion, and Education*. New York: Appleton, 1905.
17. Ibid., p. 640.
18. Dewey, John P. "Is Coeducation Injurious to Girls?" *Ladies' Home Journal* (June 11, 1911), pp. 60–61.
19. Goodsell, Willystine, quoted in Keller, *A Historical Analysis,* p. 333.
20. Lyles, Thomas. "Grouping by Sex." *National Elementary Principal* 46:2 (November 1966), pp. 38–41.
21. Karabel, Jerome. *The Chosen: The Hidden History of Admission and Exclusion at Harvard, Yale, and Princeton*. Boston: Houghton Mifflin, 2005.
22. Arms, Emily. "Gender Equity in Coeducational and Single-Sex Environments." In Susan Klein, ed., *Handbook for Achieving Gender Equity through Education*. Mahwah, NJ: Lawrence Erlbaum, 2007, pp. 171–90.

23. Leach, M. "Shelby considers same-sex classes." *Birmingham News*, November 21, 2005, http://www.al.com/news/birminghamnews/.

24. Sadker, Myra, and David Sadker. "Sexism in the Classroom of the 80s." *Psychology Today* (March 1985), pp. 54–57.

Sadker, Myra, and David Sadker. *Failing at Fairness: How America's Schools Cheat Girls*. New York: Scribners, 1994.

American Association of University Women Educational Foundation. *How Schools Shortchange Girls*. Washington, DC: AAUW, 1992.

25. Sommers, Christina Hoff. *The War Against Boys: How Misguided Feminism Is Harming Our Young Men*. New York: Simon & Schuster, 2000.

26. Sadker, David. *Single-Sex Versus Coeducation: The False Debate*. Paper presented at the First International Conference on Gender Equity Education in the Asia Pacific Region, Taipei, Taiwan, November 25, 2004.

27. Sax, Leonard. *Why Gender Matters: What Parents and Teachers Need to Know about the Emerging Science of Sex Differences*. New York: Doubleday, 2005, p. 86.

28. Ibid., pp. 227–28.

29. Gurian, Michael, Patricia Henley, and Terry Trueman. *Boys and Girls Learn Differently! A Guide for Teachers and Parents*. San Francisco: Jossey-Bass, 2001; Sax, *Why Gender Matters*.

30. National Public Radio. *Talk of the Nation*. March 8, 2004. http://www.npr.org/templates/story/story.php?storyId=1751885.

31. "The Feminst Majority." http://www.feminist.org/education/ThreatsToTitleIX .asp.

32. Monroe, Stephanie. Assistant Secretary for Civil Rights, U. S. Department of Education. Dear Colleague letter, January 2007.

U.S. Department of Education. "Secretary Spellings Announces More Choices in Single Sex Education." October 24, 2006. www.ed.gov/news/ pressreleases/2006/10/10242006.html.

Schemo, Diana J. "Federal Rules Back Single-sex Public Education." *New York Times*, October 25, 2006, p. A01.

33. Tannen, Deborah. *You Just Don't Understand: Women and Men in Conversation*. New York: William Morrow, 1990, p. 251.

34. Arms, Emily. "Gender Equity in Coeducational and Single-Sex Environments." In Klein, ed., *Handbook for Achieving Gender Equity through Education*, pp. 171–90.

Mael, Fred A. "Single-sex and Coeducational Schooling: Relationships to Socioemotional and Academic Development." *Review of Research in Education* 68:2 (1998), pp. 70–85.

Jackson, Carolyn. "Can Single-sex Classes in Co-educational Schools Enhance the Learning Experiences of Girls and/or Boys." *British Educational Research Journal* 28:1 (February 2002), pp. 37–48.

American Association of University Women Educational Foundation. *Separated by Sex: A Critical Look at Single-Sex Education for Girls*. Washington, DC: AAUW, 1998.

Hyde, Janet. "The Gender Similarities Hypothesis." *American Psychologist* 60:6 (2005), pp. 581–92.

35. Cairns, Ed. "The Relationship between Adolescent Perceived Self-Competence

and Attendance at Single-Sex Secondary School." *British Journal of Educational Psychology* 60:3 (1990), pp. 207–11; Tyack and Hansot, *Learning Together.*

36. Lee, Valerie, and Anthony Bryk. "Effects of Single-Sex Secondary Schools on Student Achievement and Attitudes." *Journal of Educational Psychology* 78:5 (1986), pp. 381–95.

37. Lee, Valerie, and Helen Marks. "Sustained Effects of the Single-Sex Secondary School Movement on Attitudes, Behaviors, and Values in College." *Journal of Educational Psychology* 82:3 (1990), pp. 578–92.

    Riordan, Cornelius. *Girls and Boys in School: Together or Separate.* New York: Teachers College, 1990.

    See also Sadker and Sadker, *Failing at Fairness.*

38. Datnow, Amanda, and Lea Hubbard, eds. *Gender in Policy and Practice: Perspectives on Single-Sex and Coeducational Schooling.* New York: RoutledgeFalmer, 2002.

    Stabiner, Karen. *All Girls: Single-Sex Education and Why It Matters.* New York: Riverhead, 2002.

39. Moore, Mary, Valerie Piper, and Elizabeth Schaefer. "Single-sex schooling and educational effectiveness: A research overview." In Debra Hollinger and Rebecca Adamson, eds., *Single-Sex Schooling: Perspectives from Practice and Research.* Washington, DC: U.S. Department of Education, 1992, pp. 7–67.

    Lee, Valerie E. "Gender Equity and the Organization of Schools," In Barbara J. Bank and Peter M. Hall, eds., *Gender, Equity, and Schooling: Policy and Practice.* New York: Garland, 1997, pp. 135–58.

    Shmurack, Carole. *Voices of Hope: Adolescent Girls at Single-sex and Coeducational Schools.* New York, Lang, 1998.

40. Lee, Valerie E. "Is Single Sex Schooling a Solution to the Problem of Gender Inequity?" In *Separate Sex: A Critical look at Single Sex Education for Girls.* Washington, DC: AAUW Educational Foundation, 1998, p. 43.

41. Shmurack, *Voices of Hope.*

42. Lee, Valerie, Helen Marks, and Tina Byrd. "Sexism in Single-Sex and Coeducational Secondary School Classrooms." *Sociology of Education* 67 (1994), pp. 22–26.

43. Bracey, Gerald. "Separate But Superior? A Review of Issues and Data Bearing on Single-sex Education." *Educational Policy Research Unit,* Arizona State University, November 2006.

    Campbell, Patricia B., and Jo Sanders. "Challenging the System: Assumptions and Data Behind the Push for Single-sex Schooling." In Amanda Datnow and Lea Hubbard, eds., *Gender in Policy and Practice.* New York: RoutledgeFalmer, 2002, pp. 10–46.

44. Reisman, David. "A Margin of Difference: The Case for Single-sex Education." In J. R. Blau, ed., *Social Roles and Social Institutions.* Boulder, CO: Westview, 1990, pp. 243–44.

45. Riordan, Cornelius. "What Do We Know about the Effects of Single-sex Schools in the Private Sector? Implications for Public Schools." In Amanda Datnow and Lea Hubbard, eds., *Gender in Policy and Practice.* New York: RoutledgeFalmer, 2002, pp. 10–30.

46. Cahill, Larry. "His Brain, Her Brain," *Scientific American* (April 2005). http://www.sciam.com/article.cfm?id=his-brain-her-brain.

47. Gurian, Henley, and Trueman, *Boys and Girls Learn Differently!*; Sax, *Why Gender Matters.*

48. Sax, *Why Gender Matters,* p. 237.

49. Ibid., p. 249.

50. Gurian, Henley, and Trueman, *Boys and Girls Learn Differently!,* pp. 44–47.

51. Martin, Emily J. *How Boys and Girls Learn Differently.* Gurian Institute Training materials. In "Title IX's 35th Birthday," *Huffington Post.* June 25, 2007. http://www.huffingtonpost.com/emily-j-martin/title-ixs-35th-birthday_b_53598.html.

52. Bracey, Gerald. "Separate But Superior?," p. 11.

   Mead, Sara. *The Evidence Suggests Otherwise: The Truth About Boys and Girls.* Washington, DC: Education Sector, 2006, pp. 14–16.

53. Hyde, Janet, and Sara Lindberg. "Facts and Assumptions About the Nature of Gender Differences and the Implications for Gender Equity." In Klein, ed., *Handbook for Achieving Gender Equity through Education,* p. 25.

54. Hyde, "The Gender Similarities Hypothesis."

55. Miller, Andrea. "The Mindful Society." *Shambhala Sun* (September 2008), pp. 58–59.

56. Maccoby, Eleanor. *The Two Sexes: Growing Up Apart, Coming Together.* Cambridge, MA: Harvard University Press, 1998.

57. Heather, Barbara. "Constructions of gender in parents' choice of a single sex school for their daughters." In Datnow and Hubbard, eds., *Gender in Policy and Practice,* pp. 304–22.

   Salomone, Rosemary C. *Same, Different, Equal.* New Haven, CT: Yale University Press, 2003.

   Streitmatter, J. *For Girls Only: Making a Case for Single-Sex Schooling.* Albany: SUNY Press, 1999.

   Hubbard, Lea, and Amanda Datnow. "Do Single-sex Schools Improve the Education of Low-income and Minority Students? An Investigation of California's Public Single Gender Academies." *Anthropology and Education Quarterly* 36:2 (2005), pp. 115–31.

58. James, Abigail N., and Herbert C. Richards. "Escaping Stereotypes: Educational Attitudes of Male Alumni of Single Sex and Coed Schools." *Psychology of Men and Masculinity* 4 (2003), pp. 136–48.

59. Jackson, Carolyn. "Can Single-sex Classes in Co-educational Schools Enhance the Learning Experiences of Girls and/or Boys."

60. Askew, Sue, and Carol Ross. *Boys Don't Cry: Boys and Sexism in Education.* Buckingham, UK: Open University Press, 1990.

   Paludi, Michele, Jennifer Martin, and Carmen A. Paludi, Jr. "Sexual Harrassment: The Hidden Gender Equity Problem." In Klein, ed., *Handbook for Achieving Gender Equity through Education,* pp. 215–30.

61. Campbell, Patricia B., and Jo Sanders. "The Legality of Single-Sex Education in the United States." In Datnow and Hubbard, eds., *Gender in Policy and Practice,* pp. 31–46.

62. Mael, Fred A. *Single-Sex Versus Coeducational Schooling: A Systematic Review.* Washington, DC: U.S. Department of Education, 2005; Bracey, "Separate But Superior?"; Arms, "Gender Equity in Coeducational and Single-Sex Environments."

63. Sadker, David. "At Issue: Should Federal Regulations Make It Easier for School Districts to Establish Single-Sex Schools or Classes?" *Congressional Quarterly Researcher* 12:25 (2002), p. 585.
64. Datnow, Amanda, Lea Hubbard, and Elizabeth Woody. "Is Single-gender Schooling Viable in the Public Sector? Lessons from California's Pilot Program." Toronto: Ontario Institute for Studies in Education, University of Toronto, 2001.
65. Woody, Elizabeth. "Constructions of Masculinity in California's Single Gender Academies." In Datnow and Hubbard, eds., *Gender in Policy and Practice,* pp. 280–303.
    Herr, Kathyrn, and Emily Arms. "The Intersection of Educational Reforms: Single-Gender Academies in a Public Middle School." In Datnow and Hubbard, eds., *Gender in Policy and Practice,* pp. 74–89.
66. Martin, *How Boys and Girls Learn Differently.*
67. Andre Boyd, quoted in *NEA Today* (May 2007). http://www.nea.org/home/17276.htm.

Chapter 9: Possibilities, Such Possibilities

1. Lederman, Doug. "Clues About the Gender Gap." *Inside Higher Ed* (January 15, 2006). http://insidehighered.com/news/2007/01/15/freshmen.
2. Burk, Martha, and Eleanor Smeal. "Why We Need an ERA: The Gender Gap Runs Deep in American Law." *Washington Post,* April 27, 2007, p. A23.
3. American Association of University Women, "Women at Work (2003)." http://www.aauw.org/research/womenatwork.cfm.
4. U.S. Department of Labor, Bureau of Labor Statistics, Employment and Earnings, Table 39, "Median Weekly Earnings of Full-time Wage and Salary Workers by Detailed Occupation and Sex," 2006.
5. Ginsburg quoted in Barnes, Robert. "Over Ginsburg's Dissent, Court Limits Bias Suits." *Washington Post,* May 30, 2007, p. A01.
6. Sommers, Christina Hoff. *The War Against Boys: How Misguided Feminism Is Harming our Young Men.* New York: Simon & Schuster, 2000.
7. Rosenthal, Robert, and Lenore Jacobson. *Pygmalion in the Classroom: Teacher Expectations and Pupils' Intellectual Development.* New York: Holt, Rinehart & Winston, 1974.
8. Kuebli, Janet, and Robyn Fivush. "Gender Differences in Parent-Child Conversations About Past Emotions." *Sex Roles* 27:11–12 (1992), pp. 683–98.
9. Siegal, Michael. "Are Sons and Daughters Treated More Differently by Fathers Than by Mothers?" *Developmental Review* 7 (1987), pp. 183–209.
10. Children's rooms were first analyzed for toy content in 1975 when the researchers found highly stereotyped playthings. In 1990, fifteen years into the gender revolution, another team of researchers found that little had changed. And the sources that follow show the trend continues today.
    Campbell, Patricia, and Jennifer Storo. *Girls Are . . . Boys Are . . . : Myths, Stereotypes & Gender.* Washington, DC: Office of Educational Research and Improvement, U.S. Department of Education, 1994.
    Golombok, Susan, and Robyn Fivush. *Gender Development.* New York: Cambridge University Press, 1994.

Rheingold, H. L., and K. V. Cook. "The Contents of Boys' and Girls' Rooms as an Index of Parents' Behavior." *Child Development* 46:2 (1975), pp. 459–63.

Pomerleau, Andree, Daniel Bolduc, Gerard Malcuit, and Louise Cossette. "Pink or Blue: Environmental Gender Stereotypes in the First Two Years of Life." *Sex Roles* 22:5–6 (1990), pp. 359–68; quote from p. 365.

Steele, Claude. "A threat in the air: How stereotypes shape intellectual ability and performance." *American Psychologist* 52:6 (1997), pp. 613–29.

11. Sperber, Jason. "Seeing Pink: Gender Stereotyping in Toys." February 26, 2008. http://www.adoptedthemovie.com/2008/02/26/seeing-pink-gender-stereotyping-in-toys/.

12. Schwartz, Lori A., and William T. Markham. "Sex Stereotyping in Children's Toy Advertisements." *Sex Roles* 12:1–2 (1985), pp. 157–70.

13. University of Texas at Austin. "Toy Buying Can Expose Children to Racial, Gender Stereotypes, Research Shows." November 29, 2005. http://www.utexas.edu/news/2005/11/29/sociology/.

14. University of Michigan. "How Dads Influence their Daughters' Interest in Math." *ScienceDaily,* June 25, 2007. http://www.sciencedaily.com/releases/2007/06/070624143002.htm.

15. Weitzman, Lenore, Deborah Eifler, Elizabeth Hokada, and Catherine Ross. "Sex Role Socialization in Picture Books for Preschool Children." *American Journal of Sociology* 77:6 (May 1972), pp. 1125–50.

16. Hamilton, Mykol, David A. Anderson, Michelle Broaddus, and Kate Young. "Gender Stereotyping and Under-representation of Female Characters in 200 Popular Children's Picture Books: A Twenty-first Century Update." *Sex Roles* 55 (2006), pp. 757–65.

17. Anderson, David A., and Mykol Hamilton. "Gender Role Stereotyping of Fathers in Children's Picture Books: The Invisible Father." *Sex Roles* 52:3–4 (February 2005), pp. 145–51.

18. Chandler, Michael Alison, "Two Guys and a Chick Set Off Tiff Over School Library Policy." *Washington Post,* February 17, 2008, p. C06.

19. American Library Association. Banned Books Week, May 12, 2008. http://blogs.ala.org/oif.php?cat=268.

20. For research summaries on the effect of reading material on development of nonsexist attitudes, see:

Sadker, Myra, and David Sadker. *Year 3: Final Report: Promoting Effectiveness in Classroom Instruction.* Washington, DC: National Institute of Education, 1984.

Sadker, Myra, David Sadker, and Susan Klein. "The Issue of Gender in Elementary and Secondary Education." In Gerald Grant, ed., *Review of Research in Education,* vol. 17. Washington, DC: American Educational Research Association, 1991, pp. 269–334.

Scott, Kathryn. "Effect of Sex-Fair Reading Materials on Pupils' Attitudes, Comprehension and Interests." *American Educational Research Journal* 23:1 (1986), pp. 105–16.

21. Sadker, Myra, and David Sadker. *Final Report: Project Effect (Effectiveness and Equity in College Teaching).* Washington, DC: U.S. Department of Education, 1986.

Sadker, Myra, and David Sadker. "Confronting Sexism in the College Class-room." In Susan Gabriel and Isaiah Smithson, eds., *Gender in the Classroom: Power and Pedagogy*. Chicago: University of Illinois Press, 1990, pp. 176–87.

If you are interested in some other studies of teacher-student interaction patterns, check out: Altermatt, Ellen, Jasna Jovanovic, and Michelle Perry. "Bias or Responsivity? Sex and Achievement-Level Effects on Teachers' Classroom Questioning Practices." *Journal of Educational Psychology* 90 (1998), 516–27.

Beaman, Robyn, Kevin Wheldall, and Coral Kemp. "Differential teacher attention to boys and girls in the classroom." *Educational Review* 58:3 (2006), pp. 339–66.

Duffy, Jim, Kelly Warren, and Margaret Walsh. "Classroom interactions: Gender of teacher, gender of student, and classroom subject." *Sex Roles* 45:9–10 (2001), pp. 579–93.

Montague, Marjorie, and Christine Rinaldi. "Classroom Dynamics and Children at Risk." *Learning Disability Quarterly* 24 (2001), pp. 75–83.

Spencer, Renee, Michelle Porche, and Deborah Tolman. "We've come a long way—maybe. New challenges for gender equity education." *Teachers College Record* 105:9 (2003), pp. 1774–1807.

Black, Susan. "Ask Me a Question." *American School Board Journal* 188:5 (May 2001), pp. 43–45.

22. Strang, Dorothy. "Sketches and Portraits." *Independent School* 52:1 (Fall 1992), pp. 19–26; quote from p. 20.

23. Hendrick, Joanne, and Terry Stange. "Do Actions Speak Louder Than Words? An Effect of the Functional Use of Language on Dominant Sex Role Behavior in Boys and Girls." *Early Childhood Research Quarterly* 6:4 (1991), pp. 565–76.

24. These stories were adapted from *Title IX, Exercise My Rights*. http://www.titleix.info/content.jsp?content_KEY=2797&t=homepage.dwt.

25. Bravo, Ellen. *Taking on the Big Boys: Or Why Feminism Is Good for Families, Business, and the Nation*. New York: Feminist Press at CUNY, 2007.

26. Pink, Daniel. *A Whole New Mind: Why Right-Brainers Will Rule the Future*. New York: Riverhead Trade, 2006.

27. Miller, Andrea. "The Mindful Society." *Shambal Sun*, September 2008, pp. 58–59.

28. Csikszentmihalyi, Mihaly. *Creativity: Flow and the Psychology of Discovery and Invention*. New York: HarperCollins, 1996, p. 9.

Index